JUL 29 1994

3 1299 00398 9077

221.6082 Out of the garden.
0

$23.00

DATE			

12/22/94 (9)

Out of the Garden

Out of the Garden

Women Writers on the Bible

Edited by

CHRISTINA BÜCHMANN

and

CELINA SPIEGEL

FAWCETT COLUMBINE
New York

A Fawcett Columbine Book
Published by Ballantine Books
Copyright © 1994 by Christina Büchmann and Celina Spiegel

All rights reserved
under International and Pan-American Copyright Conventions.
Published in the United States by Ballantine Books,
a division of Random House, Inc., New York,
and simultaneously in Canada
by Random House of Canada Limited, Toronto.

Owing to limitations of space, permissions acknowledgments appear on page 353.

Library of Congress Cataloging-in-Publication Data

Out of the garden : women writers on the Bible / [edited by] Christina Büchmann and
Celina Spiegel.
    p.   cm.
  ISBN 0-449-90692-2
  1. Bible. O.T.—Criticism, interpretation, etc.   2. Bible. O.T.—Feminist criticism.   3. Bible as literature.   I. Büchmann, Christina.   II. Spiegel, Celina.
BS1171.2.045   1994
221.6'082—dc20   93-50576
                                                                     CIP

Designed by Ruth Kolbert

Manufactured in the United States of America
First Edition: August 1994
10   9   8   7   6   5   4   3   2   1

Contents

════════ACKNOWLEDGMENTS════════

In any collection, the editors' first debt is to their contributors, without whose talent and cooperation the book could not exist. We thank them for their enthusiasm, conscientiousness, and, in many cases, advice.

This book would also not exist without the support of a number of people who helped us bring it into the world. John Herman and Georges Borchardt were encouraging from the first and set us on our way. Cindy Klein has been an unusually supportive agent; she not only managed the innumerable details of a complicated project, but served as a perceptive reader and critic, and became, in the process, a friend. At Ballantine, Mary South had the faith in us and the book to take us on, and her early enthusiasm and the freedom she allowed us were invaluable. We would like to thank her successor, Joanne Wyckoff, who heroically spurred us on, demonstrating a dedication to the project far beyond professionalism. We are grateful for her expertise, firm encouragement, and patience. We also appreciate the help of Andrea Schulz, who was a pleasure to work with, and the support of Joëlle Delbourgo, who was always reassuring and thoughtful.

We are especially thankful to Jeanne Heifetz and Jonathan Rosen, who have been extraordinarily generous and helpful in their suggestions. We are grateful for the sound advice of David Rosenberg and

Alfred Corn; their own collections of essays on the Bible were in part the inspiration for *Out of the Garden*. Robert Alter, Robert Atwan, Michael A. Bernstein, Anne Borchardt, Astrid Büchmann, Jonathan Bumas, Ingeborg Burling, Kerstin Burling, Philip Chmielewski, S.J., David Curzon, Mary Douglas, Minna Elias, David Gewanter, Dmitri Iglitzin, Peter Kupfer, Susan Larsson, Frances Lerner, Claude Lopez, Ross Metzger, Leonard Michaels, Susan Mizner, Moni and Dalit Naor, Sheila Pridmore Newbery, Noam Nisan, Laurie Parsons, Aaron and Helen Spiegel, Sharon Spiegel, Mychal Springer, Naomi Yavneh, and Joy Young contributed ideas, opinions, and encouragement.

Finally, Cindy would like to thank Peter Kupfer and Rachel Kupfer for their patience and love.

The sentimental feelings we all have for those things we
were educated to believe sacred, do not readily yield to
pure reason. I distinctly remember the shudder that passed
over me on seeing a mother take our family Bible to make
a high seat for her child at table. It seemed such a desecra-
tion. I was tempted to protest against its use for such a
purpose, and this, too, long after my reason had repudiated
its divine authority.
—Elizabeth Cady Stanton, The Woman's Bible [1]

Almost one hundred years ago, Elizabeth Cady Stanton compiled *The Woman's Bible*, an irreverent and unabashedly
earthy feminist commentary written by a group of educated women
intent on exposing the Bible's—and its traditional interpreters'—
unfair treatment of women. Stanton and her contemporaries wrote
against the religious and social authority the Bible had held over
women for centuries, while at the same time fighting its influence in
the political arena.

Much has changed in the past one hundred years. No longer is the
Bible uncritically accepted as the word of God, nor Genesis upheld
as the factual account of the beginning of the world and human society. Still, many of us today might be as shocked as Stanton at see-

ing a Bible put to use as a high chair. Rather than fighting the Bible's power over women, however, many women today are attempting to reclaim the book that has helped to shape the ways they think and live.

How, then, do contemporary women read the Bible? For this collection, we approached women writers, both Christians and Jews, whose work had in some way been influenced by the Bible. We asked each of them to choose a story, figure, or theme from the Old Testament and interpret it with this question in mind. *Out of the Garden* contains twenty-eight imaginative responses that address what it means to read the Bible as a woman today.

Most of us first encountered the Bible as children at Sunday school, in church, or in synagogue. The matriarchs and patriarchs who peopled its pages loomed like the desert mountains they were always ascending, and they seemed just as distant. It is difficult to shake one's initial impression of any book, especially a book that has had such staying power. Even if some of us have never read the Bible but are familiar with its stories (and who of us isn't?), it has most likely influenced our thinking and our imaginations—even our identities as women. Yet as an adult woman—believer or nonbeliever—whose own life experience cannot but have been at odds with this ancient book, how does one read the Bible today?

It is only recently that many of us have come to find the Bible *interesting*, no longer experiencing its claims to authority as so overwhelming as to demand mere assent and respectful attention. It takes a strong identity, and perhaps life in a predominantly secular culture, to counterbalance the Bible's weighty historical presence. In fact, one wonders whether it will ever be possible to read the Bible as one would any other book, simply for pleasure or to satisfy curiosity. Just thinking about the Bible makes many of us feel small or guilty. For women, especially, the Bible may be impossible to read independent of its authoritative claims, as its power over women has been twofold: religious and social.

For centuries, two short passages shaped almost every statement about women's character and proper place: the creation of Eve from Adam's rib, and Eve's transgression and God's subsequent curse on her. The first of these passages presents Eve and womankind as an afterthought.

> And the Lord God said, It is not good that the man should be alone; I will make a help mate for him. . . . And

the rib, which the Lord God had taken from man, made
he a woman, and brought her unto the man. (Gen.
2:18-23)

The second passage specifies Eve's effect on the world: God made it
a paradise, and woman made it the imperfect place we all know.

Unto woman he said, I will greatly multiply thy sorrow
and thy conception; in sorrow thou shalt bring forth children; and thy desire shall be to thy husband, and he shall
rule over thee. (Gen. 3:16)

War, pestilence, famine, and every sin were the price all humanity
paid for Eve's disobedience.

Ironically, while these passages were invoked by men to keep
women subordinate, from the Middle Ages on the Bible provided
most women with their only opportunity to engage in ideas. In her
history of feminist thought, Gerda Lerner has pointed out that it was
often the only book available to women,[2] and therefore a natural focus not only for protest but for all kinds of self-expression: interpretation and elaboration, devotional works (some orthodox and some
not), poetry, and fiction.[3]

BUT HOWEVER MUCH WOMEN'S relations to the Bible have
changed through the centuries, the experience of reading the Bible
remains as varied and rich as ever. Some of its figures are easy to feel
for, while others are sketched with so few lines that we have to fill
in almost every detail—and yet a number of these are among the
most vivid and memorable of all. Many of the women in the Bible
are especially sketchy figures, surfacing for a moment or two to perform a significant action, then sinking back under the text, leaving
us to guess at the larger story. In this collection, Rebecca Goldstein's
essay on Lot's wife and Norma Rosen's treatment of Rebecca and
Hagar, for example, address such memorable women and their untold
lives.

Sometimes the Bible reads like a novel, as in the story of Joseph,
or the long, emotionally complex tale of David and the people in his
court. Or it can be resigned and philosophical—our days are as grass,
we are born to trouble as the sparks fly upward. At times the Bible
offers poetry of praise for God and his world, as in a number of the

Psalms; at other times it is a call for justice. It is alternately down-to-earth, visionary, dated, and relevant as it cries out against corruption, hypocrisy, and empty religion.

Poetry, history, law—the Bible is certainly no single thing. Not in its style, not in its subject matter, and not in the time of its composition. But that only partly explains why it has looked so different, at different times, to its readers and listeners. The Bible has been used to defend, abolish, and endure slavery; it has been used to keep women subordinate even while it exhorts its readers to practice justice and equality. The Bible reflects the inconsistencies in the world, and its accounts of women are as various as its treatments of most subjects.

ONE OF THE MOST common ways of reading as a woman is to focus on women characters. *Out of the Garden* offers essays on Eve, Rachel, the Queen of Sheba, Delilah, Jezebel, and Esther, on "good" women and "bad"; and it takes up the question of how one decides who is good and who is bad—as in Anne Dailey's piece on the good and bad mothers in the story of Solomon's judgment, or Rachel Brownstein's piece on Vashti and Esther. Phyllis Trible and Fay Weldon, using quite different methods, write defenses for proverbially wicked women, Jezebel and Delilah respectively. Other essays, like Alicia Ostriker's poetic interpretation of Moses as the "nursing father" of his people, enlarge our traditional understanding of male figures by reading them from a feminist perspective, while Ilana Pardes explores the limits for a heroine in a patriarchal narrative.

Other contributors see themselves in the Bible's male heroes. Margaret Anne Doody, for example, identifies with the energetic, busy-body child Samuel, and June Jordan writes of how she formulated her ideal of friendship by admiring the heroic loyalty between David and Jonathan.

The extraordinary sustaining power that identification with Biblical figures and events can have is also attested to in the rich relation African-American culture has had to the Bible, using it "to find meaning in the most despotic circumstances."[4] The experiences of Israelite slavery and liberation, and the Psalms, with their voicings of despair and hope, have always held out a promise of a better life to those whose lives may appear to be beyond comfort. Kathleen Norris's essay on Benedictine women's relations to the Psalms emphasizes how the very act of reciting the Psalms has uplifting power—and the power to draw one immediately into an older world, collapsing ancient time with the present.

Some writers use contemporary life to lend new dimensions to a biblical tale, as in Patricia Williams's discussion of the political abandonment of the children of single black mothers, Elizabeth Swados's recreation of Job as a clown, or Louise Erdrich's unexpected encounter with Ecclesiastes on the walls of a Midwestern house. Amy Clampitt, Marina Warner, and Patricia Hampl, among others, blend their own experiences as girls and young women with literary interpretation, allowing them, as adults, to understand what they could not understand in their youth, while Daphne Merkin and Naomi Seidman, both raised in religious households, have reexamined the texts of their youth to find them more unsettling than they had previously realized. But the women who responded to our invitation to write for this collection and who chose to ignore questions of gender, such as Lore Segal, Deirdre Levinson, and Allegra Goodman, are also expressing what it can mean to read as a woman.

Perhaps it is no coincidence that three essays in this collection—those by Marcia Falk, Cynthia Ozick, and Margaret Anne Doody—center on the story of Hannah, a woman whose pursuit of her private desire, a child, brings her into public conflict with the authorities of her day. This story may have particularly compelling resonance for contemporary women, as it perhaps best embodies the tension between women's lives and social expectations. Hannah's story also brings us back to Elizabeth Cady Stanton's anecdote of the woman who sat her child upon the Bible. While Stanton describes her own reaction as a sign of the Bible's lasting authority, the same scene shows another relation to the Bible as well, namely, the mother's unself-conscious certainty that the book was hers to use. Like Hannah, this unnamed woman acted spontaneously, only to find that she unintentionally took a controversial stance with large social implications, an experience that runs throughout the long history of women's reading and responding to the Bible.

WHEN WE INVITED WRITERS to contribute to this volume, we emphasized that each one was free to bring to her essay whatever approach or combination of approaches she brought to the Bible itself: literary, feminist, religious, autobiographical, political, scholarly. She was also free to choose whichever translation of the Bible she preferred—whether for accuracy, poetic quality, or even nostalgic value. Some of our contributors have quoted from their own translations; a couple have even written their own versions, imagining scenes from an alternate perspective than the Bible depicts. Because each essay is written out of the particular tradition, influences, and interests of its contributor, in some cases we asked the writer to place her essay in context with a brief headnote.

The word "bible," with all its authority, is in fact a confusing term, since various strands of the Judeo-Christian tradition have used it for diverse selections and orderings of the scriptures. It can mean the Old Testament alone (the Hebrew Bible), or it can refer to the Old and New Testaments together. While individual essays touch on the New Testament, we have limited the scope of our book to the Old Testament, or what scholars more impartially call the Hebrew Bible (and our Jewish contributors may refer to as Tanakh or Torah), the common ground for Christians and Jews. Our decision seems to have been justified by the interests of our contributors, who often chose to focus on questions of transcendence versus family, the centrality of family and community, and the conflict between the personal and the communal, which are prominent underlying themes and issues of the Hebrew Bible. In this collection, the order of the essays follows that of the books in the King James Version, still the most widely used translation.

A word about the title of our collection, *Out of the Garden*. It may mean stepping out into a wider world; it may mean taking something from the garden with us. We can view the garden as a traditional environment of confinement for women or as a fertile place of origin that may still have something to offer. Its possible meanings mirror women's complex relations with the Bible itself, but also with the world. As Barbara Grizzuti Harrison points out in the opening essay, the dire effects of Eve's disobedience have brought us most of the things we love. Unlike the Garden of Eden, the Bible is a source women can return to, and as with all great works of literature, it is a book that changes as we change. For curiosity we were thrown out of the Garden, and with curiosity we return.

A Meditation on Eve

❦

BARBARA GRIZZUTI HARRISON

WHEN EVE BIT INTO THE APPLE, SHE GAVE US THE WORLD AS WE know the world—beautiful, flawed, dangerous, full of being. She gave us smallpox and Somalia, polio vaccine and wheat and Windsor roses; she gave me the computer I am writing on, and planted in my blood and bones and flesh a variable human love, the intoxication of the body. She (not Mary) is the mother of my children, born in travail to a world of suffering their presence may refresh. She is my sister. Even the alienation from God we feel as a direct consequence of her Fall makes us beholden to her: The intense desire for God, never satisfied, arises from our separation from him. In our desire—this desire that makes us perfectly human—is contained our celebration and our rejoicing. The mingling, melding, braiding of good and mischief in every human soul—the fusion of good and bad in intent and in act—is what makes us recognizable (and delicious) to one another; without it—without the genetically transmitted knowledge of good and evil that Eve's act of radical curiosity sowed in our marrow—we should not desire to know and to love God, we should have no need of him. We should have no need of one another . . . of a one and perfect Other. Eve, the occasion of our fall from grace, is also the occasion of our salvation. From her first issued need. She set in motion the wheels of salvation by her sin . . . such a little act, in which are contained all human actions, past and present, large and small, good

1

and evil: a cosmos in an atom. Of the salvation she engendered she will be the recipient, in heaven, where we "repent not, but smile; not at the sin, which cometh not again to mind, but at the Worth that ordered and provided."[1] In heaven there is no remorse. In that heaven for which we yearn but which we cannot imagine, Eve is united with Mary, carried by flights of angels to Mother God/Father God. She has become Mary's twin in purity, her sister. Without Eve, Mary would not be our sister. All we know of heaven we know from Eve, who gave us the earth, a serviceable blueprint: Without Eve there would be no utopias, no imaginable reason to find and to create transcendence, to ascend toward the light. Eve's legacy to us is the imperative to desire. Babies and poems are born in travail of this desire, her great gift to the loveable world.

Looking Back at Lot's Wife

REBECCA GOLDSTEIN

I

IT WAS ONE OF THE STORIES FROM GENESIS THAT MOST FRIGHT-
ened me as a child: the story of Lot's wife.

She was told not to look, and she looked; and her punishment
came swift and horrible. Frozen in the moment of her transgression,
exposed to the eyes of all in her act of rebellion, she was transformed
into a spectacle of salt, reduced to an element vaguely ridiculous, as
if to turn back any motion of pity in us. And for what? She was told
not to look, and she looked.

"Why did she look?" I asked the second-grade Hebrew-school
teacher, who was telling the story.

"It doesn't matter *why* she looked," my teacher answered. "God
said not to look, and she looked. She thought she could get away
with it, but of course she couldn't. Nobody can get away with anything. God sees all."

That God sees all was a lesson my teacher was anxious to impress
upon us at any opportunity, and it was a lesson that I, as a child, accepted without question. It was clear that God's seeing all was a consequence of God's being God. My teacher's response therefore
seemed to me irreproachable so far as its theology went. It was on the
level of human psychology that I felt it falling short.

Biblical quotations are taken from my own translation, unless otherwise indicated.

Specifically, I didn't believe that Lot's wife had thought that she could get away with it. *I* wouldn't have thought so, and I was a mere child, living in pallid, nonbiblical days. In vivid contrast was the picture of Lot's wife: fleeing the accursed city, the shrieks of the damned in her ears, and in her nostrils the sickening stink as heaven's fire and brimstone came raining down behind her. (What *was* brimstone?)

God had warned that he would come, and he had come: in the version, embellished by rabbinical tradition, told to us by my teacher, his very Presence had descended, along with a host of twelve thousand angels of destruction. It wasn't the moment in which to think that one could get away with very much of anything.

I wasn't about to press the issue any further with my teacher, but I was fairly certain that whatever it was that had made Lot's wife look back in her flight was in the nature of an overwhelming compulsion (a concept with which children tend to be well acquainted): the sort of irresistible urge that makes the whole question of whether or not one is going to get away with it pretty much beside the point.

What therefore seemed to me very much *to* the point was the question I had put to my teacher: what forced Lot's wife to look back, and—even more to the point—would I have felt driven to do exactly the same?

You begin to see why the story frightened me. Up to now in Genesis, the villains had been recognizably villainous—a brother who killed a brother, egomaniacs who brazenly questioned God's authority and erected claims to their own imagined supremacy.

But looking where one is told not to look?

Had Lot's wife, I wondered, looked back simply because she had been told not to do so, as I unfailingly sneaked a peek while standing between my mother and sisters in our pew in the synagogue during the recitation of the priestly blessing that was said on the holidays?

I had been warned by my mother, and again by my older sister, to avert my eyes from the *bimah*, where the priests were chanting their spooky melody, lest I be blinded by the Presence descending upon their upraised hands. Beneath my lowered lids I could see my two sisters turned dutifully away, facing the back of the synagogue, as all the congregation was turned away, many of the men covering their heads with their prayer shawls, as the priests themselves were doing.

Did Lot's wife and I share the same perversity of nature that compelled us to take stupid risks for no very good reason at all, for no reason that really went beyond the risk itself? And was it for this that her punishment had come swift and horrible?

Or was it rather for the whisper of a doubt, soft but irrepressible, that is perhaps always spoken in such actions as looking where one is told not to look? Were there moments in history during which God simply would not tolerate the *existence* of the skeptic?

The symbolic significance of the gesture of looking back wasn't lost on me. A child's knowledge of nostalgia is one of the mysteries of childhood. Perhaps it wasn't so much that there were moments forbidding doubt as that there were places that merited no sense of attachment. Was it the regret and longing she had directed back to her home in Sodom that had drawn God's wrath down on her?

And yet another sort, a meaner sort, of motive behind her action suggested itself, one that would remove her to a safer distance from myself: a kind of cold enchantment with the drama of death.

The summer we had spent at the seashore I had seen for myself how the crowd had gathered around the boy who had been pulled unconscious from the ocean, and how the voice and face of this crowd had quickened with a strange excitement, as if it were almost glad for the event.

Did Lot's wife have such a strong taste for the theater provided by others' tragedy that she could not keep herself from stealing a glimpse of the flaming spectacle? And was it for this that she herself had been turned, most appropriately, into the stuff of tragic spectacle?

Voyeurism or skepticism, nostalgia or bravado: who was Lot's wife, and what had moved her to look back and risk all?

II

When I came home from school that evening, I immediately went to my father with my questions. I asked him whether we knew the name of Lot's wife, and I asked him why she had looked back.

My father went to his bookshelf and took down one of his huge tomes, leafed through it for a while, returned it to the shelf, took down another book, and read. After a while he said to me:

"According to this midrash her name was Irit (some say Idit). She and Lot had four daughters. There were the two daughters who fled together with their parents out of Sodom, but there were also two other daughters, who were already married to Sodomite men. When Lot warned these two sons-in-law that Sodom was about to be destroyed, they laughed and said, 'There is music and festivity in the city, and you speak about destruction!'

"According to this midrash, Irit had pity on her two older daughters, who were left behind with their husbands. She turned around to see if they were following her and she saw the Presence and was turned to salt."

My father and I stared at each other for a few moments.

"This is only one midrash," my father finally said. "I'll see if I can find some other interpretations that will make things clearer to us."

My father was telling me that he, too, was confused by the story of Lot's wife. And from his confusion I knew many things. I knew, first of all, that in looking back at Irit, he, too, looked back with pity. But far more importantly, I knew from his confusion that my father, just like Irit, would also have looked back to see if all his daughters were following.

III

Therefore, I concluded, my father was not a righteous man, at least not in the biblical sense of the word. And for this I was extremely grateful. For what did righteous fathers do? They obeyed the word of God unconditionally, down to the last letter.

The righteous father Abraham arose early in the morning, while it was still dark, to prepare firewood for the sacrifice. He chopped the wood and saddled the donkey himself, not allowing any of his servants to perform these tasks that would ordinarily have been theirs. Evidently, out of his great love for God's word, he wished to perform for himself every part of God's request of him. And what request had that been? The sacrifice of Isaac, the son Abraham loved the best, the son who had been miraculously born when Abraham was one hundred years old and Sarah, his wife, ninety.

And when that son, on the way to the land of Moriah, turned to the father and said, "My father. Here are both fire and wood, but where is the lamb for the sacrifice?" (Gen. 22:7), the righteous father answered, "God Himself will choose the lamb for the sacrifice, my son"—adding (again in the version embellished by rabbinical tradition) "and if not, you will be the lamb."[1] At which, in this version, the son put his face between his hands and wept.

It was a tale of righteousness that could not but awe. But who would want to be a righteous parent's child?

Of course there were other fathers in Genesis.[2] There was, for example, Isaac, the child of the *akedah* now become a parent himself. (I ignored then, and forever have ignored, that Isaac is said by rabbinical tradition to have been thirty-seven at the time of the aborted sacrifice. To me he is a child, lying there beneath his father's raised knife.) Isaac married Rebekah, my namesake, who became the mother of the twin boys, Esau and Jacob, the fraternal pair who (as I saw and still see them) are the Genesis version of the mind-body problem: Esau, the lusty embodiment of throbbing desire and reckless appetite, living always in the vivid here-and-now, grabbing life with his two great hairy arms; and Jacob, for all his guile, a pure soul, emanating all the otherworldly aspirations of the born saint.

Rebekah, who seemed to me a righteous parent on the model of her father-in-law, Abraham, manages to preserve the purity of her vision of the divine priority; and in the light of this vision she subdues—or perhaps even withdraws—both love and loyalty from Esau, betraying the trust he places in her.

But Isaac, who is also a righteous father, loves Esau. He loves Esau for the things that are good in him—for it *is* good to be in love with life, and how wildly Isaac's own longing for life must have beat in him as he lay bound on his father's sacrificial altar[3]—and he's blind to the bad that's mixed in with Esau's good, as we all hope that those who love us will be similarly blind. In fact Isaac loves this prodigal, life-grabbing son so completely that he must be tricked by the clear-sighted and undivided Rebekah into giving the deserving son the blessing that will ensure the preordained dynasty.

Because she was my namesake, I wanted to love and admire Rebekah. And I did, and do, admire her. But it's Isaac whom I love. I love this blind and confused father, who can't see clearly because of love, who's so utterly and pitifully confused because of love.

IV

At my very Orthodox, all-girls high school, those of us who were making plans to continue on to college were warned of the dangers of a secular education. If we felt we had to go to college, said our teachers, then we should at least be aware that there were certain subjects that were much safer than others. Above all, we were admonished, stay away from philosophy, a most dangerous discipline that systematically subjects every article of faith and belief to corrosive analysis and doubt; and the story of the apostate Baruch Spinoza was told to us in details that were meant to horrify.

Don't even look, the teachers said.

So even before I was graduated from high school, I used one of my summer vacations to take a course in philosophy.

Later, during the years I spent as a student of this dangerous discipline, I found a restatement, although in somewhat different terms, of the old dilemma that had first been crystallized for me in the story of Lot's wife, the conflict between the demands of transcendence and the backward pull of love and accidental attachment. Actually the conflict wasn't so much in what I studied—where the claims of transcendence were pretty much one-sidedly championed—as it was in me.

Western philosophy, starting with Plato, introduced me to a notion of transcendence that transcended anything I had encountered in Genesis. Compared to the mother, Irit, Abraham was a figure of terrifying purity. But compared to Socrates on his deathbed, Abraham was a man still mired in the muck of accidental affections.

The life of the righteous men and women of Genesis was, deeply and intensely, a life of familial passions, of family loves and also hates, of family loyalties and betrayals. Qualities of action and of character, including, most importantly, righteousness, saintliness, emerged in the context of family, caught in the given contingencies of those fierce attachments determined through blood. One might be asked to temper this fierceness, and even to overcome a particular attachment if it stood in opposition to the all-transcendent bond to God. But the context as a whole was never challenged as an inextricable aspect of the life represented.

The life of the mind in Western philosophy has nothing at all like this dense emotional context surrounding it. In fact it's a vision of life as pellucid with rationality as the other is thick with the ties of blood and with the heavy decisions one is asked to make between the orders of one's love.

The first requirement of any system of philosophy is to be free from conceptual contradiction and confusion; and the philosopher asks for something similar in the life he would choose. Toward this end his allegiance is all for transcendence—in the more impersonal form, known as truth, that transcendence takes in this tradition.[4]

It's not of course that all Western philosophers have touted a life of loftiest solitude, although many have. But even among those who give to close personal ties the stamp of rational approval, the mere fact of family relationship has rarely been thought to amount to very much, philosophically speaking.

In the last hours before his death, recorded in Plato's *Phaedo*, Socrates gathers around him his friends and disciples so that they may engage in one last philosophical discussion, this one focused on the pertinent theme of the soul's immortality. But before the conversation can begin, Socrates (one of the very few "family men" among the notables in the history of Western philosophy, who, almost to a man, were bachelors) orders someone to remove his weeping wife, Xanthippe, and "the little boy." Plato also has Socrates declaring that flesh-and-blood children are of little or no account, compared with the ideas, embodied in books, and the disciples that a man leaves behind as his true progeny.[5] The good life, from the philosophical viewpoint, certainly doesn't require family and children to complete itself.

But it certainly does from the Jewish viewpoint, where childlessness itself is seen as both a curse and a divine punishment. *Ariri* is the technical term for this punishment, and there is a dispute in the Talmud as to whether *ariri* is implicit or not in the wider punishment of *koret*, which literally means being cut off and is interpreted as an early death. The Canaanite king Abimelech, who took Abraham's wife, Sarah, believing her to be Abraham's sister, was temporarily punished with childlessness. And Michal, the daughter of King Saul and the wife of King David, also suffered this punishment:

> And it was so, as the ark of the Lord came into the city of David, that Michal the daughter of Saul looked out at the window, and saw King David leaping and dancing before the Lord; and she despised him in her heart. (2 Sam. 6:16)[6]

I've always found the dramatic implications of the scene contained in this sentence to be among the richest of any in the Bible. But such considerations aside, David's wife, we are told, was divinely punished for the scorn she harbored for her God-silly husband: "And Michal the daughter of Saul had no child unto the day of her death" (v. 23).[7]

V

And yet, important as the idea of family is in the context of the righteous life, it remains, when all is said and done, only context.

I met a mystical rabbi when I was in Safed, high in the hills in the north of Israel, and he told me a strange story.

We were standing, he and I, in front of the doors of the sixteenth-century synagogue of the great kabbalistic master Rabbi Isaac ben Solomon Luria, known as *ha-Ari*, the Lion. It was exactly here, the rabbi told me, each Friday eve, right before sunset, that *ha-Ari* and his followers would gather, greeting one another and the Sabbath, as they expected at every moment to be greeting the Messiah.

One Friday evening *ha-Ari* appeared before the doors, dressed in the special white garb he wore for the Sabbath. But instead of proceeding into the synagogue, he turned wordlessly away from the door and started to walk. And all the white-robed disciples silently followed the master out of the city of Safed and across the fields.

Finally, after they had walked for miles, one of the disciples spoke up.

"Rabbi," he said, "where are you leading us? It's been hours since the Sabbath started. Our wives and our children are waiting for us and surely beginning to worry."

And *ha-Ari* sank down where he stood in the field and began to cry.

At last he was able to speak. "The moment for the Messiah had come," he said, "and I was walking to Jerusalem. But now one of you has questioned, and the moment is gone."

The rabbi who told me this story was obviously very moved by it, and I was, too, though there's little doubt that we were responding to quite different aspects. It's clear that his thoughts were all on the master and the tragedy of that lost moment, while I could only think of the disciple, who had looked back to the hills of Safed, where his family was waiting.

VI

My father did come up with several more midrashim regarding Lot's wife. One of the midrashim tried to explain why it was salt, of all things, that she became.

Irit, said this midrash, always used to skimp on the salt in the food she served. When the two messengers, who of course were angels, came to Lot's house to warn him of the imminent destruction, he ordered his wife to serve them a meal, and this time to salt the food properly. So she went around borrowing salt from all the neighbors, in this way spreading the word that the household had visitors, which was a species of persons dangerously unwelcome in the sinful town of Sodom. Because of her action a crowd of evil intent soon gathered around Lot's house, demanding that they be allowed to have a go at the strangers. The inhabitants of the house were only saved because of the angels, who blinded the men, young and old, who stood at the entrance. The blindness began with the young because it was they who had instigated the mob.

My father simply offered me this midrash, without suggesting that he thought it supplied the final resolution to the conflict we both felt on looking back at Lot's wife.

VII

On the one hand, I still remember my father's admission of confusion about Irit's fate, and the knowledge and comfort I gathered from his confusion. On the other hand, my father never could work up any enthusiasm for the luminous vision of the life of pure reason I tried to paint for him. I argued that it was the life that was the most consistent and thus right. He agreed with me that it was consistent, but he wouldn't agree that it was right. In fact he thought it was all wrong. He thought it was right for human life to be subject to contradictions, for a person to love in more than one direction and sometimes to be torn into pieces because of his many loves. I suspect he even felt a little sorry for any great man of ideas who had cut himself off, so consistently, from what my father saw as the fullness of human life.

But now, only recently, I've discovered a commentary on the story of Lot's wife that I wish I might have been able to talk over with my father.

Rabbi David Kimchi (a thirteenth-century exegete known by the acronym Radak) points out that in Genesis it is sulfur and fire that are said to have rained down on Sodom. But in Deuteronomy, when Moses, before dying, warns the children of Israel not to repeat the sins of the past, he speaks of sulfur and *salt* as having been poured onto the doomed city. In the course of explaining the discrepancy, Radak says that in fact all the people of Sodom became pillars of salt. The outcome of the physical devastation wrought upon Sodom was that the place itself became sulfur, while the people became salt.

Hence, at least if one follows Radak, it seems that Lot's wife was not the spectacular aberration I had always thought. Her fate was continuous with those who had been left behind. Suddenly I felt the whole story of Lot's wife shifting.

She was told not to look and she looked, says the Bible. And her punishment came swift and horrible, added my teacher, following the traditional interpretation I, too, had thought inevitable. But I read the story differently now:

Irit looked back to see if her two firstborn daughters were following, and she saw that they weren't and what had become of them.

In such a moment of grief one knows only one desire: to follow after one's child, to experience what she's experienced, to be one with her in every aspect of suffering. Only to be one with her.

And it was for this desire that Irit was turned into a pillar of salt. She was turned into salt either because God couldn't forgive her this desire . . . or because he could.

Rebekah and Isaac: A Marriage Made in Heaven

NORMA ROSEN

As a fiction writer I am fascinated by classical rabbinic midrash, a form of biblical commentary that asks "why" and "why not" of the Bible's stories (the word midrash *itself springs from the Hebrew, I'drash, meaning "to question"). In the process of answering its own questions, midrash invents alternative aspects of character and event, keeping all possibilities alive, in contrast to the Bible story, which allows only one. The difference between questions thrown up by the imaginations of the midrashic rabbis of the first and second centuries* C.E. *and questions that occur to us now yields further fascination. Between their midrash and ours: spaces for more questions, more midrash. I have added a midrash to the story of Rebekah and Isaac. My subtitle, "A Marriage Made in Heaven," will be seen as ironic, considering the couple's problems in a family that today might be labeled dysfunctional; yet those very words were once straightforwardly applied by the rabbis to Rebekah and Isaac's union. The duality nicely sums up the complexities of this biblical pair whose powerful hold on the imagination has not slackened over the centuries.*

To Rabbi Burton Visotzky and my fellow members of "The Genesis Seminar" at the Jewish Theological Seminary of America.

Biblical quotations are taken from Everett Fox, *In the Beginning* (New York: Schocken Books, 1983), with some alterations, unless otherwise indicated.

Their story cannot be summarized briefly; its roots go back to the parental narrative of Abraham and Sarah's story, and its branches go forward to their own children's children.

ON THE LONG JOURNEY BACK TO CANAAN, ELIEZAR, ABRA-ham's *messenger, having once before turned eloquent, rouses himself to lighten time for Rebekah. He recites a version of the story he told her family after meeting Rebekah at the well.*

"What good luck for you, Rebekah! Your future is assured. Abraham is your wise and powerful father-in-law. He smashed the old idols. True, God spoke to him: 'Take your son and sacrifice him on the mountain.' "

But before this part of Eliezar's story can reach Rebekah's hearing, a strong desert wind rises up in the space between Eliezar's mouth and Rebekah's ear and blows the words away. When Eliezar realizes what has happened, he sprints to another part of the story: "And what bad luck for you, Rebekah, that you couldn't know Sarah! A woman of courage, a beauty in her day. God also spoke to her. God personally announced to Sarah the birth of Isaac, your husband! Marvelous family. Lucky girl. Rebekah! Watch out for those sinkholes—just nudge your camel a little that way."

Another servant rides alongside. "Here's a story," he says. "There were two brothers. They had a hard life. One, a boy, a mere fourteen, was barred from the house, sent into the wilderness. Do you think any human creature came to him with a drop of water? God did. Miracles. Then the father raised his hand to kill the second son. But this boy, too, was saved at the last minute. A miracle he's still alive, your . . ."

As the servant pronounces Isaac's name, all the camels in the caravan set up a loud braying and drown out the word. The servant rides quickly away.

Then Rebekah's nurse and maids ride up to her side. They try to speak of what they've learned on the way. But Rebekah silences them. Her brother had warned, "Don't chatter on the journey, as women do! Don't pester this man with questions. He's told his story. Remember, he comes from God, or at least from Abraham's God. Keep your face veiled, your eyes on your camel, and whatever you do, don't disgrace your family!"

Thus the caravan travels in silence, respectful of the journeying bride, her ignorance, her fear, her longing, her sacred mission. Of that mission she knows only that water, and the simple daily task of drawing from the well, have washed away all that she possessed of home. And so Rebekah *remains ignorant of the* akedah, *the binding of Isaac, the man she is to marry.*

I

The passage above is an invention in the manner of midrash, a form of Bible commentary written by rabbis of the first centuries of the Common Era. It seizes upon a striking question about the Bible story of Rebekah—does no one ever tell her about the *akedah*, the binding and near-sacrifice of Isaac?—and supplies an imagined text to account for the not telling. Other aspects of the Rebekah and Isaac story are also prime midrashic moments, spaces in the story to be questioned, elucidated, imagined. Yet I do not find them among examples of midrashic literature.

The Bible recounts only the end of Rebekah's journey to meet the husband she has never seen: Eliezar, the messenger, identifies the figure of Isaac in the field. Rebekah descends from the camel. Isaac approaches.

Though much is made of the ceremony of drawing and offering water when Eliezar first meets Rebekah at the well, here, at Rebekah's first encounter with Isaac, mention of water is omitted. There is only the messenger's summary to Isaac of "all the things he had done," with their implied confirmation of Rebekah's credentials, and Isaac's precipitous taking of Rebekah into the deceased Sarah's tent, where he is "comforted after his mother" (Gen. 24:67). And that is all. No water, no refreshment. "What ceremony else?" one longs to ask, as Hamlet does over Ophelia's grave.

Traditional midrash does not address an ironic absence here, though to me the text again cries out for it. Why, when Isaac greets his bride, is there no mention of the element in which the earlier text is drenched? In this lack, this obliviousness to Rebekah's needs, accompanied by Isaac's thirst for instant comfort for himself, shouldn't we understand that for Rebekah a dry, infertile period will follow? In fact Rebekah is barren for the first twenty years of her marriage to Isaac.

What was the effect on Rebekah of having to suffer years of barrenness after her marriage to Isaac in a time when having children (sons, biblical women always said) was a woman's raison d'être? What was the effect on Rebekah of becoming the wife of a man whose father had been willing to kill him as a sacrifice to God? Might not these aspects of Rebekah's married life have contributed to the forging of her astonishing plan to rearrange the order in which her sons, Jacob and Esau, receive their father's blessings, and to her ability to carry out that plan?

Having found no existing midrash to reflect my questions, and certainly none to answer them, I undertook to write my own.

Q: What did God do after creating the world?
A: After creating the world, God studied Talmud, arranged marriages, and played with Leviathan.[1]

Q: What did Rebekah do in the twenty years of her barrenness?
A: She read novels.

By this is meant: she foresaw[2] that one day writings would appear to describe the lives of men and women, and she imagined events in these still-to-be created works. In this way one says that Rebekah "read" novels. In short she passed the time by creating midrash: She invented the story of her own life.

Rebekah's Midrash

After the excitement at the well—drawing water for the messenger, his camels—after gifts of gold—arm bangle, nose ring—after Isaac's lovemaking in his mother's tent—Sarah, who had died—I began to look about, amazed, at marriage.

I asked my maids to tell about this bridegroom—the truth, whether I liked it or not—who was so nervous, something always on his mind. What could it be, what had they heard?

They thought it safe to tell me then, like it or not: the knife at Isaac's neck, rods beneath him ready for flame, poor Yitzhak[3] trussed for burning.

"Nightsweats, heart-sinks, black mopes! That's the fun your husband had in life. Feel sorry for him," they said, "he had a dreadful youth. Went out with Abraham one day and saw his father prepared to kill him! And would have—you know Abraham!—if there'd been no ram! Since that unfathomed day sudden death is Isaac's fear. So at the mere approach of you, my dear, (maybe he's got to finish things as quick as he can!) well—need we spell it out? Because of that you won't conceive, a sin the family expects you'll take upon yourself. And we must call you barren woman."

They said I'd learn to live with it, like it or not. Sorry for me but no stopping now. What's kept in comes out, and always that way, ancient or modern.

"No one bothered to tell you the family troubles. Now you know Abraham tried to kill Isaac at God's command. And what a comedy of errors killed Isaac's mother! Fitting, really, since at God's announcement of her pregnancy Sarah laughed. Later, when the messenger came with news—'Abraham lifted his knife to slay your son, but Isaac is spared from death!'—she heard only the first part and dropped dead before clause two.[4] Because of that you never met your mother-in-law. Though what sort of relative could Sarah be to you—late-in-life mother, overprotective, yet unable to save her son?

"Don't you know that you were chosen?" my women asked. "You're married to a survivor, like it or not, imprinted deeper with our destiny than most."

They gossiped on, all secrets out, and whispered of a banished brother whose name itself was sibilant as secrets. "Ish-sh-sh-mael!" A daring, forthright man. The kind, they said, I must have dreamed I'd marry, led on camelback toward Isaac by the gold-bestowing messenger.

"No man of course takes a concubine for pleasure!" They broadly winked among themselves. "So Abraham in piety took Hagar, since barrenness was Sarah's portion. Strictly for conception—and at Sarah's urging!—for pious reasons only. Hagar might conceive a child, and did. Ishmael—it's Ishmael!"

"Why does God withhold from us?" I asked my husband.

"You call this twenty-year trifle a withholding? My mother had to wait till ninety, my father till one hundred years to have me!"

"Are we like them?" I asked.

"When we traveled through the desert once, do you remember how I claimed you were my sister? Abraham did that with my mother too. I had to see if God would speak with miracle, close for me the wombs of Pharaoh's women as he did for Abraham, should anyone dare touch you. God gave me answer. Unstained! You were unstained!"

I shuddered in remembrance of that journey. Answers felt like life or death to me: "*Are* we like Abraham and Sarah?"

"I pray I'm like my father," Isaac said, "yet dread it. I wait to see if God will strike me as he struck at Abraham. Sometimes I think God's mercy stops your bearing because of what I, too, would have to bear. The call to Mount Moriah! Once nearly sacrificed myself, to now become the sacrificer would be jeopardy of agonizing doubleness. Yet dreams already lead me there. I mount the path. My son's beside me. I feel again how all my bones turn liquid. When Abraham bound *me*! All but pierced *my* throat . . . !"

"Isaac, don't relive that nightmare time! You're safe, and in my arms!" Dread fell on me. But Isaac, like so many who stay silent, when confession's mode is on him, can't rest until the end.

"My arm goes limp, I tell you, too weak to wield a knife! I am unable to fulfill God's will! And there's no ram and no redemption. Only ashes from which nothing can rise!"

At that they say I let out piercing screams, and fell down in a faint, as Sarah did. I pity her, who never rose again. *But I will not be like her!*

I SEE THAT I, too, wait for repetition. "How like Sarah you are!" the people say. Why should I pray to have a son if he's a sacrifice? Yet not sacrificed, of course, but saved! And therefore doubly precious! Yet shocked into lifelong dread, and I like Sarah will die of it! Or maybe . . . what Isaac fears will happen? The botched call to faith, followed by shame and death!

I argue with sick thoughts. Why need this go exactly as with Abraham? Yet the voice of fear returns: Suppose God's test is meant to come in every generation? Then God must *vary* the results! Isaac might do all that's needed and *still* our son be doomed!

I am resolved. When the stealthy messenger arrives, I'll know the news. I'll intervene and go in Isaac's place, without my son. Up the mountain! Lay myself on dry sticks! Let God's angels slit my throat and light the fire, or let them set me free. And declare at last that we are chosen not for death but life.

I've made my plan. I keep my spirits up. I'm ready to laugh at a moment's notice should the angel of birth appear to say, "You'll bear a son!"

No messenger approaches me with good news or Isaac with the bad. I haven't caught him listening in the night. I haven't caught myself in laughter yet.

"Be patient," Isaac says. "Till God, remembering Sarah, fills your womb."

But what if God should vary these trials too? My child's by no means guaranteed! I will not be like Sarah!

WITH SCRAWLED ADDRESS IN hand (my women are as sharp as private eyes) I went in search of Hagar. And found her in a place not wholly hovel (just slightly better than your single-mother setup).

"How do you manage?" I asked in sympathy, thinking how my Isaac, despite all faults, is such a good provider. I saw too late that I had scratched her pride.

"Abraham," said Hagar, "sends regular contributions. Neighbors have assisted, too, though more for their own comfort than for ours. But that will all soon end."

"It's right to do mitzvot," I said, and reached for pocket shekels. Hagar raised an intercepting palm. "No charity from you! My son has expectations!"

She'd mentioned Ishmael first. That seemed to me a sign, and gave me courage. "May I speak of painful matters—how Sarah cast him out . . . ?"

"Who never should have left!" cried Hagar. " 'Cast out Sarah with Isaac, *her* son,' I said to Abraham. 'Honor your firstborn!' Ah, how he tried, poor man, to clear the way for Ishmael! Jousting with God, quibbling for definitions, searching for ways to forestall. 'Only son?' said Abraham to God. 'Who's my only son? I've two! The one I love? I love them both!' One murderous way he tried I'd shudder to speak of."

"I know it now," I said.

"God saw my son and me cast out and dying, and sent water, angels, anything we wanted! Behind the driest thicket, springs of water!"

That day still raged in Hagar. Carefully I chose my words. "Ishmael should be restored to Abraham's house, now Sarah's dead. And you be honored as well. Believe me, Hagar, I know justice is as greatly owed to you as Ishmael! As for me, I am deprived of mother-in-law and mother, and of a child, year after year! You've borne a son. But does that keep you from consideration of a daughter's dangers?"

I felt ringed with dangers, yet calm. All seemed ordained. My caution vanished. I was impelled, pulled, called! As if the world's last chance for offspring rested with me! The courage of Lot's daughters was no more than mine. Maybe my foolhardiness was like theirs too.

Still, God loves daring. Yet we earn God's wrath if we presume too much. Our tragedy's that "much" and "little" are defined not by our own perspective but by God's great sight. We see too late, our acts beyond recall. I had no choice but to press my cause.

"Since men have spouses and concubines—Hagar, please don't be offended!—then why can't women have both? By taking very little trouble, lines of inheritance could be determined, as they are with men. . . ."

"It is not with women as it is with men . . . !" said Hagar strictly.

"Yes, yes, that's true—we don't, as men do, strew our seed so wastefully. But women sometimes suffer barrenness. Who, more than you, has witnessed with more triumph? Perhaps an alternate, coming to the tent at night, could cure that cursed condition?"

I will not be like Sarah, I vowed. I will not wait for ninety years, nor let my son be taken! Before me stands the woman I emulate!

"Hagar," I cried, "come live in Abraham's house! Be mother to motherless Isaac and me! Bring Ishmael with you to father our sons. I know my powers of persuasion, I can arrange it!"

"God is great," said Hagar. "No one suffers for nothing! Once I cried for concubines' crumbs. Now my son will be father of a great nation! That promise God gave as freely as the drink of water in the wilderness when we lay parched. As for my return to Abraham's house, that would do for me as wife, not less. No more of being concubine! I speak from experience of the condition. How I remember Sarah's taunts! Now my son will be father of a great nation. It is promised! No, one doesn't suffer for nothing. No second best for us, never again! No sneaking under the shield of Abraham's covenant. We have our own! Ishmael to be father of a great nation!"

This concubine had beauty still. And strength, a resoluteness high as Abraham's. She drew my soul in admiration. Here was a mother— not like Sarah!—whose cries and prayers had saved her child! But Hagar turned on me the rage that had seethed till now.

"It's not *my* son who'll swap God's promise for a meal, however succulent your porridge, however guilefully you offer it! I'll see that Ishmael knows better than demean himself with you, and I forbid return except to see his father buried, as is right. Keep your history separate from me and mine. I scorn your triumphs, as God forbid I'd have to share your fall!"

* * *

WOMEN LOOK ABOUT THEM after marriage. Like it or not, like
Emma Bovary they pine. No one told me anything before my journey. Yet my body feels the agony of Sarah, who was—God help
me!—barren till old age. Bitter laughter she gave to God's annunciation. Then, humbled, gave her son the name of Yitzhak, "laughter,"
giving God the last laugh. Laugh and laughed-at turn about and go
on sporting with each other till our death.

My women, no less crafty at procuring than Cleopatra's were,
or Juliet's nurse, brought brawny Ishmael to my tent. He was every
inch as much as Isaac Abraham's son, maybe by several inches
more so. I was in good shape too: My arms had lifted water from
a well.

How midrash will malign you, Ishmael, call you brutish lout! Midrash, the apologetic sort, says you aimed arrows at the passing folk
and made your overtures of sex to little Isaac. Sarah banished you
with Hagar. Yet we know where Sarah's arrow aimed: inheritance for
Isaac! If I'm to pity, why not pity you, cast out by Isaac's mother with
your own, then saved from death by a miracle as great as spared my
husband? Yet the horror doesn't scar *your* psyche! Mother-in-law I
never saw put you off limits, like it or not, as if your manhood were
a spindle for Isaac's pricking. Well—Sleeping Beauty's found you.
Prick! And ghost of mother-in-law be banished!

Ishmael exulted, "Now I chisel out my fate! *Me* will your son re-
semble!" This was the message God had sent me. Ishmael would
make sons like Balzac, not like Kafka. Yitzhak, Kafka, I thought them
both one name. Laughter that caws like a crow.[5] But before we could
be known to one another in my tent, thunder boomed, lightning
glared, hailstones battered down the roof! Drenched, lit up like day,
beaten by hail whose aim was true as arrows, Ishmael cried, "Sarah
scourges me still!" and fled. After that, Isaac came to bed full-
strength, inspired by I know not what, nor dare to think about.

IN THE SAME HOUR I bore Ishmael-like Esau and Isaac-like Jacob.
They split between them again, like my husband and his brother,
Kierkegaard's fear and trembling on one side, Trollopian heartiness
on the other. Right then I swore to alter balances, set inheritance on
hardihood, not nerves. Isaac, himself, poor self-despiser, hankered to
swagger on in Esau's genes!

But from deep within the well between my thighs where destiny
awaited ladling out, I chose the child that Isaac didn't (like it or not,

a common marriage story), yet chose the child most like my spouse! Clapped bracelet pelts on hairless Jacob's arm and led him by that nose ring, mother-love, to fool his father.

I'd told my sons what Isaac suffered at *his* father's hand. I don't believe in keeping things from children. "It's quite all right to act this way," I said. "Not only is your father blind, he's also had to turn deaf ears to God for fear of what God's voice might say. He just can't hear the choice of heir God urged him toward. It's up to us to make interpretations. I always wanted you to share and get along. Remember, everyone gets something, more or less. I hope you'll make me proud and be good sports about it. Since we're clearly actors in God's play, let's make the best of all our roles. If it's to weep, we'll do so; if to exult, we must with all our might. Above all, do not draw back from what's ordained."

And so I fooled blind, dying Isaac into glory, which consists, at least in part, of getting yourself written into the right story. Then cradling my old husband in my arms, I lulled his way to rest with our old made-in-heaven song. The well, the tent, the twins, the blessing, I sang. "Look," I urged into his white-blind eyes, "look at the lengths to which the Holy One goes, for—like it not or like it—us."

Postscript: Meditation on Midrash Concerning Rebekah and Isaac

Eric Auerbach's *Mimesis* famously notes that the Hebrew Bible in its terseness expresses moral teaching above all, in contrast to Homer's storytelling mode in the *Odyssey*, where details abound and aesthetics predominates over ethics. In the Bible a detailless simplicity and almost unbearable tension: "serving-men, ass, wood, and knife, and nothing else, without an epithet; they are there to serve the end which God has commanded," says Auerbach of the *akedah*.[6] For Rebekah the well; for Isaac the *akedah*. She was generous and life-giving; he was nearly sacrificed. That is all the background the Bible accords this bride and groom, progenitors of biblical Jews, mother and father to our sacral selves.

It may be because Bible stories *are* as terse and as given to moral teaching as Auerbach describes that midrash was born. Some traditional midrash comments on Bible stories with narratives, *aggadot*, that elaborate with an interweaving of astonishing detail. They do not always express moral teaching. Sometimes detail reinforces the original intention of the Bible story; at other times it pulls the story elsewhere with seemingly absurdist and gratuitous linkings. (Samuel ha-Nagid said, "Each one explained the verse according to his fancy and according to what came into his mind." All the same, says another source, if "you wish to get to know him by whose word the world came into being—study the *aggadah*.")

The questions concerning the marriage of Rebekah and Isaac that so compel me did not compel the rabbinic commentators. They did, however, leave a great body of commentary about what did compel them. In reading through their comments I learned something about the extent to which the era in which one lives determines what one sees in a biblical text and how that is further modified by who does the seeing.

In Genesis 24:50 Abraham's servant, Eliezar, tells Rebekah's family that God led him to a wife for Isaac. Her brother and father remark, "The matter has come from the Lord." From this the rabbis infer that marriages are made in heaven. These two pieces of information, the story of Rebekah and Eliezar at the well and the midrash about marriages made in heaven that the rabbis of the early centuries spin from it, have come down to us through the ages with undying resonance, though not necessarily in their original causal connection. This midrashic gloss on marriages made in heaven may be sounding an ironic note, the very kind of note the midrash-writing rabbis loved to seize on, since the marriage of Rebekah and Isaac, with its centerpiece of marital deception, appears to be anything but ideal. Or it may be bypassing altogether the idea that the heavenly is the ideal and substituting for it the ordained, the necessary. Isaac, the traumatized, near-sacrificed man, must marry Rebekah, the water bringer, the life giver. A perfect solution, from a certain point of view, though not necessarily from Rebekah's.

In any case that is one kind of midrash—from the particular to the general. A far more prevalent kind is from the particular to the more particular. Traditional midrash can comment gravely, piously, homiletically, in support of the apparent intentions of the Bible story. But sometimes it does not. A striking feature of the rabbis' midrashic commentary, aside from learnedness, and the imprint of the time in which they lived, is that they seemed to have had no anxiety about putting the most imaginative (more bluntly: far out) conjectures to paper.

That made me wonder why it was that someone whose knowledge of Bible begins in the literary and whose immediate past contains no

pious parent or teacher—someone, in other words, like me—feels a
certain unease about letting "fancy" play in print on the lives of
these biblical personages, Rebekah and Isaac, while the pious rabbinic midrashists apparently felt no such constraint: Should I con-
clude that to live in a religious age was more liberating than we can
now conceive? If the demonic, or at least the Dionysian (for want of
a Hebraic term I'll use a Greek one), at times rose up on goat legs
and capered awhile with fancy—that, too, was from God.

In the course of learning about Rebekah, Isaac, and their in-laws,
according to ancient midrash, I learned a great deal about the imaginative freedom the rabbis accorded themselves.

Biblical Abraham does not equivocate about sacrificing Isaac: he
goes right to it. In midrash Abraham argues for Isaac's life as he once
did for the lives of the people of Sodom and Gomorah. The rabbis
felt the need to fill that gap in Abraham's nature; the midrash
changes him from a stoic to a grieving father. But another midrash
offers a nightmare version of the *akedah*. Far from reluctant, says midrash, Abraham was so intent on killing Isaac that he kept his son safe
in a casket[7] to make sure he would remain unblemished for the sacrifice. One midrash even says there was no ram provided for the sacrifice: Abraham killed Isaac; the angels brought him back to life;
Abraham killed him again. A second Isaac then arose to take his
place (a kind of mystical precursor to Freud's murdered Moses, who
was, according to *Moses and Monotheism*, replaced in the wilderness
by another man the Jews also called Moses). Midrash can be tragical-
comical or comical-tragical: Of course there was a ram! It was Abraham's pet, and he called it Isaac.[8]

Yet another midrash tells us that Isaac sustained an "unspecified
injury" as a result of the *akedah*.[9] For me this news reverberates like
the note sounded by Henry James: the obscure hurt that biographers
speculate foreclosed James's capacity for marriage. Here, I tell myself,
is a midrashic hint toward at least one question about Rebekah's marriage, although the rabbis never ask it.

As a writer of fiction I am struck by the way in which the
midrashic writing of the rabbis resembles the creation of fiction, with
one important exception: Midrash, unlike writers' revisions, comes
after the final story version, the one already in the biblical canon. In
early drafts of Thomas Hardy's *The Return of the Native*, Hardy depicts Eustacia Vye as a witch. When we think of that beautiful, mysterious, and darkly unhappy woman who appears in the published
version of the novel, it's hard to believe that Hardy would once have

so conceived of her. Eustacia Vye evolved in Hardy's imagination to one of the grand romantic heroines of English literature. Having got it right in the end, having seen that her dark-souled silences were not the trappings of Satan, but rather signs of one woman's tragic nature, Hardy does not slip back or smudge the page with his earlier conception.

But midrash can sometimes seem like alternative drafts of a Bible story. It still insists on its right to imagine what might have been, as if each character continued to possess countless possibilities beyond its Bible definition. Midrash can give voice to radically skeptical views; midrash can deconstruct.

The rabbis conjectured that the long trip to Canaan that Rebekah, Isaac's bride-to-be, took in the company of Eliezar the servant was, from Isaac's point of view, dangerous. No doubt, they said, it was miraculously speeded up to a few hours for safety's sake. All the same, midrash shrewdly conjectures that Isaac's past made him suspicious (his experience with his father!). Perhaps he thought that on the way the servant behaved improperly? Wasn't Rebekah injured, after all, in some manner? Fell off the camel at the sight of Isaac—but why? And wasn't there some blood? This in perfect disregard of what the biblical text is so eager to have us know—that Eliezar is a faithful, steadfast, loyal servant who, at the sight of Rebekah, bows down and praises God! How I envy the tranquillity with which the midrash-writing rabbis explained the verse "according to fancy"!

Midrash, through unbridled and unintimidated imagination, can also make connections of startling insight. In Genesis we read that Hagar, the concubine, is forced with her son from Abraham's house. After Sarah's death, the Bible tells us, Abraham takes a new wife whose name is Keturah. Midrash adds that the new wife is none other than Hagar. The Bible text capitulates to the power of two different versions of an event (e.g., the double creation story); the Redactor allows both versions to stand, thus making new resonances. Some midrash, taken together with Bible story, can do the same.

Traditional midrash might have helped us to trace the heroic development of a woman who began in virginal submissiveness and transformed herself into an autonomous individual, clear-sighted and courageous enough to see—and act—beyond her husband's purview. Such a midrash would walk a road not found in the Bible, yet start in the place where the Bible story begins and end where the Bible story ends.

The rabbis imagined much but never, so far as I can tell, conjectured about the effect of the *akedah* or of the twenty barren years on Rebekah's decisions and acts. Perhaps more centuries had to pass before even such close readers as the rabbis could have perceived these spaces in the story of the marriage of Rebekah and Isaac, that the rabbis once told us was made in heaven.

Rachel's Dream of Grandeur

❧

ILANA PARDES

RACHEL AND JACOB HAVE PARALLEL DREAMS OF GRANDEUR. Both strive to surmount the tyranny of time in their respective struggles against their precursors, Leah and Esau. To overcome priority means to overcome nature, to replace a concept from the natural order with one from the spiritual sphere. The biblical master of such revisions is the Creator himself, whose control over natural phenomena is unmistakable. What the Bible in fact establishes, from the very first chapter of Genesis, is a deeper rhythm than that of the annual cycle of the seasons, a rhythm that belongs not to nature but to God."[1] To gain control over natural rhythm is something both Rachel and Jacob seek to do. Their lots, however, are different. In accordance with the official hierarchy of God-man-woman, Jacob's right to imitate God is far greater. What Rachel's prerogative boils down to is to be the mimic of God's mimic in her protest against time—to be Jacob's mirror. She is to be like her husband, but not too like him, just as the first pair is created in God's image, but denied the right to become divine. And yet here as elsewhere in the Bible

This essay is a revised version of a chapter in *Countertraditions in the Bible: A Feminist Approach* by Ilana Pardes (Cambridge, MA: Harvard University Press, 1992).

Biblical quotations are taken from the King James Version, unless otherwise indicated.

hierarchies are far from being stable. There are rare moments, I would suggest, in which Rachel's story poses a challenge to patriarchal specular logic, moments in which it refuses to be a subplot whose sole purpose is to mirror the events in Jacob's plot.[2]

At first everything seems to indicate that Rachel, like her counterpart, will outdo her elder sibling. To begin with, she is granted an advantage of priority over Leah in being the first to meet Jacob upon his arrival at Aram. What is more, they meet by the well, a favorite setting for biblical betrothal scenes. Taken into the scene through Jacob's eyes, following his sudden ability to roll a huge stone from the mouth of the wall and then his weeping as he introduces himself to Rachel, one cannot but assume that such confused behavior is indicative of love at first sight. Leah is introduced only later, in a belated expository remark inserted in the midst of initial negotiations between Jacob and Laban:

> Because thou art my brother, shouldest thou therefore serve me for nought? Tell me, what shall thy wages be? And Laban had two daughters: the name of the elder was Leah, and the name of the younger was Rachel. Leah was tender eyed; but Rachel was beautiful and well favoured. And Jacob loved Rachel; and said, I will serve thee seven years for Rachel thy younger daughter. And Laban said, It is better that I give her to thee, than that I should give her to another man: abide with me. And Jacob served seven years for Rachel; and they seemed unto him but a few days, for the love he had to her. (Gen. 29:15–20)

Although this interpolated remark changes the picture, for now we are dealing with two potential brides, Rachel's success still seems ensured. She is far more beautiful than her elder "weak eyed" (as the Hebrew may be construed) sister; and Jacob, now that his feelings are explicitly revealed, is in fact wholly enamored of her, turning seven years into a few days through the force of his love. Then unexpectedly we discover that the reversal of the primogeniture law, a pivotal phenomenon in the Bible and particularly in Genesis, doesn't quite work when women are involved. On the wedding night Jacob had dreamed of for seven years, Leah is passed off to him as Rachel. The natural order is maintained: The elder sister weds first, the younger one must wait.

> And Jacob said unto Laban, Give me my wife, for my days
> are fulfilled, that I may go in unto her. And Laban gath-
> ered together all the men of the place, and made a feast.
> And it came to pass in the evening, that he took Leah his
> daughter, and brought her to him; and he went in unto
> her. . . . And it came to pass, that in the morning, behold,
> it was Leah: and he said unto Laban, What is this thou
> hast done unto me? did not I serve with thee for Rachel?
> wherefore then hast thou beguiled me? And Laban said, It
> must not be so done in our country, to give the younger
> before the firstborn. (Gen. 29:21–26)

Laban's move, as many have noted, serves as a symmetrical punishment for Jacob's cunning usurpation of his elder brother's birthright.
Just as the blind Isaac "misfeels" Jacob, so the young trickster,
blinded by love, becomes a victim of an inverted "bedtrick" as he lies
with the elder sister instead of the younger one.[3] The female subplot,
at this point, is wholly at the service of Jacob's education. Accordingly the perspectives of Leah and Rachel on this exchange are withheld.

THE YOUNG BARREN ONE VERSUS
THE ELDER CO-WIFE

Despite Laban's trickery, Rachel remains in the position of the chosen one. Jacob's love for her still surpasses his attachment to her sister. He works seven more years for the sake of his beloved. Marriage,
however, offers no sweet end to Rachel's hardships. A new problem
arises when God provides Leah (the "hated" wife) with sons, while
Rachel's womb remains closed. The motif of sibling rivalry thus
blends with a recurrent element in the annunciation type-scene,
namely the struggle between the loved barren one and the less-loved
fertile co-wife.[4] The merging of the two motifs is smooth, for the underlying pattern remains the same. The belatedness which characterizes Rachel's birth and marriage is now apparent in her deferred
motherhood. Similarly, Leah's priority in emerging from the womb is
recapitulated in her capacity to bear long before Rachel is able to
give birth.

The conflict between the two sisters is fleshed out when the narrator at last gives us access to their feelings. As if to underline Leah's fertility, the first mode of discourse allotted to her is a predominantly maternal discourse in biblical narrative, that is, naming-speeches:

> And Leah conceived, and bare a son, and she called his name Reuben: for she said, Surely the Lord hath looked upon my affliction; now therefore my husband will love me. And she conceived again, and bare a son; and said, Because the Lord hath heard that I was hated, he hath therefore given me this son also: and she called his name Simeon. And she conceived again, and bare a son; and said, Now this time will my husband be joined unto me, because I have born him three sons: therefore was his name called Levi. (Gen. 29:32–34)

While joyfully naming her firstborn, Leah expresses the hope that her success as a mother will enable her to win her husband's love. Yet the reiteration of this wish in the following naming-speeches intimates that not much has changed in Jacob's attitude toward her. Her pain at being neglected seems to increase from one birth to the next.

To the extent that these speeches are implicitly meant as taunts toward the barren Rachel, they hit the mark. In the verse that follows the description of Leah's tireless bearing and naming of son after son, we receive an explicit statement by the narrator regarding Rachel's feelings: "And when Rachel saw that she bare Jacob no children, Rachel envied her sister" (Gen. 30:1).

When Rachel's voice finally bursts out, it is very bold, impulsive, and painful: "Give me children, or else I die" (ibid.), she demands of Jacob. Her desperate craving for an offspring is inflamed by envy. In but a few words she conveys the intolerable agony of being a barren woman: childlessness means death. Rachel can wait no longer. Working against time, she is willing to do anything she can to overcome the retardation that marks her life. She ends up giving Jacob her maid, Bilhah, hoping to "be built" (*ve-'ibane gam anokhi mimena*, Gen. 30:3) in this vicarious manner. And as Bilhah gives birth "upon her mistress' knees," Rachel gains access to the discourse that previously was solely within Leah's reach: naming-speeches.

That the rivalry between the sisters is meant to mirror the struggle of Jacob and Esau in the main plot becomes conspicuous in Rachel's speech upon Naphtali's birth: "With great wrestlings [*naftuley Elohim.* lit. "a contest of God"] have I wrestled [*niftalti*] with my sister, and I have prevailed: and she called his name Naphtali" (Gen. 30:8). Her speech anticipates Jacob's struggle with the angel, which is inextricably connected with his struggle with Esau. Just as Jacob "prevails" (note the recurrence of the word) in his wrestling "with God and men" (Gen. 32:28), so Rachel, in an extremely condensed version of her husband's struggle, claims to have overcome her sister "with great wrestlings," with wrestlings of God. Once again Rachel is supposedly in Jacob's position, but not quite so. To begin with, God's role in this contest is solely figurative. Rachel's evocation of God's name to define the magnitude of the struggle with her sister may indeed disclose a desire for a different plot, a plot in which, as in Jacob's case, one is deemed worthy of struggling with the Ultimate Precursor in the process of making "the elder serve the younger" (Gen. 25:23). But God's intervention in Rachel's story remains marginal. The limited role God chooses to play in women's lives may in fact be construed as the theological correlate for the fragility of their dreams.

Even more striking is the fact that Rachel's triumph over her sister is no more than a boast of questionable validity. After all, the son she names is Bilhah's son. Her womb is still closed. This naming-speech is more the delusion of a desperate woman, trying to find comfort in the offspring of her maid.

Much like the *ficelle*—Henry James's term for a secondary character who serves to set off the protagonist's representation—Rachel runs breathless beside the coach of the "true agent," but neither manages to get her foot on the step nor to cease "for a moment to tread the dusty road."[5] In Rachel's case, I would add, her foot seems to be very close to the step, but—for one reason or another—she misses it and again ends up running behind time.

EXCHANGING PLOTS

Mutual despair brings the two sisters to a dialogue:

> And Reuben went in the days of wheat harvest, and found mandrakes in the field, and brought them unto his mother Leah. Then Rachel said to Leah, Give me, I pray thee, of thy son's mandrakes. And she said unto her, Is it a small matter that thou hast taken my husband? and wouldest thou take away my son's mandrakes also? And Rachel said,

Therefore he shall lie with thee to night for thy son's mandrakes. (Gen 30:14–15)

The exchange between the two women is tense, but it ends with a deal. Each gives up her particular prerogative in order to gain the prize she lacks. Rachel trades Jacob for a night, while Leah gives her sister the mandrakes, the fruit that promises fertility, the object that metonymically represents the son—*duda'ey beni* (the mandrakes of my son). This deal evokes the notorious bargain between Jacob and Esau in Genesis 25. In both cases the younger person initiates the bargain; in both narratives the struggle is for leadership.[6] But whereas Esau, with his terrible craving for lentils, is no match for Jacob, Leah is a rival whose merit cannot be ignored. She benefits from the deal at least as much as Rachel does. Under God's auspices both sisters become pregnant, although Leah is first.

Interestingly the story of the mandrakes is the one conspicuous spot in this double plot where a reversal of hierarchies is at work. Jacob here descends to the humiliating position of being a token of exchange between two women. To use James's metaphor once again, Jacob is, for a moment, thrown off the coach to experience what running breathless on a dusty road feels like. Patriarchal specular logic is ridiculed. The eponymous father of Israel becomes the faithful mirror of his wives: the two sisters were precisely in this position when they were circulated between Laban and Jacob in Genesis 29. Jacob is not even allowed to respond to Leah's stinging remark "Thou must come in unto me; for surely I have hired thee with my son's mandrakes." He follows her obediently. "And he lay with her that night" (Gen. 30:16).

Paradoxically, however, being momentarily in the position of the Other turns out to be to Jacob's advantage insofar as it enhances the "building" of his house. What is more, in the following episode he regains control in matters of fertility as he manipulates the mating of Laban's flocks. Using rods as stimuli, the shrewd trickster manages to increase the numbers of the speckled sheep and goats (the rare type) that Laban had allotted to him:

And Jacob took him rods of green poplar . . . and pilled white strakes in them. . . . And he set the rods which he had pilled before the flocks in the gutters in the watering troughs when the flocks came to drink, that they should conceive when they came to drink. And the flocks con-

ceived before the rods, and brought forth cattle ring-
straked, speckled and spotted. (Gen. 30:37–39)

His success as a shepherd seems to have bearing on his virility, especially in light of the fact that the names Rachel and Leah mean
"ewe" and "cow." (Jacob in fact makes a pun regarding this issue in
Genesis 31:38: "This twenty years have I been with thee: thy ewes
[rechelekha] and thy she goats have not cast their young.") Jacob is
back in business, thriving more than ever. "And the man increased
exceedingly" and had, in this order, "much cattle, and maidservants,
and menservants, and camels, and asses" (Gen. 30:43). He can at last
venture to return home to Canaan; he is ready for the decisive encounter with Esau.

JOINING FORCES

In order to leave Laban's household, however, Jacob needs to acquire
the consent of Rachel and Leah. The three meet in the field. Jacob
opens with a detailed depiction of Laban's continual abuse of him
and ends with God's request that he return to Canaan (see Gen.
31:5–13). The sisters respond with one voice:

> And Rachel and Leah answered and said unto him, Is
> there yet any portion or inheritance for us in our father's
> house? Are we not counted of him strangers? for he hath
> sold us, and hath quite devoured also our money. For all
> the riches which God hath taken from our father, that is
> ours, and our children's: now then, whatsoever God hath
> said unto thee, do. (Gen. 31:14–16)

The two have learned to cooperate in times of distress. Enraged by
Laban's usurpation of their inheritance and by their status as
nokhriyot (foreigners) in his household, they do not hesitate to join
forces with Jacob against their father. They translate Jacob's long,
calculated legalistic speech into a brief, blunt, and spicy depiction of
Laban's greed. Laban, they claim, is more than a dishonest deceiver,
he is a covetous monster who would neither stop at selling his own
daughters nor at "devouring" their money (vayokhal gam 'akhol 'et
kaspenu). In this case all three have parallel histories. They are all
victims of Laban's wheeling and dealing; and, even more interesting,

all three are foreigners: Jacob is literally so, while the sisters are estranged on a figurative level. Up until now the text focused on Laban's merciless exploitation of Jacob and the latter's attempt to deceive the deceiver. Now we get a glimpse of what has been withheld: the attitude of the two sisters with respect to their father's deeds. At this point their provocative perspective may be revealed, for it offers a critique of the oppression of women within—to use Mieke Bal's terms—the "patrilocal" system (domination of father/father-in-law), just as the transition to a "virilocal" system (domination of husband) needs to be legitimized.[7] The journey from Aram to Canaan is the concomitant geographical move.

The sisters speak with one voice against their father, yet it seems to be primarily Rachel's voice. This is at least one way to account for the order of presentation: Rachel before Leah (Gen. 31:14). The episode in which Rachel steals the *terafim* (the household gods) augments the notion that she is the instigator of the sisters' rebellion against Laban. Here, too, we have a scene that curiously evokes a central episode in Jacob's life. If one bears in mind that possession of the household gods could serve as the symbolic token of leadership in a given estate (as is evident in the Nuzi documents[8]), what Rachel is after in this case is analogous to what Jacob cunningly wrests from his blind old father. The verbal marker that links the two episodes is the verb *mishesh* ("feel," "touch"). When Laban enters Rachel's tent, he "feels" all her belongings, but fails to find the *terafim*. Stricken by male fear of menstruation, he accepts Rachel's request to remain seated: "And she said unto her father, Let it not displease my lord that I cannot rise up before thee; for the custom of women is upon me" (Gen. 31:35).[9] Feeling turns out once again to be an unreliable protection against the trickery of one's offspring.

Rachel's act is not only directed against her father. It may also be seen as yet another manifestation of the rivalry between the two sisters. Just as Jacob's tricking of Isaac is meant to secure his priority vis-à-vis Esau, so is Rachel's tricking of Laban bound up with her ongoing desire to prevail over her elder sister. Although Rachel is both a mother and the beloved wife at this point, her son is not Jacob's firstborn, which is why the *terafim* are needed. Belatedness is still a problem. The struggle between the sisters is not quite over, for the law that institutionalizes natural order threatens Joseph's status:

> If a man have two wives, one beloved, and another hated,
> and they have borne him children, both the beloved and

the hated; and if the firstborn son be hers that was hated:
Then it shall be, when he maketh his sons to inherit that
which he hath, that he may not make the son of the beloved firstborn before the son of the hated, which is indeed the firstborn. (Deut. 21:15–16)

This law, however, is often violated in the annunciation type-scene.
Thus Sarah's son, rather than Hagar's son, assumes the position of
the firstborn, just as Hannah's son, rather than Peninnah's firstborn,
is the one who becomes God's messenger. As the loved barren one,
Rachel seems to have the potential of being the elected mother of
the chosen son, but this privilege is taken away from her just when
she is about to reach her destination.

RACHEL'S DEATH

Rachel's death, perhaps even more than her life, encapsulates her
unfulfilled yearnings, her tragic exile.[10] She dies on the road—not far
from Ephrath but not fully there. The location of her tomb is not
without significance. This liminal locus intimates that she makes it
to the threshold of the royal city (Ephrath is Bethlehem) but isn't allowed to enter. The future Davidic dynasty does not spring from her
sons, but rather from Judah, Leah's fourth son.

Her final naming-speech marks her agony. "Son of my sorrow," she
calls her second son upon dying (Gen. 35:18). She who desperately
cried "Give me sons or else I die" now ironically dies upon bearing
a son. Jacob quickly changes the name to Benjamin, "son of my right
hand," perhaps to protect the newly born child from such a gloomy
name, perhaps in an attempt to mitigate the pain that characterized
his beloved's life, or possibly as a promise to the dying Rachel that
at least in the case of her sons (regardless of the lot of Leah's sons),
the younger shall prevail, just as one's right hand prevails. Later,
when blessing Joseph's sons, he will similarly switch hands, placing
the right hand on the younger Ephraim and his left hand on
Menashe.

But why does Rachel die in the prime of her life? Rabbinic interpretations stress the fatal impact of Jacob's curse:[11] "With whomever
thou findest thy gods, let him not live" (Gen. 31:32), says Jacob in
response to Laban's accusation that he stole the household gods. Although the text goes on to mitigate Jacob's harshness by making

clear that "Jacob knew not that Rachel had stolen them," one may well wonder whether Jacob, not unlike Jephthah, should have been aware of the possible consequences of his speech act.[12] Jacob knows only too well that Rachel has supported his "stealing away" (Gen. 31:20) from Laban's household. Would it have been too great a leap of the imagination to surmise that Rachel might have ventured to do some (literal) stealing? I am not trying to cast doubt on Jacob's great love for the woman he adored at first sight, but there is something about Rachel's ambitions that makes her threatening even for Jacob.

Rachel, as we have seen, ridicules Jacob when swapping him for Reuben's mandrakes. But this is a tendency one can trace, if to a lesser extent, back to their very first dialogue where she implicitly blames Jacob for her barrenness. Her cry "Give me children or else I die" (Gen. 30:1) may seem at first an irrational accusation of Jacob for something he couldn't possibly be responsible for. And indeed, Jacob's angry response reinforces this notion: "Am I in God's stead, who hath withheld from thee the fruit of the womb?" Rachel, however, is not mistaken in her choice of addressee, as the insightful midrashic elaboration of this exchange makes clear:

> *Am I in God's stead, who hath withheld from thee the fruit of the womb?* "From thee he withheld it, but not from me." Said she to him: "Did then your father [Isaac] act so to your mother? Did he not gird up his loins by her?" "He had no children," he retorted, "whereas I have children." "And did not your grandfather [Abraham] have children," she pursued, "yet he too girded up his loins by Sarah?" (Genesis Rabba. LXXI. 7)

Given the examples of his paternal precursors, who prayed for the sake of their barren wives and succeeded in procuring divine intervention, Jacob indeed should have tried to use his higher position in relation to God to help bring about the opening of his wife's womb. Rachel's exposure of his ineptness, in other words, is justifiable, and this is precisely what makes Jacob so angry.

Once Jacob is on the way to Canaan and the struggle with Laban is over, Rachel's audacity is not as beneficial as before. His curse may thus be perceived as the expression of an unwitting wish to set limits to his counterpart's plot. She is a fine mirror, but at times her mirroring comes close to self-representation. At times she goes too far in striving to become a subject, which is why her voice needs to be repressed.[13]

To be sure, Jacob will mourn Rachel for the rest of his life (see Gen. 48:7) and will love her sons, Benjamin and especially Joseph, more than Leah's sons.[14] Yet when Jacob himself approaches death, he will ask to lie at Leah's side (Gen. 49:31): he will end up preferring the traditional burial place, where Abraham buried Sarah and Isaac buried Rebekah, to being buried as an outsider, on the road, with Rachel. This is, no doubt, Leah's ultimate triumph.

DIFFERENCE IN DEVELOPMENT

Rachel remains the black sheep of the family. Unlike Jacob, she is never given the chance to be transformed. Nor does her relationship with Leah ever reach the point of an explicit reconciliation, as is the case with Jacob and Esau. The two issues are not unrelated. Jacob's inner transformation is inextricably bound up with his capacity to cope with his brother. Their reconciliation can take place only after he struggles with the angel, after he sheds the name Jacob (a derivation of the verb *'akv*, meaning "to twist" or "trick") and acquires from his divine opponent a new name, Israel. This new name marks a change in his character, a rebirth of sorts, for he seems to enter a higher state of being upon his designation as the eponymic father of the nation. I am not suggesting that Jacob becomes angelic after his nocturnal struggle, nor that the reconciliation between the brothers is innocent of tension. Nevertheless change, albeit limited, is possible in the male realm.

Transformation is the hallmark of the biblical hero, as Erich Auerbach suggests:

> But what a road, what a fate, lie between the Jacob who cheated his father out of his blessing and the old man whose favorite son has been torn into pieces by a wild beast!—between David the harp player, persecuted by his lord's jealousy, and the old king, surrounded by violent intrigues, whom Abishag the Shunnamite warmed in his bed, and he knew her not! The old man of whom we know how he has become what he is, is more of an individual than the young man; for it is only during the course of an eventful life that men are differentiated into full in-

dividuality; and it is this history of a personality which the Old Testament presents to us as the formation undergone by those whom God has chosen to be examples. Fraught with their development, sometimes even aged to the verge of dissolution, they show a distinct stamp of individuality entirely foreign to the Homeric heroes.[15]

Female characters, however, are not so "fraught with development." Their textual life-span is limited. With the exception of Eve, we have no scene that depicts the birth of the heroine, let alone rebirth. The biblical woman appears on stage only when she is marriageable, and her stay there is determined, generally speaking, by the impact of her maternal position on the status of her (favorite) son. Rachel actually dies in childbirth, but other biblical mothers simply vanish from the scene once their offspring are on their own. Their function as a foil to the men in their lives precludes the possibility of significant change: it limits the capacity of their dreams to shape reality.

DREAMS AND REALITY

In "The Relation of the Poet to Day-Dreaming," Freud analyzes the fulfillment of wishes provided in popular novels and romances. Such texts, he claims, have a "marked characteristic": "They all have a hero who is the center of interest, for whom the author tries to win our sympathy by every possible means, and whom he places under the protection of a special providence."[16]

The hero of course is bound to undergo numerous hardships, but we may maintain a feeling of security that he will find a way out of every dangerous situation, for we share the hero's own conviction of invincibility—best rendered in the expression "Nothing can happen to me!" Freud goes on to suggest that "this significant mark of invulnerability very clearly betrays—His Majesty the Ego, the hero of all daydreams and novels."[17]

The Hebrew Bible, as Gabriel Josipovici aptly shows, does not offer the comforts of fulfillment one finds in fairy tales and romances. It "takes pleasure in allowing . . . dreams their full force, but then sets them against reality—the dreams of others and the facts of life, such as failure and death."[18] Josipovici's observations hold true for both Rachel and Jacob. What they do not account for, however, is the difference, for men and women, in how their ambitions are allowed to transcend their original stations in life.

Jacob, like the hero Freud describes, is placed in a central position "under the protection of a special providence." He is God's unmistakable elect, and as such he manages to realize what he tried to do already upon grabbing Esau's heel: to reverse natural order. But Jacob is not invulnerable. He is not in the position of God, which is, in a sense, the position fairy tales end up allowing "His Majesty the Ego" to attain. Jacob's decisive victory over Esau does not enable him to live "happily ever after." The great trickster is tricked time and again: first by Laban and then by his own sons, when they present him with Joseph's stained coat, claiming his favorite son has been devoured. What is more, he must yield to death. And the length of life given him is a final frustration. "The years of my sojourn [on earth] are one hundred and thirty. Few and hard have been the years of my life, nor do they come up to the life-spans of my fathers during their sojourns" (Gen. 47:9—the new Jewish Publication Society translation). The realization of one dream is no guarantee that other dreams will be realized. In comparison with his two paternal precursors, Jacob still feels something of a loser. They had better control over time. Their life-spans were greater.

But seen against the background of Rachel's premature death, Jacob's lot does not appear terribly bleak. The restrictions reality sets up for Rachel's dreams are far greater. Although God occasionally "remembers" Rachel (Gen. 30:22), her story seems to be the obverse negative of "nothing can happen to me." The phrase that best characterizes Rachel's posture might well be, in Nancy Miller's terms, "a variant of Murphy's law: If anything can go wrong, it will."[19] Ambition is primarily a patriarchal prerogative. Thus a female character who tries to fulfill her ambitious dreams, to protest against time's tyranny, runs her head against a wall.

Rachel's dream, however, is not doomed to total frustration. In a remarkable manner she has always managed to gain much admiration for her daring aspirations and compassion for her tragic failures. She may be the black sheep of the family, but despite, or because of, this role, she has never ceased to be the favorite matriarch in Jewish tradition. This is already evident in Jeremiah, who selects Rachel, and not Leah, as the mother of the nation, as the one who is best suited to accompany Jacob in his position as the eponymous father:

A voice was heard in Ramah, lamentation and bitter weeping; Rachel weeping for her children refused to be comforted for her children, because they were not. Thus saith the Lord; Refrain thy voice from weeping, and thine eyes from tears: for thy work shall be rewarded, saith the Lord; and they shall come again from the land of the enemy. And there is hope in thine end, saith the Lord, that thy children shall come again to their own border. (Jer. 31:15–17)

In Jeremiah's famous prophecy Rachel is allowed to transcend time. Her voice rises from the dead to cry on behalf of the exiled.

The Nursing Father

❦

ALICIA OSTRIKER

"The Nursing Father," a reading of the Exodus story and of the giant figure of Moses, is taken from a longer work, The Nakedness of the Fathers, *which experimentally combines biblical commentary with fantasy, poetry, and autobiography. Writing as a twentieth-century woman and feminist, I have tried here to analyze the tremendous cultural transformation involved in breaking away from Egypt and from slavery; to understand some connections and contrasts between biblical time and our own historical moment; and to comprehend what the Exodus means to me personally, as we are enjoined to do every Passover. At the same time, I have tried to convey the exalted, heroic, and tragic struggle of Moses as he attempts to lead a people toward a Promise we have still not yet realized.*

And the Angel of the Lord appeared
unto him in a flame of fire out of the
midst of a bush: and he looked, and,

One of the epigraphs to this essay is taken from the King James Version of the Bible. Elsewhere in the essay I have at times paraphrased biblical passages, at times used phrases from the KJV.

41

> behold, the bush burned with fire, and
> the bush was not consumed.
>
> —Exodus 3:2

> This story made it possible to tell other stories.
> —Michael Walzer, *Exodus and Revolution*

WHAT WAS EGYPT, THAT GOD SENT US DOWN INTO IT AND WITH an outstretched arm brought us up out of it? A flat plane extended on either side of a great river. A place without mountains. The reifying of the abstract body. The elegance of the linear, particularly the sides and slender waists, slender and static in all the representations. No fatness, no muscularity. Among their gods and goddesses reigned a pure ancient graciousness, refined over many centuries into perfection and beyond perfection into trance.

In that aeons-long expanse of Egypt, in the stasis of its image, we discern the swollen desire of timelessness. There must nothing happen. The river floods, recedes. There are wars. There are revolutions. It is nothing. Dynasties—nothing. The same sun-Amen, the same river, the double of the cool river underground, the same priests whispering the same intrigues, the same tinted, spangled body of the goddess Nut arched as if in permanent sexual pleasure from the eastern to the western limit of the world, the same Isis and Osiris, the same Horus and Set, the same destruction and dismemberment, the same renewal and recovery. There is nothing happening and nothing to happen. No growth or decay. No death, there cannot be death, the spirit glides in her slender boat out along the dark river, jeweled and scented, arrayed and sandaled, surrounded by her playthings, and she replies to the gatekeeper Osiris, and is weighed against a feather, and passes beyond. The body, packed in resin, may wait and wait. Sealed absolutely from the air.

Upon papyrus, upon stone, upon gold, this perfect flatness or this perfectly accurate lineation. The volumes of sculpture the same. It is all luxury, calm, voluptuousness, a motionless dance. It is upon the bodies of their slaves that they dance. On the pulp of their slaves. Those whose bodies are disturbingly muscled, organisms to perform work. The subhuman. Those who, when they die, do not revive but simply rot.

I have disappeared into Egypt for four hundred years. I am enslaved there. It is my first captivity. I am a hot, foreign body of herdsmen—nomadic and seminomadic, restless, sometime hunters, sometime primitive farmers, sometime mercenaries, sometime thieves, possessing military combined with pastoral virtues. I am their stranger. I am their Other, to them an abomination. Like the God of my fathers I need to travel in order to breathe, but am trapped like a scarab in amber.

A child is born, bursts from the amber: imago, energy, genius. Tell us the story! A story! Well, to begin—even before his conception, then at his birth and in his infancy, the story is all women. You remember the two midwives who refuse to kill the male Hebrew babies? A nonconfrontational civil disobedience, they report that the Hebrew mothers are so lively they give birth before the midwives arrive. Then, you remember the mother of Moses? She doesn't kill him, either, she hides him and then she packs him (a live baby!) into a little floating basket and sets it among the reeds of the riverbank (bright green river of life, not black river of death!), where a beautiful princess who wants a baby finds him. And you know what they say? When the princess unwrapped Moses, he cried so loud, she knew he had to be a Jew. Of course she decides to keep him (women are disloyal to civilization; women want babies) and then Moses' own sister, who has been hiding in the reeds, pops out and asks Pharaoh's daughter: would you like me to find you a nurse for that nice baby? The princess says yes, so Miriam runs and fetches Moses' own mother, who then gets to breast-feed Moses for three years. Isn't that clever? Do you like the way all the brave women combine in the resistance? Of course it is also possible that the baby is really the illegitimate child of the princess. Sigmund Freud thinks so. But the essence of the story (folk essence, myth essence) is the birth, and the protected rearing in a palace, of the rebellious child.

Child of compassion, child of wrath. Moses is Egyptian, he is Hebrew, he is both/neither, he is insider/outsider. Child of the mothers in the world of the fathers. What is needed for redemption.

But the story? Stepping outside the palace for the first time in his life, like the adolescent Buddha, the young Moses encounters political reality. He sees an Egyptian foreman beat a Hebrew slave; he glances both ways, nobody is watching, he kills the foreman. Next day he sees two Hebrews fighting and chides the aggressor, who responds belligerently: Who made you our judge? Will you kill me, too, the way you killed the Egyptian? So Moses is afraid; he flees the city. Like the Buddha whose eyes were opened with horror at disease, old age, and death. No, unlike the Buddha. This anger of Moses that flares spontaneously. This hatred of slavery. This question of social justice.

What does the Buddha care for social justice? The Buddha counsels us to escape this world of suffering, from which Moses won't escape, from which he escapes to return, bearing twice his weight, bearing his infinite burden, bearing the weight of God. And the weight of the Hebrew people as well—infinitely, impossibly heavy. Already his destiny is shaped: to hate slavery, to hate violence, to be violent and enslaved—forever—to the God of the Fathers. And never to be loved or understood. Who made you judge? Will you kill us the way you killed the Egyptian? They mock him ungratefully, servilely—and they will continue to do so. Why can't we have our fleshpots, they will whine, why can't we eat fish the way we did in Egypt, instead of this boring manna, why can't we have cucumbers melons leeks onions garlic, why can't we dance around a golden calf, how do you expect us to fight Canaanites, they're bigger than we are.

Never to be loved. To bear this ungrateful people, this people without memory, this disobedient people, like a monstrous child at his breast, a mindless, colicky, sickly child—to save it but not to be loved by it. To plead with God for its life, to carry it to freedom, to build it finally into a nation and tell it what is required of it—again and again the story of emancipation. To create a memory for it. To create law for it. To create purpose. To force it into history. But never to be loved.

For God is going to use him. God doesn't care whether Moses is loved, only that he is a powerful pack animal. Of all those who were called by God and resisted the calling, Moses is most tragic—not because God abandons him but on the contrary because God seizes on him and employs him ruthlessly, to the outer limits of his extraordinary endurance. God will press him. God will squeeze him like fruit. From the day he sees the burning bush until the day of his death forty years afterward, Moses will move through life bearing the two weights. The weight of God from above, crushing him. The weight of the Israelites at his bosom, a hateful infant refusing the nipple. Because God is ready now to rupture the ancient Near Eastern timelessness.

(If God wishes to penetrate heaven's membrane, from existing beyond time to acting within time, if God wants to change from being Elohim, Transcendant Heavenly Being(s), or El Shaddai, God of the Breast-Hill-Mountain, or El Olam, Everlasting, if God desires to be named I WILL BECOME THAT I WILL BECOME,[1] then a nation is required to accept his covenant. To embody his undeclared purposes. If a nation, then a leader. If a leader, then cruelty, which in any case people understand. But also a promise.)

I write in American space and Jewish time. The space of my particular promised land. Sweet land of liberty. Land to which my grandfathers fled, with their socialist pamphlets. With Galician and Lithuanian villages burning behind them. In the village squares—it was nothing new—they were lining up the Jews. Pamphlets were being distributed declaring that Jews killed Christian babies in obscene rituals. In the village squares stood blond soldiers who would take an old man by the earlock, hold a revolver to his neck, command him to spit on his Torah.

How do I know I am a Jew in Jewish time. I am in Budapest twenty years ago, a fine restaurant. As I am leaving, the maître d' engages me in conversation for some reason, it is small talk, nothing. And you are American; yes, American. And your people . . . ? My people, my grandparents came over all in the eighteen eighties from eastern Europe. Yes, he says, with his eyes of two thousand years which I have not noticed. We call them the glückische kinder.

The lucky children.

When he saw the burning bush, he was fascinated. He walked closer. The thornbush, grown out of a rock cleft in the shrubby Midian hills, appeared to be regenerating itself moment by moment while fire bit at it and hissed around it. Inside the fire whirled twenty-two letters, like imps. He did not yet know that the bush, from which the Presence spoke, was an allegory of himself. He was regarding his own future, seething red and blue—on holy ground— where the Presence revealed itself as power. This power would use the good of Moses, his evil, his everything. Would not leave his intelligence, his imagination, his courage, his conscience, his power to persuade, his power to command—would not leave his energies alone ever again. Nor did it scruple to employ his fanaticism, his pride, his

aristocratic Egyptian haughtiness, his impatience, his violence, his
cold abstractedness—every quality a kindly man might hate in himself, the God of History used those too.

Like others called by God, Moses resisted. *Hineni*, here am I, in
the first instance. But soon: Why me, I'm only a stutterer, I'm not capable. What do you want from me and why must it be so difficult.
A wise instinct, because the God of History will lead him a little at
a time as if he were a pet dog. Or a work dog. Not the shepherd but
the shepherd's dog, yapping at the flock's heels.

Moses discovers the will of God in the bush. Here am I. In the
bush, and again in the voice, and again in the night attack from
which Zipporah saves him. A bloody husband you are to me, cries
the Hittite wife to the Hebrew husband, casting a foreskin at his feet.
Then again in the writhing snake that immobilizes to a rod. And
again in the plagues, and again in the Red Sea when a strong east
wind all night made the sea go back, and the waters were divided so
that people passed through a corridor with waters like gelatinous
walls and could see fish and other creatures of the deep captured
swimming inside, and again when the Red Sea overwhelmed the pursuing armies, finally drowning their horses, horsemen, and chariots,
and Miriam led the women in a victory dance praising God with
drums and timbrels. And again in the gift of manna (unlike the
fleshpots in Egypt), and again marching behind the ghostly pillar of
fire and pillar of smoke (unlike the image-deities in Egypt), and
again in thunder and fierce lightning and quaking and the sound of
the trumpet in Sinai that they say is a ram's horn, the same ram
Abraham slew on Moriah. Onward. Get on with it.

And again in the Commandments; and again in the destruction of
the golden calf; and again in the defeat of Amalek; and again inside
the quiet wooden tabernacle, which is like the ark of his infancy,
which is like Jochabed's uterus, where the twin carved seraphim face
each other like labia, where God speaks to Moses face-to-face as a
man speaks with a friend. Bliss then. Onward. Again when Moses
begs that the I WILL BECOME accompany the Israelites forever, separating them from other peoples, and I WILL BECOME agrees.

And again when God's anger is kindled and destroys the murmur-
ers; and strikes Miriam with leprosy for her claim that he speaks to
her; and swears by his life that none who left Egypt will enter Canaan because they are all slaves in their hearts except Joshua, so let
their carcasses rot in the wilderness. Let only the young and free possess the land. Get on with it. Any of these signs would have been

sufficient. And again when he makes the earth swallow Korah and his rebels; and again when Aaron's rod blooms simultaneously with buds, blossoms, and almonds; and when twenty-four thousand die of plague after following Moabite gods; and again when Moses is able before death to recite the entire Torah to the Israelites, and to sing that we suck honey from the rock; and again when Moses is commanded to climb Mount Pisgah, to survey the whole of the holy land, and then to die.

Any of these signs would have been sufficient.

To mediate between the king of the universe and the newly released people chosen to be his precious instrument is to endure torment. Moses' calling is completely different from the priestly function, which is rite and habit and does not devour a man's soul. To be Moses is to improvise a kind of leadership unique in history. From a despicable mob to create a free, disciplined, self-governing nation. With a rule of law. With stress on social justice; commandments of generosity to the poor; periodic release of debts and slaves; periodic release of the land, which, it is understood, belongs to God, not to human beings, so that all "private property" is temporary. A commandment not to afflict widows and orphans in any way, because if they cry at all to God, he will surely hear their cry, and his wrath will wax hot, and he will kill you with the sword, and your wives will be widows and your children fatherless. A commandment to love God (love! with all your heart, mind, and strength) and your neighbor as yourself. Repeated reminders that the law applies equally to rich and poor, to native and stranger. Repeated, repeated injunctions against oppressing the stranger, because you know the heart of the stranger, because you were strangers in Egypt.

All of which appears impossible, since the people are constantly backsliding and seem unable to remember from one day to the next even a simple thing like God's getting them through the Red Sea, much less a complicated set of laws. The fact is nobody likes this project of liberty very much.

Egypt, Succoth, Sea of Reeds, Marah the Bitter, Horeb, Sinai, Moab, Gilead, Pisgah, Canaan.

Babylon, Rome, Ethiopia, India, Persia, Spain, Portugal, the Low Countries, Germany, Poland, Russia, England, France, America.

Auschwitz, Bergen-Belsen, Buchenwald, Theresienstadt, Dachau, Treblinka, Chelmno, Sobibor, Belzek, Majdanek.

Montgomery, Little Rock, Greensboro, Nashville, Atlanta, Albany, Birmingham, Washington, D.C., Jackson, Meridian, Harlem, Chicago, Watts, Selma, Memphis.

Wilderness.

> *Oh, freedom. Oh, freedom. Oh, freedom over me.*
> *And before I'll be a slave, I'll be buried in my grave*
> *And go home to my Lord and be free.*

A song learned at the same time as I learned the others. Go down, Moses. We shall not be moved. Long may our land be bright, with freedom's holy light. Study war no more. Around the Pioneer Youth Camp campfires the girls and boys sat in separate whispering clumps, passing forbidden candy. The counselors would move around the fire swiftly, featureless shadows, throwing more wood on or adjusting logs at the edges. I wondered how they could dare to go close to it, this fire that to me seemed so great and hot, hurling huge flickering reddish lights among us.

What we did in the dark was sing. I loved the sound of our voices together. Oppressed so hard they could not stand was like when the kids in my building at home ganged up on me. Grabbed my books, tossed them in the gutter, taunted Who do you think you are, Einstein? I am only a junior pioneer but already know about the world we are working for, the no more hatred and persecution, the no more war, no more cruel oppression, one world. An end to ignorance and prejudice. I know the words of the songs and can harmonize the way my father showed me. Around the flames the campers sway from side to side with our arms around each other's small bodies. If I had a hammer . . . I'd hammer out love between my brothers and my sisters, Aaall over this land. We watch the red sparks flying from the top of the fire.

After the campfire we have to find our way through the woods to our cabins. I wandered off the narrow dirt trail, banged against standing trees and dead ones, scratched by invisible branches. Fell in a sea of dry leaves. Starting to crawl instead of walk. Starting to cry, hearing the unbroken mockery of crickets, the voices of the older campers still singing.

Nobody understands this project of liberty, it is far too difficult. They do, however, understand terror. Whoever is on my side (God's side), go out into the camp and every man slay his brother, his son, his friend and neighbor. They do understand intolerance. No other gods. No images, no idols, no interbreeding, no whoring with the Others, whom the God of History has not chosen. What if the Others are great and we are little? Still they are the unclean, the not-us. Division of clean from unclean. Pure from defiled. Righteous from unrighteous.

The universality of God—this monotheism that is now digging its massive root down to the core of the planet—leads along one branch to universal love and compassion, an infinite cherishing of life, a new ethics: They shall not hurt nor destroy in all my holy mountain. Along another branch it becomes the laws of science. Gravity, motion, everywhere reasonable, everywhere predictable. This selfsame logic, says Johannes Kepler, the Creator placed in our minds so that we might share in his ideas. Along yet another branch, Sinai feeds the tenacious pride of those who consider themselves chosen, who will rejoice at the death of the unbeliever, the death of the apostate. It is a pride that will precipitate oppression, suffering, and martyrdom, the spilled blood of century after century, in religion after religion. It is a pride that will encourage the narrowness of the narrow in spirit, let there be no mistake. And as for the flower of intellectual evil that has most fully blossomed in our own century, the doctrine of racial purity: this, too, with its rhetoric, its simple appeal, is rooted in Sinai. For what is a Master Race if not the distorted mirror image of a Chosen People, at which all the devils in Gehenna laugh until their sides split?

But as for Moses, our pack animal, destruction of the wayward is not his desire. When they worship the golden calf, Moses prevents God from destroying all the Israelites—the Egyptians will laugh at you and think you're crazy, remember what you promised Abraham, Isaac, and Jacob, shouts Moses at the Almighty; then he goes down the mountain and orders the massacre in which three thousand men are slaughtered; then desperately climbs Sinai again and demands: forgive them! And if you will not—then blot my name from your book! And when they all weep for meat instead of manna, Moses turns on God: why do you lay this burden on me? Did I beget this people? Did I give birth to them, that you require me to carry them like a nursing father on my bosom, to the land you promised their fathers? Where am I to get meat for them? From my own body? Kill me, then! They are too heavy for me to bear.

AND ALL THE WHILE Egypt is being defeated. Instead of Image we possess Word. An alternative beauty bursts into existence, through the tongue of the stutterer Moses. It is the triumph of Language. Nothing remains to be seen—God is perfectly invisible, impalpable—only to be heard. Listen! The Lord thy God, the Lord is One, says Moses. One gives us the Law. Therefore the Law and the Prophets, the Law and its interpretations, all oral tradition, all written commentaries, all words regarding the Word shall become portions of Torah, twigs on a tree of life, rooted in Sinai, exfoliating in time and space.

Gives us a Book, gives us therefore the life of the mind, gives us the intellectual power to survive in exile—and if in that act is a perpetual bondage, there is also a perpetual liberation from bondage: for are we not commanded by the text itself to interrogate, to engage in dialogue with each other, with the text, with God? Turn it and turn it, says Talmud, for everything is in it. Talmud says, There is always another interpretation. For words, unlike images, are powerful yet indeterminate, slip and slide and escape when you think you have them pinned, contain immeasurable dark interiors.

An image is motionless, timeless. It gives itself to you immediately. But language moves, it exists only in time, in history, the past melting and rushing toward the future, provoking you, dancing away. Infinitely heavy, infinitely plural, ungraspable—like God—a perpetual guarantee against slavery.

But remember the women in the story. What do the women say? The women say that the triumph of the Word is the repression of the Mother. Sensuous perception is subordinated to intellectual principle. The invisibility of God means the paternity of God. For the Father must be deduced, while the Mother remains evident to the senses. And so Mother must be disempowered, whether she be mortal or goddess.

Elsewhere when one people conquers another, the number of gods increases. The new ones join the old, some are promoted and some demoted. Witness Hinduism, the textbook case of syncretism in which augmentation is the rule, nothing is lost, and dozens of divinities coexist in layers of various provenance as if no deity once alive can ever die. With the God of Moses it is different. When this one descends on Canaan, the rest must disappear; we must all agree that they never existed.

But what if a god once alive can never die?

They are denied, that is to say they are eaten. Devoured, swallowed, absorbed, their bundles of attributes digested. They wait. And sometimes one feels them kick.

"Come not near your wives," commands God to Israel before Sinai—and so we suddenly learn that women are perhaps not included in the covenant? Yes, it is in the life of Moses that we see the women disappear. We see the flash of their backs as they dive, like dolphins, beneath the agitated surface of the text. Where are they now, bold midwives, mothers, sisters, disobedient princesses, bitter talking-back wives? Submerged; objects of the law; apparently passive. You shall not suffer a witch to live. A daughter is her father's possession. He may sell her if he wishes. A woman's husband is her lord, she cannot initiate divorce, she cannot inherit property except where there is no male heir. The punishment if a bride is not a virgin, or a woman is convicted of adultery, is death by stoning. The woman, the mother, the cycle of maternity, is now said to be intrinsically unclean. Her menstrual blood defiles. Her secretions are the paradigm for every kind of pustulence or running sore, diseases requiring isolation and ritual cleansing. Leprosy is figuratively a female disease: Miriam but not Aaron is punished by it. Before and after menstruation a woman is unclean. She is also unclean after childbirth, and longer if the child is a girl. If she touches you during these periods, you become defiled. If you touch her bed or something she has sat on, you are defiled.

Yet do prohibitions not draw one's (secret) attention to that which is prohibited? Do these prohibitions not make the defiling thing at once disgusting and attractive? Not even to touch the place where a menstruating woman, or a woman after childbirth, has sat. One almost wishes her to sit, to have sat, everywhere. So the reduction of the woman's power, the elevation of the abstract father whom one cannot see, contribute to the power of the covenant? The woman pollutes? Very well: exorcise her, isolate her, erase her (she will rule your dreams).

The subduing of the image, then, is complete. Instead of a graven image, God is language. But the subduing of the body, the subduing of woman? Apparently defeated yet far from defeat, she invisibly propagates, increases, and multiplies throughout the laws, statutes, and ordinances designed to contain her. Because no substitute exists for her sexual vitality, her practical capacity, here in the world of generation, which God has made according to his will. (Where is the promised land? It is of the earth, earthy. If it were abstract, it would be Egypt.) And if *ruach*, spirit, is a woman; if *hokhmah*, wisdom, is a woman; if *rachmanes*, compassion, derives from the mother's womb; if the Sabbath is a bride; if the Shekhina is daughter, bride, mother, moon, sea, faith, wisdom, and speech; and if Torah herself is the king's child who shows herself little by little to her lovers—then it is inside the language, the place of interpretation, the place of dialogue, interrogation, commentary, laughter, the place of holy disobedience, the site of persistent stubbornness, wrestling, and the demand for blessing, foreseen eternally by the Holy One who has curiously chosen this rebellious people for his especial treasure—here in the place of metaphor is where woman waits.

And therefore the rabbis say the Shekhinah, who is the feminine portion of God, became the spouse of Moses, replacing Zipporah. They claim that the Shekhinah accompanied him always and filled him with secret joy. And telling of his death, they say that on Mount Pisgah Moses refuses to die. God sends the Angel of Death for him, but Moses thrice rejects the summons. Finally God says he will permit Moses to live on condition that Israel dies. Only then does Moses surrender to God and consent to die; and the Shekhinah bends down and kisses him on the lips. On this kiss his spirit travels to heaven.

Leaving me behind to possess the land and lose it, possess it and lose it. Leaving me to be hated, derided, exiled, imprisoned, raped, tortured, flayed in strips, castrated, put to death by the sword, burned at the stake, gassed, shot, shoved into ovens, my ashes smeared over Europe. Leaving me at my desk, at my typewriter. Leaving me in the library among floors of books as the sands of the sea. Setting me on fire with words. Throwing me into a classroom. Putting paper at my disposal and salvation in my mind, generations of voices in my ears, and they argue, and sometimes they sing. Commandments, promises, who can obey enough, hear clearly enough.

Leaving always a remnant telling the story, intoxicated by time future. Next year in Jerusalem. Soon the promised land.

What is the promised land, that the Almighty drives us to it? A child runs by the oceanside, dashes barefoot into the surf, runs giggling to the mother. The grandmother hitches her pruning hook over a long branch. In the evening the man under his fig tree and the man under his vine argue politics; the wives join them, and nobody makes them afraid.

Milk and honey, the desert blooms, spacious skies.

The promised land really exists, it really doesn't, are we there yet. Borders unspecified, we will know when we've arrived. Profusely fertile, agriculturally a heartland; good also for grazing; room for cities. Are we there yet. The land of opportunity, these truths to be self-evident, it is necessarily elsewhere, from sea to shining sea. No more auction block. Take this hammer, carry it to the captain, tell him I'm gone. Emancipate yourself from mental slavery. If you are not for yourself, who is for you; if you are for yourself alone, what are you, and if not now, when. Keep your hand on that plow, hold on. No more sin and suffering, no pharaoh, no king, one man one vote, are we there yet, no grinding the faces of the poor, are we there yet, no bribing of judges, are we there yet.

An impossible place, let freedom ring in it. We've been to the mountain. We've seen the land: a terrain of the imagination, its hills skipping for joy. How long, we say, we know our failure in advance, nobody alive will set foot in it.

In Search of Pharaoh's Daughter

❦

PATRICIA J. WILLIAMS

"Have mercy! Lord, have mercy on my poor soul!"
Women gave birth and whispered cries like this in caves
and out-of-the-way places that humans didn't usually use
for birthplaces. Moses hadn't come yet, and these were the
years when Israel first made tears. Pharaoh had entered
the bedrooms of Israel. The birthing beds of Hebrews were
matters of state. The Hebrew womb had fallen under the
heel of Pharaoh. A ruler great in his newness and new in
his greatness had arisen in Egypt and he had said, "This
is law. Hebrew boys shall not be born. All offenders
against this law shall suffer death by drowning."
—Zora Neale Hurston, *Moses, Man of the Mountain*

Who has been to blame for the riots? The rioters are to
blame. Who is to blame for the killings? The killers are to
blame. . . . I believe the lawless social anarchy which we
saw is directly related to the breakdown of family structure, personal responsibility and social order in too many
areas of our society. . . . Our cities are filled with children
having children; with people who have not been able to
take advantage of educational opportunities; with people
who are dependent on drugs or the narcotic of welfare. To
be sure, many people in the ghettos struggle very hard
against these tides and sometimes win. But too many feel

Biblical quotations are taken from the King James Version.

they have no hope and nothing to lose. This poverty is, again, fundamentally a poverty of values. . . . When families fail, society fails. Children need love and discipline. They need mothers and fathers. A welfare check is not a husband. The state is not a father.

—Vice President DAN QUAYLE,
speech to the Commonwealth Club of California,
May 19, 1992

Were baby prices quoted as prices of soybean futures are quoted, a racial ranking of these prices would be evident, with white baby prices higher than nonwhite baby prices.

—Sixth Circuit Federal Court of Appeals
Judge RICHARD POSNER and Professor ELIZABETH LANDES,
"The Economics of the Baby Market"

I ADOPTED MY SON EXACTLY ONE WEEK AFTER DAN QUAYLE made his Murphy Brown speech. My child, in other words, was guided into the world not by the stork or the stars but by the flaring political runway that culminated in the 1992 Republican National Convention. I remember it particularly because *family values* was the buzzword of the day, and amid all the excitement and joy of the baby's arrival, I remained vaguely aware that in some sectors of this nation my use of the word *family* might be seen as purloined. I am so many of the things that many people seemed to think were antifamily—"unwed," "black," "single," everything but "teenage." Add "mother" and it began to sound like a curse. Stand in the mirror and say it to yourself a few times: "I am an (over-the-hill) black single mother."

"Why are you doing this to yourself?" asked my mother dubiously when I began the adoption process. "You're only forty. The right man could come along any day now. Women are having babies into their fifties these days." I had been hearing my mother say this since my thirtieth birthday, when women were said to be having babies well into their forties. Her quiet, unblinking slippage into the next decade made me realize that while *her* hope sprang eternal, I was starting to get stiff from all that sitting on the porch in ruffled sateen with a gardenia behind my ear.

My father was plain grumpier about the prospect: "I'll be a hundred years old before this child reaches college."

"No, you won't," I said sourly. "You'll barely be ninety."

The rest of my family was delighted but worried that I had not adequately taken into account the degree to which having children would cut into the indulgent Buppy lifestyle of which they so rightly accused me.

I have really hated disappointing everyone, but thus far motherhood has been the richest, most satisfying of rewards. While my son has indeed restricted my ability to eat in fancy restaurants, he has opened up the way to new and far better indulgences, like playing, like learning to be silly again. He has made walking the streets of New York unexpectedly interesting: People smile at me—at him—more. They establish eye contact. They talk in streams of uncontrolled amiability. The other day as I stood waiting to cross the street, a young man with a ruby-henna'd mohawk and a ring through his nose said very gently, "What a cute baby. God bless you." My son—bless him indeed, for I can take no credit for this—brings out the best in other people, even a hard case like me.

It bears emphasizing that I am an especially privileged mother—whether single or not. I am a lawyer, pretty well established in my career, and my employer permitted me to take off a few months when the baby arrived. My life is such that I have time enough to sit down and muse about single motherhood in print, and I am well aware of how uncommon a luxury that is.

But what is striking to me, despite the tremendous privilege of my shining lawyerly middle-classness, is how much social resistance I have encountered nonetheless, and I take that difficulty as an indication that if some things are this hard for me-who-has-everything, it has got to be unbearably difficult for women with much less. The following is more or less a collage of stories that have been echoing in my head, particularly after I recently reread the story of Moses' secret birth and subsequent adoption by Pharaoh's daughter. It is a kind of pendulum of parables, a call-and-response patchwork of tales over time, in which there seems an odd consistency of theme out of a diversity of peoples and histories.

> Now there arose up a new king over Egypt, which knew not Joseph. And he said unto his people, Behold, the people of the children of Israel are more and mightier than we: Come on, let us deal wisely with them; lest they multiply, and it *come* to pass, that, when there falleth out any

war, they join also unto our enemies, and fight against us, and so get them up out of the land. (Exod. 1:8–10)

If, as Dan Quayle says, the state is not a father, then I guess it is long past time to rethink the old, unifying illusions of Uncle Sam and the Founding Fathers, George Washington and the Puritan patriarchs. And if that is true, then it is also long past time to rethink the way in which we metaphorize our sense of belonging or exile, nationality or identity, race or allegiance, enmity or defensiveness. A sense of kinship, whether mythologizing fatherly relation or not, has in most cultures provided the protective legacy and legitimizing reinforcement to civic and community participation. But in the United States of America, kinship—to say nothing of community, to say *nothing* about that dangerous, endangered little clot of connection called "the family"—is an increasingly complicated affair.

Quayle's notorious attack on the television program "Murphy Brown" was an intriguingly complicated expression of social resentment aimed against single women, particularly black women, and their children. In Quayle's attack on Murphy Brown, a fictional white upper-upper-middle-class newscaster who has a child out of wedlock, the Vice President specifically linked *her* purported lapse in basic family values to the riotous social collapse in South Central Los Angeles in the wake of the acquittal of the police officers who beat Rodney King. The not-very-subtle subtext of this speech is of course that all those rioters were the unfathered wild children born of loose wombs, not of "legitimate" mothers. It bears underscoring that if Quayle had implied nothing more than that, his remarks would scarcely have raised an eyebrow and certainly wouldn't have generated the controversy that actually ensued. But the ingredient that so distinguished Quayle's remarks was his bold equation of Ms. Brown's morals with those attributed to real women of color. What made Quayle's remarks so controversial was his mixture, not mere juxtaposition, of images of white and black women's unmarried bodies—corrupt by virtue of their autonomy, their uncontrollability. It was a challenge to the usual hierarchy of black women as surrogate vessels, strong-walled if chipped pitchers, as opposed to the fragility of little white uterine hostesses. That challenge is seen as profoundly undesirable, the offspring alternately perceived as the innocent but irremediably ruined victim of the wild woman's willful profligacy, or else the riotous, hydra-headed reassertion of it.

Dan Quayle's attack on Murphy Brown made me think of the attacks, some thirty years ago, on Elvis Presley. Elvis's gyrating hips, "Nigra" music, and loose, wet lips were widely rebuked as corrupting the (white) youth of America, inciting them to civil insurrection and, worse, parental disrespect. No wonder Murphy Brown was so threatening: gyrating up there on national TV to that Negro music (Aretha Franklin, specifically), imitating the morals of those loose Negro women. Does that sort of behavior produce proud statesmen like Dan Quayle? No, it does not, ladies and gentlemen. It incites their unruly, illicit, overexcited offspring to RIOT.

Yet in an odd way the fates of Murphy Brown and her poorer, browner sisters are very much linked. When Bill Clinton attempted to appoint Zoë Baird to the post of attorney general of the United States, the revelation that she had hired noncitizens to take care of her children and then had not paid taxes on their salaries directed new inquiry into the range of day-care options for working women. While that ever-too-brief but spectacular debate focused almost exclusively upon middle- and upper-class working women, the lack of decent, accessible day-care facilities is directly tied to the not-so-underground exploitation of poor women who work as domestic servants for scandalously low wages. And I am not convinced that room and board should count as part of what domestic servants are paid, particularly when they have families and children of their own to provide for somewhere off the premises. The conceit that a domestic worker is really being paid $1,000 a month to live at such a "fashionable" address must also imagine a status value and a cash value that can be translated into edible benefits for her family and the children she will see only on holidays.

Until the day-care crisis for all women is addressed in material terms, the cost of having children remains prohibitive yet strangely unacknowledged, for poor working women and for middle-class women alike—and God help women on welfare. This is so regardless of whether one is married, although the burden obviously falls disproportionately on poor single women.

> Therefore they did set over them taskmasters to afflict them with their burdens. And they built for Pharaoh treasure cities, Pithom and Raamses. But the more they afflicted them, the more they multiplied and grew. (Exod. 11–12)

In my own child-care quest I ended up relying heavily on sporadic baby-sitting by family and friends. The unreliability of this alternative meant that my son came to work with me a lot (yes, another luxury as these things go). For the first seven months of his life, he suffered through all my committee meetings, listened to me tap away on the computer, or snoozed in the Snugli while I droned on about things that bored even me. He even went on live radio with me (hooray for WBAI), burbling once or twice but otherwise calm in the face of my great and foolish faith. "I just wanted to say hello to the baby," called in one kind listener.

All this is, again, the description of a very privileged option, but I wonder if it need be so. Increasing numbers of corporations have experimented with on-site day-care facilities with great success and enhanced productivity of their workers. Such a system could be cost-efficient and emotionally reassuring for both parents and children. Yet in a rapidly downscaling economy I fear that such measures are denied to all but a few management-level employees. "A woman's place is in the home" seems to be the slogan response, as though women's liberation were responsible for ruining the global economy.

It's odd, but during the Great Depression "spinsters," widows, and single mothers were allowed more of a certain kind of deference— albeit a condescending, pitying one—than in today's business world; by contrast married women (then the overwhelming majority) were ignored, routinely denied jobs so that "men with families" could be employed. In today's recession/depression, in some inverted reiteration of that old order, it is increasingly "women with families" who have been most severely penalized, for not filing themselves more economically under the heading of men's dependents.

This shift in public perception of who deserves what slice of a dwindling resource has been accompanied by and fed by a growing assumption that single mothers ruin their children. That is an interesting notion, since at least in some of its aspects it is quite recent. The Horatio Alger myth, after all, was all about captains of industry who came up the hard but noble way, the proud products of struggling widows, urban single mothers. And peaking in the 1930s there was a whole genre of Depression-inspired literature in which single mothers and their resolute sons plowed the fields and wrassled coyotes, milked their bone-dry cows with faith and patience, and told each other stories. Then a miracle would happen and they'd be graced with just the right amounts of rain, hay, and milk.

Somehow the years have eroded this mythology: single mothers, who now bear a greater responsibility for raising the children of this society than ever before in our history, are demonized as never before. Complex economic forces and social migrations are only part of what has contributed to the fragmentation of civic, political, and extended family systems, not only in this country but around the world. For all the nostalgia for the nuclear family of the 1950s, the notion of the nuclear family was itself only the idealized side of what was even by then the loss of a settled extended family in an increasingly mobile, industrialized society. The cruel mother-in-law jokes so popular in vaudeville have vastly diminished in popularity, not, I would guess, because of the women's movement but because they are so rarely a constant feature of anyone's family life today. Those with a live-in mother-in-law are more often seen as richly blessed with a reliable, live-in, tax-free baby-sitter.

Telling single women to get married in the face of decades of demographic and economic tumult is the silliest, most simplistic of antidotes. Nor does it treat as real the social factors that make couples as well as single parents so frequently isolated. I think that if the children of single women are suffering disproportionately from the effects of poverty, we should be examining the continuing ghettoization of women in the workplace, the continuing disparity between women's and men's salaries, and how these inequalities are directly linked to the greater rate at which women fall below the poverty level than men. Nor should we forget to consider the effects of lost jobs, declining standards of living, and poverty as contributing to the breakdown of marital relations. We should be asking not about what happened to the two-parent household but what happened to our kinship circles. A friend of mine from Ghana could not even fathom what single motherhood meant. "If a girl has a child, she always has her family to turn to, yes?" "No," I said. "Her tribe?" I shook my head. "Her language group?" he persisted with diminished conviction. "Yeah, sure," I said in my best American idiom.

> And they were grieved because of the children of Israel.
> And the Egyptians made the children of Israel to serve with rigor: and they made their lives bitter with hard bondage, in mortar, and in brick, and in all manner of service in the field: all their service, wherein they made them serve, was with rigor. (Exod. 1:12–14)

An important part of what has happened since the Great Depression, of course, is that the politics of single motherhood have been racialized. Horatio Alger has turned into Willie Horton, and his regal, hardworking mother who always gets her just deserts in the end has turned into a shiftless welfare queen who always gets more than she deserves. This is a powerful ideological myth that has somehow trumped every bit of empirical reality, even in the minds of well-educated policy makers. Most Americans still believe that blacks are having more than their fair share of babies, that blacks account for most welfare recipients, and that women on welfare are "addicted" (as Dan Quayle implied) not just to drugs but to being on welfare—so much so that women have babies on purpose, just to get more welfare checks. Yet, again, the facts are that most welfare recipients are white women, many of whom have come out of bad marriages with bad settlements, and that welfare in New York, to use an example of a state that has long been considered "too generous," pays only two dollars a week more in benefits for a new child—a dead loss, and certainly not an incentive. Contrary to public opinion, births among black women have been decreasing since the 1960s; infant mortality rates are scandalously high (higher in Harlem than in Bangladesh); and shortened life expectancy, unattended medical problems, and lack of health care are such serious dangers for blacks that once women enter their twenties, complications from pregnancy become a serious health risk. In other words it makes biological sense, if not normative social sense, to have one's children while in one's teens under such circumstances. And while I am all for population control, I'm curious as to the eugenic implications of that argument as it is applied to blacks exclusively while simultaneously a major industry in fertility has arisen for a principally white clientele—providing more eggs, more motility, more births. I have no problem with the idea of trying to curb a population explosion—if there is one—but I think constitutional notions of equality demand evenhandedness as to both class and race if we are to engage in the game of who deserves to be a parent or not.

I am fascinated by the power of this mythology: it has visited me on occasion, and I am taken aback by the cruelty, condescension, arrogance, and just plain in-your-face-ness I have encountered. When my son was one month old, I engaged in a spirited public debate about the upcoming presidential election. At the end one of my opponents stood up, shook the hand of the woman on the other side of me, and said, "Thank you for being so polite. It's obvious *you* come from a two-parent household." When my son was five months old, I called him "sweetheart" in the presence of a neighbor. My neighbor snapped, "You'd better stop talking to him like that unless you want to see him putting Nair on his legs by the time he's seventeen." When my son was eight months, a young white male law student chided me publicly for not caring about "young black males" because I had adopted a son as a "black single mother."

I cite the personal litany not because of how all this makes me feel—wretched!—but because it seems so prevalent as a political force and so unbelievably misguided in terms of its sense of cause and effect. Some people act as though single mothers are vacuum-sealed in a world without men yet live in a perpetual state of sexual overindulgence. No role models, just pimps. While I am not a great fan of idealization of any sort, I have begun to long for just a touch of countermythology. Say, mythic black single mother educates her young 'uns against all the odds and wrassles urban coyotes, all the while stretching that two-dollar welfare check over twenty-one meals till Sunday.

At some level this whole debate is about sex, sin, and what lives are worth living. It is also about disguising the class problems of our supposedly classless society, primarily through the filter of certain kinds of discussions about race and the shiftless, undeserving, unemployable black "under" class. (Which is most emphatically not to say that we shouldn't be talking about the great power of racism in this society: what I mean to say is that welfare is not primarily a black problem, yet the impression is that it functions to disguise how broad the scar of poverty truly is.) What results is a powerful schema of thought justifying significant intrusions into the lives of black and white women, and of poor young women in particular. (The intrusions into the lives of poor young men deserve a book of their own.)

The wholesale demonization of "the black single mother" is quite focused upon black patterns of sexual behavior as deviant from larger social norms. I would like to see this voguish literature concentrate a little less on black women's reproductive and man troubles and more on encounters with those gatekeepers with whom contact is supposed to guarantee entry into the Promised Land, yet who effectively barricade the borders of their isolation—employers, schoolteachers, hospital workers, and police officers—the lived encounters that make it hard for them to raise a family at all. I would like to see the high rates of black teenage pregnancy framed less by moralistic attributions of black "social disorganization" and more by comparative patterns of the widespread sexual activity among all teens (or for that matter among all politicians, to name a random population whose social indiscretions might take volumes to describe). I would like to see direct, rather than quite subtly implied, links made between pregnancy rates and the availability of health education and reliable birth control as economic resources. Otherwise one is left with the impression that the rights to children, intimacy, and privacy are the rewards of wealth; one is left with an image in which mainstream society's punitive and oppressive desire to make poor blacks literally disappear wins acceptance when reexpressed as *their* uncontrolled desire for babies *they* can't afford.

"Family Values" in the context of these social divisions becomes nothing more than a boundary, a marker of those who are part of the society to which you should only be so lucky to belong versus those "others." At the 1992 Republican Convention Dan Quayle and the folks at the Christian Coalition behaved like the kids who shout "your momma" over their shoulders as they run for the shelter of their own. Such taunts have less to do with your momma's actual life than with drawing a line in the playground sand. And yet they have the psychological effect of producing a mad scramble to be on the safe side of the line, the icon of one's own mother above reproach.

At stake in this debate is the definition of "family" itself. To what extent does the nineteenth-century proposition endure that "[b]ourgeois men and women ... tended to see any woman who was sexually active outside of marriage as a prostitute"[1] and therefore as delegitimized and thus functionally disenfranchised? In conjunction with the disinheritance that rendered slave children "illegitimate," the concept of family is not merely a biological marker but a boundary by which civic participation is delineated.

Thus the 1992 Republican attack on single mothers was not merely a ploy to reiterate the hallmark Willie Horton campaign of the 1988 presidential campaign but represented a subtle blend of "your momma" (1992) and "black rapist" (1988) into the quintessential schoolboy fighting word "motherfucker." In 1988 Willie Horton, stereotyped as the typical inner-city black rapist, was used to coalesce a broad coalition of anger. Blacks and whites against rapists; class-privileged against the "underclass"; whites against blacks; suburbs against inner cities; conservatives-who-hate-crime against liberals-who-supposedly-wallow-in-it-by-inviting-Willie-Horton-home-to-meet-their-daughters.

To the extent that Willie Horton personified an object for all this wrath, "black men" became the source of all problems—rather neat and tidy: All you need is someone willing to control *them* and your problems are solved. Furthermore the Willie Horton ads deflected attention from the fact that most rapists are white and known to their victims; and from the fact that confirming one-quarter of—or even all—black men will not stem the epidemic of violence and sexual abuse among mainstream whites who live in suburbs and who have money and who have never been to jail and who just might even be priests or executives or Pat-Buchanan-Republicans.

Similarly, to the extent that unruly women—Murphy Brown, Hillary Clinton, or black single mothers—personified an object for Republican wrath in 1992, other pressing social issues became isolated and forgotten. As in 1988, it was a strategy of packaging complexity neatly: Control *them*, and your problems are solved. And, again, a whole range of social boundaries were drawn, pulling together identity groups formed neither out of common nor self-interest, but rather out of guilty allegiances of the threatened gut: white versus black, men versus women, married versus single, straight versus gay, working mom versus sainted stay-at-home mother (for whites), and working woman versus demonized promiscuous, eternally pregnant welfare queen (for blacks).

> And the king of Egypt spake to the Hebrew midwives, of which the name of the one was Shiphrah, and the name of the other Puah; and he said, When ye do the office of a midwife to the Hebrew women, and see them upon the stools, if it be a son, then ye shall kill him; but if it be a daughter, then she shall live. But the midwives feared God, and did not as the king of Egypt commanded them, but saved the men children alive. And the king of Egypt called for the midwives, and said unto them, Why have ye done this thing, and have saved the men children alive? And the midwives said unto Pharaoh, Because the Hebrew women are not as the Egyptian women; for they are lively, and are delivered ere the midwives come in unto them. (Exod. 1:15–19)

In a sense much of today's demonization of single motherhood conforms to the kind of theorizing first associated with anthropologist Oscar Lewis—the assumption of a "culture of poverty" that creates destructive intergenerational behavioral archetypes. These purportedly self-perpetuating archetypes mask the larger society's perpetuation of its own *stereo*types, thus making this form of sociology the subject of heated debate.

I have to think that some of this is an unconscious ordering, and quite old in our cultural history. My great-great-grandmother, whom my mother's family called Mammy Sophie, was a twelve-year-old slave when she was impregnated by one Austin Miller, her white slavemaster and a lawyer. Recently my mother told me how she was raised to be absolutely contemptuous of Mammy Sophie's memory. Sophie bore Miller a daughter, my great-grandmother, Mattie. Miller's white wife, Mary, raised the slave daughter, Mattie, to be "moral," "Christian," and contemptuous of her mother. My mother grew up, through this understanding, thinking of Sophie as immoral because she had been raped by Austin Miller starting at the age of eleven. My mother says she grew up resenting Sophie the way that Austin's white wife must have resented Sophie—as wild, godless, and disruptive. As an embarrassment to "the family," although I wonder just whose. Mary raised the light-skinned black Mattie to be tame, Episcopalian, and a palliative racial mediator. Mattie was married at the age of seventeen to a man named Morgan, also light-skinned and thoroughly bred, and together they were given the task of setting up a black Episcopal church, so that they could intercede like oil upon the waters and spread the word of God to the heathen. Mr. Morgan died of consumption at a very young age, and Mattie married again, to my great-grandfather, a French Canadian Cherokee, a man whom I grew up hearing about only as Mr. Ross.

My mother paused, then came to the point of the anecdote: A neighbor and black contemporary of Mattie died, having contracted consumption from his white family, like so many servants-who-were-also-family. At the wake Mammy Sophie said to the widow, "My condolences; I know just how you feel." The widow rose up and said, "I was legally married to a husband. You have no idea how I feel." Then Sophie's daughter, my great-grandmother, Mattie, rose up and spoke against her own mother: "And I've had two legal husbands; you can't possibly know what it's like."

My mother said she grew up with that as a cautionary tale about how awful Sophie was—how loose and irredeemable, how she produced children without mothering them. My mother, in her turn, taught me that black teenage motherhood was deplorable. It was not until I started writing about it, my mother says, that she started rethinking the valuations in this account.

Therefore God dealt well with the midwives: and the people multiplied, and waxed very mighty. And it came to pass, because the midwives feared God, that he made them houses. And Pharaoh charged all his people, saying, Every son that is born ye shall cast into the river, and every daughter ye shall save alive. (Exod. 1:20–22)

Black children and interracial children are like the wet dreams of this society; the carelessly spilled seed, the sinfully expended potency; the wasted hopes of a nation otherwise relentlessly committed to creating gardens in the wilderness of God's promise to the Puritans. Blacks, even black children, are treated at every level like an abomination against nature, a mistake in the scheme of things, a deviance denied in hyperdefensive, warring terms.

For example, when arson destroyed a home in an all-white section of Queens, New York, which had been scheduled for the placement of six "boarder" babies, then–police commissioner Benjamin Ward observed, "I do know most of the babies are minority babies. Maybe that's inside."

"Are they still going to be here when they grow up?" asked Richard Blasi, 11 years old. He meant the six babies.

"This is heartbreaking," said Gretel Strump, a 46-year resident of the block. "Listen, we have nothing against babies. But the mothers, the dope addicts. My husband says, we will never be safe any more. It's nothing but dopists."

"I know it's a selfish kind of feeling but I moved here because it is the way it is," Mrs. Sawicki said. "I have my daughter here. These houses are worth a lot of money. There's got to be a better place for them than smack in the middle of here."[2] (I cannot help but notice how the word *better* is a loaded term in the context of that sentence. *Better* does not seem to mean better for the babies, but better for the Sawickis: someplace "else," someplace where the daughters and houses are worth less. Better from the reference point of the babies, in other words, means not better at all but worse.)

Fliers handed out in opposition to making the house into any sort of a group home said, "We do not want our stabilized residential areas turned into garbage. We do not need more CRIME, VIOLENCE, BURGLARIES, TRANSIENT PEOPLE or PROSTITUTION."[3] (Again the language is quite remarkable: the mere presence of six babies is a kind of reverse Midas touch, a noxious contaminant, a garbage-y breeding ground for flies, prostitution, and all the world's vices.)

"The battle over the house began in September, when the owners put it up for sale. John W. Norris, the head of a local civic association, the Auburndale Improvement Association, said the owners asked $325,000, about $100,000 more than the market price for other houses on the block. . . .

"The city signed a rental agreement last Friday to pay $2,400 a month for the house, which neighborhood residents said would bring about $1,100 on the open market.

"Mr. Koch did not say why the city had agreed to that rent, other than to cite 'supply and demand.' "[4]

There is a peculiar and powerful inversion at work, in which "worthless" children drive up the price to corrupt or unattainable heights; the poorer and blacker the child, the farther out of reach the price rises. Meanwhile the more valuable, legitimate daughters get to live in the high-rent district for cheap.

> And the woman conceived, and bare a son; and when she saw him that he was a goodly child, she hid him three months. And when she could not longer hide him, she took for him an ark of bulrushes, and daubed it with slime and with pitch, and put the child therein; and she laid it in the flags by the river's brink. And his sister stood afar off, to wit what would be done to him. (Exod. 2:2–4)

I think that history is filled with mirrors in whose stark reflections we must find the lessons for change. Recently I have been haunted by the story of a twelve-year-old girl who gave birth alone in a corridor of her Brooklyn project house and threw the newborn down a trash shute. The building's maintenance men heard cries just as they were about to activate the trash compactor, and the baby was saved. According to all the papers, no one knew she was pregnant—not her mother, not the neighbors, not the teacher of her sixth-grade slow-learner class. It turns out the father of the baby was her twenty-two-year-old uncle. He was being prosecuted for statutory rape. The prosecutor's office announced its intention to prosecute the twelve-year-old girl for attempted murder.

> And the daughter of Pharaoh came down to wash herself
> at the river; and her maidens walked along by the river's
> side: and when she saw the ark among the flags, she sent
> her maid to fetch it. And when she had opened it, she saw
> the child: and, behold, the babe wept. And she had com-
> passion on him, and said, This is one of the Hebrews' chil-
> dren. (Exod. 1:5–6)

In recent neo-Victorian mythologies such as Dan Quayle's, women's
bodies are increasingly depicted not as autonomous but as extensions
of collective will and state interest. If in Victorian times husbands
controlled their wives' bodies, the state, through the political device
of fetal protection, has become today's agent of control in place of
husbands. Take the abortion debate.

If you are a pregnant woman thinking about an abortion, how do
you resist, never mind resolve, the voices that would blame you for
your sexual activity, blame you for getting pregnant, blame you
for not having a child, blame you *for* having a child, for being a child
while having a child, for not having a perfect child, for not being a
perfect mother, and for *permitting* yourself to get knocked up to begin
with? These are the voices that would blame a child for being a
child, a teenager for being a teenager, and an adult for never being
young enough. And that's not even counting the voice of the doctor,
should you be so lucky to find a still-operative abortion clinic, who
would engage you in a state-sponsored tête-à-tête in order to dissuade
you.

There is a bumper sticker I have seen that says, "There Is No
More Dangerous Place on Earth Than a Woman's Womb." How do
you seek your own counsel and resist such pervasive misogyny? How
does a woman guard the corporal integrity that is all any of us has
in life; is there any reinforcement available for the idea that the decision to give a part of yourself and your body new form in the process of childbearing is yours alone? That gift has increasingly
been redescribed as an obligation—either to family or to race, religion, the nation—as well as a kind of confused contract, in certain circumstances, "required" in exchange for the "investment"
of sperm.

How to resist the voices that denounce abortion *per se* while carving a more sinister ideological separation between a woman and the
egg/embryo/fetus within her, by metaphorizing women and fetuses as
equal, independent, rational, atomized individuals? The mystery of

two hearts beating in one body is neither captured by the zealotry of hyperindividualism nor sustained by philosophies in which personal integrity has no voice in the face of the demands of a group to propagate itself.

There are lots of voices that tell women that abortion is a sin of genocide—against blacks, against whites, against Jews, against Gentiles, against girls, against boys, against future Nobel Prize winners. But genocide is not accomplished by individual women who, in the absence of either the urge or the community to mother children, follow their instinct to abort. Genocide is wreaked upon whole populations by state action that devalues all choice about reproduction, that forecloses reproduction altogether. In the United States of America we might better be worried about the kinds of quiet federal policies that made sterilization free for poor women but provide no funding at all for abortion; that provide no counseling about birth control but insist on a squeal rule for teenagers who consult doctors; and that give no subsistence, never mind assistance, for those who are not just "preborn" but born.

How, in these times, to resist romanticizing—as appears to be the vogue—either motherhood, adoption, or abortion? Giving birth or giving up a child for adoption is a good thing for some women, but it is, no less than abortion for others, ofttimes filled with a similar sense of permanent loss and terrible regret. There are no easy, liberatory, perfect answers. And with all the frenzy about making childless couples happy, it must be hard to remember that you have no personal obligation to act as someone else's breeding vessel, no matter how much you are paid, in either gratitude or dollars.

The decision to bring a pregnancy to term is a personal decision about whether to reproduce oneself into a community of caring. Without the confidence of that larger caring, which proceeds not just from the circumstances of conception but includes all one's life circumstances, no one will be served, not a woman, not the community, not God, and least of all a child.

The gift of reproduction will best be received either into a family, whether of a single mother's love, or extended into that of the larger world when women find the inner confidence that such love exists in the world, for them, for their progeny. And the failure to find that confidence is not a sin, but sometimes nothing less than a most reasonable instinct of self-preservation. I deeply believe that the unresolvability of the intimate complexity that is pregnancy cannot be legislated by outlawing or counseling against abortion but rather by working to make the rest of the world a happier, more viable place in which we are all able to enjoy the instinct to self-perpetuate, in the fullness of our humanity.

> Then said his sister to Pharaoh's daughter, Shall I go and call to thee a nurse of the Hebrew women, that she may nurse the child for thee? And Pharaoh's daughter said to her, Go. And the maid went and called the child's mother. And Pharaoh's daughter said unto her, Take this child away, and nurse it for me, and I will give thee thy wages. (Exod. 1:7–9)

I think that the current spate of blaming single mothers for the troubles of this country is an unfortunate yet pervasive way of not seeing the fiscal, racial, and political catastrophes that so beg for our attention. Poverty and dysfunction among single mothers and their children is a symptom, not a cause. The vicious stereotypes with which my son and I have been greeted by significant numbers of random strangers have nothing to do with me or my son—who is the most delightful, intelligent young man in the world—whether it's assumptions that unless I am earning the equivalent of Oprah Winfrey's salary, my child will inevitably grow up asking society for handouts and stealing for a living or that, even if I were making Oprah's salary, I would still sabotage and "feminize" my son's mythic warrior spirit. I think that these stereotypes, so commonly misunderstood as the "difficulty" with single motherhood, are more accurately seen as part of the daily battle that all parents must wage with the world in order to create the space in which our children may grow into gentle, wise, and loving adults with the emotional resources to do bigger battle than street war. And this in turn is a daily struggle that we all— black, white, female, male, parents, or not—ought to be engaged in anyway, whether on behalf of our children or of ourselves.

It is time to stop demonizing single mothers or anyone else who makes family where there was none before. Children, in their happy irrationality and complete dependence, are perpetual reminders that we are all members of a larger community, that we can never quite attain the atomistic nuclear status to which the sweet nostalgia of Happy Days sometimes tempts us. Raising children, even for black single mothers on welfare, is dependent on the very wonderful belief that community is possible; that there is family not only within but beyond the walls of one's home; that there is regeneration for oneself and a life for one's child in the world at large. This belief is what makes me such a tenacious, annoying, finger-shaking, communitarian moralist ("Socialist!" says my sister with a sigh). But I really believe that if we could just see that family is not only about individuals acting autonomously within some private sphere but is also communally inspired and socially dependent—if we could just refrain from penalizing the nonformulaic (even as we defer unduly to the nuclear formula even when domestic abuse rules the roost)—if we could but act on all this in even modest fashion, then we might begin to see to it that no "single" mother need ever be alone and that no child raised in this supposed "man's world" should be without dozens of good men to look to for protection. Cultivating the extraordinary richness of what children offer us depends on neither a mother nor a father alone but is a responsibility that extends to grandparents, friends, neighbors, and civic community—across fences, across religion, across class, and across town.

And the woman took the child, and nursed it. (Exod. 1:9)

At a glitzy New York Christmas party with lots of great hors d'oeuvres, I mingle with a group of high-powered lawyers. A beautiful woman, an ex-runway model who has spent her life getting paid to stay thin, observes that the answer to the Third World's problems is to convince them to "stop having so many unwanted children." I turn away from her, too pained to respond, and push through the Tom Wolfe-ish crowd, in search of Pharaoh's daughter.

Samson and His Women

FAY WELDON

And the children of Israel did evil again in the sight of the Lord, and the Lord delivered them into the hands of the Philistines for forty years. (Judg. 13:1)

AND THERE WAS THIS CERTAIN MAN, MANOAH, AND HIS woman (she never gets a name), who was barren, but the Angel of the Lord appeared unto her and said, "Lo, thou shalt conceive and bear a son: and no razor shall come on his head. For the child shall be a Nazarite unto God from the womb, and he shall begin to deliver Israel out of the land of the Philistines." And she did conceive, to everyone's astonishment.

So you can imagine how Samson was brought up. Shrieks and wails if a razor went near his head, and the whole community involved. Only, as soon as he was grown into the biggest, strongest man around, he started causing trouble by bedding and wedding Philistine girls, not his own kind, to the distress of Manoah and "the woman," who now at least becomes "his mother," though she still never gets to have a name.

Biblical quotations are taken from the King James Version.

And she [that is to say, Delilah] made him sleep upon her knees, and she called for a man, and she caused him [the man] to shave off the seven locks of his [that is to say, Samson's] head: and she began to afflict him, and the strength [that is to say, his potency] went from him. (Judg. 16:19)

Samson, according to the Bible, *loved* Delilah: he didn't just "go with her," as he did the other Philistine women, including his unfortunate wife, who got burned to death as a result of Samson's incessant feuding. And herein, if you ask me, is the reason for Samson's downfall. Nothing like true love for bringing the temple pillars crashing down. Sex is a doddle, compared with love. No wonder the story so alarms men. Love a woman and if she afflicts you, that is to say, starts telling you what to do, you'll do it, and then everything will end in ruins. Many a strong man—and what man isn't a Samson in his head?—has a stronger mother, the kind who insists he never get his hair cut, or never marry outside the tribe, or always polish his shoes, whom he runs from all his life. If his mother catches up with him in the form of his own true love, he's had it! So has the love object, of course, but never mind. Who in the Bible cares about the women? At least Delilah gets given a name.

The story of Samson and Delilah, which renders men aghast, is at least a source of some small satisfaction to a certain kind of woman. Look at it this way. Bring a strong man to your knees, and just possibly you'll bring him to his. Cut off the hair his mother told him to grow while he lies trusting, sleeping, loving, and you'll have him in your control. Fetch me my handbag, dear! The poor, genderless, impotent ox! So what if the temple comes crashing down: all that's in the future, and doesn't he have a hard time with his own gender anyway: isn't it all binding, blinding wage slavery and treadmilling imposed by other, more powerful men; executive attacks in the dark, stabs in the back and concrete boots out there in the male world? Isn't he better off with me, the femme fatale? And isn't it better to be the power behind the throne than to have no power at all? To entrap by love if there's no other way of getting by in the world?

Love me, Samson: I love you! But it's lies, all lies. Some women act like this anyway—not most, I hope, but enough for the rest of us to feel guilty. Who, me? I'm no Delilah! I'd never do a thing like that to *you*—women like men strong, not weak, honestly. All that new-man stuff isn't for me: oh, no. You be a real man, I'll be a real woman. Cook your dinner, iron your shirts, plod after you through the desert. Of course.

The Old Testament is a wonderfully nonpolitically correct document. Patriarchy personified, in the form of Jehovah—but then, did we ever doubt it? The Words of the Desert God still ring in our ears. Take that, Eve! Insults, calumny, blame! That's what you get for showing an intelligent interest in an apple, taking an independent line. Now see what you've done—your fault, Eve, everything from the very beginning, so don't come running to us men with your complaints. Of course childbirth hurts, kills: you brought it on yourself, you offered that apple to Adam. He'd never have eaten it otherwise. No chloroform for you until the late nineteenth century: no contraception allowed, here, there, and everywhere; still no terminations allowed in most places in the world: in pain shalt thou bring forth; it says so in the Bible, and *that's that*. So you thought you'd leave home, did you, Ruth? We'll soon have you in tears amid the alien corn. Wanted to have a good time, did you, Jezebel? All that'll be left of you will be the palms of your hands. The dogs will have eaten the rest. So Joseph raped you, did he, O wife of Potiphar, then told the world he tore his garment trying to *get away* from insatiable you? That was his story. Who's ever going to believe yours?

Women in Judges are responsible for all kinds of evil. Look what happened when Ephraim (chap. 19) took home a concubine. (She doesn't get a name either.) She chose to go back to her father. Ephraim then had to go all the way back to fetch her. On the way home they met up with some hostile Benjamites. He managed to quiet them by giving her to them for their pleasure and usage. In the morning he picked her up from where she'd fallen upon his threshold, took her home and then divided her with his knife into twelve pieces. He sent a piece to all the countries of Israel, because he said they were all so lewd and foolish, they really ought to consider the matter and take advice. After that another great bout of internecine battle broke out, with hundreds of thousands dead, and obviously all the woman's fault. Concubines should just stay *home*.

I suspect the story of Samson and Delilah, more of a folk myth than actual history, and one in which the woman gets to be powerful, escaped the censor's pen—or perhaps chisel?—only because its deeper significance as a cautionary tale to men outweighed any gratification it might have offered women.

How the story of Samson and Delilah gets the men going! He gets caught and Delilah gets the blame—as Eve gets the blame for

Adam's weakness—and then his fellow men blind him and set him to low-grade domestic work (the treadmill) as if he were a woman. "Dark, dark, amid the blaze of noon," wrote Milton in *Samson Agonistes*, "Irrecoverably dark, total eclipse. Without all hope of day."

Milton was blind himself, and notoriously disagreeable to his wife (cf. Robert Graves's *Wife to Mr. Milton*). One thing Milton couldn't abide, as many a man before and since, was a powerful woman. The story preyed upon his mind, as it did later on William Blake's, though the latter was rather more sympathetic to Delilah. Milton saw Samson as married to Delilah and obliged to live, once blinded, as "uxorious to thy will, in perfect thralldom." The ultimate fear: what Jane Eyre does to blinded, helpless Rochester. "Reader, I married him." Milton, like Blake, assumes Samson to have "married" Delilah. Ephraim "has a concubine"—but he is described as "her husband." And wives are such dreadful, dangerous creatures! More *Samson Agonistes*:

> *Seeming at first all heavenly under virgin veil*
> *Soft, modest, meek, demure,*
> *Once joined, the contrary she proves, a thorn*
> *Intestine—far within defensive arms*
> *A cleaving mischief—*

Let them know their place. As Milton has his chorus declare,

> *Therefore God's universal law*
> *Gave to the man despotic power*
> *Over his female in due awe,*
> *Not from that right to part an hour,*
> *Smile she, or lour;*
> *So shall he least confusion draw*
> *On his whole life, not swayed*
> *By female usurpation, nor dismayed.*

The whole narrative poem an act of reproach to Delilah, who stepped out of line!

Another story from Judges. Shall we consider Samson's relative, the daughter of Jephthah? Jephthah was a judge of Israel, at the time engaged in a conflict with the Ammonites. Jephthah vowed to the Lord that if the Lord would deliver the children of Ammon into Jephthah's hands, Jephthah would sacrifice whatever first came forth out of his door when he got home. Victory against the Ammonites was secured, and alas it was Jephthah's only child, a daughter, who came running out to greet him. Jephthah rent his clothes but said there was no way out of his dilemma; his daughter was going to have to die. (Even with all this drama, she doesn't get a name.) She said, "Give me one month to go on up the mountainside with my friends to bewail my virginity, then so be it" (Judg. 11:37). And so it happened. She went up, bewailed, came down, and got sacrificed to God, still nameless. I hope to heaven she did more about her virginity up that mountainside than bewail it. After that all the daughters of Israel were allowed four days a year to go up the mountaintop to lament and bewail the virginity of Jephthah's daughter—but not the manner of her life or the cause of her death of course, just her general unavailability to men thereafter.

Now, it seems to be part of human nature to believe that if things go wrong, someone has to be to blame. It can't be just chance. God is good by definition, so misfortune must be of human origin. If the weather's bad, we feel obscurely that it's the government's fault (at least we do here in Britain); if the ozone layer thins, why, then, our vanity is responsible—too many of us using aerosol hairsprays and deodorants. If we the Israelites have been in servitude for forty years, someone's sinned, and it's probably sexual sin at that, and that means women, so the best thing for everyone is to keep women in order. A philosophy of life still popular with Islam today.

The human race, in its obsessive regard for its mishmash of holy texts, its passion to believe something, anything, as being the word of God, divinely inspired, is truly remarkable. Though you can see that a belief system, once established, which keeps women firmly in their place, setting them up as the next best thing to camels, though rather more easily disposable, is likely to be popular with the men and have a lot of staying power, no matter how the women chafe. The older, pagan religions, with their many gods and goddesses, were too female-based for patriarchal comfort. Let there be one single, vengeful, male God, keep the women in order and populate the desert. Abzam of Bethlehem had thirty sons and thirty daughters, which must have kept a lot of women busy.

When I was a child at a Catholic school, the Bible was forbidden literature, arcane knowledge, interpretable only by priests. I thought this was because they didn't want us to read the sexy bits. I can now see—forget the sex—they didn't want the likes of me exposing their sacred texts to ridicule and doubt, taking issue with the judges of Israel, challenging Jehovah himself. The God of Exodus and Judges, with his constant exhortations to massacre and castrate, wipe out cities and sacrifice children, demonstrates himself to the contemporary eye as sexist, racist, vengeful, willful, punitive, and all the things we see these days as really, really bad. In retrospect the general feeling of the church fathers, that the less the faithful knew about the source material of their belief the better, turns out to have been wise. Hard, in the modern context, to admire, say, Jacob, that liar, sneak, coward, and thief, so disliked in the valleys he was turned out of one after another, simply because he was "beloved by God." What kind of God could love Jacob?

Catholic mass was recited, in the days of my childhood, in Latin. Confuse and baffle! Promise heaven, threaten hell! Keep the people obedient, iron out dissent. If they think it's God's will to pay taxes, they will, for fear of the consequences. Most people are not very bright, and never have been. Kings and priests collude to keep them quiet, keep the wheels of society running smoothly. Lenin and his friends abolished God and served up Marxism instead, an even more punitive and controlling belief system, that God has now overthrown. What next? I have a feeling we're all on the verge of worshiping Carl Gustav Jung, the god of therapy, but that's from a European perspective. As G. K. Chesterton once observed, when people cease to believe in God, they do not believe in nothing, they believe in anything.

At home, too, the Bible was forbidden literature. I came from a nest of self-sufficient female atheists—grandmother, mother, sister, me—and the Bible was seen as superstitious nonsense; reading it could only render me stupid. Forbidden fruits are sweetest: compare Eve and the apple. She tempted me: I fell! I've been reading the Bible ever since.

There were Bibles openly on sale in the local bookshop of my youth: rather shocking to come across them, like those books on how to make nuclear bombs out of kitchen ingredients. Here I sneak-read the beginning of Genesis and received the female primal shock of discovering that Eve was an afterthought. Adam was fashioned from clay—bad enough—but Eve, just to keep Adam company, fashioned from Adam's *rib*? Intolerable. Though, come to think of it, if God had stuck to his original plan, so that people were born from man's rib, easily and painlessly, and not from out between women's legs, a lot of pain and distress would have been saved.

As a child I also acquired a copy of the Anglican prayer book. It had thin, papery pages, thinner and finer than the communion wafers I could never eat because I hadn't been baptized and was therefore doomed to limbo. No one talks about limbo very much anymore. It was where you went when you died, if you happened to have been born before Jesus came along to save mankind, or if, one way or another, you hadn't been lucky enough to hear about him. Others could get you out of Purgatory by praying for you, but once you were in limbo, that was that. *Nothing* happened in limbo. The nun described it to me as others have since described depression. Gray, flat, featureless, never ending, without hope. I read the prayer book by torchlight under the bedclothes. I learned psalms by heart and whispered prayers for the preservation of the monarch and those at sea, and for the scattering of our enemies. I didn't learn and whisper in order to get to heaven—that was out of the question anyway—but because I liked the language in which my forebears addressed the deity, and because there was no TV and I had to entertain myself somehow.

In lieu of the Bible at school we little girls were given a strange potpourri of religious reading matter—from *Little Lives of All the Saints*, a detailed and stirring account of how various female saints were put to torture, which acted as a hymn to the delights of masochism, to *A Child's Guide to the Bible*. This was illustrated with color plates of desert landscapes, complete with palm trees and oases, done by someone who'd obviously never been there, through which scurried European-looking men in long robes with sandals, or drooped rather darker women, mostly weeping. They didn't show my favorite, Jezebel, in action, or Joseph with Potiphar's wife of course, but there was at least a scantily clothed Delilah whispering in Samson's ear. How beautifully his long hair flowed over bare, burnished shoulders; how pillarlike his legs! In the background a lion roared. The artist had been inspired: oily limbs touched, promising sex, complicity, treachery, disaster! Samson and Delilah, the story that got away.

According to my 1911 *Encyclopedia Britannica*, "the stories of Samson's exploits are plainly taken from the mouths of the people and have all the appearance of folk-tales, not unmixed with mythical motives. Points of similarity between Samson and the Babylonian Gilgamesh, the Egyptian Horus-Ra and Hercules, have been observed by many writers, and it has been inferred that the whole story of Samson is a solar myth." What's this? What's a solar myth? Oceans of ignorance! Do I know nothing?

I look up Samson and solar myths in Barbara Walker's *The Woman's Encyclopedia of Myths and Secrets* and all is made clear, or clearish. Here Samson appears as the Hebrew version of the sun god called Shams-On in Arabia, Shamash in Babylon, identical with Egypt's Ra-Harakhti; just as Ra was "made weak" by Isis, so Samson was made weak by Delilah, a word that itself means "She Who Makes Weak." Hair cutting, we are told, was a common mythic symbol of castration, since according to ancient Eastern beliefs, phallic power was supposed to reside in a man's hair. Delilah is the equivalent of Hercules' deadly consort Deianeira, the instrument of the hero's destruction. Blinding also meant putting out the "phallic eye." I daresay there's no disproving it, just as there's no proving it. Hair cutting equals castration: blinding equals impotence. Samson becomes the archetype for male fear of women—though personally I think he just didn't want his hair cut because his mother told him not to. It was guilt that weakened him, lost him his potency, not Delilah.

But look at this! "When a man's phallic stance is inflated, priapic, it becomes necessary for a man to be cut down to size, a process experienced by the man as profoundly humiliating." So says Eugene Monich in *Castration and Male Rage*. Change the book and change the message: just because one version of our existence makes sense doesn't mean another version can't make equal sense. *The Woman's Encyclopedia* presents a rich and secret world founded on Jungian principles of ancient symbols and hidden forces. Monich, a Freudian, has a concept of a universe that leaps into life the moment a man is born, and not a second before. Penis envy and death wish can be reborn every minute: there is no need for the accumulated energies of the past to be involved at all. As for today's man, so for Samson. What's the difference? Your myth, my truth. Your truth, my myth.

Let me try and link the two—join the new feminist religion, which worships the ancient dark female forces, allowing the story of Delilah and Samson to be the old castration myth, stirring and disturbing men and women both, while giving you Delilah's version of the incident.

"Whatever it takes," says Delilah, "whatever it takes to get you through the lonely nights. And you know how hot those nights in the valley of Sorek could be. I'd lie on my striped rug in my little mud hut with the door open, trying for a breath of air, a scrap of sleep, and who'd I see standing there, blotting out the moonlight, blotting out the stars, but Samson. I knew from the beginning it was bad news. The Israelites are the lowest of the low, always on the move, regular Mad Maxes; hair all over the place and circumcised, so you can always tell. They can't pass as Philistines. A lot of the girls won't go with them. And this Samson was a wanted man. I knew that. There was a price on his head for mass murder. I should have informed on him at once, but my dear, those shoulders, those hands! He'd stand in the doorway, all smile and muscle, built like a giant, hair almost down to his waist. I love a man with hair: mostly if you come across them they're Nazarites and religious nuts, but who am I to argue? I never asked him to pay, so he reckoned I loved him. Perhaps I did. He told me why there was a price on his head, how he'd married a Philistine wife. They'd been living with her family; there'd been a stupid tiff about a riddle, and he'd gone back home in a huff.

"'What was the riddle?' I asked.

"'Out of the eater came something to eat,' he said.

"'And out of the strong came something sweet.'

"It had been going the rounds for years. No one knew the answer. Samson would tease his in-laws with the riddle to upset his wife, prove to everyone he was brighter than they, which he clearly was. I asked Samson what the riddle was about, and he told me how he'd once strangled a lion with his bare hands and a swarm of bees had settled in the carcass and made honey. I said how could his wife's family be expected to know an idiotic thing like that. He said, after he'd calmed down, he'd realized exactly that and gone back to her, only to find his father-in-law had given her to his best friend. All the father-in-law had to say was sorry, and couldn't Samson make do with his wife's little sister? Samson was so upset by this, he set fire to his father-in-law's fields; in retaliation the Philistines burned his wife alive. Samson naturally went after them and killed everyone in sight. A man has to do what a man has to do! He then lit out to the mountaintops—where the Israelite girls go to lament the virginity of Jephthah's daughter—perhaps he met up with some of them, because pretty soon three thousand of his own people came after him, brought him down, and handed him over to the Philistines. He just burst his bonds—an easy trick if you know how—slaughtered another thousand of them with an ass's jawbone, and was off.

"They did nearly get him once, Samson told me. He was visiting yet another Philistine girl and the authorities closed the city gates to trap him, but Samson just walked out with the gates on his shoulders. A real Incredible Hulk!

"Look, even allowing for some exaggeration, I was sleeping with a mass murderer, but at that time and place who wasn't? The sex was good at first, I'll say that. I like a man with some size to him, and he was gentle enough with me, so I let it go on. But then he fell in love with me; you know how that can put a girl off; some giant of a man staring at you with soppy eyes saying, 'Did the earth move for you too?' and you lying, 'Oh, yes.' And the more his hair needed washing, the more he'd douse it in oil. Though you can get a taste for that. Hot, so hot, that summer!

"And then the CIA, or their desert equivalent, pressured me and said, 'Delilah, we know what's going on, we need some pillow talk here. What's the secret of Samson's remarkable strength? We want this man alive, not dead, and we don't want to get hurt taking him.' I didn't like to say what I always felt: 'It's not that he's so strong, it's that your lot are so weak.' You don't say that kind of thing to the CIA, you do what they say and live to earn another day. Whatever it takes! I pretended to go along with them, but I didn't mean it. I was exhausted, but I was satisfied, and I prefer a circumcised man, I don't care what the others say. I fobbed them off.

"But I began to get tired," said Delilah the timeless. "I needed sleep. I'd say, 'Samson, you're too much for me, what are we going to do about it?' He joked and said try tying him down with green withies, in other words bondage, but it only turned him on the more. And I'd taken the CIA's money and I was getting desperate and complained a lot, and one night he said, 'The only way you'll ever get enough sleep, Delilah, is by cutting my hair. That'll put me off my stroke.' So I thought I'd try it. I told the watcher behind the arras (there always is one) to slip in and cut off all that beautiful hair. It hurt me as much as it hurt him to see it go. After that he simply couldn't get it up anymore, and it was the same night after night. Hairless, he just wasn't a man. Guilt, I suppose: disobeying his mother, getting his hair cut. So what was the point of having him around? I turned him in and didn't think much more about it, though how the world keeps harping on. Samson and Delilah, one of the world's great stories! Mind you," said Delilah, "We harlots of the desert tribes get a better deal than the wives, any day. All having a husband earns you is the likelihood of being burned, raped, chopped up, or given away. We free women just get to earn our own living, enjoy a bit of sexual variety, and learn how the world works. You live to find out that the thing most likely to put a man off his stroke is his mother, and that's always worth knowing!"

Ruth and Naomi, David and Jonathan: One Love

JUNE JORDAN

"ENTREAT ME NOT TO LEAVE YOU OR TO RETURN FROM FOLLOW-ing you; for where you go I will go, and where you lodge I will lodge; your people shall be my people, and your God my God. Where you die I will die, and there will I be buried. May the Lord do so to me and more also if even death parts me from you" (Ruth 1:16–17). From earliest childhood, I remember one or another version of these passionate words. As far as I knew, they were the only memorable, and even startling, thoughts attributed to any woman in the Bible. And, as a little girl, I appropriated the fierce loyalty, and the all-out loving commitment embodied by this passage, as an ideal towards which I could and should eagerly aspire. But the story around those unparalleled declarations remained rather wan, and confused, and confusing, in my mind, until this past summer.

Yes, I knew it was a woman named Ruth who had so declared her-self to Naomi. But I did not understand why. And, as a child, it was not necessary for me to clearly get the context for their relationship, or even for me to clearly fathom their reasons for knowing each other. What mattered to me was that, finally, somewhere, in that big Holy Book, there were words uttered by somebody female to anoth-er somebody female. And, what was most important was that her

Biblical quotations are taken from the Revised Standard Version.

words matched up to the heroic qualities of the other biblical figures I came to memorize and assimilate inside the pantheon of my young heart.

I distinctly remember, for example, my time at an all-girls' camp, Robin Hood, in upstate New York. Whenever any of us decided there was need to ceremoniously remark our friendship, we would invent a secret name for ourselves, such as The Dare Devils, and we would mix blood from the inside of our wrists, thereby becoming "blood brothers." Blood sisters simply would not fly; what would that connote? Where was the precedent for "blood sisters" in any literature, or film, or theater piece? Ruth and Naomi, maybe. But did they ever do anything like stealing into the night in order to set loose all of the rowboats, or taking an increasingly perilous walk through the woods—a walk punctuated by bigger and bigger crevasses over which it was necessary to jump—or else retire, humiliated, as a coward?

And were they sisters? I was never sure. But I was certain about David and Jonathan. I knew that Jonathan had been the son of King Saul. And King Saul frequently rushed into battle against the Philistines. And one of the Philistines was Goliath, that huge freak of a warrior on the wrong side. And young David, as just a slender boy, came and slew the giant Goliath with his slingshot. And the King was much impressed. As were all the rest of the Israelites. But none was more moved by the gallantry and intelligence of David than Jonathan. "Jonathan loved him as his own soul" (1 Sam. 18:1).

And after that victory, King Saul insisted that David come and live in the royal palace. But the women of Israel sang, "Saul has slain his thousands, and David his ten thousands" (1 Sam. 21:11), and the King heard this popular outcry of comparison and he became truly jealous. And from that day forward, he eyed David with malice aforethought and, in every way possible, tried to devise David's death. Again and again the King sent young David into battle, hoping that he would be killed. And, even beyond that, the King schemed for David's execution. But, again, and again, the King's son, Jonathan, raced from the palace to warn his friend David and, thereby, saved his life. And after many battles, and much fight and much flight, finally it was obvious that the Lord was with David and that David was, therefore, invincible. And David prevailed. And when David learned of the eventual war deaths of King Saul and of Jonathan, who loved David "as his own soul," David tore his clothes and raised a lamentation that concludes,

How are the mighty fallen
in the midst of the battle!

Jonathan lies slain upon thy high places.
I am distressed for you, my brother Jonathan;
    very pleasant have you been to me;
    your love to me was wonderful,
    passing the love of women.
                                (2 Sam. 1:25–26)

So Jonathan had defied his father for the sake of David. And repeatedly he had rescued David from the nefarious intent of his father, the King, thereby jeopardizing his own, otherwise natural, succession to the throne of Israel. And when the King died, David did not rejoice because the King had been "the Lord's anointed." And when Jonathan died, David did not rejoice because to him, Jonathan's love "was wonderful / passing the love of women." Theirs was great reciprocal love. The dimensions of the interaction between the two men approached the mythical in scale. And the content of their intersecting histories is the very stuff of spectacular movie suspense, climax, and triumph.

This summer I became one of the too many thousands of women who must fight breast cancer. From the surgery to determine whether or not there was a malignancy through the surgery for removal of the malignant tissue (a partial radical mastectomy) and the removal of lymph nodes to determine whether or not the cancer had spread, I suddenly became wholly dependent upon the kindnesses of my friends. I had to depend on my friends for my personal care, for the walking of my dog, for the securement of groceries, for the cooking and serving of food, for the cleaning up of the kitchen and of the house, for transportation to and from the doctors, for the handling of correspondence and for diplomatic dealing with innumerable phone calls: for my life.

At different points, you would find an elaborate schedule for every day of every week, sometimes broken into hourly segments. Slotted into each segment of each day you would find the name of one or another or yet another friend—a woman friend. And I felt overwhelmed by the exhaustive, seamlessly graceful, and indispensable caretaking organized by these women. How could I possibly have survived any of the ordeal of this fight, and how could I possibly hope to heal, and defeat this cancer, without the unstinting love given to me?

It was Angela, for example, who read everything published on breast cancer and who drove me to the doctor on the morning when the doctor told me that the cancer had spread to the lymph nodes and that, consequently, he was revising his prognosis from 90 percent likely to survive to 40 percent. It was Angela who drove me away from that terrible news to a neighborhood hairdresser whom she begged to "do something" and who, in fact, created a small fire on the top of my head: an electric orange stripe that she bleached into my hair.

It was Adrienne who washed my back and cleansed the wound and told me there was nothing horrible about that horrible procedure, while she changed the sterile dressing. And it was Adrienne who slept through the nights in a chair next to my hospital bed.

It was Lauren who brought bananas just perfectly not quite ripe. And Stephanie who organized my friends into a computer wizardry of a fail-proof network.

And it was the other Adrienne who traveled all the way from Santa Cruz to bring lunch and laughter and new anthologies of poetry. And Martha who came from New York.

And it was Camille who came at midnight with medicine when the pain was quite unbearable. And Pratibha who came from London.

And it was Sara who talked me through yet another nightmare of giving blood so that the hospital could run necessary, pre-op tests. And Phyllis who watered the garden several times a week, on her way to work.

And on and on for several months. And I thought, "This is the love of women. This is the mighty love that is saving my life. And where are the public instances of praise and celebration of this love?"

And I found my Bible and, when I could read again, I looked up the story of Ruth to see if I could make better sense of it now.

And I could. And I did.

"In the days when the judges ruled there was a famine in the land" (Ruth 1:1), and for this reason Naomi and her husband and their two sons left Bethlehem and went to a more promising country, the country of Moab. While they stayed there, Naomi's husband died. Her two sons took to themselves two Moabite wives, Orpah and Ruth. And then Naomi's sons died. And Naomi decided she would return to Bethlehem, since the famine had now ended. And so she arranged to bid her widowed daughters-in-law farewell. And one of them, Orpah, wept, and kissed Naomi, and accepted her counsel: She would stay in Moab. But the other daughter-in-law, Ruth, refused to separate from Naomi, and she said, "Entreat me not to leave you or to return from following you." And when Naomi saw that Ruth could not be dissuaded, she allowed her daughter-in-law to return with her, to Bethlehem.

Now when the two women returned there, they could not provide for themselves; neither of them was married; neither of them had a husband to protect and feed and honor her. And it was very hard. But Naomi was not about to give up and perish. Nor was she about to permit Ruth to become prey to wanton depredations, or hunger. Therefore, Naomi conceived of a plan whereby Ruth would become appealing to a wealthy farmer and kinsman. Ruth obeyed Naomi and she succeeded in pleasing the kinsman so that he made her his wife. And then Ruth bore the kinsman, whose name was Boaz, a son. And that son became the joy of Naomi's old age. "Then Naomi took the child and laid him in her bosom, and became his nurse" (Ruth 4:16). And Naomi was no longer without family and shelter. And the son of Ruth and Boaz was Obed. And Obed was the father of Jesse. And Jesse was the father of David. Here ended the Book of Ruth.

At first, I was dismayed. The evident dependency of both Naomi and Ruth upon their menfolk struck me as extreme. It was not as though they had set up house together and/or started up a small subsistence farm that then became an amazing commune for other stranded women. And, really, Ruth had to literally put herself at the very feet of Boaz in order to gain the favors of his attention. And suppose Ruth had not found Boaz attractive, or kind, or fun?

And then I realized I was being obtuse. Ruth and Naomi had made brave choices in a circumstance that allowed them no freedom. And they had chosen to do whatever would allow them to stay together, without undue penury, or censure by the townspeople of Bethlehem. And, yes, they could not ride horses into battle and slay the sources for their grief or slay the enemies of their joy. And, yes, they were neither princes nor kings, but, rather, slaves to a social environment that would not permit them any liberty, any respect, any safety, any assurance, even, of work with the reward of food—unless at least one of them became somebody's wife.

But is it not marvelously true that Ruth's love for Naomi was the equal of Jonathan's great love for David? And is it not wonderfully true that Ruth's love for Naomi surpassed her love of men even as David's love of Jonathan surpassed his love of women?

And is it not fitting that the child of Ruth and Naomi should become the father of the father of David? From Ruth and Naomi through David and Jonathan we possess the fabulous history of one love. And, yes, differences of gender have made for huge differences in the documented public display of their differing but always passionate and virtuous attachments. But it is one love. It is love that supersedes given boundaries of birthright or birthplace or conventions of romance or traditions of loyalty. It is one love that yields to no boundary. It is one love that takes you to its bosom and that saves your life.

And we would be foolish to neglect the cultivation and the celebration of such love within our own heroic and our own quite ordinary passage here, on earth.

Hannah and Elkanah: Torah as the Matrix for Feminism

CYNTHIA OZICK

WHAT IS FEMINISM? BETTY FRIEDAN ENCAPSULATES IT IN A word—the "personhood," she puts it, of women. On that everyone can agree, and it may be that we ought to stop at the definition that promotes agreement. But definitions promoting *disagreement* are not without their importance. The revelation implicit in the study of Talmudic method is that, though not all analysis is equal because only one will carry the decision, all analysis is open to view. In that spirit, then, I want to offer a perhaps controversial definition of feminism—through a biblical look at an instance of personhood.

The beginning of personhood is not, contrary to what we often hear, that Johnny-come-lately term humanism. The beginning of personhood lies in Jewish civilization. Without the Jewish *religious* idea—and this I offer without apology to the moribund Marxists—no concept of personhood is possible: it could not have come into the world.

Consider, by way of illustration, Hannah, the mother of Samuel: a heroine of Jewish civilization. She is counted as a heroine because she was a barren woman who prayed to have a child and got one.

This essay was adapted from a talk delivered at the American Jewish Congress America-Israel Dialogue. Biblical quotations are taken from the King James Version.

Now a hard case can be made that none of this is exceptionally heroic, however exceptional the child turned out to be. What it is, in fact, is a story of conformity in an age not very different from our own, an age when woman's personhood is defined by her ability to be the mother of a son. Hannah in her story is a woman of conventional expectation—she wants to have her dignity, and the only way under patriarchy she can aspire to it is through achieving motherhood. Without motherhood she has no personhood—she is nothing. And she is, accordingly, treated as nothing.

She goes up to the House of the Lord and speaks a prayer "in her heart; only her lips moved, but her voice was not heard" (1 Sam. 1:13)—so immediately, of course, Eli, the man in charge of the House of the Lord, thinks she's a bag lady, a drunk, and advises her to "put away thy wine from thee" (v. 14). Well, she certainly *looks* like a drunk, muttering away to herself like that—no woman, after all, is expected to own a spiritual dimension.

And yet is this the only reason Eli is crucially misled? Hannah is not suspected of an act of prayer; she is suspected of an act of drunkenness. Why? It is not only because a woman of no visible prestige is off mumbling in a corner. It is also because the House of the Lord, in this period, has not yet become a *bet tefilah*, a House of Prayer. The synagogue has not yet made its appearance in history, and neither Eli nor anyone else in his world has ever been witness to inward prayer sent out within sacred walls. The Tabernacle, predecessor of the Temple, is a place of high ritual, of incense and animal sacrifice: a summing-up, so to say, of ancient styles of worship, all expressed on one site in one collective voice, so as to bring an end to the multiple loci of such rites, with their temptation toward multiple *genii loci*, or polytheistic backsliding. Until the moment Hannah speaks "in her heart," all liturgical speech in the Tabernacle has been public, representative, communal, a gathering-platform to inculcate a teaching vision of the One Creator.

Hannah is a heroine of religious civilization because she invents, out of her own urgent imagining, inward prayer. Without bringing a sacrifice, without requiring priestly attendance, soaring past every liturgical convention, she rides her words up into the holy air of the House of the Lord; and in that instant she alters forever what we mean by "prayer." Hannah is an originator, a genius of envisioning: she imagines a Lord of History who not only can command event, but who can also listen to a still, small voice; she imagines the power of that still, small voice itself to influence event. On a lesser plane, one might say that she is the inventor of the inward force of psychology.

But the *content* of this inward force is less innovative. Hannah, genius of lyric outcry though she is, originator of prayer-speech though she is, is nevertheless perfectly conventional in her most pressing desire: she wants to do exactly what society expects her to do. She prays to have a son; she prays to own prestige through motherhood. The inventor of prayer is, simultaneous with her genius, a woman obedient to the rules of patriarchy.

Hannah is the first we would take for a religious heroine. She is the last we would take for a feminist heroine. Hannah's gift is incandescent; but there is nothing feminist in her story.

Until we have a look at her husband, Elkanah. He, after all, is living in the same patriarchal society. He has another wife, Peninnah, who *does* bear children, and no doubt Hannah is jealous of Peninnah because Hannah, in common with her society, cannot conceive of personhood without motherhood. Not so Elkanah. "Hannah," says Elkanah, "*lameh tivki*? Why weepest thou? And why eatest thou not? And why is thy heart grieved? Am I not better to thee than ten sons?" (v. 8). Now *nothing* is more valuable in the world of Hannah and Elkanah than a son, and ten sons ten times that—so that in asserting the value of his individual personhood to Hannah, Elkanah is also asserting the value of Hannah's individual personhood to himself, even without the achievement of motherhood. Hannah has value even if she cannot be the instrument of generation.

It is a tremendous metaphysical moment, the earliest declaration of intrinsicness, a new idea of woman, an unconventional idea, a radical idea—metaphysical in the transcendent sense, and also in its nonattachment to physicality. Hannah, cries Elkanah, with or without sons *you have value in yourself*! What Elkanah—a feminist hero—has discovered in himself is the first principle of feminism: the ethical passion that expresses itself against instrumentality, against woman-as-instrument, against woman-as-the-instrument-of-societal-policy.

It *is* a transcendent moment: it precedes Immanuel Kant's formulation of the same principle by several thousand years. Kant spoke of a Kingdom of Ends: let every human being be treated as an end in herself or himself. Intrinsicness declares itself against instrumentality.

But where does this ethical passion against instrumentality derive from? From the Enlightenment? No, it is older than the Enlightenment. From humanism? No, it is older than humanism.

The ethical passion against instrumentality—intrinsicness, personhood—derives from the beginning of the beginning of Jewish civilization. We will find it in the first verse of chapter 5 of the Book of Genesis: The human being is made in the likeness of the Creator.

And this is where I want to offer a view of feminism that is not entirely in consonance with the views of many self-designated feminists today. I want to affirm what I have been repeatedly told is an old-fashioned, an obsolete, idea of feminism. I think of it, however, as classical feminism, and consider that departures from classical feminism have been departures from feminism itself. I speak of the idea of feminism as the transcendence of biology. Now we have heard it said again and again, in the current mode of corporeal feminism, that "biology is a factor." Yes, biology is a factor. How can it not be a factor? Each of us is a kettle of organs; the brain, the seat of human thought, is a mere organ; we are all biological creatures; we are organisms.

But the urgency of classical feminism, which many have forgotten, or ignore, or dissent from, or believe we have evolved from, was precisely the fight against the notion that anatomy is destiny. If anatomy is destiny, then every woman, and every man, is by definition an instrument of blind biology, and the human being no longer lives in the aspiring Kingdom of Ends, but wholly and savagely in the Kingdom of Instrumentality. If feminism is not meant to transcend the biological, then there *is* no feminism. We have heard Jewish "feminists" call for the renewal of New Moon ceremonies as an innovative pursuit for the advancement of Jewish women: is the celebration of the recurrence of the menses feminism, or is it a ceremony honoring instrumentality? We have even heard a call for a technological disclosure that would extend the capacity of women to bear children into old age, as a pursuit of so-called biological equality with men—an ideal, it seems to me, so regressive that it strips Hannah once again of intrinsic value.

Classical feminism took as its starting point two inviolable negative principles: first, that woman was *not* to be considered an instrument for policy goals, whether explicitly of the state or implicitly of the society; and second, that biology was *not* to be the governing motif of a woman's value.

What these negative principles led to was a definition characterized by simplicity, strength, and purity—namely, that feminism means equal access to the great world, access founded in capacity and merit. It means participation in the professions and in the arts, and in every other human enterprise that makes the world go—and all the rest is private life, filled with private choices. For classical feminism, tyranny enters in with the politicization of the personal. For classical feminism, when biology enters in, at that instant feminism ends. In this view, if rape is considered a "women's issue" rather than a societal issue (it is, after all, the crime of a man who victimizes a woman, and might better be termed a "men's issue"), if abortion is considered a "women's issue" rather than a societal issue, if day care is introduced solely as a "women's issue" rather than a societal concern, what all that marks is not the beginning of a wider feminist arena but the erosion, at its absolute center, of feminism itself.

The idea of classical feminism was to bring an end to the segregation of women; to the notion of women as a separate class or species with a separate outlook, a separate psychology, a separate destiny. In this view, insofar as emphasis on segregation and psychological separateness is promulgated, to that extent is feminism eroded.

What is the source of this uncompromising exclusion of the biological?

The source is the great feminist source itself, the first source in the history of all civilization to declare against instrumentality and for the Kingdom of Ends—and that is Genesis 5:1, those words about being made in the likeness of the Creator.

In the Jewish vision the Creator has no likeness in any terms that human beings can see or know or imagine. The Creator is an imagining of the unimaginable. The revolution in the Jewish idea is that the Creator is not an incarnation, neither of man nor of woman nor of beast nor of anything else that can be found in biological reality. Since the beginning of the history of the world, there is no other religious vision on the planet, from animism straight through Zoroastrianism—that's A to Z—that does not incarnate or image divinity in physical or biological reality. In the Jewish vision, and only in the Jewish vision, the nature of the Creator is dissociated utterly from the biological: because the biological is the fount and origin of instrumentality.

For Jews, to be made in the likeness of the Creator means that you may not be made into the likeness of anything or anybody else; that no one may fashion you into an instrument for his or her own use.

This is the power of Torah—that it declares against instrumentality. Intrinsicness is precisely the theme of Jewish history. Israel, an idea luminous with holy continuity, remains the exemplum of Jewish steadfastness within the intrinsic. It was so for Abraham, and it is so for us. How did exile, which drew Rachel's tears, come to be reversed in our time and undone, and Jerusalem restored? Because every day in every generation there were those, women and men, who passionately and yearningly pronounced the name of Jerusalem. "We will no longer be buffeted, we will no longer be the instruments of the policies of others," said the sovereign soul of the Jewish people, set in the likeness of the Creator.

And now it is the turn of Jewish women to say the same.

I want to dare to observe that if Jewish feminism does not emerge from Torah, it will disintegrate. The hope derived from Enlightenment tolerance is an idol that will not serve women as it turned out not to serve Jews; Voltaire found room in his liberalism for anti-Semitism. The hope invested in contemporary manifestations of humanism is an idol that will not serve women as it turns out not to serve Jews; observe how the advocates of "human rights" have for decades stood in the gutter with other Jew-haters to support or whitewash the lords of terror.

Those who say that Torah offers only "male models" forget that justice is neither male nor female, but an idea; and ideas have no anatomy. Those who say that Torah as a source of feminism cannot possibly appeal because religion is the illusion of the superstitious are themselves opium eaters who have shut out insight into the origins of ethical civilization; they lack the moral imagination.

And it is just this—the moral imagination, Torah's mammoth gift—that lifts Elkanah, the husband of the inventor of the language of inward vision, out of the parochialism of patriarchy and into an understanding of personhood. Service to Torah can make no woman and no man into a thing of servitude. And who is to say that Hannah, in her singular service to the Creator, did not inspire Elkanah to see singularity?

Reflections on Hannah's Prayer

❦

MARCIA FALK

EVERY YEAR, ON THE FIRST DAY OF THE HOLIDAY OF ROSH HA-shanah, Jews read in synagogue the story of Hannah's prayer:

> There was a man from the highlands of Ephraim named Elkanah.... He had two wives, one named Hannah and the other named Peninnah. Peninnah had children but Hannah was childless.... Her husband Elkanah would ask her, "Hannah, why do you weep, and why do you not eat, and why is your heart so heavy? Am I not more good to you than ten sons?"
>
> Once Hannah rose after eating and drinking at Shiloh while Eli the priest was sitting at the entrance to the temple of God. Her spirit was greatly pained and she prayed to God, weeping profusely. She vowed a vow, saying: "O God of Hosts, if you will look upon and see the plight of your servant, if You will not forget but remember your servant and give your servant a son, then I will dedicate him to God for all the days of his life, and no razor shall ever touch his head" [that is to say, she would enter him into the Nazarite service of God].

Biblical and Talmudic quotations are from my own translations.

94

As she continued praying to God, Eli watched her mouth. Hannah spoke in her heart; her lips moved, but she uttered no sound; and Eli took her for a drunkard. Eli said to her: "How long will you go on behaving like a drunkard! Put away your wine!"

Then Hannah replied, saying: "No, my lord, I am a woman in anguish, and I have had neither wine nor hard liquor, but have been pouring my heart out before God. Do not regard your servant as a worthless woman, for I have been speaking all this time out of the greatness of my concern and out of my vexation."

Then Eli answered, saying: "Go in peace, and may the God of Israel grant the petition you have asked of Him." She said: "May your humble handmaid find favor in your eyes." The woman went on her way, and ate, and her face was no longer sad.

Early in the morning they arose, worshiped before God, and returned to their home in Ramah. And Elkanah had sexual relations with his wife, and God remembered her. And in due time Hannah conceived and bore a son, and she named him Samuel (*Shemu'el*) because she asked him (*she'iltiv*) of God.

When Elkanah went on pilgrimage with his household to make the yearly sacrifice to God and to fulfill his vow, Hannah did not go, but said to her husband: "Not until the boy is weaned. Then I will bring him to appear before God, and he will stay there forever." ... So the woman stayed, and she nursed her son, until she weaned him. When he was weaned she took him with her ... and brought him to the house of God in Shiloh. And the boy was still young. They slaughtered the sacrificial bull and brought the boy to Eli.

And she said: "O my lord, as surely as your soul lives, my lord, I am the woman who stood here next to you praying to God. For this child I prayed, and God gave him to me, God gave me what I asked (*she'elati asher sha'alti*). And so I too will lend him (*hish'iltihu*) to God, all his days he will be lent (*sha'ul*) to God."

And they worshiped God there. And Hannah prayed. . . . (1 Sam. 1:1–2:10)

Hannah has long been a character close to my heart—for many reasons, but perhaps above all because she is a woman misunderstood.
In this story she is misunderstood twice: as she weeps—in her
sorrow—by Elkanah, her husband; as she prays—in her yearning—by
Eli, the high priest. Yet Hannah has a voice; she means to be heard.

Hannah's husband, Elkanah, asks her why she weeps: "Am I not
more good to you than ten sons?" And Hannah doesn't answer, because she knows from the way he puts the question that he has not
understood. After all, he already has sons and daughters (not to mention two wives). And although Elkanah loves Hannah, and gives her
double portions of his sacrifice, and speaks to her not without tenderness, he is far removed from her pain. As a father, with all the benefits that fatherhood bestows on him in that patriarchal world, he is
in no position to suggest that Hannah should be satisfied without
children; is he promising to provide for her, as children did for parents, in her old age? And it is outright presumptuous of Elkanah to
expect his spousal love to fulfill Hannah's yearning to be a mother.
Elkanah reveals with his question—"Am I not more good to you
than ten sons?"—how differently he views relationships from his
wife. For Hannah cannot think of the love that she is ready to give
her child as replaceable by the love she has for her spouse—or indeed for anyone else. She doesn't answer Elkanah's question because
she knows that even if she did, he still would not understand.

Trying myself to understand Hannah, I think of two other biblical
stories that touch on the relations between parents and children. I
think first of King David and his rebellious son, Absalom. When
Absalom is killed by David's own army, David is rent and cries out,
"My son Absalom, my son, my son Absalom, would that I had died
in your place, Absalom, my son, my son" (2 Sam. 19:1). His grief is
inconsolable, undiminished by his ties to others: presumably none of
his eleven wives, nor any of his more than a score of offspring, can
compensate for the loss of his Absalom—his son, his one and only
Absalom.

The other story I think of is the story of the binding of Isaac
(which, as it happens—surely not by coincidence—is read in synagogue on the second day of Rosh Hashanah). When God decides to
test Abraham's faith by commanding him to sacrifice Isaac, this is
what God says: "Take your son, your only one, the one whom you
love, Isaac, and go to Moriah and offer him up on a hill that I will
point out to you" (Gen. 22:2). There is a problem—what medieval
commentators call a "difficulty"—in this verse: Why does God say

"take . . . your only one"? What about Ishmael? Abraham had *two* sons, and this seeming inconsistency in the text has for centuries afforded translators and commentators opportunities to speculate and excuses to amend. But I think there is in fact no inconsistency here; the language of this command is perfect in its emotional truth. For in this terrible context—at the singular and absolute moment when Isaac's life is threatened—the storyteller knows that Isaac *is* to Abraham an *only*—absolutely, singularly *only*.

We don't hear Abraham's answer: what could he possibly say at such a time? And we hear nothing at all of Sarah. What must she have felt that morning as she watched Abraham take Isaac up the hill, Abraham carrying wood and a knife, and no sacrificial lamb with him? What did Sarah see in the eyes of her son, her only son, the beloved child of her old age, for whom she, like Hannah, must have wept and for whom she finally laughed?

As the mother of an only child—a much wished-for child of my middle (if not old) age—I live all the time with the unspoken and unspeakable terror of Abraham and Sarah, the *ordinary* unspeakable vulnerability known as parenthood. I used to think that my vulnerability was worse than that of some others because I have only one child, and at my age will probably not have more. But a friend, the mother of two grown sons, said to me, "More doesn't help, doesn't matter. I don't have two children: I have two ones, two onlys."

What my friend knew (what perhaps all parents know?) was that in the context of loss, each child is an only to her or his parents. Human relationships do not fill in for, do not substitute for, do not replace each other. So when Elkanah asks Hannah why she weeps, when he asks if he can't substitute for the child she so desires, he may be trying to help—but he's missing the point.

But you are perhaps wondering how I got from Hannah's *longing* for a child to David's inconsolable *grief* over the loss of a child, to Abraham's and Sarah's *terror* in the face of such loss? Because Hannah is not yet a mother, you may assume that she cannot possibly know parental grief or terror. You may, perhaps, even find her a bit greedy: after all, she has a devoted husband; why is she not satisfied? Indeed, if one has not experienced Hannah's longing, it may at first be difficult to understand that Hannah's sorrow *is* a kind of grief, that her yearning is a kind of terror—the fear that what one so desperately desires—what one, in a way, already loves—will be forever denied.

Difficult as it often is to grasp someone else's pain, it is easy to judge another's behavior. So Eli the priest doesn't hear Hannah's silent prayer; he sees her lips moving and calls her a drunk. And Hannah does not seem surprised by Eli's reaction. Perhaps she expects it. Respectfully, employing the language deemed appropriate to her social station and to his, she tells him that she is deeply distressed and that she has been praying, and she asks him not to judge her harshly. After all, he is an authority who has, at the very least, the moral power to judge and to condemn. She, in contrast (and in her own words), is a mere "servant."

The social politics of this situation are at once ordinary and extraordinary. A seemingly ordinary woman, a woman immersed in longing, Hannah prays from the depths of her heart, silently, privately. In this behavior she follows no convention—and she becomes extraordinary. At this moment, talking to God, she does something entirely on her own: She stands at the sanctuary—the sanctuary where priests officiate as men offer up their sacrifices—and she prays, using her own words and her own voice, without intermediaries. Her act is all the more extraordinary in that, by all accounts, she is the first woman—indeed the first "ordinary" person—to pray in any sanctuary, at this point in time before institutionalized prayer has replaced sacrifice as the means of public worship.[1] In so acting, Hannah stands poised to become a symbol for rabbinic Judaism, providing for the early rabbis—the Amoraim—a model of authentic prayer, which is to say, "the prayer of the heart"—although all Hannah has *meant* to do is to speak her *own* heart. We may call her intentions spiritual, but the result of her action is both spiritual and political. Hannah discovers her own voice, and herself legitimates that voice.

And the high priest—no ordinary man but a man of spiritual authority, which is of course also political authority in that time—sees her, rebukes her, and deems her out of line, out of her mind. This, alas, is the predictable part of the story—the disturbingly ordinary part.

Hannah's response to Eli combines both the ordinary and the extraordinary. Though she speaks deferentially, respecting convention and the social order, the fact that she speaks at all, that she asserts herself and *explains* herself to Eli, is surely an act of courage. Hannah has self-respect, and she means to be heard. Her protest—do not condemn a person until you have stood in her place, until you are sure she is guilty—is a political act. From it the rabbis will later devise the ruling that one must not let a false charge to oneself go uncorrected: one must defend oneself and not be apathetic to what others think (Babylonian Talmud, Tractate Berakhot 31b).

So impressed were the rabbis with Hannah's prayer *and* with her defense of it to Eli that they interpolated the following words into those of the Bible story: "Hannah said to him [Eli]: You are no person of authority in this matter, and the Spirit of Holiness is not upon you, since you have been suspicious of me in this matter," and further, "You are no person of authority, nor is the divine Presence or the Spirit of Holiness with you, since you have presumed me guilty rather than innocent. Are you not aware that I am a woman in anguish?" (Babylonian Talmud, Tractate Berakhot 31b).

This bit of Talmudic midrash, which imputes to Hannah somewhat more chutzpah than the biblical author allows her, invites us, too, to enter into the story with our imaginations; once there, it is hard not to speculate about other changes we might like to see. For example, we might wonder how the story would have looked if Hannah's prayer had been met with a different reaction from Eli the priest. What would it have been like if instead of automatically assuming that this woman talking to herself was a drunk, Eli had paused to listen to Hannah, bearing witness to her spiritual expression? Might he have learned, from the woman who called herself his servant, about the prayer of the heart? Might the meaning of spiritual authority have been altered at that moment?

Indeed, the rabbis of the Talmud seem to suggest that Hannah's response to Eli appropriately raises the whole question of spiritual authority. Yet, tragically, the rabbis did not go on to revise the social order. On the contrary, the bitter irony is that these very rabbis, in creating communal prayer, neglected to give Hannah's daughters— the women of Israel—a place in it.

And we might further speculate: What would it have been like if Hannah's grief had been met with a different response from her husband? What if instead of attempting to talk her out of her feelings, Elkanah had simply respected them? Might the meaning of comfort, of empathy—of relationship itself—have changed in that moment? Had Elkanah ceased patronizing and begun listening, might he have begun to glimpse the possibility of reciprocity in marriage? Might Hannah have become Elkanah's equal in his eyes at the moment when he stopped condescending to her pain and began instead to respect it? Might Hannah have become Elkanah's teacher in matters of the heart?

And what would it have been like if centuries of interpreters and commentators had taken Hannah seriously, on her own terms—as the rabbis of the Talmud began, but ultimately failed, to do? How differently might the tradition have been shaped if, over the millennia, Hannah's voice had clearly and consistently been heard within it? What turns of plot might the midrashic narratives have taken, what concerns might have been addressed in the legal debates, what images might have emerged in the evolving liturgy? The thought of what has been lost in the silencing of Hannah's daughters is overwhelming—the cause of genuine despair.

We might, then, choose to reframe these questions in a more hopeful way. Instead of lamenting, we might take it upon ourselves to pick up where the rabbis left off. We could begin by asking what it might mean for us—as individuals and as communities—to hear Hannah's voice today. We might also ask what it would be like to create a community of empathy, where silent pain is given a voice. What, indeed, would it be like to have a truly inclusive spiritual community, a community of equals, where all could pray together in the language of the heart? What might communal prayer sound like if it included everyone's voice?

The recitation of Hannah's story, with its triumphant ending, can turn the festival of Rosh Hashanah into an excruciating experience for Jews who—like Hannah—suffer the grief of infertility but whose prayers—unlike Hannah's—go unanswered. And the synagogue can be a painful place for Jews who—like Hannah—need to pray from their hearts, in words that are an honest expression of the heart.

For many Jews today—and especially many Jewish women—the traditional Hebrew liturgy, constructed by male authorities and entrenched over time by male usage, does not express the language of the heart. In particular, in its address to an exclusively male divinity, this liturgy denies Jewish women their full humanity—that humanity which is created in the image of the divine. And in its dearth of meaningful imagery that speaks to their reality, this liturgy often leaves both women and men feeling unrepresented and unfulfilled. Yet these Jews count themselves as members of *klal Yisra'el*, the community of Israel; they want, like Hannah, to be heard; they do not want to be exiled in their longing. Hannah is a woman misunderstood, unheard, invisible—and she lives here among us today.

But those who lack authority and centrality and power are often invisible, their speech—like Hannah's prayer—inaudible, at least to those accustomed to hearing their own voices echoing loudly in the sanctuaries and other meeting places. How, then, do we begin to hear these silent prayers and give them voice? In the words of the feminist theologian Nelle Morton, we need "to hear each other into speech," so that listening becomes the stimulus for expression instead of—as we are more accustomed to having it—speech being the stimulus for our hearing. This means, first, listening to those who have had the least opportunity to have their voices heard. It means, for example, listening to the new liturgies being created today by women— listening and making room for them in the sanctuaries, and not rushing in to silence or condemn. It means, in other words, reversing our expectations and our norms.

Indeed, reversals are what so poignantly mark the biblical narrative of Hannah's prayer. Not the least of these comes at the end of the story, when Hannah the petitioner becomes Hannah the benefactor, who approaches even her relationship to God with self-respect and with the assumption of reciprocity. The Hebrew author emphasizes this reciprocity with a play on words: Hannah will lend Samuel to God because God has, as it were, lent ear to her voice and granted her request.

And reversals are what Hannah explicitly celebrates in her second prayer, the public one that comes at the end of the story (and that was, undoubtedly, added to the story at a later date, but that nonetheless fits there beautifully). In this prayer, said aloud for the whole community to hear, Hannah unfurls a vision of a world in which the arrogant are humbled and the mighty fall, while the weak are strengthened, the hungry are sated, and the disempowered gain access to places of honor. The voice of Hannah, misunderstood by the men of her day, has been fully heard by God and strengthened by Hannah's own experience; with great power it moves outward, extending the meaning—and the politics—of the story into broader realms, and into the future:

> The bows of the mighty men are broken and those who stumble are girded with strength. Those who had plenty to eat now have to go to work to earn their wages, and the hungry are no longer hungry. . . . God raises the poor up out of the dust, and lifts the beggar up from the gutter to be set beside princes, so that they will inherit the throne of glory. (1 Sam. 2:4–8)

This is truly a story of reversals—a story that Hannah enters as an ordinary woman, a woman desiring to be a mother, and that she leaves as an extraordinary woman, a prophetess seeking a new world order. She has tested her inner voice, allowing it to pour out, and it has ultimately been heard (and even answered!). No wonder, perhaps, that her legacy has been silenced; and no wonder that it should—and will—persist in being heard.

Infant Piety
and the Infant Samuel

❦

MARGARET ANNE DOODY

"Do you read your Bible?"

"Sometimes."

"With pleasure? Are you fond of it?"

"I like Revelations, and the Book of Daniel, and Genesis and Samuel, and a little bit of Exodus, and some parts of Kings and Chronicles, and Job, and Jonah."

"And the Psalms? I hope you like them?"

"No, sir."

"No? oh, shocking! I have a little boy, younger than you, who knows six Psalms by heart; and when you ask him which he would rather have, a gingerbread-nut to eat, or a verse of a Psalm to learn he says: 'Oh! the verse of a Psalm! angels sing Psalms,' says he; 'I wish to be a little angel here below'; he then gets two nuts in recompense for his infant piety."

"Psalms are not interesting," I remarked.

—Charlotte Brontë, *Jane Eyre*[1]

THE TEN-YEAR-OLD JANE EYRE STANDS UP WELL UNDER THE INterrogations of the intimidating Mr. Brocklehurst. When he inquires

Biblical quotations are taken from the King James Version, unless otherwise indicated.

as to her Bible reading, he is doubtless surprised by the literalness of her reply. Jane's particularity swerves out of the mode in which his questions are set. She gives no impression of "piety"—it is as if she did not know about that. She does give a considerable impression of literary authority and individual taste. She obviously likes books of prophecy with grand and disturbing images, for she cites Revelation and Daniel first in her ad hoc canon. The other works that appeal to her are narratives. She places Genesis first among these, as is conventional, but she breaks convention by following Genesis with the Book of Samuel. Only when she has got that work safely in, that combination of the prophetic and the narrative, does she double back to a selective Exodus. She then continues with the stories of Samuel and of Saul, David, Solomon, and their descendants as narrated in the stirring historical books, Kings and Chronicles. Jane Eyre's last implicit category concerns the trials of great survivors of tribulation—the innocent Job and the guilty Jonah being united in those qualities that Jane herself shares.

The tone of Jane's interest disconcerts Brocklehurst, who endeavors to get the conversation back on track. Cleverly he seizes on her omission of the Psalms. Jane rejects these nonnarrative and meditative works. She remains unmoved by his urgent example of the virtuous little boy who gets gingerbread-nuts for learning Psalm verses. Undoubtedly Jane has seen enough of little boys in her cousin John Reed to be skeptical about the desirability of following this little male's example, and Brocklehurst, in boasting about his son, inadvertently shows that his son has very early learned to manipulate his father. Unlike the frank Jane Eyre, the horrid Brocklehurst boy gets his way by guile and hypocrisy. Brocklehurst is in some sense a victim, a victim of his own attitudes, for he has been well taken in. He is susceptible to the image he tries to create, the image of "infant piety." Statements made in the Psalms, of love, awe, and humility, are thought particularly suited to the child (in relation to its elders). The childhood lisping of Psalmic sentiments is clearly an aspect of cultural theater. Jane insists on not colluding, on not participating in this form of theater. She utters her comically strong and simple repudiation: "Psalms are not interesting." Brocklehurst at once retorts, "That proves you have a wicked heart." Jane's "wicked heart" is a narrative heart that prefers story to stasis. She values actions and the strong delineation of character. Jane also tells us, "I had read Goldsmith's 'History of Rome,' and had formed my opinion of Nero, Caligula, &c" (p. 8). The historical is the raw and the real. That the

Psalms (at least used in Brocklehurst's way) are bland is perhaps inadvertently acknowledged by Brocklehurst himself, for the verses
must be helped down by a spicy "gingerbread-nut" or two, as an an-
tidote. The books Jane likes have their own ginger.

Jane's mode of reading is presented to us as a child's mode of reading. Behind the brave Protestant who holds her own before Mr.
Brocklehurst we can sense the adult Jane, amused as she relates this,
and beyond her the implied author. Both of these characters know
that Jane's style of reading is a childlike style, and we are not held
to any belief that the adult Jane, or Charlotte Brontë, at present does
not care for the Psalms. Yet the child Jane's manner of reading has
a certain validity, and through it Brontë poses an interesting case of
the girl reader who reads the Bible. Charlotte Brontë sets Jane up as
an appropriate and entitled reader of the Bible—and this is certainly
not the role Brocklehurst would allow her. In his eyes she ought to
be a submissive, not an active, reader of a sacred Scripture that
would teach her humility. He is not comfortable with his own potential recognition that reading Daniel, Samuel, Exodus, Kings, and so
on may not lead at all to the acquisition of humility and reverence
for one's betters. Bible reading is supposed to have—according to a
theory to which he subscribes—a salutary and repressive effect. But
the reading of the Bible by a child does not necessarily lead to "infant piety."

One great model for all that is understood by the phrase *infant piety* is the young Samuel. There is a famous painting by Sir Joshua
Reynolds entitled *The Infant Samuel* that looks soulful and expressive.
Someone in our house owned a reproduction of that painting. Perhaps at some point one of the three children received it as a present
or a Sunday-school prize. Ours was a clerical household, and we had
a fair share of religious pictures. It may have hung in my father's
study; the figure of Samuel was important to my father, probably as
representing his own early sense of his vocation as a clergyman—a
clergyman not at all of the Brocklehurst type. He was a witty, sunny-
tempered, deeply humane man, and, as the son of an English coal
miner, he felt a kinship to all mankind, particularly those who suffered or were heavy laden. I think his own calling seemed to him
something miraculous, though he *never* talked about it in that way.

I early knew Reynolds's image of the infant Samuel, who here exhibits some of the tendencies approved by Mr. Brocklehurst. He is in
prayerful posture, thus humble, and his eyes are above things of this
world, such as gingerbread-nuts. He might, however, get a nut or two

through this effective exhibition. He was in marked contrast to the figure in a picture I liked much better, a large picture in my father's study showing Christ among the doctors. Jesus, a twelve-year-old Jesus with masses of deep black hair under his cap, stands confidently among the learned men in the Temple, amazing them with his knowledge and his answers. And they visibly *are* amazed, really impressed. I don't think I felt exactly "religiously" about this picture—hence I do not here capitalize the *he* and *him*. Yet I was impressed with it. In this picture Jesus is obviously a know-it-all, a show-off of the supernal sort, a smart kid—and people approve of this, and it is right to be interested in books and questions and ideas. Jesus was not humble, and *not* obedient. He stayed at the Temple when he should have gone home with his family. His mother was upset: "Son, why hast thou thus dealt with us? behold, thy father and I have sought thee sorrowing" (Luke 2:48). But none of that mattered.

The youthful Christ in the Temple among the doctors is engaged with other people, obviously talkative, as Reynolds's Samuel is not. But I don't think I put much stock in the painted Samuel. He was too babyish and too sweet; I liked better the character in the story.

The story of Samuel I originally read was not in the Bible. Unlike *Jane Eyre*, I did not in childhood read large portions of the King James Version by myself, although I did read some of it, and certainly heard the Bible (King James Version) read aloud in church Sunday after Sunday, so that I knew some passages by heart. But for current and pursuant reading of the Bible, we children turned to a compendium entitled *Hurlbut's Story of the Bible*, "a continuous narration of the Scriptures told in one hundred and sixty-eight stories."[2] This enormous work by Jesse Lyman Hurlbut (1843–1930) had first appeared in America in 1904 and was published repeatedly in various editions with illustrations and maps. Hurlbut's model is undoubtedly Charles and Mary Lamb's *Tales from Shakespeare* (1807), and he is certainly a simplifier, but the narrative desire of the young reader was satisfied by swinging along through the 168 stories from Genesis to Revelation, and the early reading made indelibly familiar all sorts of persons and events. The book was satisfying, such a wonderfully large thick substantial book. Stretched on your tum by the fireplace, with Hurlbut's *Story of the Bible* lying companionably on the floor too, somewhere beneath the chin, you were very well set up for a rainy or snowy winter afternoon.

In reading the Bible in any form, or in hearing it read, I think we children took some special interest in any stories about children. I know I did. Certainly from ages seven through thirteen I felt a kind of age-loyalty in relation to characters. This could be stretched pretty far. When we had family Shakespeare readings and did *As You Like It*, for instance, I decided Rosamund must be my closest chronological neighbor in the story, though admittedly she was obviously a lot older. The Bible provided more children than Shakespeare, and Bible children are certainly not like Shakespeare's when the Bard of Stratford does deign to let them in on the plot. Shakespeare's children are all little boys of the most sophisticated sort, like the little Princes in *Richard III*. Shakespearean kids are very knowing and precocious, palace-wise and given to wisecracking; they seem just like Hollywood children, or at least like the Hollywood children we get told about. The Bible's kids aren't Hollywood, or Beverly Hills, they're not visibly on their way to being politicians or rock stars—though of course many of them do become politicians and some, like the musical young David, have a touch of the rock-star about them. There aren't many more girls in the Bible than in Shakespeare, it's true. When Moses' sister stands guard over the baby in the ark among the rushes, the girl is not given a name, though she's obviously important, and so is Pharaoh's nameless daughter. We like to suppose that the loyal older sister was Miriam, Miriam the prophetess, who leads the people in a song of praise in Exodus 15:20–21. But she is called the sister of Aaron and may not be Moses' sister. When we meet Esther and Ruth, they are quite grown up. It is easy to imagine a childhood for Leah and Rachel, but we meet them in their prime too. A girl child features importantly among the New Testament miracles: Jairus's daughter. Still, it had to be admitted that Jairus's daughter didn't actually *do* anything, except get out of bed and walk.

The boys in the Bible stories were much more active and thus more interesting—especially a hero like David. David as child or youth, however, is more interesting when he is a loner, tending his flocks, or equipping himself to fight Goliath, and the youthful David could not be seized upon by parents as a model of childlike obedience. I think most parents, guardians, pastors, and masters have also been a bit shy of pressing the example of young Joseph, who shows off outrageously and antagonizes his brothers by hubristic boastfulness. He doesn't quip like one of Shakespeare's precocious little horrors, but Joseph is truly too self-involved to be set up as exemplary, a model for good children. One would be hard put to create a picture of the infant *Joseph* at prayer. Samuel seems safer. That's probably why there was (and is) a hymn about Samuel in our Episcopalian and Anglican hymnbooks. In the British *Hymns Ancient and Modern* it is found in the section "For the Young," right after "All things bright and beautiful." Hymn 574 presents Samuel to "the Young" as a model. It does seem odd to sing a five-stanza hymn that begins with the idea of silence and the hushing of hymn singing, but I think that paradox is part of the charm of the piece when performed:

> *Hush'd was the evening hymn,*
> *The temple courts were dark;*
> *The lamp was burning dim*
> *Before the sacred ark;*
> *When suddenly a Voice Divine*
> *Rang through the silence of the shrine.*
>
> *The old man, meek and mild,*
> *The priest of Israel, slept;*
> *His watch the Temple child,*
> *The little Levite, kept;*
> *And what from Eli's sense was seal'd*
> *The LORD to Hannah's son revealed.*[3]

Hannah's son—yes. How easily in childhood I passed over the ordeal of Hannah, which is the beginning and the framework of the story. Hannah feels slighted, passed over, worthless, because she does not bear any children. We begin the story with Hannah's suffering. We see from her perspective. Hannah is one of a set of two, one of Elkanah's two wives. The story is full of doublings, substitutions, and difficult equations. At first Hannah seems to be negative, signaled by a minus sign: "and Peninnah had children, but Hannah had no children" (1 Sam. 1:2). Her husband, Elkanah, seems a loving and generous man, in the brief glimpse we have of him. Seeing Hannah lamenting and weeping, he asks her "why is thy heart grieved? am not I better to thee than ten sons?" (v. 9). One feels the generosity of spirit and the deep affection in these words. In an era in which women were valued only or primarily for childbearing (really sonbearing), Elkanah says it doesn't matter, that the love between the two of them is what counts. He offers himself as a substitute son—or rather ten sons. That is Elkanah's substitution. That is his equation: 1 husband = 10 sons. But Hannah doesn't want her husband to be a son, and there is an unnerving suggestion of the childish as well as the strong in Elkanah's well-meant equation. Hannah is not in the least comforted by these words. They seem in fact to exacerbate her condition, so much so that she gets up the courage to go to the Temple and pray out all her agitation and despair and pleading. And there she makes her vow to the Lord: "If thou wilt indeed look on the affliction of thine handmaid . . . and wilt give unto thine handmaid a man child, then I will give him unto the Lord all the days of his life" (v. 11). That is Hannah's doubling and substitution, her new equation: 1 Hannah's son = 1 gift to the Lord.

Hannah is watched in her prayer by Eli, the priest, who "sat upon a seat by a post of the temple" (v. 9). Eli doesn't in the least understand what Hannah is about, or the depth of feeling that moves her. He misreads her body language; "only her lips moved, but her voice was not heard: therefore Eli thought she had been drunken" (v. 13). Eli doesn't have the kindness to keep his suspicion to himself, but speaks aloud to the strange woman, rebuking her bad behavior in the Temple precinct: "And Eli said unto her, How long wilt thou be drunken? put away thy wine from thee" (v. 14). That is Eli's first doubling, his substitution and equation: Woman moving lips = drunkard. The idea that women might have feelings, inward lamentations, that they might make prayers to God that are not intended to be heard by mortals, not even men, not even the priest—this is not an idea that has occurred to him. Eli seems comically stupid. His tremendous obtuseness and the fundamental ineffectiveness concealed beneath his authority (concealed first of all from himself) are all magnificently and dramatically revealed here. Eli is first heard uttering a misplaced rebuke. He finds fault where it is easy, blindly rebukes where he should not—and never succeeds in rebuking where he should. As the narrative of this first chapter moves on, his insulting words offer Hannah the opportunity of reply and explanation. She becomes loud and articulate. If Eli was waiting for a *voice*, he has now got one. In this narrative he first gets into trouble, sitting inertly at his post, because he cannot hear or is not able to hear a voice . . . and then finds that the voice has really uttered, but not for or to him. That will, of course, be his situation in the central story. At this point, however, Eli redeems himself in the reader's eyes by listening to Hannah, blessing her, and endorsing her prayer. Thus he may be felt to have some instrumentality in answering her prayer, in conceiving a son; the moment of blessing makes him Samuel's spiritual father.

Hannah finds, then, as in all the best stories, that her wish is gratified, her prayer is answered, her dream comes true—but at a price. She does conceive and bear a son: "She bare a son, and called his name Samuel, saying, Because I have asked him of the Lord" (v. 20). The ideas of both *desire* and *voice*, so we are told to believe, inhere in the hero's very name; but in fact Hannah's wordplay is mistaken; the word that would equate with her meaning is the name *Saul*, whereas *Samuel* means "his name is El," that is, "this person is God" or "a reflection of God." Why did the author(s) play with a false etymology? Commentators have suggested that some element of the story of Saul (who will appear in the book of Samuel) got transferred to Samuel.[4] But perhaps, too, the author(s) could not resist the introduction of voicing into the name of Samuel, as *voice* is a key concept in the narrative, and the story works in a pattern of asking, speaking, and replying. Hannah has to abide by her original equation, which was her vow. When she has weaned the child, the family journeys back to the Temple, slays a bullock in sacrifice, and delivers the child to Eli. Hannah's great prayer or psalm of thanksgiving is, for Christians, the background and type for the song of Mary called the Magnificat (Luke 1:46–55). Mary's song, however, comes at a joyful moment, after the conception, when she hastens to her cousin Elizabeth, and Elizabeth saluting her recognizes the wonder that has happened. At the human level the announcement of one woman to her friend and relative that she is pregnant is a cause for celebration. Mary exults, "He hath put down the mighty from their seats, and exalted them of low degree. He hath filled the hungry with good things; and the rich he hath sent empty away" (vv. 52–53).

Hannah in her triumph likewise praises a God of transformation and reversal who does not adhere to worldly standards and expectations: "The Lord maketh poor, and maketh rich: he bringeth low, and lifteth up. He raiseth up the poor out of the dust, and lifteth up the beggar from the dunghill, to set them among princes" (1 Sam. 2:7–8). Hannah expresses joy and thanksgiving in a moment of paradox. Mary's song is a rejoicing at fulfillment. Hannah's a substitution for loss. Hannah becomes poetical and powerfully verbal, giving voice at the very moment of most intense pain, the loss of her son. Her canticle, her voicing, is a substitution for the child she is in the process of losing.

Nowadays when I read the story, I wonder how as a child I passed over Hannah's story so lightly, how I remained so unmoved. But unmoved, on the whole, I was. For myself as a child reader Hannah was just *background*. Her presence proved that Samuel was supremely

wanted, and that was enough. I myself liked to think that I was supremely wanted, and the children we meet in stories are customarily
wanted very much by their true parents, before some ogre or witch
steals them away or some mischance betides them. Hannah was like
the parents in fairy tales, like the queen in "Snow White," who
wishes so ardently for a daughter and is given one at the price of her
own death. Hannah, however, does not die, so she has little to complain of. She seemed suitably occupied, to me, in making her child
clothes; I liked that because our mother made a lot of our clothes.
Hannah and her pious husband come to the shrine every year, and
Eli is pleased to see them and blesses them, saying to the husband (of
course he's not good at talking to women), "The Lord give thee seed
of this woman for the loan which is lent to the Lord" (1 Sam. 2:20).
And Hannah is rewarded, with doubling and redoubling and substitution: "And the Lord visited Hannah, so that she conceived, and
bare three sons and two daughters. And the child Samuel grew before the Lord" (v. 21). This is a profitable equation indeed: 1 child
given to the Lord = 5 children. Certainly the author(s) of this book
did not want us to feel that Hannah was shortchanged. Yet the text,
having introduced her momentous gift, her loan, and her loss, can
never quite get rid of the sense of her loss. While she may rejoice in
her five new children, the very first is absent: "The child Samuel
grew before the Lord"—in that clause we see that Hannah is missing,
even among the cluster of her five children. Samuel grows before the
Lord, not in her sight. She has lost the child who might play near
her, in the room or in the dooryard, who might be schooled nearby
and learn a trade and marry some nice neighbor girl and come
around of an evening. All the vivid home hopes and daily affections
are cut off. That suppressed desire to be part of Samuel's life, to surround him with her love, emerges in the annual gift Hannah brings
to her "Temple child." "Moreover his mother made him a little coat,
and brought it to him from year to year, when she came up with her
husband to offer the yearly sacrifice" (1 Sam. 2:19). Jacob, besotted
with the child of his old age, his clever Joseph, made for him (or had
made up for him) a coat of many colors (Gen. 37:3). Hannah can
create nothing very spectacular; like a child at a boarding school,
Samuel has to look suitably attired. "But Samuel ministered before
the Lord, being a child, girded with a linen ephod" (v. 18). Simplicity and purity are the order of the day. Here is another substitution:
For words of love and playfulness, for kisses and hugs, there is substituted the making of an object and then just the object.

This substitution already verges on the problematic and dangerous, for much of this part of the narrative is taken up with improper use of and fixation on objects. The sons of Eli, Hophni and Phineas, are priests who have no sense of vocation, but harbor a greedy love of objects. They make their servant hook up with "a fleshhook of three teeth" (1 Sam. 2:13) all the sacrificial meat he can carry off. They help themselves to the fat parts before the meat is sacrificed or even cooked. They also lie with women "at the door of the tabernacle" (v. 22).[5] One realizes that, with a father like Eli, these hulking sons can see women only as objects. What are only slight or venial tendencies in Eli become strong sins in his sons. Eli himself has a great indolence about him. Almost every time we hear of him, he is sitting or lying down. Later, on his death day, when he hears that the Philistines have captured the ark and slain his sons, Eli is sitting on a seat by the road. Struck by calamity, "He fell from off the seat backward by the side of the gate, and his neck brake, and he died: for he was an old man and heavy. And he had judged Israel forty years" (1 Sam. 4:18). We sense the heaviness, the lethargy of Eli's judgment in his bodily configuration. Even his very death is a figure of inertia.

Eli's sons are less inactive, but they, too, have the physical desire for flesh that has already turned Eli's body fleshy. They devour everything, and women are just other pieces of meat to consume. The two sons have no sense of the spiritual, nor of women. If they respected others, they could not abuse those persons' sacrifices in the heartless way they do. Globose, self-contained, sucking in everything that comes their way, they are caricatures of Eli and satires of the priesthood. Eli rebukes them, but so feebly that his scolding has no effect. Eli doesn't have the guts to fire his sons and send them away from the Temple. He does nothing even when he hears a remonstrance and prophecy delivered to him by another man, a man of God who comes to him and tells him off:

> Thus saith the Lord . . .
> Wherefore kick ye at my sacrifice and at mine offering
> . . . and honorest thy sons above me, to make yourselves
> fat with the chiefest of all the offerings of Israel my people? (1 Sam. 2:27–29)

Eli cannot admit that he is honoring his sons more than God, letting his sons weigh more. Fat, weighty, incapable of change, the family of Eli with the line of their priesthood drops toward the earth beside the springing, active shoot of the new priest, the prophet who has been brought into their midst, like the cuckoo into the nest.

To a novelist or dramatist perhaps the most powerful part of the story would be Hannah's or Eli's. The story of Eli and his sons is a situation ripe for the exploration of an Arthur Miller, or perhaps, in another tone, suited to the laconic elaborations of Harold Pinter. Like Pinter characters, Hophni and Phineas are somewhat menacing, blocked in communication, devious and internally self-involved, taciturn even in selfishness. Eli is garrulous but inaudible: "They hearkened not unto the voice of their father" (1 Sam. 3:25). In this story the personages perpetually wait for or expect voices, and yet ignore them, partly or wholly, when the voices utter.

Despite the pathos, the ironies, and the dramas, the story of Hannah, and the story of Eli and his sons, were not attractive to the child reader who was myself forty-some years ago. Grown-ups were fundamentally uninteresting to me, interesting only in their relation to the central figure, the child waiting to assert itself. I don't think that is a "wrong" reading, either, for the story told by the author(s) of this book is the story of the decline of a priestly line and a new beginning, a new form of fulfillment, of which the child is the symbol and the agent—and the grown-ups must at last, very properly, be relegated to the background. But what I now see, or perhaps *feel* would be a better word, is that Samuel enters upon a situation fraught with emotion, pain, and difficulty. Like most well-treated children, he is able to ignore a large part of the pain swirling around him, for to him that is merely history, and he treats history rather as Henry Ford did. The Samuel who is a child here seems very wrapped in his own affairs. His own affairs include serving in the Temple, but for him (as not for the unfortunate and passively guilty Eli) that service is unproblematic. Samuel is innocent not only of sin, of guilt— but also of pain. His mother lost him, but he registers no particular need or desire for her. Samuel is a still center, a point about which the others and their emotions eddy and swirl.

The position of naive quietness, of a happiness that is not inertia and an activity that is not stressful, is the position uniquely perhaps of the Temple Child as type. Admittedly no other Temple Child is found in the Bible, so there is no "type," save in the Christian figurative sense, in which the child Samuel in the Temple is a "type" or figure of the young Jesus in the Temple among the doctors. But antique literature offers us another example of the Temple Child, in a work of pagan fiction written some four or five hundred years after the Book of Samuel was first written. In Euripides' *Ion*, a play first produced about 420 B.C.E., the hero is a Temple Child, in infancy abandoned by his mother and taken in by the priestess of Delphi. After an introductory explication by Hermes, the play opens with this child, now a youth, entering with a broom made of laurel twigs to sweep the outer porch of the Temple. Ion (with Chorus) sings of the beauty of the new day, and of the pleasure and order of his work:

> *Now I will sweep the temple—*
> *My duty here since childhood—*
> *With a broom of laurel-branches,*
> *And purify the entrance*
> *With holy wreaths of flowers;*
> *Sprinkle the floor with water;*
> *And with my bow and arrows*
> *I'll send the wild birds flying*
> *That foul our temple treasures.*
>
> *I have no father or mother;*
> *All I would owe to them*
> *I give to Apollo's temple,*
> *Which nursed my orphan childhood.*[6]

Ion is holy, innocent, and happy. His serene but never inactive life is about to be disrupted, for the next set of pilgrims who come to the shrine proves to be his parents. The parents' story is complicated, and, in the case of the mother, extremely unhappy. Creusa was the victim of a rape—as she believes, a rape committed by the god Apollo. In youth she kept the result of this horrifying experience a secret, and abandoned the child. Her present husband, Xuthus, does not know of her story, or her curse, which ironically is childlessness. Creusa now wishes to find out what happened to the lost child. Her boisterous husband, however, has his own story. Xuthus, it turns out, committed a rape (*the* rape) during the Bacchic rites at Delphi. Now he wants to adopt Ion. Ion is thus claimed by parents who are in conflict about the nature of his conception, about the meaning of sexuality, about the nature and role of male and female humans—and of the gods. Ion tries to keep free of his parents. He tries to reject Xuthus's offer of adoption, explaining that he doesn't want position and money: "A simple, untroubled life is what I want; that is what I have here, Father; and I have been happy" (p. 61). Ion cannot, however, escape the meshes of parentage, conflict, and history. He must leave the temple service to go with these difficult parents.

I have said the story of Hannah, like the story of Eli, might attract a dramatist. Euripides in some respects is that dramatist. He gives us what the biblical author(s) of Samuel cannot allow to enter—the reunion (the problematic reunion) of mother and son. Lost child and lost mother are reconnected; the simple split that Hannah experienced, whereby the child was donated once and forever, is not allowed to occur in Euripides. Creusa's story, with her childlessness, her loss, is a variant of Hannah's.[7] Yet Creusa's anger is overwhelming, whereas Hannah cannot be allowed to feel or express anger.

The primary difference between Euripides' story and that of Samuel is that the central deity is questioned in one work and must not be questioned in the other. Given that fundamental difference—and granting to Euripides an unusual degree of skepticism mixed with an offbeat religious feeling—we may yet find a strange similarity between Ion and Samuel. Ion is somewhat the older—he is a youth who has been the Temple Child all his life. But both are youthful characters in a state of unconscious refusal, and both are about to be awakened—not with the "normal" awakening to sex, but with a (supposedly) abnormal awakening to religious and moral problems.

Both Ion and Samuel live originally in a state of brisk serenity. Yet both youths are active. Ion likes doing things. Some of the things that he does as part of his religious service are "feminine" (sweeping, washing), and he has been brought up by a priestess whom he regards as a substitute mother. Samuel is more cut off from the feminine. Yet both children enjoy the obverse of their deprivation; they have the Peter Pan luxury of doing without parents. And both of these Temple Children know their way around the edifice and their work, displaying self-sufficiency, self-command. As they understand order so well, we may suspect a bossy streak in both of them. This is certainly exhibited by Ion at the beginning of the play, when he tells the crowd of pilgrims and tourists the rules: "You may not go inside the temple unless you have sacrificed sheep . . . look round at everything that is open to the public" (p. 48). Ion seems to act as a bridge, door, or gateway between Inside and Outside. He keeps outer spaces clean (cleansing, scaring away the birds). Samuel plays no such role in relation to the public—it is Eli's sons who rove about the perimeter, taking women in the doorway. But Samuel, like Ion, knows about ritual actions and ritual spaces. In both stories (one dramatic, one narrative) there are strong representations of holy edifice and spaces. Both youthful characters, the Temple Children, are at home in the various spaces, and they are at home (so they think) with holiness. They are the ultimate Insiders, who do not even have to think of themselves as Insiders, because being at the center of holiness is part of daily life, undifferentiated and unremarkable. They are Unconscious Insiders, characters in a state of superb latency.

Samuel represents the Unconscious Insider. Ion we see first gracefully at an outer perimeter of the temple edifice; Samuel at his most important moment is deep within, in the heart of the shrine. He is yet without feelings of dread, awe, or excitement in this holiest of places:

> And ere the lamp of God went out in the temple of the Lord, where the ark of God was, and Samuel was laid down to sleep:
> [Then] the Lord called Samuel: and he answered, here am I.
> And he ran unto Eli, and said, here am I; for thou calledst me.
> And he said, I called not; lie down again. And he went and lay down. (1 Sam. 3:3–5)

The hymn of J. D. Burns has cheated at this point. The hymn gets a good effect of hushed stillness, of night, of one holy lamp burning amid the darkness, but the hymn writer can't let the story alone. He must meddle to make Samuel more perfect—that is, to make Samuel not the Unconscious Insider but the Conscious Insider: "His watch the Temple child,/ The little Levite, kept." Samuel must be keeping a watch, conscientiously at attention. He must be vigilant. That Samuel is conscious and purposeful is also suggested in the added flourish of Burns' description of him as a "little Levite." Nowhere in this narrative is it said that Samuel is of the tribe of Levi. The hymn writer wants Samuel to be proper, ordained for the ministry, consecrated to his vocation like a good Scots scholar. But that is not what is given us in the biblical narrative. We should not lose sight of the fact that Samuel is asleep. This is an aspect of his childlike greatness, or the greatness of the childlike. He is laid down to sleep in the holiest place of Israel, slipping happily into unconsciousness beside the great Ark of the Covenant. If we saw an adult doing that, it might seem blasphemous, or daring—certainly some intention or thought would seem to be involved. But for Samuel there is no thought. This is normality. This is home. I think that is one of the things I enjoyed as a child about this story. Samuel is not fussed by holy surroundings. He makes his home among them, he is practical. He goes to sleep promptly in the Temple every night, without concern, with the good sleep of childhood.

Yet Samuel is awakened or aroused to attention by the voice. He is obviously an active child, for he *ran* to Eli. Samuel's alacrity and promptitude have impressed readers, both adults and children. Adults remarking on Samuel's "Here am I" generally overstress his promptitude and usefulness. They like to imagine he is the sort of child who doesn't have to be asked twice to mow the lawn. It would be pleasant if children could be persuaded to be useful, to bring a parent the saw or the sewing basket with dispatch, to go off at once to the store for two pounds of flour and some Mazola without grumbling, argument, or delay. That's what adults try to teach children, really, when they talk about Samuel's obedience, forgetting that the story has its ironies. Eli didn't need anything, and Samuel was barking up the wrong tree. The real obedience was demanded by God, and that is the only obedience that ultimately counts. But adults writing *for* children have never failed to stress *obedience* as an aspect of Samuel's virtue. This is the line taken by the hymn writer. We are to pray for Samuel's ear ("Alive and quick to hear / Each whisper of Thy word"), for Samuel's heart ("A lowly heart, that waits"), and Samuel's mind:

> Oh! give me Samuel's mind,
>   A sweet unmurmuring faith,
> Obedient and resign'd
>   To thee in life and death;
> That I may read with child-like eyes
> Truths that are hidden from the wise.

Those last two lines seemed right on the money when I was in my youth. And asking for the ear that is quick to hear seemed a sound notion. I was not then, nor am I now, convinced, however, that Samuel's heart was "lowly" or that there was anything particularly "sweet" about him—nor did I want there to be. Samuel's virtue was not obedience (what child ever thought that of much value!) but energy. Samuel got right up and went in to look after Eli, and he did this three times. What I saw in Samuel was a very take-charge little chap. Eli was logy and slow, had now become old and couldn't see very well. I didn't think much of Eli. I thought he was rather a weight on Samuel's hands, a responsibility. But Samuel, being bright and energetic, was perfectly able to cope, the way kids are able to cope, and if Eli was tiresome, that's the way adults are and Samuel was reasonable enough not to get upset about it. Samuel's patience is an aspect of his energy—the alertness that allows him to wake up at once and go rushing along a corridor. I know that we do not know the age of Samuel at the time and that it would be reasonable to picture him as a youth, a stripling—like Ion—even a young adult of eighteen years. But I prefer to think that he was the child Samuel—to that extent faithful to the tradition of Reynolds. I always thought of him as eight years old at the time of his calling—maybe ten. Not a great big boy like Jesus at his Bar Mitzvah, but a little kid. I could see him twinkling along through the temple in his pajamas, the way I went to the bathroom in my pajamas in the middle of the night. But Samuel got up to look after somebody. He wasted no words, never got pettish, and wasn't afraid of the dark.

It took a while, but Eli at last figured out that there was a reason why Samuel had been called by God. Eli turns up trumps for once in telling Samuel what to do, and Eli shows the saving humility that turns out to be quite admirable—for he must recognize that God is not talking to him but has made a prophet and saint out of his protégé:

> And Eli perceived that the Lord had called the child. Therefore Eli said unto Samuel, Go, lie down: and it shall be, if he call thee, that thou shalt say, Speak, Lord; for thy servant heareth. (1 Sam. 3:8–9)

It's like "Cinderella," it's like Ruskin's "The King of the Golden River"—the youngest and least thought-of member of the party is the important one. That's how good stories should be. "That I may read with child-like eyes / Truths that are hidden from the wise." Father does *not* know best. Tradition, the fathers, the priests, and the learned need not necessarily know best. God skips over learning and tradition and the institution and the recognized authorities—looking for somewhere where he can make a breakthrough. I wanted to be one of the "wise," it is true, and to become one of the Doctors instead of one of the prophets. But there was some subtle encouragement to women in the story of Samuel, for if God gets fed up with the holy mess created by the holy orders and skips about ignoring the hierarchies of the institutions, why, then, there's no reason why the vision of God, the word of God, the truth of God might not strike suddenly the least likely person—the female. Samuel as a consecrated male and Temple Child was not the least likely person—he just looked that way. Samuel had obviously not indulged in any of the saccharine piety and heavy-breathing prayer suggested in Reynolds' picture—otherwise he would not have been so able and practical at seizing the Lord's meaning. He was a good listener. At first, like other characters in the story, he listens imperfectly. The word of God is hard to catch. He misunderstands the source of the voice. But once he knows it, Samuel very practically says the words suggested by Eli, and he really does hear.

So far we get something compatible with what might be called the sweet version of the calling of the prophet. But hymn writers and writers for children and so forth tend to want to tune out just what is said by the Voice Divine. Samuel may be the chosen prophet, but that doesn't mean that what God says to him is pretty. God tells Samuel in no uncertain terms that he is going to judge Eli and his house, "because his sons made themselves vile, and he restrained them not" (1 Sam. 3:13). It is all that thunder that Samuel has to carry about with him until morning, wondering whether to let it out. "And Samuel lay until the morning, and opened the doors of the house of the Lord. And Samuel feared to shew Eli the vision" (v. 13). In the morning Samuel moves from the center of God's house to the periphery, from the ark to the door. Like Ion, he greets the morning at the doorway. When Ion first did that, his mind was free—it was soon to become oppressed and puzzled. Here Samuel is for the first time oppressed and puzzled. Samuel could have said with Ion "a simple, untroubled life is what I want." That simple, untroubled life is not going to be possible for him either. The emotions and iniquities swirling around Samuel have at last gotten through to him also. God has taken him out of latency and given him unwanted knowledge. Samuel is faced with a problem: Should he tell Eli these unpleasant things? Should he not utter them? Eli begs him to hide nothing from him that God has said. Samuel fulfills the job of a true prophet: "And Samuel told him every whit, and hid nothing from him" (v. 18).

Samuel's first act of prophecy is not a success. His speaking of what God has said makes no difference. Eli says only "it is the Lord: let him do what seemeth him good." Eli doesn't have the gumption to say, "Well, yes, I should get after my sons, and they shouldn't be priests another day—they are a disgrace to their profession and they are damaging themselves, and I won't have them peculating and cheating one moment longer!" Eli can't say these things, still less act on them. It must have been grievous to Samuel the energetic to contemplate the great dearth of energy that is Eli. That Samuel was fond of Eli there can be little doubt, though I think it was a fondness of an unconsciously patronizing kind, as bright children can feel fond of rather dull but kind grown-ups. God couldn't speak to Eli because Eli could not—would not—listen. Eli made doublings and equivalents and evasive equations. To Eli it seemed just as good for God to talk to Samuel as to himself, and just as good for God to punish him and his as for Eli to try to set matters right. Eli thinks in equations and balances; his balancing means not the wisdom of good judgment but the poise of stupid inertia. Samuel is the new Eli, an equivalent or double, the true priest. But he is not exactly a priest, not tied to that formula. He is a new being, a prophet, and is to bring in a new spiritual life. There is no equation anymore, for Samuel doesn't just equal the sum of something else. He is different.

The adult writers who tell children about obedience and cite Samuel as the exemplar deserve to hear their auditors cry "Foul!" For what Samuel learns in this story is that he is far superior to his elder, who is certainly not his better. And when God tells Samuel some very unpleasant home truths, Samuel has to deliver that sharp stuff to Eli. Samuel is really the model for disobedience of certain kinds, for answering back, for speaking out, for telling it like it is. The child who tells the parent not to smoke, not the child who fetches the Mazola, is the truest successor of Samuel. Samuel is not cowed by affectional ties or the grandeur of office. We see in this story that the official often becomes a hollow sham, not because of evil in the office or in the structure itself but because of human defects. It is useless to pretend things are working well when they are not. Samuel has no pretense about him, which makes him a rather startling companion. Eli can afford to be, as the hymn writer says, "meek and mild," because that is a strategy the old man has for getting through the world. If he weren't so meek and mild, he'd have stood up to Hophni and Phineas. Eli *likes* being "meek and mild," but Samuel has no use for meekness and mildness, and no need for them.

Perhaps Samuel errs the other way; he learns very quickly the art of telling others their faults that God teaches him. There is a certain officious quality already present in the youthful Samuel; it is part of his energy and his unaffected charm. He also has a good deal of curiosity. Curiosity and officiousness help to get him up on a dark night to go running in to the old man he thinks called out to him. Samuel the adult won't be happy unless he's managing other people's lives—not an amiable trait. In the child in his pajamas twinkling promptly along the dark corridor, popping in and saying, "Here am I," there are premonitory glimmers of that officiousness that was to be so vexing to the royal house of Israel. But as a child reader one sees with gratitude the vision, the voice, the energy of Samuel—undepressed though things are falling to pieces around him. If only Eli had realized that he should boot out his two sons. That was one equation Eli couldn't make—that his son in the spirit could be substituted for his dreadful sons of the flesh. Eli in fact could do nothing. That meant it was up to Samuel to do it all. I think children often feel that way about their elders—not just about their immediate friends and relations, but about the world the adults have cobbled together and left to them. Samuel is not a particularly resigned personality, either in childhood or later on, but he has to resign himself to the fact that Eli will do no more and can do no better.

Energy and inertia, there they stand side by side—or sit rather—Samuel the child, the runner, the hearer, and Eli the slothful, the heavy man. They are friends, bound by ties of affection, yet they are in perennial opposition. That opposition is rather distressing to grown-ups, parents, and teachers to think about. They have tried to tame the child Samuel into a picture of sweet obedience, because otherwise children will realize that Samuel is a picture of the child turning upon its elders. Samuel does not turn upon his elders in rage or resentment—that's precisely what makes his judgment so fearsome. Here is a happy chap, serene in himself, confident, curious, level-headed. He has no reason to feel the personal animus of a Jane Eyre. Yet in depicting the encounters between Mr. Brocklehurst—another priest—and young Jane, Charlotte Brontë has endorsed the energy and truth telling of a young Samuel. In the child Jane Eyre's two encounters with Mr. Brocklehurst, we see a reflection of the story of Samuel and Eli. Mr. Brocklehurst, grim and vicious, is apparently a far cry from the kindly, fat Eli, but in Brocklehurst, that "black pillar," that "black column," that "piece of architecture . . . looking longer, narrower and more rigid than ever," we recognize the principle of inertia expressed as rigidity. Here, too, is the temple taking false precedence over the Voice of God. Brocklehurst, deluded by his greedy son, is a failed priest, a member of a troop in which Eli ranks near the head. This "black marble clergyman"[8] must be set aside so that the true young prophet, Jane herself, can be heard, as well as the voice or voices that speak through her. At every such point of the inevitable if sad conflict between a Samuel and an Eli, we see human life lurching out of latency and into history, into the world where progress and change are possible. The dynamic if stormy reigns of Saul and David, the taking of Jewish national life into the full tide of history, are possible only when a Samuel has risen and an Eli fallen. In an obstinate profession of well-meaning men, Eli can do a good deal of damage, but he is finally a superfluous man, and must disappear, as Brocklehurst, too, disappears from Jane's narrative. Brocklehurst tried to cancel Jane's voice, saying she was a liar, but he shrivels under the torrent of Jane's powerful voicing of her life. And with the inspiration of a Jane Eyre replacing the failed institutions of a Brocklehurst, a new national and spiritual life for women is also signaled as possible. We should be frightened of the Samuels, for they mean a change is on the way.

Energy, persistence, openness to divine revelation, and unnerving candor—these qualities accompany a certain heartlessness on the part of children. Children understand this quite well themselves, and grown-ups don't want to know about it. Infant piety is a frightening thing. Either it is feigned (as in the case of Brocklehurst's little boy), in which case it is a sticky piece of hypocrisy. Or it is genuine, which means the child who is listening to God and not to us will be capable of startling revelations, and will refuse to be taken in by our show.

The Psychopathology of King Saul

(1 SAM. 8–31)

DEIRDRE LEVINSON

"The king's heart is in the hands of the Lord."
A king is history's slave.

—LEO TOLSTOY, *War and Peace*[1]

THE CRUCIAL THEOLOGICAL QUESTION ARISING FROM THE narrative of Saul's reign—namely, why God chooses this man from among all Israel as the first king of Israel, only to deem him unfit at the earliest opportunity—points to an archetype underlying the text, which is of the king himself as the sacrificial offering. Saul as archetype is the scapegoat of an angry God, appointed by him to pay the price for Israel's unholy demand for a king, to demonstrate in his increasingly demented being God's initial repudiation of the institution he compels Saul to inaugurate. Similarly Saul's pivotal historical role, as it was to effect the transition from the rule of the judges to monarchical rule, thereby opening the way for David's conversion of the

My heartfelt gratitude to Allen Bergson for his indispensable contribution to my reading of the text.

In addition to using the King James Version of the Bible, I consulted *The New English Bible*, Oxford study ed. (New York: Oxford University Press, 1976); and *The Book of Samuel* (New York: The Judaica Press, Inc., 1976).

123

Israelite tribal confederacy into a nation state, might well be seen as
a sacrificial one too. But if the narrative reveals enough of Saul as
victim to scandalize such readers as require that the Hebrew God
(contrary to the overwhelming documentary evidence of his nature)
comply with human standards of fair play, this is emphatically not
the point of view of Saul's chroniclers. For them it is not the nature
of Saul's role in itself but (in contrast to his son Jonathan, who plays
his appointed part—also a sacrificial one—in accord with God's will)
his resistance to it that makes his life a disaster. The dice may be
loaded against Saul from the start, but, as in Sophocles' *Oedipus*, the
chief interest of this narrative is in the way its protagonist
characterologically plays out his predestined role in history. The story
thus lends itself to a psychological reading; but more particularly in
that, tellingly as it dramatizes the development of Saul's character
in the course of his progress from youthful naïveté to adult criminal-
ity, it still leaves so much unexplained. How, for instance, does one
account for Saul's eagerness to sacrifice his son Jonathan at
Michmash? How does one account for the onset of Saul's mental collapse and how does one understand its symptomatology when all the
text tells us is that "the Spirit of the Lord departed from Saul, and
an evil spirit from the Lord troubled him" (1 Sam. 16:4)? Why does
he break down precisely at this point, and what clues prepare us for
it? In this essay I have attempted a psychological reading of Saul's
character in the belief that such a reading can clarify certain opac-
ities in the text without violating its spirit.

The story begins ominously. The elders of Israel, with the cata-
strophic leadership of Eli's corrupt sons and the Philistine seizure of
the ark of God still fresh in their memory, and now with the bleak
prospect of only an aging Samuel and his two venal sons as judges
over them, propose to Samuel that he appoint them a king, "to judge
us," as they say, "like all other nations" (1 Sam. 8:5). Samuel's instant response to this request is to take such offense on his own account that God, unprecedentedly in this prophet's lifelong term of
office, has to remind him sharply of his proper priorities ("they have
not rejected thee, but they have rejected me, that I should not reign
over them" [v. 9]), before charging him to apprise the people pre-
monitorily of "the manner of the king that shall reign over them."
Samuel thereupon rehearses before the people the price that a king
will surely exact for his services; and he does not mince matters. "He
will take," he says, "he will take . . . he will take" (vv. 11–17). Still
the people stand firm: "Nay; but we will have a king over us; that we

also may be like all the nations; and that our king may judge us, and go out before us, and fight our battles" (vv. 19–20). The combined function of judge and military leader is not new to Israel: The earlier judges served as military leaders, Gideon so successfully that he was offered a hereditary appointment as ruler—an offer he promptly refused ("I will not rule over you, neither shall my son rule over you: the Lord shall rule over you" [Judg. 8:23]). But not within living memory have the people been led by a warrior judge: neither Eli nor Samuel has been a military leader, and their self-serving sons have discredited the office of judge as a hereditary position. It is a measure of their desperation that the people seek a new order now; the greatly intensified threat, at this point in their history, of the reinforced military power of the Philistines prompts their appeal for political normalization, to be "like all the nations," to be led by a king who, like other kings, is discernible to the human eye. Not that Israel's plight, in the view of either their dethroned God or their superannuated judge, justifies their demand. It is under the direction of a smoldering God that the displaced and resentful Samuel proceeds to make them a king.

If, in light of this inauspicious prologue, the prospects for Saul's reign look forlorn, his initial appearance in the narrative is not so unpromising. In the first place he is, as well as strikingly handsome, a head taller than any of his compatriots. Both sources of the text make this claim,[2] and the Samuel of the later source, though he holds no brief for kingship, is, despite himself, mightily impressed: "See ye him whom the Lord hath chosen," he declares when he presents Saul to his subjects, "that there is none like him among all the people" (1 Sam. 10:24). Saul, as he enters the narrative, utterly unaware of what God has in store for him, is in single-minded pursuit of his father's lost asses. Failing to find them, despite a lengthy search, he proposes to his servant that they return home, "lest my father leave caring for the asses, and take thought for us" (1 Sam. 9:5). An irreproachably filial young man, Saul is introduced to us, though not untenderly, in this charming passage, as something of a simpleton. His father, judiciously, won't have him go on his own to seek the lost asses. "Take now one of the servants with thee" (v. 3), he instructs his son; and indeed all the initiative in the course of the search comes from the servant. Saul seems not to have heard of the famous seer (though he was known, as we are told earlier, to all Israel "from Dan to Beersheba" [1 Sam. 3:20]), but his servant has. It is at the servant's suggestion that they go to consult him; and when Saul demurs on the grounds that they have nothing left with which to pay the holy man, it is the servant who produces the needful. Samuel, to whom God has already given notice of Saul's arrival, is waiting for him at the city gate. "Behold the man whom I spake to thee of! this same rule over my people" (1 Sam. 9:17), God tells Samuel, while Saul, still with no other end in mind but recovering his father's lost asses, is inquiring of him where the seer's house is. Thus this first of the fateful series of encounters between the first of Israel's kings and the last of Israel's judges is presented to us as one between the young man who knows nothing and the old man who knows all.

Saul's unknowingness, easily his most salient trait so far, is even now hinted at as a form of unconscious resistance to knowing that is later to characterize him. The protocol of the sacrifice, which is to become so crucial an issue between Saul and Samuel, has already been mentioned while Saul is still on his way to the seer. The girls Saul inquires of describe Samuel specifically as the man who presides over the sacrifice; and it is first of all in connection with the sacrifice at the hill-shrine that Samuel identifies himself to the backwoods youth who had thought of the seer only as the man able to divine the whereabouts of vagrant asses: "I am the seer: go up before me unto the high place; for ye shall eat with me today" (v. 19). Only then does he go on to set Saul's mind at rest about the lost asses, while in the same breath announcing the news of his appointment as king: "And as for thine asses that were lost three days ago, set not thy mind on them, for they are found. And on whom is all the desire of Israel? Is it not on thee, and on all thy father's house?" (v. 20).

The asses Saul seeks have been found; the king Israel seeks has been found. The implied comparison is not lost on the agitated young man. "Am not I a Benjamite, of the smallest of the tribes of Israel? and my family the last of all the families of the tribe of Benjamin? wherefore speakest thou so to me?" (v. 21), he asks with a tremulousness that contrasts sharply with Samuel's rocklike self-assurance and that is validated by "all that knew him beforetime," when they witnessed him subsequently, the divine charisma upon him, prophesying among the prophets. "What is this that is come unto the son of Kish?" they ask each other, astonished. "Is Saul also among the prophets?" (1 Sam. 10:11). His sense of his unworthiness, hardly mitigated by Samuel's reiterated denunciation of the people at his election at Mizpeh, is further underscored by the account from the later source of his attempt to escape his royal appointment. Like his father's asses, "when they sought him, he could not be found" (v. 21). He has concealed himself so effectively that the people are obliged to consult God as to his whereabouts: "And the Lord answered, Behold, he hath hid himself among the stuff" (v. 22).

The qualities that are so engaging in the character of Saul as a commoner—his ingenuousness, his rustic simplicity, his contentment with his humble station in life, his horror at the prospect of having greatness thrust upon him—while not in themselves boding ill for him as king, hardly amount to those qualities required to take the strain of his unprecedented office, encumbered as it is with the unallayed resentment of the kingmaker himself.

Even with Saul's first stunning demonstration of his military prowess in his decisive victory over the Ammonites—upon which, at Samuel's own prompting, the people march to Gilgal to "renew the kingdom there" (1 Sam. 11:14)—comes Samuel, like a skeleton at the feast, to make them rue it. Conspicuously withholding from Saul the congratulations he surely deserves, the displaced old prophet deliberately sets out to eclipse Saul's illustrious victory in a savage harangue that (despite God's earlier emphatic reproof) blatantly advertises his wounded *amour propre*. Samuel begins as if to announce his resignation of the leadership by calling the people to witness the unimpeachable nature—as against the relentlessly extortionate nature of the king he had earlier prefigured for them—of his own performance in office: "Whose ox have I taken? or whose ass have I taken? or whom have I defrauded? whom have I oppressed? or of whose hand have I received any bribe to blind mine eyes therewith?" (1 Sam. 12:3). Having thus established his moral preeminence over his royal successor, he goes on to claim, only somewhat less baldly, the same for himself as a military figurehead: of the six leaders he names in the course of enumerating "all the righteous acts of the Lord" (v. 7) in delivering the undeserving Israelites from their enemies, the first is Moses, the sixth is himself. As for this battle against the Ammonites, its sole significance, according to Samuel, is in marking the juncture at which the people insisted upon a king to reign over them, "when the Lord your God was your king" (v. 12); and as for this substitute of theirs, he seems like nothing so much as a figure of scorn for Samuel to point his dismissive finger at: "Now therefore behold the king whom ye have chosen, and whom ye have desired!" (v. 13). If, at Mizpeh, Samuel threw cold water upon the designs of the electorate assembled there, here, at Gilgal, he threatens literally to drown them in it: "I will call unto the Lord, and he shall send thunder and rain; that ye may perceive and see that your wickedness is great, which ye have done in the sight of the Lord, in asking you a king" (v. 17). God accordingly sends a storm so life-threatening that the terrified people abjectly implore their old inter-cessor, "Pray for thy servants unto the Lord thy God, that we die not; for we have added unto all our sins this evil, to ask us a king" (v. 19). Whereupon Samuel, mollified, promises not to abdicate his irreplace-able role after all ("God forbid that I should sin against the Lord in ceasing to pray for you" [v. 23]), but to continue teaching them "the good and the right way," failing their adherence to which, however, he concludes with one last lunge at Saul, "ye shall be consumed, both ye and your king" (v. 25). Thus Saul's reign is launched, and thus simultaneously his oedipal struggle with Samuel, to the grave and beyond.

The narrative, as if signaling Saul's repression of his feelings about this prophet, who has in private insisted, in the teeth of his protests, on anointing him king only to disgrace him in public at the very mo-ment of his triumphant accession, makes no mention of Saul's feel-ings at all. But they must be unbearable to him, for, in light of the subsequent narrative, it is evident that he summarily banishes them to his unconscious, never to be acknowledged, only endlessly acted out. Already characterized less by what he does have in him than what he doesn't, Saul, lacking the inner resources to counter Samu-el's assault, never recovers from it. On the contrary, it sets in motion a chain of reactions in him that, unidentified, always unconscious, makes his ruin inevitable. Significantly the chapter immediately fol-lowing Samuel's fateful tirade has as its subject Saul's first act of dis-obedience.

In accordance with God's stated purpose in appointing him king ("that he may save my people out of the hand of the Philistines" [1 Sam. 9:16]), Saul's next undertaking, after routing the Ammonites, is to launch an all-out offensive against the Philistines, commencing with his son Jonathan's attack upon their garrison at Gibeah. The Philistines duly counterattack with an army of such titanic propor-tions as to send the terrified Israelites flying for cover. At this, Saul, having observed to the letter, neither less nor more, the seven days' waiting time appointed for Samuel's arrival at Gilgal, now seeing his army evaporating, takes it upon himself to offer the propitiatory sacrifice—a venture no sooner concluded than "behold, Samuel came" (1 Sam. 13:10). Saul's glib rationalization for trespassing upon the prophet's turf—"I forced myself" (v. 12) is how he puts it—cuts no ice with Samuel. He speaks to Saul's real motive, that is, his bid to supplant him by intruding himself between God and God's prophet: "Thou hast done foolishly: thou hast not kept the commandment of the Lord thy God, which he commanded thee" (v. 13). As he prefaces his terse announcement of Saul's ensuing forfeiture of a dynasty, so he concludes it: "But now thy kingdom shall not continue ... because thou hast not kept that which the Lord commanded thee" (v. 14). For the reader the authority of Samuel's indictment here, with its deep reverberations of the expulsion from Eden, is witness enough to his authenticity as God's conduit, to the indivisibility of his word from God's. As for Saul, he gives Samuel no argument; but we are shortly to witness in full measure his retaliatory reaction to the desolating judgment his symbolic father and insuperable rival has pronounced against him.

Samuel makes no appearance in the scene immediately following his announcement that Saul is to be deprived of the royal prerogative to father a line of kings; it is Saul's eldest son, Jonathan, who plays the lead here. Unbeknownst to Saul, Jonathan and his armor bearer entrap the Philistines who are holding the pass at Michmash, thus causing a wholesale stampede in the Philistine camp. The moment Saul's watchmen apprise him of this spectacle, he orders a count to be taken of the men who are with him: "and when they had numbered, behold, Jonathan and his armourbearer were not there" (1 Sam. 14:17). So he knows who is responsible for the "very great trembling" (v. 15) in the enemy camp; and he knows who is not in his audience when he adjures his men, on pain of death, to abstain from food all that day "that I may be avenged on mine enemies" (v. 24)—a megalomaniacal statement of purpose sorting oddly with his concomitant demonstration of religious zeal. A most untimely demonstration it is too, as Jonathan observes when, only after refreshing himself with some honeycomb, he hears of his father's veto. The fast has done nothing but hinder the people—a view the narrator apparently shares: "The men of Israel were distressed that day ... the people were faint ... the people were very faint" (vv. 21–31). In fact, the people are so famished by the evening ("they flew upon the spoil" [v. 32]) that Saul is hard put to stop them violating, as the ironic consequence of his unauthorized ban, the Mosaic proscription against eating meat with the blood on it. Nevertheless Israel speeds so well that day that, at the end of it, Saul proposes, subject to the oracle's go-ahead, to continue spoiling the Philistines all night too. But the oracle makes no answer. Immediately imputing this to a violation of his decreed fast, Saul loses no time in pronouncing sentence of death on the as-yet-undiscovered culprit in a vociferous oath that plainly betrays his intent: "For, as the Lord liveth, which saveth Israel, though it be in Jonathan my son, he shall surely die" (v. 39). Equally plainly the procedure he lays down for the drawing of lots to ascertain "wherein the sin hath been this day" (v. 38) is calculated to ensure the success of his aim. He has all Israel stand on one side, he and Jonathan on the other; and when the lot falls on his side, "Cast lots," he says, "between me and Jonathan my son" (v. 42), as if his own life can endure only at the cost of his son's; and indeed, as the lot falls upon Jonathan protesting, "I did but taste a little honey . . . and, lo, I must die" (v. 43), his reply, "God do so and more also, for thou shalt surely die, Jonathan" (v. 44), positively trumpets his relief. But at once, in a consummately ironic reversal that brings Saul's elaborate stratagem tumbling about his ears, the people, invoking with passionate sincerity that God whom Saul has so speciously called to witness in each step toward his murderous objective, defy him in unison, resolved to save Jonathan's life for what may be the very reason Saul sought to destroy it: "Shall Jonathan die, who hath wrought this great salvation in Israel? God forbid: as the Lord liveth, there shall not one hair of his head fall to the ground; for he hath wrought with God this day" (v. 45).

It is Jonathan, as the people avow, not Saul, who has won the day for Israel. As his soldiership—on the evidence of his earlier assault upon the Philistines at Gibeah (an enterprise Saul claims for himself [1 Sam. 13:3–4]), and now of his virtuoso performance at Michmash—demonstrably surpasses his father's, it may be that this has roused Saul to murderous jealousy. But if so, that is only his more apparent and conscious motive. At a deeper level his deadly design upon Jonathan is an expression simultaneously of his unconscious conflict with his punishing surrogate father and his identification with him. Projecting upon his son the same rivalrous feelings toward him that he himself harbors for Samuel, Saul contrives to entrap Jonathan by maneuvering him into a position analogous to his own at Gilgal. As he disobeyed Samuel's sacrosanct command there, so he sees that Jonathan disobeys his trumped-up injunction here; and as Samuel pronounced his doom then, so (mimicking Samuel's "What hast thou done?" [1 Sam. 13:11] in his incriminating "Tell me what thou hast done" [1 Sam. 14:43]) he pronounces Jonathan's now. In this particular, however, he quite outmatches Samuel; for, as his identification with his surrogate father is a function of his unremitting rivalry with him, what lies at the bottom of all his bloody contrivance against Jonathan is his rage to best Samuel, to forestall the fulfillment of his prophecy at Gilgal by killing his heir apparent himself.

Yet, for all the increasing evidence of an ingrained and pervasive corruption in Saul, he remains a superlative fighting man; continuously waging war "against all his enemies on every side, . . . whithersoever he turned himself, he vexed them" (v. 47). But there is one enemy, namely the Amalekites, that is in a class of its own. As the first to assail the Israelites, when, barely out of Egypt, they were most vulnerable, the Amalekites constitute a special case and one of the utmost gravity. The anathema God pronounced upon them then was subsequently embodied in the Law expounded by Moses to Israel, in the form of a twofold charge to the people: to look back to Amalek's outrage—"when ye were come forth out of Egypt; how he . . . smote the hindmost of them, even all that were feeble behind thee, when thou wast faint and weary; and he feared not God" (Deut. 25:17–19)—and forward to the vengeance to come, when, settled in the Promised Land, Israel is to "blot out the remembrance of Amalek from under heaven." Now that Saul has made the kingdom relatively secure, Samuel comes with a commission to him to settle the ancient score with the children of Amalek.

No doubt mindful of the disaster at Gilgal, Samuel goes to great lengths this time to make his communication proof against any possible misconstruction. Thus he repeatedly stipulates that it is at God's express command that he brings Saul this charge to slaughter the Amalekites wholesale, "and utterly destroy all that they have, and spare them not" (1 Sam. 15:3). Meticulously nailing down every bolt hole his slippery customer might conceivably wriggle through, he leaves no asset of the Amalekites unmentioned: "slay both man and woman, infant and suckling, ox and sheep, camel and ass" (ibid.). But the more emphatically Samuel spells out his instructions the more he excites Saul's compulsion to defy his authority. The rivalry is all on Saul's side now, for it seems that Samuel, reassured of his indispensability to Israel, has made peace with the kingship—has indeed, in his austere way, come to love the king. When God apprises him of Saul's nonfeasance, "it grieved Samuel; and he cried unto the Lord all night" (v. 11); and though, with this flagrant proof of Saul's obduracy, he must permanently sever relations with him, "nevertheless Samuel mourned for Saul" (v. 35), so protractedly that, for the second time in his life, God has to call him to order. But between his heartbreak now and the narcissistic umbrage that prompted God's first rebuke of him lies a world of difference; and this is the measure of how far the old prophet has traveled emotionally in the course of his association with Saul.

For Samuel God's will is the sole and immutable determinant of what matters. From this moral law within him he derives his unshakable sense of his own identity, the ego strength that enables him ultimately to forgo his resentment, reconcile himself to the new political order, and accept his rival. But Saul, lacking any such touchstone by which to adjudicate his hateful feelings, cannot likewise develop. Thus the unknowingness that was no discredit to him in youth has, in the absence of an internalized moral standard, given place in his mature years not to understanding but to cunning, and the country boy's natural diffidence has given way not to self-confidence but to presumption. But it is not till this scene leading off from God's disclosure to Samuel of Saul's culminating act of disobedience that we see the full extent of Saul's spiritual destitution.

First, evidently anticipating Samuel's prompt appearance at Carmel, Saul gives him the slip there, compelling the old man to trail him to Gilgal (Israel's sanctuary, the place of Saul's coronation and of his first disobedience), to be greeted, through the din of bleating sheep and lowing oxen, with bland insolence: "Blessed be thou of the Lord: I have performed the commandment of the Lord" (v. 13). In reply to Samuel's last-ditch struggle to make Saul understand what Saul, in his unremitting resistance to recognizing any higher authority than his own, will never understand—"the Lord anointed thee king over Israel, And the Lord sent thee on a journey" (vv. 17–18)—Saul only treats him to more of his cant: "Yea, I have obeyed the voice of the Lord, and have gone the way which the Lord sent me, and"—with a derisive flick of his forked tongue at Samuel—"have brought Agag the king of Amalek, and have utterly destroyed the Amalekites" (v. 20). As for the preservation of the best of the Amalekite livestock, which, he confesses with odious sanctimony, "should have been utterly destroyed" (v. 21), he imputes this to the people's desire to provide for a sacrifice at Gilgal.

Refusing to comment upon Saul's personal souvenir of his victory, Samuel addresses himself undividedly to this matter of the sacrifice, its meaninglessness as the mere form without content, as the show of deference devoid of obedience that Saul, in his emptiness, would have it be: "Hath the Lord as great delight in burnt offerings and sacrifices, as in obeying the voice of the Lord? Behold, to obey is better than sacrifice, and to hearken than the fat of rams" (vv. 22–23).

From there he goes on, in a similarly explanatory vein, not merely to reiterate his original pronouncement upon Saul's first obedience, but this time, as if to point to the inner being as the place where God's law resides, to represent God's alienation from Saul as the direct counterpart or mirror image of Saul's alienation from God (a concept his ghost is later to put most succinctly when he says God has become Saul's enemy): "Because thou hast rejected the word of the Lord, he hath also rejected thee from being king" (v. 23). But since words for Saul, God's word notwithstanding, serve only to be manipulated, even as he confesses "I have sinned: for I have transgressed the commandment of the Lord, and thy words" (v. 24) (still refusing to accept the two as inseparable), he makes shift to explain his transgression not as the sin of commission it is but as contingent upon his fear of disobeying his men: "I feared the people, and obeyed their voice." All the while maintaining an unbroken silence on the subject of Agag, he seeks to reverse the judgment against him, urging Samuel to "turn again," return with him to make his penitential supplications to God, entreating him, clutching at his robe, all in vain. Only with his abject plea to have Samuel return with him just for appearances' sake, to save his face in the presence of his people, does the old prophet—perhaps recalling how brutally he discountenanced him before all Israel at his coronation—relent so far as to grant Saul this favor, upon which only one thing remains to be done before he turns his back upon him forever. Disregarding all the rest of the forbidden spoil, "Bring ye hither to me Agag the king of the Amalekites," he addresses Saul for the last time (v. 32). Then, in a monstrously ironic demonstration of the primacy of obedience over sacrifice, there, in the very place consecrated to sacrifice, "Samuel hewed Agag in pieces before the Lord in Gilgal" (v. 33).

The remainder, or part two, of the Saul narrative spans the years between Samuel's parting prophecy to Saul at Gilgal and the reiteration of it by his ghost at Endor on the eve of Saul's death. As Samuel makes abundantly clear when Saul, in a desperate attempt to detain him, "laid hold upon his mantle, and it rent" (v. 27), God has already taken the kingship from Saul: "The Lord hath rent the kingdom of Israel from thee this day, and hath given it to a neighbor of thine, that is better than thou" (v. 28). In his penultimate appearance in the narrative Saul, failing to get an answer from the oracle the night before what is to be his last battle, resorts to having the sorceress at Endor call up Samuel's ghost. "I am sore distressed; for the Philistines make war against me, and God is departed from me, and answereth me no more" (1 Sam. 28:15), he explains himself, very poignant now that he is *in extremis*, yet still thinking to draw a line between God's prophet and God. "Wherefore then dost thou ask of me," Samuel's irate ghost demands, "seeing that the Lord is departed from thee, and is become thine enemy?" (v. 11). Samuel, no less in ghostly than in fleshly form, can always be relied upon not to pull any punches. The whole of part two can be read as an explication of the ghost's blunt statement.

The characterization of Saul in part two is developed with far more explicitly psychological aim than previously: it is directly to Saul's inner man, which has become indeed the perfect mirror of God's enmity, that the narrative now calls our attention. There is murder in Saul's heart. Samuel knows this and knows he is its target. "How can I go?" he falters, when God, briskly dismissing his mourning, commands him to go and anoint Saul's successor, "if Saul hear it, he will kill me" (1 Sam. 16:2), whereupon God, in a witty affirmation of Samuel's own recent exposition of the inconsequentiality of sacrifice relative to obedience, prescribes the sacrifice as his means of cover. Meanwhile the king's state of mind is alarming his court, for, though the cause is hidden from them, the effect of Samuel's secret transfer of the divine charisma to Saul's successor comes home to Saul at once and with a vengeance in the shape of what his attendants, as well as the narrator, call "an evil spirit from God" (v. 5). Biblical exegetes commonly diagnose Saul's condition as melancholia, acute depression; but depression is the consequence of anger turned inward, against the self, whereas—as we have already observed in his masked offensive against Samuel, and as we are shortly to see in undisguised form—Saul habitually directs his rage outward. This lethal rage, though bedeviling him since Samuel's savage slap-in-the-face at his coronation, has hitherto only worked underground. But now, with the final maledictory rejection of him by the prophet who, albeit his object of hate, was also his indispensable mainstay— his rage has become uncontainable. This is Saul's malady. The narrator remarks explicitly in preface to both occasions upon which Saul hurls his javelin at David that "the evil spirit from God" (1 Sam. 18:10; 19:9) has come upon him again. What the evil spirit from God signifies is Saul's paroxysmal murderous rage. It is the nether side of that spirit of God that alighted on Saul when he was anointed and empowered him to prophesy with the prophets.[3]

As Samuel exits from Saul's life and David enters it, Saul's character, hitherto portrayed largely in the context of his vexed relationship to his predecessor and adversarial father figure, is now to be rendered largely in the context of his relationship to David, his secretly anointed successor. The two accounts of David's introduction to Saul—in the role of healer, in the earlier source; in the later as an untried warrior—differ without contradicting each other. Multifaceted, diversely gifted, the soul of grace, David is everything Saul is not.

The intense and superabundant life that characterizes David emanates from his wellspring of faith in the God he calls "the living God" (1 Sam. 17:26), empowering him like a dynamo. Harking back to an event in his past to support his suit to fight Goliath (in whose height, defiance, and final decapitation the narrator perhaps intends an ironic glance at Saul), "The Lord that delivered me out of the paw of the lion, and out of the paw of the bear, he will deliver me out of the hand of this Philistine" (v. 37), he assures Saul, the poetic energy of his language itself as if animated by the living God. Saul, apart from the two occasions when God's spirit alights on him uninvited, has no experience of God, no relationship with him; God never speaks to him directly. His idea of God is an abstraction exploited by Samuel to thwart and ruin him. But David's buoyant self-confidence, his mobility, freedom, and joyousness, his prudence and wisdom ("David behaved himself wisely," we are told repeatedly, "he behaved himself very wisely" [1 Sam. 18:24])—as against the increasing bedevilment, paranoia, and stasis of the frantically insecure and impulse-ridden Saul—every aspect of David's being proclaims his harmony with God, his perfect trust, his ardent delight in him. Hence, without fear and expressly to exalt the God of Israel, he goes to meet the preposterously armed Goliath with only five stones and a sling, "that all the earth may know that there is a God in Israel. And all this assembly shall know that the Lord saveth not with sword and spear: for the battle is the Lord's" (1 Sam. 17:47–48). David's radiant imagination of God is the direct antithesis of Saul's, as the living God's immanence in him is the direct antithesis of the ever-expanding void at Saul's center.

Everybody loves David, including Saul ("he loved him greatly" [1 Sam. 16:21]). But his love for the man who has worked his cure is, very shortly after David's felling of Goliath and ensuing rout of the Philistines, to yield to adverse feelings fomented in him by the women (who "came out of all cities of Israel, singing and dancing, to meet King Saul" [1 Sam. 18:6]) tumultuously acclaiming the superiority of David's warriorship to their king's, as if Saul's role as their warrior-leader were already defunct. "Saul was very wroth" (v. 8): characteristically projecting his unconscious aggression, he perceives it as David's intention to usurp him: "what can he have more but the kingdom?" As Saul gives himself up to his jealous and paranoid rage ("Saul eyed David from that day forward" [v. 9]), accordingly, the following day, the evil spirit from God, which David's music has so far held at bay, promptly returns. But his illness is now incurable. He no longer wants to be cured, as he demonstrates by twice hurling his javelin with murderous intent at his erstwhile healer—to no effect ("because the Lord was with [David]" [v. 12]), except that now Saul is racked with unremitting fear of David, ever increasing with David's increasing success and popularity: "he was afraid of him. But all Israel and Judah loved David" (vv. 15–16).

As fear dictates cunning, Saul temporarily controls his impulse to assassinate David. Intending to have the Philistines do the job for him, he promises David the hand of his elder daughter, Merab, asking as the bride-price "Only be thou valiant for me," before adding, as he recalls that this is the man for whom the battle is the Lord's, "and fight the Lord's battles" (v. 17). Saul reneges on this promise, however; but soon, informed that his younger daughter, Michal, loves David, he resorts to his former plan ("I will give him her that she may be a snare to him" [v. 21]) and forwards it this time with much ceremonious pomp, asking "not any dowry, but a hundred foreskins of the Philistines, to be avenged of the king's enemies" (v. 25). When David brings in double the stipulated number of foreskins, Saul, obliged to honor his promise, accordingly loses his daughter to David. At this point the narrative dwells at unusual length on Saul's perception of his situation: "Saul saw and knew that the Lord was with David, and that Michal, Saul's daughter, loved him. And Saul was yet the more afraid of David; and Saul became David's enemy continually" (vv. 28–29). What he now perceives as following directly from God's affiliation with David is that David is engrossing the love—his own daughter's as well as his people's—that is Saul's due; that David's gain is his loss; that the more the love attaching to David, the more the fear accruing to Saul.

Even so, Saul has yet to learn that Michal's love for David is such that far from countenancing her father's intent, she loses no time in alerting David to it, letting him down through a window, and contriving to hold off Saul's hatchet men until David makes his escape. Nevertheless, of the love for David that is so repeatedly remarked upon in part two, it is Jonathan who is its supreme exponent. Even as Saul's initial love for David makes its swift about-face, we learn that "the soul of Jonathan was knit with the soul of David, and Jonathan loved him as his own soul" (v. 1), whereupon he immediately makes a covenant with David and invests him with his own royal insignia. The ready instrument of God's will through his abiding love for the man who is to supplant him, Jonathan is the first to perceive that David is destined to be the next king of Israel.

Devoid of jealousy of David, slow to believe evil of Saul, Jonathan is the obverse of his father. It is a measure of his greatness that he contrives, in the teeth of the enmity between Saul and David, to remain ever faithful to both, steadfastly protecting David from Saul while striving simultaneously to protect Saul from himself. Unambivalently committed to the man he knows from the first to be his father's successor, still he never forgets that he is Saul's son and that this, too, incurs obligations. Thus on David's final flight from the court Jonathan, as he blesses him ("the Lord be with thee, as he hath been with my father" [1 Sam. 20:13]), requires him on oath—twice insisting upon it—to keep the covenant between them, not in his lifetime only but forever; and when they part in the wilderness of Ziph, never to meet again (for by this time there is open war between Saul and David), renewing the pledge that inaugurated their undying friendship, "they two made a covenant before the Lord" (1 Sam. 23:18). But even as Jonathan wholeheartedly accepts and promotes David's succession, he is at pains to ensure that his house will not be blotted out of Israel's history. That Jonathan is thereby faithfully serving his father's only authentic interests Saul himself ultimately bears out in (according to the earlier source) his last words to David, when he asks from the bared depths of his heart the same oath of David that Jonathan has already secured: "Swear now therefore unto me by the Lord, that thou wilt not cut off my seed after me, and that thou wilt not destroy my name out of my father's house" (1 Sam. 24:21–22).

Saul's rage, because it cannot be vented upon its real object, makes him an increasingly demented murderer. Its real object is Samuel, whose twice-repeated prophecy of transferring the succession to a more deserving candidate, with its implications for Saul's very manhood, let alone his kingship, he labors to defy. His progressive madness is the expression of his resistance to the inevitability of David's succession, to admitting Father Samuel's triumph over him, to acknowledging that his issue will not reign after him: it is the expression, in sum, of his increasingly frantic resistance to what he knows.

To add to this radical, unremitting conflict, Saul's feelings about his object of hate are conflicted too. Thus the first time he orders Jonathan to kill the man he has just made his son-in-law, helpless to explain himself and inwardly ambivalent, he "hearken[s] unto the voice of Jonathan" (1 Sam. 19:6), who persuades him of the sin of slaying David "without a cause" (v. 5). So Saul is reconciled to David for a while; but the next time David returns victorious from slaughtering the Philistines, Saul's impacted rage explodes again. He hurls his javelin, this time following up his failed attempt with murderous pursuit, castigating his daughter Michal for aiding the escape of her husband, whom—still without explanation, as if to voice his unspoken fear of David's succession were to confirm Samuel's prophecy—he merely calls "mine enemy" (v. 17). But, so much for Saul's secret. David's ensuing flight to Samuel in Ramah only the more loudly proclaims his destiny. For here, in a display of power that dwarfs Saul's, God himself directly intervenes, first causing all three of Saul's dispatch units successively to prophesy with the Prophets, "Samuel standing as appointed over them" (v. 20); then, turning Saul's rage inside out, the Spirit of God alights upon him while he is in hot pursuit, so that he, too, "prophesied before Samuel in like manner" (v. 24). Under Samuel's aegis, not only is David unassailable, Saul's will to assail him is abrogated. For this, Saul is eventually to avenge himself upon Samuel in the most horrendous act of his life.

David is never again to set foot in Saul's court, though he does return to its vicinity, fleeing there from Ramah expressly to convince the still-incredulous Jonathan that Saul is in earnest: "there is but a step between me and death" (1 Sam. 20:3). To this end David proposes a plan to test Saul's intent, the upshot of which leaves Jonathan permanently rid of any shadow of doubt. While, so far, as David has observed, Saul has taken unusual pains to conceal his intent from Jonathan, "lest he be grieved" (ibid.), now seeing that the crown prince himself is bent on protecting the pretender, his rage detonates in Jonathan's face. It all comes out—his sexual insecurity (he curses Jonathan as the son of a whore) and his furious jealousy at Jonathan's love for David—as he screams aloud the thing he has not dared voice until now: "As long as the son of Jesse liveth upon the ground, thou shalt not be established, nor thy kingdom. Wherefore now send and fetch him unto me, for he shall surely die" (ibid.). As Jonathan, pointedly overlooking his father's vital disclosure, only asserts David's blamelessness. Saul, whose will to revenge, even in the face of his own opposing interests, is always his priority, hurls his javelin at his heir apparent. This action, by which Jonathan sees that his father will stop at nothing in his rage to kill David, marks a crucial turning point in the progress of Saul's madness.

With this attempt upon Jonathan's life, Saul's paranoia rises steeply. The report that the fugitive David (now joined by "all his father's house" [1 Sam. 22:1] and some four hundred assorted malcontents) is assembling an army provides Saul with ostensible justification for roundly reproaching his own men, whom he first reminds of his all-inclusive bounty (David's increasing corps of malcontents notwithstanding); then, with the shameless self-pity his paranoia lets loose ("there is none of you that is sorry for me" [v. 8]), he accuses them of concealing from him his own son's alleged collusion with the son of Jesse to ambush him.

To this blatantly paranoid projection nobody in his audience responds, except one Doeg the Edomite; but Doeg's embellished version of what he witnessed of David's recent exchange with the priest Ahimelech at Nob gives Saul pretext enough for venting his fury upon an older and bitterer enemy than either of his alleged assassins. Ahimelech, whose scrupulous fealty to his king has been most meticulously illustrated in the account of his proceedings with David, being thereupon summoned with all the priests of Nob for interrogation ("Why have ye conspired against me?" [v. 13]), and Saul's footmen refusing his order to "Turn, and slay the priests of the Lord" (v. 17), Doeg obliges, massacring "on that day fourscore and five persons that did wear a linen ephod" (v. 18) and slaughtering, more comprehensively than Saul did the Amalekites, every living thing in the priestly city of Nob. Thus, by way of exterminating these innocent priests of God who had no part in abetting David at Nob, Saul wreaks his revenge upon Samuel, the prophet of God, and upon God himself, for protecting David from him at Naioth in Ramah.

That Saul, immediately after this—when, with civil war already afoot, he besieges David and his men at Keilah—can actually delude himself that God is on his side ("God hath delivered him into mine hand" [1 Sam. 23:7]) only further attests to the accelerated disintegration of his darkened mind. God is in fact directly supervising David's activities in Keilah, and in the wilderness of Ziph, where Jonathan comes to him "and strengthened his hand in God" (v. 16), assuring him of the impotence of Saul's malice: "the hand of Saul my father shall not find thee; and thou shalt be king over Israel, and I shall be next unto thee; and that also Saul my father knoweth" (v.

17). With this, his historical function in aiding David's succession concluded, the great-hearted Jonathan, shortly to die fighting by Saul's side against the Philistines, makes his last exit from the narrative.

With the imminence of David's succession (apparent now even in his increasing appropriation of the narrative space) and his impending transformation of the former tribal confederacy into a nation-state, what remains of the story of Saul's life is infused with the pathos of the old order he represented, its obsolescence prefigured in the crumbling of his psychic defenses. Failure upon howling failure of all his ploys to defeat Samuel's prophecy has brought him to the brink of collapse without his knowing it. Though he mobilizes an army of three thousand men to pursue David in the wilderness of Engedi, no sooner does David show him proof that, far from seeking the life of "the Lord's anointed" (1 Sam. 24:10), he has actually saved it, than Saul breaks down completely: "Saul said, Is this thy voice, my son David? And Saul lifted up his voice and wept" (v. 16). The obverse side of his malignity toward David, long obscured by his fear and deadly jealousy, reappears as his defenses collapse; and with their collapse he is at last freed to voice unreservedly the truth he has so long, at such terrible cost, striven to deny: "I know well that thou shalt surely be king, and that the kingdom of Israel shall be established in thine hand" (v. 20). The king himself has said it. Precisely at this point in the narrative Samuel dies, his overseeing function discharged, as Saul, implicitly affirming his prophecy, voluntarily yields the succession to David.

Yet despite Saul's capitulation at the end, there is no redemption for him. His last days, the unhappy dénouement of the ill years that preceded them, are terror-stricken, as if fear (the rage it fueled burned out now) is all that is left him. The warrior-king whom God had appointed specifically "that he may save my people out of the hand of the Philistines" (1 Sam. 9:16), who has intrepidly waged war after war against them, is now so unstrung at the sight of the Philistine host that "his heart greatly trembled" (1 Sam. 28:5). His stealthy recourse to the sorceress at Endor, though he himself had outlawed necromancy, is the envoi to the history of his indurate enmity with God, which Samuel's implacable ghost rearticulates; "tomorrow shalt thou and thy sons be with me" (v. 19). Falling flat on his face at this disclosure, "straightway all along the earth" (v. 20), Saul experiences now all the terror of his God-forsaken condition. Yet he goes into battle the following day and dies in the role he was appointed for, fighting in Israel's defense. Far outmatched as Saul's military virtue comes to be in the course of his reign by the enormity of his personal vice, the narrator (more humane than Samuel) brings us back to its full-circle in the epilogue. The people of Jabesh-Gilead hearing what the exultant Philistines had done to Saul, "all the valiant men arose, and went all night" (1 Sam. 31:12) to retrieve his mutilated body and the bodies of his sons, because it was in the defense of Jabesh-Gilead that Saul mobilized the concerted manpower of Israel and Judah to fight the first battle of his reign, and gloriously won it.

The Judgment of Women

ANNE C. DAILEY

TWO PROSTITUTES COME BEFORE KING SOLOMON, EACH claiming to be the mother of an infant boy. When Solomon calls for a sword and threatens to divide the child in two, the first woman gives up her claim to the child so that he may live, while the other woman refuses to do so, demanding that he be divided. Upon hearing their responses, Solomon lays down his sword and proclaims the first woman to be the true mother of the child.

The familiar story of Solomon and the two mothers gives us the Bible's most direct and powerful commentary on the meaning of human justice. The short tale introduces us to a wise sovereign, an inspired method, and a right decision. Or does it? As our focus shifts from the king to his subjects, as we attempt to understand the plight of the two unhappy prostitutes, as our interpretive grasp reaches down beneath the biblical metaphor, a terrible uncertainty emerges. The contrasting images of motherly love and female vindictiveness, of the first woman's sacrifice and the other woman's jealous deceit, play upon stereotypes we sense we cannot trust. Who in fact are

I would like to thank Steven Ecker and Laurie Parsons for their valuable comments and suggestions.

Biblical quotations are taken from the Jerusalem Bible.

142

these nameless women? And how are we to interpret their cries—
"Let the child live!" "Cut him up!"—without knowledge of the context of their lives? Did King Solomon make the right decision, or did
he instead inflict a great injustice on the women and child standing
before him?

OF DIVINE WISDOM
AND HUMAN UNDERSTANDING

Then two prostitutes came to the king and stood before
him. "If it please you, my lord," one of the women said,
"this woman and I live in the same house, and while she
was in the house I gave birth to a child. Now it happened
on the third day after my delivery that this woman also
gave birth to a child. We were alone together; there was
no one else in the house with us; just the two of us in the
house. Now one night this woman's son died; she overlaid
him. And in the middle of the night she got up and took
my son from beside me while your servant was asleep; she
put him to her breast and put her own dead son to mine.
When I got up to suckle my child, there he was, dead. But
in the morning I looked at him carefully, and he was not
the child I had borne at all." Then the other woman
spoke. "That is not true! My son is the live one, yours is
the dead one"; and the first retorted, "That is not true!
Your son is the dead one, mine is the live one." And so
they wrangled before the king. "This one says," the king
observed, " 'My son is the one who is alive; your son is
dead,' while the other says, 'That is not true! Your son
is the dead one, mine is the live one.' Bring me a sword,"
said the king; and a sword was brought into the king's
presence.

"Cut the living child in two," the king said, "and give
half to one, half to the other." At this the woman who
was the mother of the living child addressed the king, for
she burned with pity for her son. "If it please you, my
lord," she said, "let them give her the child; only do not
let them think of killing it!" But the other said, "He shall
belong to neither of us. Cut him up." Then the king gave
his decision. "Give the child to the first woman," he said,

"and do not kill him. She is his mother." All Israel came
to hear of the judgment the king had pronounced, and
held the king in awe, recognising that he possessed Divine
Wisdom for dispensing justice. (1 Kings 3:16–18)

The story of the two prostitutes is intended to illustrate the dazzling
acuity of Solomon's newly acquired wisdom. In the passage immediately preceding the story, God comes to Solomon in a dream and
asks him what he would like, to which Solomon responds, "A heart
to understand how to discern between good and evil" (v. 5). Pleased
by Solomon's already evident wisdom, God grants his request by giving him "a heart wise and shrewd as none before you has had and
none will have after you" (v. 12). Solomon's God-given power of
judgment—his wise and shrewd heart—then immediately displays
itself for us in the drama of the two mothers.

The story portrays Solomon as more than simply a merciful sovereign willing to give of his time to two common prostitutes; it dramatizes Solomon's profound capacity for comprehending human
nature, his ability to penetrate the exterior appearances of the two
women to judge them on the basis of their true selves. The accidental death of the first infant boy has thrown the motherhood of the
two women into question, and they come to Solomon seeking judicial resolution of their dispute. Once before the king, they unexpectedly encounter the violence of the sovereign's own sword as it is
raised above the body of the second child. For one frantic moment
it appears that motherhood and justice are to be sacrificed to King
Solomon's arbitrary, and deadly, whim. As the sword is lowered, all
Israel stands in awe of Solomon's wisdom in using a seemingly brutal
threat of death to discern the compassionate love of true motherhood.

Solomon's decision to adjudicate the claims of the two women by
raising a sword over the child is certainly a bold legal technique,
even for a powerful king. Yet given the paucity of evidence in the
case, how else is Solomon to determine the true mother? He has no
modern blood tests to help him, no witnesses, no fathers; he has only
his own understanding of human nature to assist him. Solomon trusts
that the threat to the child's life will incite the women to speak.
More surely than the sword he wields, Solomon's wisdom falls upon
the women with incisive accuracy, opening up their true selves to his
judicious gaze.

Solomon decides the substance of the dispute by declaring the first woman to be the true mother of the child. She is the paradigmatic good mother: self-sacrificing, willing to take upon herself a grievous loss for the good of her innocent child. Her virtue springs from a place beyond her deliberate control; as the story tells us, her body "burned with pity for her son."[1] The woman shows a degree of empathy and compassion for the infant boy that overwhelms her desire to keep the child for herself, a desire that had first brought her before the king. And the story dictates that because Solomon intuitively understands how a true mother behaves, he succeeds in recognizing her.

King Solomon's wisdom may also be understood to extend beyond an instinctive recognition of biological motherhood; his final judgment may rest upon a normative conception of what a good mother should be.[2] The "true" mother of the child is the woman who, biological tie or not, conforms to the social ideal of motherhood. The law of Solomon thus understood reflects an aspirational justice, a judicial articulation of the norms that guide social behavior. When Solomon declares, "She is his mother," his words may not confirm a preexisting truth but help to constitute an unfolding one. From such a normative perspective Solomon's divine wisdom encompasses the vast potential for human virtue.

Solomon's judicial temperament appears to display a profound understanding not only of the rights of the two women but also of the needs of the child. His decision eventually places the child with the woman who it seems will best care for him. It is perhaps the ultimate measure of King Solomon's insight into human nature that, with the simple raising of a sword, he exercises his sovereign power for the good of an innocent child.

King Solomon eventually adjudicates the conflicting claims of the two women with clarity and conviction. Yet things are not always so straightforward in the world of Solomonic justice; all is not necessarily what it appears to be. A seemingly loving mother reveals her jealous deceit, and an apparently brutish tyrant ultimately rules with an understanding heart. The simple thematic oppositions between deceit and truth, violence and law, selfishness and altruism, propel the narrative story line and shape the moral of this biblical tale. The story teaches us that divine wisdom entails the capacity to see beyond human appearances, to recognize and reward the true inner virtue of compassionate love. Yet perhaps we, together with the people of Israel, overlook the deeper implications of Solomon's decision to raise the sword over the infant child. Perhaps Solomonic justice itself is not the fair and insightful ideal of law that it purports to be.

THE VIOLENCE OF S/WORDS

Although Solomon's divine wisdom leads to the celebrated reunion of mother and son, his form of human understanding lies far removed from the gentle compassion of mother-love. Solomon's call for the sword is a violent, even shocking, act, a profoundly tyrannical gesture at the opposite extreme from the principle of fair procedure inherent in the rule of law.[3] It is in fact against this image of the tyrannical sovereign that Solomon's divine wisdom emerges with such force. Not only has the king judged with understanding, not only has he realized the ideal of legal certainty from the midst of human disorder, but he has also reaffirmed the supremacy of law over the arbitrary power of the sovereign's own sword. Although he could just as easily have divided the child in two, Solomon ultimately resolves the dispute between the two women with the force of his law.

Yet despite the ultimate safety of the child, Solomon's use of the sword remains ambiguous: The story never reveals whether Solomon would have followed through on his threat to kill the child if the first woman had not given up her claim. We may be inclined to believe that the sword was merely a procedural device, a kind of legal trick for inciting the women to speak the truth. Indeed it seems we must believe so if we are to accept Solomon's Divine Wisdom as a form of human understanding, for a truly inspired judge would surely not kill an innocent child. Yet even if we as readers suspect that Solomon would not have harmed the child, the women had to believe that he would. The story as traditionally understood depends upon their trust in Solomon's stated intention to divide the infant boy.

The traditional reading of the story focuses on the second woman's apparent inclination to permit the child to be killed. Her willingness to harm the child, yielding to a higher authority, recalls the earlier biblical story of Abraham's near-sacrifice of his son Isaac.[4] Complying with God's request, Abraham brings his son to a mountaintop, binds him upon an altar of wood, and raises the knife to kill the boy (Gen. 22:1–9). Before the knife falls, God intervenes and promises to shower blessings on Abraham and his many descendants. In vivid contrast to this reward for Abraham's show of faith, the woman in the Solomon story is condemned for her eager complicity. Her willingness to sacrifice the child signifies not spiritual faith but moral failure.

The traditional focus on the second woman's violent disposition ignores the obvious point that it is Solomon who orders the sword to be raised over the child and who threatens to divide the child in two. How is it, then, that the violence of the story is attributed to the other woman? Presumably it is her words, "Cut him up," that shift the moral responsibility for the child's death from Solomon onto her. Solomon's raised sword is understood as the mere catalyst for eliciting the other woman's violent instinct; it is her words, and not his hand, which threaten to bring the sword down upon the child.

Although Solomon's sword is understood to be the other woman's moral responsibility, shouldn't we question Solomon's responsibility for raising the sword in the first place? Had he not called for the sword, the other woman might never have expressed her seemingly violent impulse. Why, then, is Solomon judged wise rather than murderous by the people of Israel? The violence of Solomon constitutes a legitimate exercise of power as compared with the unnatural, unacceptable violence of the other woman. As king he exercises institutional violence, the power of the sovereign/state/judge to enforce his will on his subjects/citizens/litigants. It is in the nature of judicial power that the judge may command those who come before him to submit to his will. The raised sword now stands as a literal representation of the violence always implicit in the act of judging; behind King Solomon's will lay a royal army ready to enforce his wise decision.[5] At the heart of this story of divine justice and natural law lies a decidedly positivist lesson: Law—even divinely inspired—exists only at the point of the human sword.

We have faith in King Solomon's sword, violent as it is, because we believe it ultimately serves to reveal something important about the women's true natures. The sword shows us that the first woman would choose the child's life over her own needs, while the second would choose to see the child killed. But does the second woman really *choose* to have the child killed? Maybe she would have picked up the sword and slain the child with her own hands, but we certainly do not know that. All we know is that she says, "Cut him up." Her response may have represented many things besides a heartless desire to see the child killed: futility, hopelessness, anger, or perhaps a disbelief that Solomon would follow through on his murderous threat.

We might even find in the second woman's brief response a courageous act of self-determination. The prostitute directly confronts Solomon's arbitrary use of violence by refusing to back down at the sight of the sword. Instead she stands up to the king. "Cut him up," she tells him. Her words dare him to take responsibility for his own threat; a defiance of the raised sword, they have no power, or intention, to cut. Her speech forces Solomon to recognize that he must choose *for himself* whether the child will live or die. By her unwillingness to submit to his threat of violence, the second woman refuses the moral responsibility for the child's death—and places the burden on Solomon.[6]

The institutional violence that the two women confront in the sword of Solomon mirrors the violence that women face in their everyday lives. Women are expected to back down, negotiate, settle, and accept the arbitrary assaults of men at home, on the street, and in the workplace. They are expected to respond with the self-sacrifice of the first prostitute. And when they do not, when they defiantly transgress the laws of men, women must endure, Eve-like, the punishment meted out to them. Like the pain of childbirth, women are made to suffer the consequences of being judged a jealous liar. That the two women in the Solomon tale are prostitutes renders this reading of the story all the more poignant: they are women for whom submission is a way of life. The fact of their profession makes it all the more dramatic that the second woman finally chooses to stand up to perhaps the most powerful man in her life and all of Israel.

Blind faith in the correctness of Solomon's judgment can be maintained only because we hear so little from the women. When the sword is raised and the command given to divide the child, the women know that they have but moments to plead their case. Their speech is uttered in a fearful rush, a female cry in the face of seemingly arbitrary male violence. Had Solomon recognized that the women's initial responses were incomplete, had he desired to *know* these women rather than judge them immediately according to a preconceived ideal, then, had he been truly wise, he would have listened with a patient ear to all they had to say.[7]

Solomon's raised sword is not only a weapon for the silencing of women. In the hands of the listener-judge it also precludes a truly empathetic response, identifying the listener as someone who will hear without compassion or understanding. Solomon succeeds in resolving the dispute over the child in a swift and expedient manner, but he fails to comprehend the cost in human terms of doing so. By judging the women on the basis of a few frantic words, he erases the fullness and complexity of their lives. Relying on the sword, he opts for silenced rather than open speech, for legal certainty over female experience.

The people of Israel respond to the judgment of King Solomon with awe. Yet it is the judgment of the two women, their different responses to the raised sword, that commands my attention and respect. One chooses to give up her claim for the good of the child, her judgment grounded in her empathy for the innocent boy. The other woman chooses to challenge King Solomon's show of violence, her judgment grounded in self-respect and courage. Solomon raises his sword and reduces the complex narrative of their lives to a simple story of good and evil. Had Solomon instead listened with greater care to the words of the two women, he might truly have judged with wise understanding. He might even have decided that the child should belong to both.

In and Out of the Fold:
Wisdom, Danger, and Glamour
in the Tale of the Queen of Sheba

(1 KINGS 10:1–13; 2 CHRONICLES 9:1–12)

MARINA WARNER

ALONGSIDE THE POLYPS IN ALCOHOL JARS AND THE GIANT, stuffed armadillos, beside the star maps and wampum belts in the cabinets of curiosities where connoisseurs collected the wonders of the world, there would sometimes also be displayed small-scale models of ancient and sacred buildings, among them the Church of the Holy Sepulchre.[1] It was the holiest place in Christendom, the place of the Lord's death and resurrection, the heart of the Holy City, Jerusalem.

Made of smooth nutmeg-colored wood, inlaid with mother-of-pearl in the Damascene style, these replicas of the Holy Sepulchre can be taken apart; they are made like expensive doll's houses, with movable parts—the domes come off and the walls slide out to reveal the apses, the narthex, the ambulatory, the choir, the nave, the antechapel where Mary of Egypt, she of the long hair to her feet, suddenly realized she could not enter such a sacred place with her polluted body but must repent of her life of voluptuous pleasure. The assembly of architectural elements in these pilgrims' models anticipates with odd, ironic accuracy the divisions of the building today, no longer simply architectural but political, ecclesiastical—and vicious. On any day of the week, and more violently on Sundays, the

Biblical quotations are taken from the King James Revised Authorized Version.

rival churches within present-day Christianity will hold their services at the same time in their allotted portions of the building: the Copts give full cry to their liturgy at the side chapel that backs on to the Syriacs, who will chant theirs ever louder; the Greek Orthodox have walled up the choir altogether so that their ceremonies can be held out of sight of other, heretical sects; the Catholics, the Protestants, share out the rest between them and vie to outdo one another in show and noise. Each of those exquisitely crafted chambers in the cabinet of curiosities' model church has today been segregated for exclusive sectarian use.

Of all the Christian churches represented, the Ethiopians have drawn the short straw; they have been relegated to the roof of the Holy Sepulchre, the most distant spot from the sacred site of the Savior's tomb. And yet they have more space under the sky above Jerusalem than the Syriacs or the Copts, who huddle so much more closely to the center, in the dark and captive passages around the high altar. The Ethiopians spread out through a series of different chambers between the shallow, whitewashed domes of the Holy Sepulchre's flat roof, rising in shallow swellings until the area looks like an upside-down baking tray for a giant's baps or scones. For the church they have established on the roof doubles as their home in exile in Israel, their embassy, their social club, their living quarters. There's a monastery up there, a series of whitewashed cells with azure-painted wooden doors; carpets and animal skins are laid out under square, fringed awnings of saffron and vermilion and slung from tasseled pole to pole for gatherings and audiences. The priests and their followers flow with dark, indigo-dyed robes, or sun-whitened, equally voluminous white drapery.

No spectacle in Jerusalem rivals for theatrical authority the sight of these Ethiopian prelates on the roof. And Jerusalem is a city where men—and some women, but mainly priestly hierarchies, mainly men—have perfected competitive pageantry, from the Knights of Saint John swirling through the streets of the Old City with their blood-red crosses emblazoned on white satin cloaks to the black-garbed Orthodox patriarchs with the grizzled shovel beards of Assyrian lion slayers.

In the chapel where the Ethiopians worship, a painting tells the story of the founding parents of this branch of the Christian faith. Not Adam and Eve, but Solomon and Sheba. It depicts the king and queen's encounter in Jerusalem, not far from the Holy Sepulchre; the painting fills one of the side walls in the small shrine, and it unfolds the tale in episodic, strip-cartoon style, the figures boldly outlined and crowded to the edges of each squared section, with hugely magnified black eyes and, again, the saffron, ochers, vermilions of the Arabian landscape.

Solomon and Sheba: emblematic figures of male and female wisdom, they also embody Judeo-Christian ideals of masculinity and femininity, and in the story of their changing, reciprocating relations, it is possible to find broader codes of orthodoxy, religious and sexual. The Ethiopians have claimed Solomon and Sheba as their direct genealogical forebears; and in some ways, which I hope to unfold, Solomon and Sheba are an exemplary couple for all the people of the Book, an ancestral pair in a shared symbolic past. Even as a common mother, another Eve, Sheba does not, however, quite belong to the main trunk of the family tree; just like the Ethiopians, who keep her memory more fervently than any other sect, she stands to the side of the mainstream tradition, never wholly belonging. She's not Solomon's exact correlative in female form, but she retains a flavor of the outsider. This tension, between Sheba's legendary character as a figure of female beauty and virtue and the anomalousness, foreignness, and alterity that simultaneously mark her, makes her, among the many women of the Bible, a richly layered subject of feminist study.

It is often startling how brief the appearances are of famous, towering characters in the Old Testament, how rich the afterlife of faces glimpsed only for an instant in the crowd of the Bible: household names like Cain, or Lot, or Noah. Some are more mythopoeic than others: the murderous, the incestuous, the miraculous survivors. Sheba doesn't commit a crime, nor is she the subject of a miracle. The scant verses of the first book of Kings, in which she makes her appearance, number only eleven all told; they are repeated almost verbatim in the second book of Chronicles.[2] In these passages the Bible emphasizes her wealth, describing the train of laden camels she brings in tribute to King Solomon: "And she gave the king an hundred and twenty talents of gold, and of spices very great store, and precious stones: there came no more such abundance of spices as these which the Queen of Sheba gave to King Solomon."

But besides this inventory of her gifts, it's her mind the writers invite us to admire. Her mind—for this, Sheba is a very unusual woman in the biblical Christian pantheon. The passage opens, "And when the Queen of Sheba heard of the fame of Solomon concerning the name of the Lord, she came to prove him with hard questions."

Biblical commentators' cross-references direct the reader to other passages where such "hard questions" are put, and in all cases they concern male heroes and prophets: Samson, who set the riddle of the lion's carcass that brought forth sweetness; Daniel, who interpreted all the dreams and visions put to him by Nebuchadnezzar.

The Book of Kings then goes on to say, "And when she was come to Solomon, she communed with him of all that was in her heart."

Reciprocating, Solomon shares all his knowledge with her: "And Solomon told her all her questions: there was not any thing hid from the king, which he told her not."

Solomon, the wisest man on earth, trusts Sheba with all he knows and understands. She becomes "breathless" when she hears him, and exclaims that reports of his wisdom have fallen short of the true dimensions of his brilliance. In consequence she acknowledges that the god he worships is the true God and calls down blessings on Him for installing Solomon on his throne. She can then return to her own country, saved.

But before she leaves him, there is a further exchange: King Solomon gave the queen "all her desire, whatsoever she asked." So she is represented expressing desire: her body moves, her flesh breathes in a way that Solomon's does not. Though they are matched in wisdom (and in wealth, almost), and now share belief in the same god, their styles of articulating their meanings differ. The Bible then continues that Solomon indeed gave her "all her desire, whatsoever she asked," and adds, "beside that which Solomon gave her of his royal bounty." So his gifts included something more than material goods.

The distinction drawn between his "bounty" and the fulfillment of other desires she may have expressed led hearers and readers of the Bible since the sixth century to imagine the passionate and fertile love of the king and queen. The Ethiopians, for instance, believe that when Solomon granted all her desires, they bore a child, Menelik, who became the fabled father of the Ethiopian race; medieval painters, who decorated *cassoni*, or trousseau chests, with the meeting of Solomon and Sheba conceived of it as a traditional bridal procession, in which the woman comes to her groom's bed bringing with her a rich dowry. Such interpretations seize on the equivalence in the story between Sheba's submission to Solomon's god and erotic surrender. When a woman capitulates, her head, her heart, and her body act as one. It is she who is "breathless"; Solomon retains his composure. The story adds to Solomon's glory and magnifies his deity; Sheba's wisdom and beauty enhance his stature; lesser tribute from a lesser personage would count for less. But her response is complicated, inevitably, by her woman's body and by the possibility that carnal knowledge played its part among all the other secrets they shared.

THE QUEEN OF SHEBA, in the West, remains unnamed in the Bible, and she's generally given the name of her country, by a kind of metonymy. In the eastern tradition, both Ethiopian Christian and Islamic, she's called Bilqis. But I shall continue to call her Sheba in this essay, for it is as "Sheba," with all its connotations and echoes, that she fascinates me and directs my thoughts. Sheba is the kind of name English children give to the coal-black kitten of a litter; it is in fact the brand name of a certain luxurious kind of catfood that features a slinky creature of the night on the container. The manufacturers are rubbing the magic lamp of the queen and her associations. As William Butler Yeats writes, catching the drift,

> *Sang Solomon to Sheba,*
> *And kissed her dusky face.*[3]

In biblical exegesis Sheba became a prototype of the Church, beloved of Christ, who is prefigured by Solomon; and both of them were identified with the lovers in the Song of Songs. The poet and praise singer himself was identified with Solomon in the first line of this sapiential book, and indeed in the Protestant English Authorized Version the book is called the Song of Solomon. The object of his blazons—the smitten Shulamite who responds with languishing verses about her own passion—merged with the figure of the Queen of Sheba in medieval commentaries, in the impassioned allegorical sermons of Saint Bernard for instance. In the Song of Songs, the beloved woman says, "I am black, but comely" (*nigra sum, sed formosa.*) (Song of Songs 1:5). As such she in turn foreshadowed the Virgin Mary, the culmination of all female prophetic figures, the symbol of Mother Church (*mater ecclesiae*), the embodiment of Divine Wisdom, (*"sedes sapientiae"*), the moon to her child's sun, and so forth. The verse from Solomon's song was adduced to justify all those Black Madonnas who work miracles in ancient shrines all over the Christian world, at Montserrat, Le Puy, Rocamadour, Guadalupe. The eclectic, omnivorous and yet ultimately orderly imagination of the Catholic theologians found in one female figure the proleptic silhouette of another and interlaced them into a kind of chorale, a paper chain of similar yet individual outlines.

That's a very telltale *but*, that *sed* in the Vulgate translation of the Song of Songs' line "I am black but comely." It functions to mark a contradiction, unlike the original Hebrew, in which *v* means *and* as well as *but*. The Vulgate's *sed* carries the Church's ambivalence about otherness, color-coded in the livery of the underworld, with its double power of dread and fascination.

The blackness of the Queen of Sheba was taken for granted, naturally, by the Ethiopian Christians and their artists. Solomon, in the story scrolls and paintings, is ocher-colored, by contrast. Solomon and Sheba figure today among the immediate ancestry of the Rastafarians, who have identified themselves with Ethiopia; but beyond the groups of devotees, in their different enclaves scattered across the world, the Queen of Sheba isn't always black. Sometimes there's a kind of feeling that European artists are skirting the issue.

Renaissance painters will sometimes hint at her origins, by introducing a maid from Africa into her train, as in Piero della Francesca's fresco cycle *The Legend of the True Cross*, in Arezzo, where such a figure plays a background role, literally placed in the middle distance to one side and behind the dominant group of gracious quattrocento white, patrician Tuscans—Sheba and her attendants. The maid, signifying in this reticent manner the foreignness of Sheba's origins, wears a beehive-shaped African cap of bound reeds or maybe even ivory—Piero likes millinery to indicate origin, and this hat is exactly the kind of exotic curio that connoisseurs would later collect to ornament their cabinets. A painting attributed to Hieronymus Bosch and his school also includes a single black maidservant in the queen's train; Tintoretto multiplied this single figure, including several Moors of both sexes in his processional tableau in Vienna, which shows elephants' tusks among the treasures Sheba unloads on the quayside to give to Solomon. Only rarely in European iconography will the queen herself be black: in a German tapestry of 1540, for instance, now in the Pringsheim Collection, Munich; and in a drawing by Rubens, in the Courtauld Collection, London. But consistently, by some sleight of hand, the Queen of Sheba's arrival from an elsewhere far away is always marked.

As a child I had absorbed the Queen of Sheba as the most exotic, luxurious, sensual, and exciting woman in the Bible; the name Sheba conveyed heat and perfume and riches, and given the cast of mind that an English child of my background develops, this configuration

of qualities was essentialized as blackness as surely as myrrh oozed
from the sap of faraway trees. Almost the first poem we learned by
heart in English lessons was John Masefield's "Cargoes," which condenses the attitudes of the seaborne Britannic Empire to its far-flung
possessions, both imaginary and political: "Cargoes" begins:

> *Quinquereme of Nineveh from distant Ophir,*
> *Rowing home to haven in sunny Palestine,*
> *With a cargo of ivory,*
> *Of apes and peacocks,*
> *Sandalwood, cedarwood, and sweet white wine.*

The associations were unmistakable: These woods were known only
from the Bible, and specifically from the Temple Solomon built, the
same Solomon who had lived and ruled in "sunny Palestine," and
the cargo resembled the tribute the Queen of Sheba brought to lay
at Solomon's feet to thank him for his great wisdom. For after enumerating the spices and the gold and the precious stones, the biblical
passage immediately digresses: "And the navy also of Hiram, that
brought gold from Ophir, brought in from Ophir great plenty of almug trees, and precious stones."

No matter the non sequitur between the queen's gifts and the navy
of Hiram's freight from Ophir—Masefield was drawing on biblical
evocations of sumptuousness, and I, at the age of fourteen or so, as
I learned "Cargoes" by heart, learned, too, the colonial northerners'
dream of the warm south, its mysterious substances and essences, captured by those seductive, perfumed words—*almug, sandalwood,* and
quinquereme. As I write the lines down, I remember that we did not
only learn the poem by heart but sang it, too, for an interschool
choir competition, and that the music slowed down to long-sustained
dreaminess on the spondees of the last line; and the nun who taught
us music, Sister Miriam, conducted us to a prolonged hush to give
the words their maxim languorousness. In this way I became an Ori-
entalist, in the sense of the term as explicated so memorably by
Edward Said. My appetite for sensual stimulus was directed toward
distant places and distant peoples, toward everything I was not allowed to be and led to believe I could not be, except in fantasy. Like
many children of my generation with a Catholic background, I was
awakened to the life of pleasure through the aesthetic sensorama of
the Mass, but it was firmly interdicted as a pursuit in the here and
now. Heaven, however, faraway and blissful, overlapped with Eden

and paradise—and where was paradise? To the east, to the south—in the Orient.

The geographical position of the land of Sheba was—and is—hazy. Saba, in southwest Arabia, became fabulously wealthy, but only much later than Solomon's time; Seba, in the Hebrew Bible, is identified more closely with Cush, or Ethiopia—one of the reasons for the Ethiopians' sense of lineage. Archaeologists are digging today in the Yemen in what are considered the remains of the queen's realm, which stretched, in the opinion of the editors of the Jerusalem Bible, to include Sabean settlements in the north of the Arabian Peninsula. Josephus, however, interprets the queen's origins as African, and this tradition overlaps with that of the Ethiopians, though it locates her territory farther south and west.

The imaginary geography of Sheba is much more precise than the historical record. In the figure of the Queen of Sheba the beckoning Orient is relocated and broadened to encompass Eastern exoticism far beyond the Arabian Peninsula; Sheba, or Saba, represents the Levant, the place of the rising sun, as Ultima Thule describes the far north, and Tarshish in the Bible enciphers the western limits of the earth. The transmission of the queen's story, in western Christian iconography and folklore, makes her territory march not only with the original cradle of civilization in Mesopotamia but with the garden of Eden. For the receivers of her story in the Middle Ages and Renaissance, this location merges her possessions with Islam's later extensive dominions. Whether Arabian or African or from the hinterlands of present-day Iran and Iraq, she's identified with the Moor's sphere of influence, and her biblical encounter with Solomon encrypts proleptically the promise of a Moor's conversion to the future Christian faith, the return to the fold of a heathen potentate. The Queen of Sheba is a Muslim before time, and she becomes a Christian before time, just as Solomon is a forerunner of Christ, one of the just who will be drawn from limbo at the Crucifixion.

Her condition as a heathen outside the fold, who receives enlightenment and abjures her native faith, is intertwined with her femaleness: she acts as the reciprocating Other who completes the male principle of wisdom, embodied by King Solomon; she symbolizes the carnal condition of woman in its fullest form—vitality, seductiveness, fertility, and . . . wisdom too. This added element, Sheba's reputation for wisdom that matches Solomon's, her status as his peer and natural partner, gives a different, mixed flavor to the heathenness, the heat, the meridian, the Moorishness of her persona. She's both an insider and an outsider, anticipating such ambiguously positioned characters as the *alemah*, the figure of the wise dancing girls in eighteenth-century Egypt, who recited poetry and were adept at all civilized pleasures.

THE CURRENTS OF SYMPATHY that were set flowing in me by Sheba's story were divided: As a white Catholic, instructed to believe in the firmness of Peter's rock and the marginal, outcast, hellbound condition of other Christians, I was meant to feel at one with Solomon, the precursor. Yet as a Catholic in England, where the Old Religion had only been granted freedom of worship and civil rights in the 1830s and still bore the scars of its suppression (no medieval cathedrals to worship in, for one thing), I was tugged toward Sheba, the excluded foreigner. And, as I say, I felt the spell of her glamour. She was both a phantasm of difference, in her gorgeous, quinquereme-style of being, and a mirror of my fantasy self, as something of an outsider, too, by virtue of my "foreign" faith (I was a Catholic through my mother, who is Italian), and my necessarily fleshly fallenness as a woman.

We all share the right to create our own savage, as Clifford Geertz has remarked, and oddly enough, the perception of Sheba as outside the fold does not belong exclusively to the Catholic tradition but is at the heart of the Islamic tradition about her as well. Within Muslim culture she also acts as a pivot on which orthodox self-definitions and self-affirmations turn. Indeed, in the passage of the Koran that concerns her, and in the commentaries and folktales that surround it, Sheba's strangeness becomes more deeply explicit. And her Koranic role helps to illuminate, in turn, the part the queen plays in evolving Christian perception of women's sexuality and—by extension—in the formation of ideas about body and spirit, "them" and "us," "you and me" in the mind of a woman like myself.

Just as Sheba in the Old Testament realizes the truth of King Solomon's God, so she does in the Koran.[4] Solomon is as vital a persona in the Muslims' holy book as he is in the Bible, but much more of a fairy-tale wizard. Attended by djinns and magic animals, he can perform wonders and enchantments greater than any other king, and when he hears, from his messenger the hoopoe, that a fabulously rich queen has come to the throne in the south, he becomes curious. She worships the sun, he's told, not Allah: thus she stands in relation to this Muslim Solomon as a pagan, just as she does to the Jewish proto-

Christian king in the Old Testament. In the Koran Solomon orders
the queen to come to him "submissively," and with his prodigious
powers of goety, he performs various tricks to bring her to him, including conjuring a stream across the floor of his courtyard that looks
like water but is really mirror. When the queen arrives, the Koran
continues,

> She was bidden to enter the palace; but when she saw it
> she thought it was a pool of water, and bared her legs. But
> Solomon said, "It is a palace paved with glass."
> "Lord," she said, "I have sinned against my own soul.
> Now let me submit with Solomon to Allah, Lord of the
> creation."[5]

This highly compressed encounter is indecipherable without addi-
tional information, without knowledge of the accompanying lore
that attributed a peculiarity to the Queen of Sheba, a deformity lo-
cated under her dress. Legends clearly predating the writing of the
Koran spread the rumor that she had ass's hooves, or otherwise monstrous nether parts; in more genial variations she simply suffers from
hairy legs. Some of the stories tell how the stream cures her
affliction—it miraculously turns to healing water. In other versions,
doubtless popular in the bazaar, where her problem is merely hairi-
ness, Solomon comes to her rescue, naturally, in this as in other matters, and with the assistance of his djinns invents a depilatory cream.

   In the Muslim sacred book the queen's exposure of her legs brings
about her recognition of the true god. When Solomon's magic makes
her show her physical malformation, she comes to the realization
that she is spiritually impaired as well. Her body articulates her soul:
the Islamic Sheba shares her biblical counterpart's integration of
flesh and spirit, because, as woman, her flesh carries the messages of
her interior state, for good or for ill.

   The storyteller Ibn Al-Athir (d. 1234 C.E.) elaborated romantically
on the traditional tale and gave the Queen of Sheba a fabulous et-
iology to explain her physical anomalies: out hunting one day, a warrior sees two snakes fighting, and as one is getting the worst of it, he
orders his attendants to kill the assailant. Whereupon the snake in
distress turns into a most personable and youthful prince, who gives
his rescuer a wish in return for saving his life. The warrior asks for
the hand of the former snake's daughter in marriage. His wish is
granted, but only on condition that she is never refused anything or

ever contradicted in any way. Bilqis, the future Queen of Sheba, is born the child of this union, the daughter of a snake-princess who could never be thwarted, and when she inherits her father's realm, she rules it in her own right.[6] Thus, in Ibn Al-Athir's tale, Sheba's descent is magical and her authority derived and exercised beyond the usual norms. The outer sign of her deviance appears on her body, which she keeps hidden until King Solomon exposes her. In Al-Athir's fairytale Solomon cures her snaky lower parts and she then marries him—accepting due process in social arrangements of rank as well as the true faith.

This medieval Muslim folklore explicitly links heterodoxy with femaleness in the myth of Sheba. In these curious and indeed entertaining stories the queen is doubly a stranger to the center commanded by Solomon: in body and soul, she has parts to keep hidden, to be ashamed of, and he acts as her savior, who establishes her conformity, her orthodoxy of shape, and hence thought, bringing her into the fold.

These Islamic stories conjure the difference of woman in demonic terms and then free her from the taint. Sheba is admitted to the true faith and the human race; that she stood in need of vindication on both counts finds echoes in the Western legends, too, which spring up from the Bible account and join the Islamic stories, and begin to leave traces from the fourteenth century onward, as crusaders and pilgrims return from the Holy Land and bring with them new stories about her. In early fifteenth-century prints, which appear in German towns on the pilgrim routes such as Ulm, the Queen of Sheba displays her deformed foot—usually webbed. At Kutna Hora, the monastery outside Prague, a fresco, also fifteenth-century, shows the Queen of Sheba wading the stream in front of King Solomon: through the water, her broad, webbed goosefoot can be seen. Poems relate the story of her simultaneous cure and conversion. The deformity captured the popular imagination and merged with Christian imagery of witches' distinguishing marks: the pagan queen, outside the fold, becomes lame in one foot, like the character in the children's game called Old Witch. It is still played today, and the "It" has to pretend to limp, in imitation of the devil and his followers, as he or she tries to catch all the other players. The metonymy of legs or feet for the genitals occurs frequently in language, both waking and dreaming; it does not necessarily represent a fetishistic displacement but merely a symbolic translation, a kind of euphemism, making it possible to talk of certain unspeakable things, of the dangerousness of women's sexual parts, their need for purification through the words of a wise man representing God.

The biblical Queen of Sheba who is familiar to us, from Piero della Francesca's fresco cycle for instance, would seem to have none of these bizarre, less-than-human blemishes. The serene geometry of the sequence in the chapel of San Francesco in Arezzo belies the outlandish and vulgar (in the proper sense of "popular") character of the stories it relates. Yet the same observation could also be put differently: that Piero's graphic calm, his poise and lucidity, match the import of the tale he tells. He is setting to rights disorder and deformity, he is rounding off jaggedness and incoherence, and the Queen of Sheba is only one of several outsiders in the story cycle who becomes an insider, saved through the power of grace, working through the wood of the cross.

Besides the Book of Kings, Piero's source for the frescoes of *The Legend of the True Cross* in the chapel at Arezzo was the *Golden Legend*, the thirteenth-century calendar of saints' lives by the Dominican Jacobus de Voragine, which embroiders fancifully the biblical account of the meeting of Solomon and Sheba. The entry for May 3, the feast of the Finding of the Holy Cross, tells the story, and it develops suggestively the themes of exclusion and inclusion implied by the Old Testament.

As the queen makes her approach toward Jerusalem, she comes to a footbridge across the stream of Kidron, flowing below the mount where Solomon built his Temple; this footbridge is made of the wood destined to become the cross on which the Savior will be crucified, and the Queen of Sheba refuses to set foot on it but instead kneels in worship on the bank. The *Legend* then includes many apocalyptic prophecies that the queen makes to King Solomon; she foretells, for instance, that the cross will bring about the end of the kingdom of the Jews.

On the end wall of the chapel Piero depicts the next phase in the tale, with Constantine, the first Christian emperor, in bed dreaming of the cross that will bring victory. After the fulfillment of his dream Constantine converts the whole Roman Empire, and then dispatches his mother, Helena, to find the relics of the true cross in Jerusalem. Queen Helena has Golgotha excavated—the theme of one of the strata on Piero's left-hand wall—and she identifies Christ's cross by holding it over the body of a sick youth, who is cured by its powers.

The popular narrative of the true cross thus condenses and reorganizes time, in the same way as Piero's pictorial storytelling telescopes space; but it also selects homologies across the centuries in order to provide a rhyming structure to the disparate episodes, and this returns us to the Queen of Sheba's pivotal role in establishing orthodoxy by the very fact of her difference: in the story one unbeliever after another is transformed by contact with the true cross, and each of them represents another quarter of the globe, another dominion for the universal catholic church—first Sheba from the South, then Constantine from the West capitulate to the faith. To complete the global conquest, Piero depicts, in the final frescoes, the defeat of the heathen East—of the future Islam, in the victory of the Byzantine emperor Heraclius in the seventh century over the Persian king Chosroes. Vanquished, Chosroes and his entire army with him submit to Heraclius's will and are baptized into the Christian fold. Banners fly above the heads of the warriors and horses engage in the panoramic battle, and on one prominent enemy flag appears the head of a Moor—the same trophy that the Crusaders displayed on their arms after they had fought with another stripe of unbeliever, the Saracens, for repossession of the holy places, including Jerusalem. Thus, as Sheba is to the South, Constantine to the West, Chosroes stands to the East and to the dominion of the Moors, which looks forward to Islam; each is represented as in turn succumbing through time to the truth of the faith and the embrace of the Church, the outstretched, welcoming arms of the cross.

The formal plan of Piero's narrative thus unfolds Divine Providence's all-encompassing love, universal forgiveness, salvation—or, in other terms, its will to power, its catholic reach, its imperium.

The Queen of Sheba plays her part in this when she acquiesces to Solomon's superiority, as in the Bible and the Koran, and by so doing is interpreted, in the medieval tradition, as a future Christian granted a vision of the cross's destiny. Though the struggle between the believers and the unbelievers isn't couched directly in terms of sexual conflict, either by Piero or his source, the *Golden Legend*, so much of the surrounding hagiography prescribes different conduct for men and women and insists so inventively on the dangers of sexuality, that the story of the encounter between Solomon and Sheba, even in Piero's measured and harmonious rendering, crystallizes, in a *coincidentia oppositorum*, the attraction and repulsion of the sexes, the struggle for equality, which so often resolves itself into a struggle for mastery.

* * *

I HAVE FOUND THE Queen of Sheba's encounter with Solomon a continuing inspiration. In a short story I dramatized the Koranic episode in the present day, as a young woman's fascination with a powerful man and dread of his sexual aggression (a dread that turns out to be justified, when he tricks her into showing her legs);[7] I've also attempted to undo the Otherness of her figure in a comic opera for children (*The Queen of Sheba's Legs*), in which I spliced her story with "The Emperor's New Clothes," so that at the end, when the queen does cross the stream and lift her skirts, Solomon and his court discover, to their surprise, not something monstrous, terrifying, in need of cure, but:

> "*Your legs are the ordinary human kind.*"
> *And Solomon admits:*
> "*. . . we feared the worst*
> *The sleep of reason begets monsters at first.*"[8]

It's been my lifelong experience to be drawn to an image, a persona, an ideal, and to suffer when it/she/he turns out not to be an illusion exactly but to be so complex, so fine-meshed and intricately structured that a response of simple worship or love or yearning no longer expresses my needs. It's true of Sheba too: she holds out such promise when she appears with her fabulous wealth and reputation and wisdom in the Old Testament, a match for Solomon in all his glory. But on examination she turns out to be a vital part of the Christian will-to-rule—even if by understanding and forgiveness—so that my childhood fascination with her exoticism developed logically from the implicit power relations in her story: She is there to be dominated, taken over, and the more spirit she shows, the better for her victor, for the one who gathers her testimony. What a crux this is! Sheba stands for all the richness and contradictoriness of the outsider/insider, and in this she reproduces, or I feel her reproducing, my desired but oh-so-uncomfortable relationship to the center—that male-gendered mainstream of orthodoxy and authority—my wanting to belong and yet not belong at one and the same time, to be included but free to mark my exclusion if I wish.

Postscript

When the children's opera *The Queen of Sheba's Legs* was in production with the English National Opera, I received a call asking me to come to a meeting with a representative from the Race Relations Board. There had been a complaint. I became scared and confused—the Rushdie affair was into its second year, and I had been afraid from the start of the project that my use of the Koranic story for an opera buffa might offend Muslims among the families of the children taking part. But it turned out, when we reached the Royal Retiring Room at the London Coliseum opera house, where the meeting was being held, that there had been no complaints about the libretto. The designer, English-born, with a Caribbean mother, of Northern Indian blood, had resigned on the grounds of racial prejudice within the organization—he was the only black on the (tiny) team of composer, producer, director, music director, and writer (myself), and he felt the whole atmosphere of the project was structured along prejudiced lines. Julian Grant, the composer, pointed out that he was the only gay Slav on the team, a lighthearted intervention that fell completely flat in the tense atmosphere.

We all beat our breasts to uncover the faults of racism we had committed. The English National Opera's education program sees itself in the vanguard of liberal "multiculturalism"; my proposed opera had won approval partly because Solomon and Sheba belong to the tradition of three of the major religions and thus might avoid the sin of Christian ethnocentrism. The surnames of the cast, two hundred children from six inner-city primary schools, read like the United Nations.

Eventually, after the meeting ended, the feeling of discomfort and—in some cases—anger, had grown far more acute than they had been before and continued to rankle long after the production was over, in a series of recriminatory letters between various parties. The designer did not withdraw his resignation, and another was appointed, on very short notice. The designer told a friend in the company, privately, afterward, that he could not work with a South African—the director, a woman who was born in South Africa though she has lived and worked in London for some time. He did not say this at the meeting, perhaps because he could not do so to her face, perhaps because the arbitrator of the Race Relations Board might have pointed out it was a racist position to take.

This unpleasant trouble isn't entirely beside the point of this essay. In a sense the English National Opera, a broad church indeed, represented something all the participants were being invited to become a part of, to acknowledge its wisdom. The designer stresses his own Otherness by exotic dress (long robes, a modernist variation on Indian clothes), hair halfway down his back, swept back smoothly and loosely tied at the nape of the neck, and a total commitment to black-identified productions and arts media (such as carnival costumes for instance). He presents himself as different, as foreign, as exotic. On the telephone, however, it would not be possible to hear him as such: everything about his speech is mainstream, native British. Indeed he is aware of this and alluded to it in the course of the Race Relations meeting, pointing out that his mother had wanted him to have a good education and learn to speak English like an Englishman, otherwise she knew he could not succeed. He was included, in some ways he wanted to be included, but in the last analysis he found a reason to stay outside, to refuse. His exoticism, if he had accepted to be accepted, somehow would no longer count, it would be subsumed into the embrace of the authority who was welcoming him; it could only have a point if he entrenched it, by his apostasy toward the very liberalism that extends tolerance to his difference in the first place. But, by a further irony, this very refusal pleased the management in some deep and subtle way, though it created such practical difficulties with the immediate production. It proved his authenticity, his priorities, his irreducibility, his integrity: multicultural liberalism needs otherness to prove its own vaunted elasticity, universality, truthfulness. He was immediately reengaged, in another venture.

So who can tell who ultimately predominates in this need for the defining Other: the one who occupies its site voluntarily or the one who seeks it out and helps define it by the urgency and force of desire?

Though I consider the young designer's stand unreasonable and even opportunistic, he helped me see the labyrinth in which the Queen of Sheba twists and turns as she seeks to find her way. And it is the same maze we all find ourselves in when we seek to tolerate and be tolerated, when we try to slip the leash of inherited values and prejudices and resist absorption or incorporation, for we take one turn only to find that we have lost the way again.

The Odd Couple: Elijah and Jezebel

❧✦❧

PHYLLIS TRIBLE

This essay brings together two bitter enemies: Jezebel, the Baal-worshiping queen of Israel, famous for the slaughter of Yahweh's prophets and for her own brutal death, and Elijah, the stern spokesman for Yahwism, who becomes a towering figure in Judaism and Christianity.

ACROSS THE CENTURIES ELIJAH AND JEZEBEL HAUNT MY world. Though Sunday-school teachers, scholars, and theologians have kept this couple apart, I propose to bring them together. The medium for the proposal is a verbal diptych; the method, exegesis; and the message, convergence of opposites.

SELECTING THE SOURCES

To craft the diptych requires selecting material from the Bible and from scholarly research. The two books of Kings constitute the primary source. There within a narrative on the reign of King Ahab and

Most biblical quotations are taken from the New Revised Standard Version (NRSV); my own translations are marked with an asterisk (*).

his successors (869–842 B.C.E.) appear stories about Elijah and Jezebel. He enjoys the bigger portion. An editorial introduction in 1 Kings 16:29–34 sets the stage, naming Jezebel of Sidon as the wife of Ahab.[1] A cluster of stories focused on Elijah extends from 1 Kings 17 through 19. Chapter 21 brings Jezebel to the forefront (21:1–16) and then juxtaposes Elijah (vv. 17–29). Another cluster focused on Elijah extends from 2 Kings 1:1 through 2:12. It completes his appearances. The last story about Jezebel occurs in 2 Kings 9:30–37.

THE DEUTERONOMISTIC HISTORY

Two areas of scholarly research inform the background of this essay. The first concerns the theological framework that shapes the books of Deuteronomy through Kings. Scholars refer to this complex as the Deuteronomistic History.[2] It evolved in two major editions, one compiled in seventh-century B.C.E. Judah and the other in sixth-century B.C.E. exile, plus subsequent revisions. The central thesis of this History declares that obedience to Yahweh brings reward and disobedience brings punishment. Overall, the work advocates an ideology that accounts for the destruction of the northern kingdom, Israel, in 722 B.C.E. and the southern kingdom, Judah, in 586 B.C.E. Israel receives the harsher condemnation. Having broken away from the Davidic monarchy in Jerusalem (992 B.C.E.), it is accused of abandoning Yahweh. But Judah's transgressions against Yahweh also merit punishment. In the end the Deuteronomists offer little hope.

Set in ninth-century B.C.E. Israel, the Elijah-Jezebel stories supply abundant fodder for the theological appetites of Deuteronomistic historians. As a prophet upholding Yahwistic faith, Elijah suits their purpose. To portray him sympathetically, indeed gloriously, feeds their condemnation of the North. Just as importantly, but with reverse emphasis, Jezebel, the imported Phoenician princess, falls prey to their ideological scheme. As a worshiper of the god Baal, she represents the antithesis of Yahwistic faith centered in the Jerusalemite cult. To portray her unsympathetically, indeed ignominiously, also feeds their condemnation of the North.

CANAANITE-PHOENICIAN RELIGION

The second area of research concerns Canaanite-Phoenician religion. It permeates the Elijah-Jezebel stories. Twentieth-century discoveries at the ancient city Ugarit on the Syrian (Phoenician) coast provide firsthand accounts of the religion, uncontaminated by biblical bias.[3] They depict a patriarchal and polytheistic faith interested in cosmogony and fertility: the establishment of order and the maintenance of life. El the father god heads the pantheon, but Baal plays the central role as storm god and cosmogonic warrior. After defeating chaos, represented by the god Yamm, he becomes king. With lightning as his weapon and clouds as his attendants, he exercises great power over the earth. He appoints the seasons of rain so essential to Canaanite agriculture. Fertility marks his domain. Mot is Baal's enemy. Sterility marks his domain. When Mot swallows Baal, rain ceases and drought prevails. The reversal comes through violent actions of Baal's sister-consort Anat, who kills Mot and sows his remains in the earth. In time Baal revives. Crops grow; the land yields produce. Life wins over death. But every seven years the entire process repeats itself. Never-ending combat poses an ever-present threat.

In addition to Anat, the goddess Asherah appears in Canaanite texts. She is the consort of El and mother of the gods. Whether she has a place within ancient Israelite religion remains an unsettled issue. Debate hinges on the meanings of the word *asherah*. It specifies the personal name of the goddess; it also specifies a wooden pole or perhaps a tree. Though the pole symbolizes the goddess, in time it seems to have become a cult object independent of her. In other words, the pole "outlived the cult of the goddess who gave her name to it."[4] Only once, in 1 Kings 18:19, does the Bible clearly mention the goddess Asherah. Numerous other occurrences of the word *asherah*, including one in the Elijah stories, probably identify only the wooden pole.

The Deuteronomistic introduction to the reign of Ahab (1 Kings 16:29–33) condemns him because, among other sins, he erected an altar and temple to Baal and "made an asherah" (a reference to the cultic object). In the first cluster of stories Elijah challenges Baal's presence and power by announcing to Ahab neither rain nor dew in Israel except by the word of Yahweh (1 Kings 17:1). Thus he sets the stage for the later contest on Mount Carmel (1 Kings 18:20–46). Then he flees north into Phoenician territory. Upon his return he orders Ahab to gather at Mount Carmel "the four hundred and fifty prophets of Baal and the four hundred prophets of Asherah who eat at Jezebel's table" (v. 19). Though this reference specifies the goddess, she plays no role in the narrative.[5] The contest opposes Baal and Yahweh. The one who answers by fire is god in Israel. Only Yahweh answers. After the victory, rain comes. Yet the outcome settles nothing, for subsequent stories continue the conflict between the deities. It exacerbates the polarities between Elijah and Jezebel.

REVISIONIST SCHOLARSHIP

Whereas scholarly research supplies information for crafting a diptych of Elijah and Jezebel, with few exceptions it makes the task difficult. Like the Deuteronomistic History, it favors Elijah. A notable exception comes from the Canadian scholar Stanley B. Frost.[6] He observes that in the Bible and in the history of interpretation, Jezebel has been tried and condemned without mercy. Yet a fresh trial would show that she does not deserve the censure. Arriving in Israel through an arranged marriage, she is the result, not the cause, of Ahab's Canaanization policy. She forges an unusual relationship of equality with her husband. (By contrast his other wives receive no mention despite the fact that Ahab had seventy sons.) Strong character, marital devotion, and religious fervor characterize her role. These traits prevail as she opposes Elijah. By refusing to concede defeat, even in the contest on Mount Carmel, she weakens his victories for Yahweh.

Frost observes further that as a foreign woman of power Jezebel is hardly unique in Israel. But although foreign women such as Rehab, Jael, and Ruth receive approbation even while engaging in treason, murder, and seduction, Jezebel reaps condemnation. The difference? They support Yahwism; she does not. She remains faithful to another vision, profound in its own right as it beholds the mysteries of life and death. Jezebel tries to make Israel into the image of Sidon, rather than recognizing the distinctiveness of Israel's Yahwistic stance. For that political and religious failure Israel condemns her. Though in conclusion Frost sounds an unclear note, he yearns for a rapprochement between Israel and Jezebel. By retrying her as a woman wronged, he has questioned the weight of witnesses over millennia.

Recent analysis of the Naboth incident (1 Kings 21) strengthens the case for Jezebel. In its present form this story convicts her for the murder of the Jezreelite man, Naboth, who refused to give Ahab his vineyards. But the Israeli scholar Alexander Rofé has shown that the present account reworks an older story in which Ahab, not Jezebel, was solely responsible for Naboth's death.[7] Some four centuries later editors intent on protesting intermarriage shifted the blame to her.

They manipulated and maligned Jezebel to personify the evils of foreign wives. Studies of this type suggest that no woman (or man) in the saga of Israel has received a more distorted press than Jezebel.[8] Surely the tendentious nature of the judgment against her protests too much.

CRAFTING THE DIPTYCH

Informed by the Bible and scholarly research, each panel of the Elijah-Jezebel diptych presents four events: the introduction of the character, the role in the drought, the role in the incident of Naboth's vineyard, and the ending of the character. Through point and counterpoint these two pictures stand side by side, hinged to yield a larger picture.

INTRODUCTION

The Deuteronomistic introduction to the reign and character of Ahab provides the context for the introductions of Jezebel and Elijah. The device of inclusio, whereby the opening and closing of a literary unit correspond in vocabulary and emphasis, delineates the context. At the beginning and at the end stereotypical language stresses that Ahab did evil and provoked the Lord "more than all who were before him" (1 Kings 16:30 and 33). Within this devastating indictment comes a recital of his sins. Jezebel heads the list. Ahab "took as his wife Jezebel daughter of King Ethbaal of the Sidonians." The words *wife* and *daughter* surround the name Jezebel; husband and father define her. Their status as kings sets the boundaries for her as Israelite queen and Phoenician princess. The narrated discourse allows Jezebel neither speech nor independence. Instead it encloses her in both patriarchal structures and hostile Deuteronomistic ideology.

Like her father, the daughter has a Baal name. Ethbaal means "with him is Baal." Jezebel means, "Where is the Prince?" In the Ugaritic myth, when vegetation dries up, the cry goes out "Where is Baal the Conqueror? Where is the Prince, the Lord of the Earth?" The question anticipates the return of fertility, the release of Baal from the power of Mot. If the daughter's name asks the question, the father's supplies the answer. The myth declares, "for Baal the Conqueror lives, the Prince, the Lord of the Earth, has revived." The faith Jezebel espouses, her name announces. "Where is the Prince?"

The Deuteronomistic theologians who censure Jezebel in strong language support Elijah by the absence of discourse. When he appears, they step aside. Abruptly he takes center stage (1 Kings 17:1). No patriarchal lineage identifies him, only a geographic location in Transjordan: "Elijah the Tishbite of Tishbe in Gilead." Unlike Jezebel his identity depends not upon others but comes through his own speech. He declares to Ahab, "As the Lord the God of Israel lives, before whom I stand, there shall be neither dew nor rain these years, except by my word." Elijah challenges the power of Baal. Moreover, claiming Yahweh as his authority, he dares to elevate his own word to equal authority. The meaning of his name underscores the point. *Eli* ("my God") and *jah* (abridged form of Yahweh) match the oath "Yahweh, God of . . ." The faith Elijah espouses, his name announces. "Yahweh is my God."

Contrasting portraits highlight the couple. Jezebel is female and foreigner; Elijah, male and native. She comes from the coastlands, he from the highlands; she from a sea climate, he from a desert climate. She belongs to husband and father; he has neither uxorial nor paternal identity. Entrapped by hostile editors and male lords, she appears as object without voice or action. Free of narrated restraints, he appears as subject, announcing himself in word and deed. Yet they both hold privileged positions, royalty for Jezebel and prophecy for Elijah. Both have theophoric names that unite them in opposition: Jezebel the Baal worshiper; Elijah the Yahweh worshiper. Juxtaposed through the details of an economic text, the two stand poised to interact.

DROUGHT

The second section of the diptych relates their activities in time of drought. Interaction begins subtly when Elijah departs his land for hers. Hiding from Ahab, he dwells for a time in "Zarephath, which belongs to Sidon" (1 Kings 17:9). There in the kingdom of Jezebel's father, an unnamed widow gives him food, drink, and lodging. Though the storyteller attributes these gracious ministrations to the presence and power of Yahweh, the subtext suggests another meaning. Jezebel and Elijah exchange venues but encounter different receptions. While she lives unwelcomed in his land, he sojourns safely in hers.

If Jezebel subtly haunts Elijah in her homeland, she foreshadows him upon his return to Israel. Murder seals the bond. The storyteller reports that she has "killed the prophets of the Lord" (1 Kings 18:4*). Yet her efforts meet only partial success because a man named Obadiah has hidden a hundred prophets. Elijah, on the other hand, annihilates Baal's prophets with total success. After the victory for Yahweh on Mount Carmel he orders that all the prophets of Baal be seized, specifying that not one of them is to escape. Then he "brought them down to the Wadi Kishon and killed them there" (v. 40b). Elijah emulates Jezebel even as he surpasses her.

Their coalescence in violence continues when Ahab reports to Jezebel all that Elijah had done, "how he had killed all the prophets with the sword" (1 Kings 19:1). Immediately she sends Elijah a message. For the first time Scripture assigns her speech, albeit reported through a messenger. Its content has survived in two versions. The Septuagint, the ancient Greek text of the Hebrew Bible, quotes her as saying, "If you are Elijah, then I am Jezebel!" The marvelous juxtaposition of their names bespeaks the theological battle. Yahweh opposes Baal; Baal opposes Yahweh. The juxtaposition also encapsulates the human battle. Despite Elijah's victory on Mount Carmel, Jezebel repudiates the defeat. Unbowed, she takes him on. Though he initiated the contest "with the four hundred fifty prophets of Baal and the four hundred prophets of Asherah, who eat at Jezebel's table" (1 Kings 18:19), she now hurls the gauntlet directly before him. United in violence, the two remain mortal enemies. "If you are Elijah, then I am Jezebel!"

In the Hebrew text, however, Jezebel never utters this sentence. Instead her first words begin with the second sentence in the Greek version. She takes an oath: "So may the gods do to me, and more also" (1 Kings 19:2). The formula parallels the words that first introduced Elijah. He, too, began with an oath, "As the Lord the God of Israel lives" (1 Kings 17:1). These verbal debuts share a genre though not a deity. Elijah has used a Yahwistic oath to announce death in the land. Jezebel uses a Baalistic oath to announce his death because of the slaughter of her prophets. "So may the gods do to me, and more also, if I do not make your life like the life of one of them by this time tomorrow." As Elijah has emulated Jezebel in murder, so Jezebel promises to emulate Elijah in murder. No wonder he fears and runs away. His victory has become his defeat; a death threat hangs over him. Though Jezebel never enacts it, she remains the nemesis of Elijah. Enemies intertwine.

NABOTH'S VINEYARD

The story of Naboth's vineyard (1 Kings 21) occupies the third section of the diptych. Reflecting the misogynous and xenophobic biases of post-exilic editors, it provides narrative perspective rather than historical veracity. The story divides into two scenes: the securing of the vineyard for Ahab (vv. 1–16) and the aftermath (vv. 17–29).

Scene one begins with Ahab sulking because Naboth the Jezreelite refuses to relinquish his vineyard to the crown (vv. 1–4). It continues with Jezebel getting for her husband what he wants (vv. 5–16). In all the narratives only this scene accords her a major role. She prevails in both structure and content. An inclusio forms the limits of the unit. Her words to Ahab come at the beginning (vv. 5–7) and the end (vv. 15–16) of the scene. They enclose her successful efforts on his behalf (vv. 8–14).

The beginning of the scene (verses 5–7) mirrors in miniature the structure of the whole. Words of Jezebel to Ahab surround his response, with narrative introductions identifying her as "his wife." "*His wife* Jezebel came to him and said, 'Why are you so depressed that you will not eat?'" He tells her about Naboth's refusal. She then gives a three-fold reply, prefaced by "*His wife* Jezebel said to him." Her opening words allow various interpretations. "*You* now, you act as king over Israel" (v. 7*). In intent the sentence may be interrogative, asseverative, or hortatory. By the emphatic use of the second-person pronoun Jezebel may be twitting her husband for his impotence even as she reminds him of his power. Next she orders him to start eating and stop sulking. "Get up, eat some food, and be cheerful." At last, by the emphatic use of the first-person pronoun, she contrasts herself to him as she promises him the vineyard. "*I, I* will give to you the vineyard of Naboth the Jezreelite" (v. 7*). In the structure and content of this unit Jezebel, wife of Ahab, surrounds her husband with solicitude, encouragement, and assurance. The text reports no response from the sullen and defeated king, neither question nor objection. In silence Ahab acquiesces. Jezebel takes charge.

The center of the overarching inclusio reports her activity and its successful outcome (vv. 8–14). Through an elaborate ruse she has Naboth charged with blasphemy, convicted, and stoned to death. To accomplish the deed, she writes letters in the name of Ahab and uses his seal. These procedures probably follow the conventions of patriarchal and royal prerogatives. For certain they mislead no one. The men of the city know that the letters convey Jezebel's, not Ahab's, word (v. 11). Yet they cooperate fully. When the deed is done, they send her the message. Jezebel triumphs.

Unlike the beginning, the end of the overarching inclusio does not mirror the structure of the whole. This time, rather than enclosing Ahab, the words of Jezebel free him to move (vv. 15–16). Parallel narrated introductions set the context for her and for him. "As soon as Jezebel heard that Naboth had been stoned and was dead" finds its sequel in "as soon as Ahab heard that Naboth was dead." For Jezebel the introduction leads to speech. She said to Ahab, "Go, take possession of the vineyard." For Ahab the introduction leads to corresponding action. He "set out to go down to the vineyard of Naboth . . . to take possession of it." Again, Ahab acquiesces in silence. Jezebel remains in charge. Throughout the first scene of this story she prevails on behalf of him.

Scene two counters Jezebel's victory. Elijah dominates on behalf of Deuteronomistic venom (vv. 17–29). The scene opens and closes with the rubric "the word of the Lord came to Elijah." In the opening (vv. 17–19) he meets Ahab in the vineyard and convicts him, not Jezebel, for the murder of Naboth and subsequent possession of his property. Elijah predicts a vengeful death for the king. Dogs will lick up his blood in the place they licked up the blood of Naboth. The scene continues with Ahab's brief response and a lengthy excoriation by Elijah (vv. 20–24). It uses the stereotypical language of doing "what was evil in the sight of the Lord," announces the total annihilation of Ahab's house, and singles out Jezebel for a vengeful death that matches the prediction about Ahab. "Also concerning Jezebel the Lord said, 'The dogs shall eat Jezebel within the bounds of Jezreel' " (v. 23). Though cast as predictions, these oracles developed as prophecies after the event. Editors added further condemnation, claiming that no one surpasses the evil of Ahab, "urged on by his wife Jezebel" (vv. 25–26). In the closing of the scene the word of the Lord postpones the evil on Ahab's house to his sons (vv. 27–29). But the verdict against Jezebel holds firm.

In the two scenes of this story Jezebel and Elijah do not interact, not even through messengers. She never mentions him. Though he denounces her, he does not confront her. Remaining apart, they dominate their respective scenes as they exercise authority on behalf of others. Jezebel writes letters in the name of Ahab; Elijah speaks words in the name of the Lord. She takes initiative; he receives initiative. Never does she call upon her god Baal; he repeatedly calls upon his god Yahweh. Violence characterizes their stances. She acquires the vineyard through the murder of the one man Naboth. He announces for revenge the annihilation of Ahab's entire dynasty as well as the horrendous death of Jezebel. Thus are drawn the lines for battle unto death. From separate narrative encampments Jezebel and Elijah await their endings.

ENDINGS

The fourth section of the diptych presents the endings. In the biblical narrative Elijah goes first; Jezebel follows after many chapters. His departure comes near the close of the Ahab dynasty; her demise near the beginning of the Jehu dynasty. The order corresponds inversely to their introductions: Jezebel first in a Deuteronomistic summary; then Elijah in a series of stories. Structurally Jezebel envelops Elijah while narratively he triumphs over her.

These endings begin with prior scenes. Before his departure Elijah engages in a lengthy and spirited confrontation with the successor to Ahab, King Ahaziah. He has sent messengers to ask Baal-zebub, the god of Ekron, if he will recover from illness. Meanwhile Elijah sends Ahaziah a death notice through the same messengers. Not knowing Elijah's name, they describe him to the king by his sartorial makeup: "A man, owner of haircloth, and a belt of leather tied about his waist" (2 Kings 1:8*). Ahaziah identifies him immediately. "It is Elijah the Tishbite." Before her demise Jezebel engages in a brief but spirited confrontation with King Jehu, who overthrows the Ahab dynasty. He has come to Jezreel complaining of no peace in the land "so long as the many whoredoms and sorceries of . . . Jezebel continue" (2 Kings 9:22). (Apart from this reference the text gives no evidence for the accusation.) As she prepares to meet him, the storyteller describes her cosmetic makeup. "She painted her eyes, and adorned her head" (v. 30). Jehu has no trouble identifying her. United in their opposition to Israelite kings, Elijah and Jezebel offer striking contrasts in physical appearance: he in haircloth and a belt of leather; she with painted eyes and decorated head.

From elevated positions they behave in similar ways. Sitting on top of a hill, Elijah taunts Ahaziah (2 Kings 1:9–16). Looking down from the window, Jezebel taunts Jehu (2 Kings 9:30–37). Elijah descends the hill to repeat his question: "Is it because there is no God in Israel that you are going to inquire of Baal-zebub, the god of

Ekron?" Jezebel stays at the window to ask her question, "Is it peace, Zimri, murderer of your master?" She alludes to an earlier Israelite king Zimri, who murdered to secure the throne. If Elijah shows no fear in taunting Ahaziah, Jezebel shows no fear in taunting Jehu. But the outcome diverges radically. Elijah wins. Ahaziah dies "according to the word of the Lord that Elijah had spoken" (2 Kings 1:17). Jezebel loses. Jehu orders her murdered. But long before that happens, Elijah has disappeared.

The Bible never says that Elijah dies. Instead he is "taken up by whirlwind into heaven" (2 Kings 2:1*). The motif of translation permeates the narrative (vv. 1, 3, 5, 9, 11). In it new characters appear, namely "sons of prophets," who are members of prophetic guilds, and Elisha, the companion of Elijah. Repetition and travel impede the pace of the story to build suspense. As Elijah and Elisha journey, three times Elijah instructs Elisha to stay behind, but invariably he refuses (vv. 2, 4, 6). Together they go from Gilgal to Bethel to Jericho to the Jordan River. Sons of the prophets witness from a distance as Elijah takes his mantle, rolls it up, and strikes the water. It parts on either side. Elijah and Elisha go over to Transjordan on dry ground. Their movement brings not only physical but psychic and spiritual separation. From ordinary times, places, people, and events, Elijah and Elisha cross the threshold to the numinous.[9]

Only the final separation awaits. As they walk and talk, suddenly Elijah ascends (vv. 11–12). Fiery language defines the boundary. "A chariot of fire and horses of fire separated the two of them." Four Hebrew words, repeating the motif of translation, capture the climactic movement. "And-went-up Elijah by-whirlwind to-heaven" (2 Kings 2:11*). Elisha exclaims enigmatically, "My father, my father!* The chariots of Israel and its horsemen!" Immediately the narrator renders the vision invisible. "And he saw him not again" (v. 12*). In Transjordan, the land from which Elijah the Tishbite mysteriously appeared, he now disappears without a trace. In his end is his beginning. What a triumph!

But Jezebel lives on in Jezreel, awaiting the violent end forecast by Elijah (1 Kings 21:23). Meanwhile an unnamed young prophet elaborates on it. As he anoints Jehu king of Israel, he quotes the Lord: "so that I may avenge on Jezebel the blood of my servants the prophets" (2 Kings 9:7). He continues, appropriating Elijah's words: "Jezebel the dogs shall eat in the territory of Jezreel."*[10] Then he adds his own: "And no one shall bury her" (vv. 1–10).

When Jehu arrives in Jezreel, the vengeful prophecy comes to pass.

He does not answer Jezebel's taunting question "Is it peace, Zimri, murderer of your master?" Instead, lifting up his face to the window, he asks a counterquestion: "Who is on my side? Who?" (v. 32). Two or three eunuchs look out at him. As Jezebel has taunted him, so now he taunts them. He dares them to side with her. They do not. Whereas the sons of the prophets and Elisha supported Elijah when he approached his ending, the eunuchs attending Jezebel betray her when she faces her demise. In a single Hebrew word Jehu commands, "Throw her down." In a single word they obey: "So they threw her down." Rather than declaring her dead, the narrator describes the gruesome scene. "Some of her blood spattered on the wall and on the horses, which trampled her" (v. 33). Her blood atones for the blood of Naboth (1 Kings 21:19) and the blood of the prophets (2 Kings 9:7).

After witnessing the event Jehu "went in and ate and drank" (v. 34). He has satisfied himself. One detail remains: to give royalty a proper burial. So he issues an order that yields an Israelite epitaph for Jezebel. "Attend, pray, to the cursed female, this one, and bury her, for the daughter of a king is she" (2 Kings 9:34*). "The cursed female." Her name he never uses. Further, he derives her royal identity from her father. The phrase "daughter of a king" echoes the introduction of her as "daughter of King Ethbaal of the Sidonians" (1 Kings 16:31). Male bonding, even between enemies, motivates Jehu. Jezebel as queen he discounts. As in the beginning, so in the end she remains captive to male power.

Jehu has exercised total control; his every command has been obeyed. This time, however, is different (1 Kings 9:35–37). He cannot achieve a proper burial for Jezebel because the attendants find "no more of her than the skull and the feet and the palms of her hands" (v. 35). But Jehu is undaunted. He avers that these remains but fulfill "the word of the Lord, which he spoke by his servant Elijah the Tishbite, 'In the territory of Jezreel the dogs shall eat the flesh of Jezebel'" (v. 36). And Jehu adds a prophecy never before recorded: "The corpse of Jezebel shall be like dung (dōmen) on the field in the territory of Jezreel, so that no one can say, 'This is Jezebel'" (v. 37). His words play off the prophecy of the young man, "That no one shall bury her." In the beginning Jezebel forfeited her Phoenician homeland for Israelite territory. In the end this land not only obliterates her but it defecates on her identity and memory. Scholars suggest a horrendous wordplay between the Hebrew words dōmen ("dung") and zebel (also "dung").[11] For Jezebel the vocabulary of disgrace knows no bounds. She disappears without a trace. What ignominy!

The dramatic endings of Elijah and Jezebel come as polar opposites. Relational, spatial, and physical imagery separate the two. Prophets fittingly and harmoniously attend him. A royal retinue fittingly yet hostilely attends her. His departure happens in an isolated region of Transjordan with only Elisha and the narrator as witnesses. Hers happens in the city Jezreel with a host of witnesses. Whirlwind sweeps him up; eunuchs throw her down. Chariots and horses transport him; horses trample her. He ascends into heaven; she descends to earth. He leaves no telltale signs; her blood spatters. And when the dogs have had their feast, her skull, feet, and palms remain, but only for a time. As Elijah first appeared, so he disappears, mysteriously unconnected to human relationships. As Jezebel first appears, so she disappears, tenaciously identified as "daughter of a king." The numinous clothes Elijah; excrement clothes Jezebel. At last, however, witnesses behold them similarly. The narrator reports that Elisha saw Elijah "not again." Jehu declares, "No one can say, 'This is Jezebel.'" In their disparate endings neither Elijah nor Jezebel has a burial place. Both vanish.

PONDERING THE ODDITIES

Crafting a diptych of Elijah and Jezebel has disclosed an odd couple. In the entire biblical narrative they never speak face-to-face, nor do they even meet. Moreover asymmetric depictions skew the relationship between them. Elijah receives major attention and sustained adulation. Jezebel receives less attention and resounding condemnation. Yet through point and counterpoint the text links them in their introductions, their roles in the drought, their roles in the story of Naboth's vineyard, and their endings. These links portray the couple as strong, ambitious, and dedicated. They have power, and they use it to get what they want. Both the Yahweh worshiper and the Baal worshiper manipulate, scheme, and murder.

Understandably, the Bible sides with Elijah and vilifies Jezebel. A Phoenician telling of the story would no doubt reverse the judgment. It would censure Elijah for murdering prophets, for imposing his theology on the kingdom, for inciting kings to do his bidding, and for stirring up trouble in the land. The epitaph for him might be, "See now to this cursed male." By the same token Jezebel would be held in high esteem for remaining faithful to her religious convictions, for upholding the prerogatives of royalty, for supporting her husband and children, and for opposing her enemies even unto death. The epitaph for her might be, "My mother, my mother! the chariots of Sidon and its horsewomen." Juxtaposing the biblical account and a presumed Phoenician version elucidates the similarities of this odd couple. In Elijah, Jezebel resides; in Jezebel, Elijah resides. No wonder each threatens the life of the other. To condemn her then is to condemn him; to exalt him is to exalt her. Context exposes the biases of judgment.

In behavior and mode of being Elijah and Jezebel become mirror images. Despite any wedge that Sunday-school teachers, scholars, and theologians have driven between them, they are inextricably hinged through the convergence of opposites. What tradition has put asunder, the diptych has joined together. As adversaries Elijah and Jezebel hold hands to haunt the ages.

Chosen Women

❁

RACHEL M. BROWNSTEIN

IN OUR SOPHOMORE YEAR AT BARNARD, IN THE FALL OF 1955, my friend Doris and I were hired to teach Sunday school in Tuckahoe, a bedroom community north of the Bronx. It would be a mistake for you to picture a pair of white-faced, pious girls, long-sleeved and observant; we were nothing like that—nothing like what you would expect, as we liked to congratulate ourselves then. We took pleasure in eluding expectations and categories; we saw ourselves grandiosely as different, nonconforming individualists, unaffiliated observers, citizens of the world. Friends from high school, we were even pleased by our difference from one another. Doris was tall and athletic and political, while I was literary: I nominated her for class president so that she could get the intellectuals' vote. The significant thing we had in common, aside from rudimentary Jewish educations that we valued very little, was an ebullient sense of ourselves as superior and smart. If asked why on earth we set up as Sunday-school teachers, we probably would have balked at calling ourselves perverse, but would have owned up precociously to ironic. That we should be hired by the Jewish Center of Tuckahoe—I don't remember how we came by the jobs—struck us as a pretty good joke. At the interview we had made it clear to the tall, unmarried rabbi that we were unenthusiastic Jews, and if he was too dense or too dazzled to take this in—he seemed to be sizing up Doris as a possible *rebbit-*

zin—it wasn't our affair. Could we help it if we were so engaging that he couldn't believe we were truly disengaged? It would be a lark, we thought, to escape the parental apartments that stifled us on weekends, to travel up to Tuckahoe together early Sunday mornings, make (I think) ten dollars apiece, see the fabled horrors of suburbia for ourselves, and strut our stuff.

The level of arrogance we floated on then is hard to credit now, especially since the 1950s has been pegged as a dark period in the history of American womanhood. Heady with ambition and success, we were dizzy as if on the cusp of outright rebellion, which we had not yet tried. Of course we must have been a little frightened too— McCarthy had just scared the whole country; everyone knew you could ruin your whole life by not being careful, by stupidly signing the wrong thing or getting pregnant. But to be young can be very heavenly even in a conservative dusk, even in a Playtex girdle. Later on Doris and I would be vocal in deploring the feminine mystique and the sexual unfreedom of the 1950s, the terrifying divide between good girls and bad ones. But at the time we were sublimely confident. For we were the best and could prove it—on paper, where everything important got proved. Passing the test to get into Hunter College High School had proved us the best in the city; scoring high on the Regents Scholarship Test had proved we were best in the state; getting into Barnard, one of the exclusive women's colleges in the country, then getting mostly A's our first year there, made us the best in the country. Which of course was the best in the world. About the universe we did not speculate, and we were rather inclined to snicker at people who did. We signed on to teach in Tuckahoe because we didn't take religion seriously, also because we felt authorized to operate in any kind of classroom. Bored, bad Jews that we were, we were very good at school.

"JANE GOES TO ANOTHER SCHOOL / Isn't she a little fool / And when I meet / Her on the street / I tell her! / O, I hardly mention why / For it leaps to every eye / What a wonderful, marvelous, wonderful, marvelous, marvelous creature am I!" Hunter College High School, a school for girls, had hardly trained us as feminists; the cause of women bored us as it had bored Gertrude Stein. Our high school anthem—ironic, of course, the work of our kindly, clever music teacher—was joking but to the point: we thought we were better than people in general and other girls in particular. It was an article of our faith that nothing like us had ever walked the earth, certainly not in female form. Partly for that reason, partly because feminist literary criticism had not yet been born, it did not occur to Doris and me to consider the Bible stories we taught in Tuckahoe from a feminist point of view, and choose to focus in our classrooms, with didactic intent, on strong women such as Deborah, Judith, and Jael. (Anyway, my personal favorite Bible story was the one about the young Abram—not yet Abraham—breaking up his father's idols, and being approved of for doing so.)

We would have hooted then at the very idea of role models, although in retrospect it seems to me we could have used a few—not because we lacked self-esteem but because our goals were so huge and amorphous and because we believed so absolutely in the absolute opposites of excellence and mediocrity, success and failure. Dead set on being marvelous creatures, it never occurred to us to consider the female figures in literature as inspirational or prescriptive models, or indeed as representations of actual women. We were not, of course, reading the Bible as doctrine or revelation; and it seemed naive to assess and judge people in books as if they were real. The English courses we took had taught us to give short shrift to plot and character while we probed for ever-deeper meanings. We read to observe how realistic-looking narratives put particular events and settings and persons in telling relation to one another so as to intimate larger, vaguer, higher things. In other words, we were trained in the hermeneutic approach, which is one traditional way of reading the Bible: the teacher or rabbi will point out, for instance, that the idol-making father set up against the youthful Abram adumbrates the significant themes of faith in God versus human love and loyalty that will be elaborated later in Abraham's story when he himself comes close to killing his son.

If we had been feminists, we might have looked, in the hermeneutic spirit, at the several pairs of contrasted women the Bible presents. The conjunction, for example, of Abraham's barren wife, Sarah, and her Egyptian servant, Hagar, whom she gives to her husband so that he may have a child, then spitefully has banished, with the child, into the desert. Or of Rachel and her sister, Leah. Jacob falls in love with the beautiful Rachel and agrees to work for her father seven years to earn her; at the last minute the father substitutes unmarriageable Leah, heavily veiled, for her sister at the altar. Leah, who had to be veiled to be married, is brutally described as weak-eyed. (The legend that she wept her eyelashes away anticipating forced marriage to Jacob's brother, hairy Esau, is a nice extratextual fillip of poetic justice.) Jacob's crafty father-in-law forces him to work seven more years for Rachel. He marries her as well, and for the rest of their lives the women (and his concubines) live together and compete to produce his sons. For years Rachel appears to be barren while Leah is fertile; at one peculiar point Rachel begs one of her sister's grown sons to give her a (surely phallic) mandrake root he uprooted, and Leah wheedles, in exchange, Rachel's promise that she can have Jacob to lie with her for one night. The rabbis have pondered these anecdotes to richly ingenious and various effect, but the insistent theme, from a feminist point of view, is only too obvious: absolute male privilege and dominion over women, and piteous feminine rivalry for lovers and sons. The victory of the favorite Rachel over her lesser sister is thorough in the end: Leah has more sons, but the more beloved wife's children, Joseph and Benjamin, are the ones most prized by their father and God. Yes, Leah is denominated a Mother of Israel along with Sarah, Rebecca, and Rachel; and true, Hagar's son, following God's covenant with her, does prove to be the father of a great nation; but there is no question of who the important woman is, no question what and who make her important. And no question that the other, lesser woman functions in the story largely to underscore and emphasize the chosen one's superiority.

Had we noted them—but I don't recall that we did—Doris and I might have been made uncomfortable, in our highly critical youth, by the victories of the first and more legitimate wife, and the more beautiful sister: we might have called Abraham henpecked, and Jacob a sucker for a pretty face. But it would have been extremely hard for us to quarrel with the reiterated message implicit in those stories that the best woman is chosen to win over the lesser one, who loses. For it was our pride to be winners; and what was that status based on but similar invidious comparison? We had not yet begun to question the mechanics of meritocracies, or what winning might entail for others and for ourselves. And we were already fatally hooked on applause.

TO GET TO TUCKAHOE, we took the Woodlawn line of the subway, which was elevated part of the way. Standing between the cars of the train for the air and the sun, even in winter, Doris and I talked over our Saturday nights, trading veiled innuendoes about levels of sexual venturesomeness and alcohol consumption. Face-to-face with the pale early-morning sun drying up the sleep in your eyes, shot across the Bronx with nobody else in hearing, you could (at the top of your lungs) say things, hint things it surprised you to hear. Speeding on our way to enlighten the parochial and unsophisticated, we buoyed each other up, egged each other on, felt dangerously free and urbane and conspiratorial.

A bus from the train took us to the raw, new Jewish Center on its plot of still-muddy ground and to our separate classrooms, really the basement recreation room divided by an accordion-pleated plastic door. There we moved the neatly dressed nine- and ten-year-olds through the Hebrew alphabet and the stories in the Bible, paying special attention, as directed, to the holidays. We spent a good deal of time supervising the production of things to take home and hang on the walls to prove we'd been busy, using up the colored paper and oak tag the center was pleased to allot us as signs of its prosperity. On those mornings when we had decided, on the train, that Doris had the more serious hangover, we opened the folding door after one hour, and for the rest of the time I led both the classes (not very well, but better than she could) in Hebrew songs; if I had complained most loudly about my night before, and the weather was good enough, the classes got together outside for the second half of the session, and Doris supervised us in volleyball, which the rabbi came out to watch or even join in. Though I didn't enjoy the game, I loved the effective blend of covert rebellion and pleasing compliance we managed with it, the way we were flouting the authorities and simultaneously knocking them dead. The rabbi's helpless admiration, and the cantor's (he was married, but young, too), would be the targets of our hilarity over lunch.

This we ritually had before going back to the city, at Patricia Murphy's Candlelight Restaurant, always at the same dark table toward the back. The unwritten rule was that we both had to order either pork or seafood. This breaking of the law of *kashruth*, which our parents observed, put the finishing touch on our Sundays; it celebrated our rebellious, unclassifiable selves. Sitting decorously before a pink tablecloth with a lighted pink candle on it, sucking clamshells in the dimness at noon, we gloried in our independence of the Jewish community that paid the salaries we were blowing. More than the food or atmosphere of the fussy suburban restaurant, we enjoyed the bland literal-minded *goyishness* of Patricia Murphy's, which would not have been nearly so delicious at any other time.

Now, over thirty years later, when Doris and I lunch at more in-

teresting restaurants, we tend to talk some of the time about education. We didn't then. Teaching was the mere unexceptionable pretext for our gay Sunday-morning excursions, a mild workout for our
quick wits. We liked having to prepare so little and getting away
with so much. The significant audience we performed for was not the
children but the benighted synagogue officials and provincial parents
in the wings. But of course for all our Olympian distance from our
pupils, we came to care about them, especially the few bright and im-
pudent boys and girls who seemed likely to shake off the bourgeois
shackles we deplored. And for all that we didn't acknowledge it, we
did profoundly believe in education: look what school had done for
us. For these reasons and others we eventually were obliged to recon-
sider at least one insistent moral of the Bible stories we had so glibly
undertaken to "teach" or retell.

THE BINARY OPPOSITION BETWEEN women that the Hebrew Bible
reiterates is more comprehensive and perhaps even more compelling
than the later antithesis between Virgin and Whore, or Good
Woman and Bad. Among women as among nations, the text insistently suggests, the important distinction is between the Chosen and
the Not Chosen. (In the case of Sarah and Hagar the Egyptian, the
categories Women and Nations overlap.) If Doris and I were in no
position to observe this years ago, it was mostly because we believed
it. Contemptuous as we were of mere orthodox femaleness and the
conventional overvaluation of primacy, legitimacy, and beauty—the
reasons for Sarah's superiority to Hagar, Rachel's to Leah—we were
also reflexively bent on being the best. So while we might have questioned the grounds on which Sarah and Rachel are chosen over their
rivals, we could not but have taken it for granted that comparison
and contrast, rivalry, and conclusive choice were mandatory and inevitable.

These different, tangled matters presented themselves to us dramatically in Tuckahoe in the early spring, in connection with the
story of Esther. She is the most glamorous of biblical heroines, the
queen of the holiday celebrated, in Sunday schools in America, as a
festival for little girls. On Purim, when Jews read the Book of Esther
and commemorate its heroine's feat of marrying the great King Ahasuerus, foiling his powerful evil minister, Haman, and saving the
Jewish people from destruction, there is a lot of merrymaking: singing, game playing, noise making. Children traditionally dress up in

costumes, the boys choosing from a range of roles, king or sinister
minister or Esther's wise, long-bearded cousin, Mordecai, while the
girls get themselves up as gorgeously as possible as Queen Esther. If
they must vie for one role only, it is the best one: Esther is beautiful
and good, a reigning queen and a savior. She is the heroine of the
holiday, the eponymous heroine of the last book of the Hebrew
Bible—a light, according to legend, that points to the future.

Because of her primacy in the Purim story, Esther is sometimes
called a feminist heroine, but it is hard to make a very persuasive
case for that. Young and beautiful and good, she is living obscurely,
alone with her guardian, Mordecai, in the city of Shushan, when
suddenly the great King Ahasuerus throws out his wife, for the reason
that Vashti has disobeyed his summons to show herself at a banquet
where he has been drinking with friends, and the king has been advised by his counselor that no man in his dominions will be master
in his own house unless a royal example is made of her. Vashti summarily banished, the king announces he will hold a beauty contest,
the winner of which will be his new queen. Esther is sent by Mordecai to enter the contest under a false name (evidently so as to conceal her Jewishness). With the other contestants she docilely spends
months being creamed and groomed and polished to perfection; finally judged the fairest of them all, she wins and marries the king.
Her strategic position very soon proves to be invaluable: the evil
courtier Haman is planning to persuade Ahasuerus that the Jews are
plotting against him and must be destroyed. Esther introduces Mordecai into the palace and ultimately ensures Haman's destruction
during a banquet in her quarters. Where Vashti lost her place by refusing to be the king's guest, Esther charms him by being his hostess.
And where Vashti enraged her husband by not revealing her (bodily)
charms, Esther's beauty induces the man even to embrace her newly
revealed Jewishness and her Jewish relatives.

Obviously Queen Esther is by no means an embarrassment to
women. A canny political actor who manages to rule a king, she is
a far cry from those homey Mothers of Israel who want only sons.
(Also to her credit, from my point of view then, was the fact that she
is allowed, nay encouraged, to marry a *goy*, which my parents would
not have tolerated, king or no king.) On the other hand, she falls
short of being a cause for feminist celebration. Esther conceals her
real name, Hadassah; evidently she has no problem being less than
true to herself. There is no evidence that she has ideas of her own:
she is the puppet of her wise and good male guardian. She submits

without question to the exotic cosmetic treatments and complai-
santly exhibits her body to the gaze of evaluating men. Finally her
great achievement is to get what she wants by duping her doting husband over dinner, as in an episode of "I Love Lucy."

What alerts the prefeminist woman reader to be disturbed by all
this is the shadow presence of Vashti—the not-Esther or anti-Esther,
the queen who dared to say no to being a sex object (being pushed
around, we said then), who refused to exhibit her beauty on demand
to a party of drunken men. Was it because she was shy or severe, or
because she had no beauty to show? Because Esther's beauty is so important in the story, the reader in the habit of polarizing women—
beautiful and unbeautiful, chosen and dismissed—is tempted to
assume that Vashti is Esther's opposite, to imagine a faded older
woman opposed to a pretty young one. But the Book of Esther gives
no cause for doing so. These two are not rival queens; they do not
confront each other, as Sarah and Hagar or Rachel and Leah do.
Vashti's story precedes Esther's and is its necessary prelude—she has
to be banished so that Esther may be queen; also it intimates the second story's significant theme, the vanity of tyrants, absolute power's
terrifying selfishness and arbitrariness. The two women's stories are
parallel tales about people in perilous positions: there are two exhi-
bitions of women's bodies, two banquets, two pieces of advice given
to a nervous and insecure king who wants to continue to be all-
powerful. The stories reflect each other, and the echoes between
them suggest another theme of the holiday of Purim (the word is al-
legedly a Hebrew plural of a foreign word for "lots," the kind one
casts or draws): the theme that life is a gamble rather than a fair test
in which merit prevails. Self-respecting Vashti, arbitrarily dismissed
for no good reason, is not a woman to be disdained or pitied. So it
is altogether inappropriate that, when the contest for Queen Esther
is held in Jewish Sunday schools in connection with the celebration
of Purim, and the prettiest girl in the best costume is awarded the
crown, the role of Vashti should be merely a consolation prize.

Yet this was the tradition—which is to say, the way things had
been done at the Sunday school in Tuckahoe the year before and (in
another building) the year before that. In celebration of the holiday,
there was to be a masquerade, followed by an enactment, in dumb
show, of the Purim story, while the rabbi read it aloud. The children
with the very best costumes would be chosen to act out the play, by
a committee made up of the rabbi and the cantor and the president
of the congregation, and Doris and me. As the holiday approached,

there was mounting excitement among the nine- and ten-year-olds, bribes, deals, bets and coalitions, secrets and spite. In the past the contest to choose a Queen Esther had crowned one brilliant success and one failure—the charmless child people felt sorry for. Vashti was a bad queen, the children were already saying; she had to be punished because she didn't do her job and listen to her husband. Doris and I objected that this husband was a drunk and a fool, a man manipulated by his counselors and his greed for power, but nobody was persuaded. The compulsion to binary opposition prevailed over the text: if Esther was wonderfully good, it had to follow that Vashti was not good. As the contrasting pairs of chosen and unchosen women in the Hebrew Bible demonstrate, this is not only children's logic. Indeed some respected rabbinical readers, thinking along the standard lines, constructed a wild early life for Vashti, who (before unaccountably repenting) liked to dance naked for the king and his pals (and presumably gave them the idea of demanding her presence at their party—i.e., it was all her fault).

The children of Tuckahoe were not so lubriciously imaginative. Vashti was not Jewish, one little girl protested, when we tried, with deliberate subversiveness, to talk her up; we pointed out that the king wasn't Jewish, either, and were told that that didn't matter since he was the king. Doris and I turned abruptly serious about the mixed academic and moral values (dispassionate logic, fairness, close reading, good humor) that we were failing to instill. We even went so far as to seek out the rabbi, whom we otherwise elaborately avoided. There were two decent roles for girls in the Book of Esther, we argued, and fairness required that they both be presented; wouldn't he come and help us convince the kids that Vashti was a pretty good queen? It would stop the nasty competition among the girls that was spoiling the atmosphere of the classes. The rabbi laughed and assured us we were looking for easy ways out, that the kids would see right through him, that everyone knew the holiday belonged to Esther. The beauty of Purim, he insisted deafly, was that it allows every girl to be a queen.

The deck was stacked against us. Ellen, blond and cute-faced, a smug goody-goody who was the most popular child in both groups, was destined to be the reigning Queen Esther; Rhea, dark and bespectacled and awkward, was fated to be Vashti. Over our shrimp cocktails at Patricia Murphy's, Doris and I invoked Sir Walter Scott: Rowena and Rebecca, we groaned, savoring the irony of the rabbi's playing Saxon Ivanhoe and choosing the blonde. Use your imagination, we urged the little girls the next week; imagine what a Vashti would be, how she would be different from an Esther. We can have two different *kinds* of queens, two different kinds of costumes. More than one of you can be the best. Of course it didn't work. All the girls came dressed up as Queen Esther, and Ellen won. When we argued, during the judging, that—blue-eyed and pink-cheeked and done up in frilly yellow to go with her gilded crown—she was more a fairy princess than a Middle Eastern queen, the rabbi and the cantor and the president of the congregation laughed as if we had said something girlish and charming. We were outnumbered, and furthermore embarrassed by hearing our secular selves arguing for fidelity to the Hebrew Bible.

THE WOMEN IN THE Bible are so sparely described that they invite hermeneutics—also projection, identification, embroidery. Like real and imagined women elsewhere, they have been conventionally understood by being put in opposition to one another, even when this mandates a distortion of the text. The vexing importance of gender, the aesthetic imperative of symmetry, the weird need to say at once that women are all the same and that there are two opposite kinds of woman, conspire to make for strange conjunctions and distortions. Recently, in a museum, I saw a seventeenth-century French oak chest on which a carving of Potiphar's wife, reaching out for Joseph's garment, is balanced by one of Judith bagging the severed head of Holophernes: contrasting a seductive sinner and a righteous arm of the lord, the artist simultaneously makes a connection, through the similar swag of fabric on both panels, between sexual and violent woman. Together the comparison and contrast make the misogynistic point.

Rereading the Hebrew Bible and its critics, feminist scholars have helped us to useful new emphases. Phyllis Trible, notably, has offered Hagar the Egyptian, who experiences a theophany in the desert, as a worthy heroine. Working along these lines, following the lead of Islamic artists, one might argue rather more speculatively for Potiphar's wife as a feminist heroine of desire—Zuleika the dreamer, who sees in a vision the beautiful youth who is an interpreter of dreams. My favorite biblical woman, partly for old time's sake, remains Vashti. As I am still unwilling to wave the flag for exemplary images, I like her not so much for daring to say no—and demonstrating that that's not easy—as for her structural function, the way her story inverts Esther's in a minor, tragic key. Vashti is cast off because she refuses to obey her husband, whose domestic power is a model for every husband in his kingdom: her story demonstrates the common interest—and anxiety—of tyrants large and small, and interestingly indicates that one woman's rebellion makes all men feel endangered. It also begins to suggest that women (just like men) may have much in common. Vashti is not the heroine's opposite or foil; she is not the defective Other Woman we have come to expect in stories. We know only that she is strong-minded and not as lucky. By foreshadowing Esther's, her career demonstrates the cruel constraints that limit and shape any woman's chance for success in the world, the humiliations that attend on being obliged to please, the real risks of not playing the game. Her presence in the Book of Esther subtly undercuts the heroine's triumph and gives the text something like a novel's density.

In retrospect, at least, it seems to me that when Doris and I urged a double crowning in gilded oak tag of Vashti as well as Esther, in Tuckahoe in the spring of 1956, we acted as agents of a Vashtian irony that invites one to question the rule that only the best woman wins, and to wonder if losers have to exist in order that winners may feel chosen. We weren't quite aware of this at the time; the sense of irony we were so proud of then was jejune and self-deluding. To our profit and loss, life would instruct us in greater, more painful ironies later on.

The World Remade: The Book of Esther

❧

CELINA SPIEGEL

The Book of Esther has always struck me as one of the strangest books in the biblical canon. Even the Jewish celebration of the story, the carnival holiday of Purim, when all Jews are commanded to get drunk, is an anomaly among Jewish holidays. All cultures have their carnival—but only when I realized that the literary genre most closely connected to carnival is the satire did the Book of Esther come into clearer focus for me. Suddenly Esther was no longer the straightforward virtuous heroine I had always thought her. And for the first time I began to understand why the story bears her name when so much of the credit for the salvation of the Jewish people belongs to Mordecai the Jew.

A JEWISH ORPHAN WHO WINS A BEAUTY PAGEANT, BECOMES queen, and then thwarts a wicked official's plot to annihilate the Jews, Esther has been called a savior of the Jewish people, a feminist hero, and a clever beauty. Yet even though I felt queenly and beautiful as a young girl when I dressed up as Queen Esther for the holiday of Purim, I never quite felt like the hero of the day. Even as

Biblical quotations are taken from *Tanakh: The New JPS Translation According to the Traditional Hebrew Text* (Philadelphia: The Jewish Publication Society, 1985).

a child I sensed that Esther's guardian-cousin, Mordecai, was the brains behind Esther's success.

It is Mordecai, after all, who saves the king's life, learns of Haman's evil plot, instructs Esther how to behave, and at the end is granted the privilege of wearing the royal colors and the crown. While Esther risks her life for her people, her resistance to Haman lies primarily in her obedience, at best a passive sort of activism. The first plan she devises, twice refusing King Ahasuerus's forthright offer to carry out her any wish and instead inviting him to a two-day wine party, smacks of cowardice, if not outright stupidity. Why, then, is the Book of Esther not Mordecai's book? In a story noted for its overt ironies, reversals, and unsettling exaggerations, the title of the Book of Esther is perhaps the most striking inversion of all.

THE ONLY BOOK OF the Bible besides the Song of Songs that does not once mention God, Esther has always been one of the more controversial biblical texts: rejected by the Essene community at Qumran (it is the only biblical book for which no fragment has been found there), it did not make its way into the canon until as late as 90 C.E. Christians, in general, have responded uneasily to the story's "happy" ending, a killing spree in which Jews are allowed two days of bloody revenge; in fact the Greek variant of the Hebrew Esther, today part of the Catholic liturgy, includes long prayers to God, which lend the story a more palatable theological tone.

Unanswered questions lurk at the center of this strange and violent story that has come to stand as the paradigmatic tale of Jewish persecution and self-defense. Why does Ahasuerus's first queen, Vashti, refuse to appear before the king? Is her disobedience mere insolence, a political stance, or an act of modesty in accordance with the strict Persian customs that condemned any public display of a married woman's beauty? The early biblical commentators seemed befuddled enough to speculate that the king's real command was that Vashti enter naked, or that she was embarrassed to reveal her leprosy. Why does Mordecai instruct Esther to keep her Jewish identity from the king? And what of Mordecai's refusal to bow to Haman, which provokes Haman's wrath and sets the entire plot into motion? Mordecai's defiance is never directly explained in the story. (One commentary has it that Mordecai the Jew could not bow before the idol whose image Haman wore around his neck.) Why the grotesque double killing of Haman's ten sons?

Despite the story's own claim to being a historical document written to describe the events that led to the establishment of Purim, and despite the efforts of historians, who have identified Ahasuerus as Xerxes I, there is no historical evidence of a Jewish queen of Persia or of her impertinent guardian. Although critics have tended to concede isolated moments of farce and invention, the Book of Esther is filled with historical improbabilities, exaggerations, coincidences, and neat ironies that point to a reading of Esther as satire, expertly structured to mock the established order while empowering the Jews.

Though it plays with history, subverts and challenges it, satire is the most antihistorical of literary genres. It is not just an imagined vision of the world but, in Aristophanes's words, a vision of the "world remade,"[1] the British Empire reduced to Lilliputian size or the Russian Revolution led by pigs. Its spirit is a carnival one, rooted in the ancient saturnalian tradition, which can be characterized by the well-known words of the Book of Esther itself—"*ve-nahafokh hu*," "it was turned upside down." The story playfully, yet willfully, takes the familiar world and turns it on its head, exposing its underside for all to see.

In reading Esther as satire it becomes clear why the story of a people's near extermination lends itself so readily to the boisterous celebration of Purim, the only Jewish holiday on which all are required to drink without restraint until the drinker cannot distinguish between blessing Mordecai (not Esther!) and cursing Haman. That satire is born of tragedy is evident throughout Esther, where the loftiest and most crucial issues of identity and survival are in constant tension with a farcical lightness and comic exaggeration.

Evidently written at a time when Jewish identity was in crisis, poised between ease and uncertainty, conformity and self-preservation (apparent in the double name of Esther/Hadassah—and as Mordecai's insistent tag "the Jew" unsettlingly reminds us in our own time), the Book of Esther addresses the fears of diaspora Jews, ultimately empowering them through a fiction in which the reader, like the riotous celebrant in the Purim festival, is drawn into the tale, compelled to participate in its fantasy. The story serves as a much-needed relief from law (emphasized by an absent God) while paradoxically upholding its very values; if the Book of Esther's means are different from those of any other book of the Hebrew Bible, its goal is the same—to strengthen the identity of the Jewish people.

* * *

THE BOOK OF ESTHER opens in Shushan, the royal fortress where King Ahasuerus has thrown a 180-day banquet for his officials and courtiers, displaying for them his splendors and his wealth. He then prepares a seven-day feast for all the people of Shushan, high and low alike:

> [Hangings of] white cotton and blue wool [were] caught up by cords of fine linen and purple wool to silver rods and alabaster columns; and there were couches of gold and silver on a pavement of marble, alabaster, mother-of-pearl, and mosaics. Royal wine was served in abundance, as befits a king, in golden beakers, beakers of varied design. And the rule for the drinking was, "No restrictions!"

The narrator's delight in objects—their colors, textures, and value—exhibits an indulgent attention quite unlike the terse, suggestive descriptions elsewhere in the Bible. These opening lines make clear that in entering the Book of Esther we have left behind the stark world of the patriarchs, matriarchs, and prophets. Marked by excessive luxury, unlimited drinking, and the inclusion of mighty and common alike, this Persian celebration, with its suspension of prohibitions and social hierarchies, is our first hint of the saturnalian—an unbridled exuberance that will rear its head throughout the story.

This opening glimpse into a world of sensuous objects and inexhaustible pleasures sets the stage for replacing one queen with another in a beauty pageant of prolonged and detailed preparation. When Queen Vashti refuses to display her beauty at Ahasuerus's stag party, the enraged king banishes her. But if this seven-day drinking festival, at which Vashti hosts her own party, is indeed a saturnalia, her behavior is not disrespectful or improper. Such a festival, in ancient practice, was the one opportunity for every person, man or woman, to speak his or her mind; the satires of Horace, for example, use the saturnalia as an occasion for slaves to criticize their masters freely.[2] During this one week, in which the great are not distinguished from the lowly, Vashti may have her only sanctioned opportunity to disobey the king.

If this is the case, Ahasuerus's reaction to Vashti's behavior is without justification. Yet her disobedience wounds his pride, and he comes to believe it threatens every man in his kingdom. His advisers recommend that he issue an irrevocable royal edict banning Vashti from his presence—and that he command all wives throughout the kingdom to respect their husbands, great and humble alike:

> For the queen's behavior will make all wives despise their husbands, as they reflect that King Ahasuerus himself ordered Queen Vashti to be brought before him, but she would not come. This very day the ladies of Persia and Media, who have heard of the queen's behavior, will cite it to all your Majesty's officials, and there will be no end of scorn and provocation!

The drunken king's edict, which continues with the stipulation that each man rule in his own home and speak the language of his own people (as opposed to the language of his wife?), merely restates the status quo with absurd force, while exposing the king and his ministers' insecurity as rulers, as men, and as husbands.

While the king's edict is foolish, in the context of satire its significance becomes clearer. Vashti's refusal takes place on the last day of the festival, when there arises an increasing anxiety that the festivities will not end with the holiday, that the lowly will refuse to relinquish their newfound privileges, and that chaos will reign. This anxiety, inherent in the close of any carnival, is of course most threatening to the king, whose royal position emerges as somewhat precarious, even arbitrary. In requiring each man to rule over his home and speak his own language, and each woman to respect her husband, Ahasuerus, then, is reasserting his power by declaring a return to preexisting customs—customs as they were before the holiday began. Ironically, his refusal to partake in the spirit of his own festivities makes him appear ridiculous. When he sobers up and his anger subsides, he remembers Vashti, and his regret only emphasizes his failure as king and lord of his home. The sexual politics and intrigues so common to satire here suggest Ahasuerus's foolish impotence. But where Vashti fails in her role as queen, Esther reveals herself to have a shrewder understanding of the stirrings of men.

AN ORPHAN WHOSE TRUE name, we are told, is the Hebrew Hadassah, Esther (a variant of Ishtar, the Assyrian and Babylonian goddess of love and war) is first introduced in the story as a young beauty. It is her physical appeal, we sense, that prompts Mordecai to adopt her in the first place ("The maiden was shapely and beautiful; and when her father and mother died, Mordecai adopted her as his own daughter"), and, again, her beauty that wins her "the admiration of all who saw her." When the king's scouts enter her in the competition for the queenship, she charms Hegai, the guardian of the virgins. And she is evidently as pleasing as she is beautiful, for after spending the night with the king at the end of the requisite year-long beauty treatment, she wins his "love" over the other young virgins.

While Vashti is characterized by her refusal to obey the king, when Esther is placed in the king's harem, she does not disclose her true identity, "for Mordecai had told her not to reveal it." And when brought before the king, "she did not ask for anything but what Hegai, the king's eunuch, guardian of the women, advised." We learn that even after Ahasuerus selects Esther as his queen, "Esther still did not reveal her kindred or her people, as Mordecai had instructed her; for Esther obeyed Mordecai's bidding, as she had done when she was under his tutelage."

Esther heeds Mordecai, never questioning her cousin's reasoning—even while he insists on loudly proclaiming his own Jewishness. Yet nowhere in this supposed historical document is there a hint of anti-Jewish feeling in Persia—if there were, would the king so blithely allow the Jews their revenge? Why, then, must Esther hide her identity? Mordecai's determination that she conceal the name of her people seems more the ploy of a narrative strategist intent on dramatic revelation than the request of a fearful or assimilated Jew.

Mordecai takes an unusually active interest in his beautiful cousin. "Every single day Mordecai would walk about in front of the court of the harem, to learn how Esther was faring and what was happening to her." In his relentless attendance at the palace gate after Esther is chosen as queen, Mordecai overhears a plot to kill the king and tells Queen Esther, who is in a position to report his good deed and ensure that his name be placed in the royal records. Yet despite his clear propensity for good deeds, Mordecai, in contrast to Esther, is largely characterized by his emphatic insubordination. His primary objective throughout the story is to make a buffoon of Haman, and in doing so he acts the role of the wise fool, a stock figure of satire, who gains power and explodes ironies through seemingly naive manipulation.

When Haman is promoted to the highest position of all the king's officials, Mordecai refuses to bow before him as is required. "Why do you disobey the king's order?" the king's courtiers ask day after day, "and [Mordecai] would not listen to them," explaining only that he is a Jew. When Haman, in his revenge, takes Mordecai's personal slight to the extreme and plots to annihilate the entire Jewish people, he prepares Ahasuerus by arguing, "There is a certain people, scattered and dispersed among the other peoples in all the provinces of your realm, whose laws are different from those of any other people and who do not obey the king's laws." The solitary disobedience of Mordecai the Jew, as he is called, extends to embody the disrespect of the entire Jewish people and emphasizes the issues of obedience and identity in the story.

Mordecai's epithet, "Mordecai the Jew," odd in a text that is part of the Jewish canon, underscores his role as the allegorical every-Jew, a Jew who, in his defiance of Haman, represents his people. Although Mordecai's initial antagonism is never explained, the story assumes a level of biblical familiarity on the part of its readers. Mordecai is introduced as a descendant of Kish, the father of Saul; Haman as the son of an Agagite. By refusing to bow before the descendant of an Amalekite, the Jews' ancient enemy, Mordecai perpetuates the blood feud first encountered in Exodus and then in Deuteronomy. And Haman responds in kind, as if aware of the allegorical dimension of Mordecai's act, by plotting to destroy all the Jews in the kingdom as his revenge. Haman's extreme response—"he disdained to lay hands on Mordecai alone"—has its precedent in God's annihilatory commandment to King Saul, whose disobedience in sparing the life of King Agag and the healthiest sheep and oxen ensures his demise as the king of Israel, and ensures that the rivalry between Amalek and Israel will live on.

Haman, a descendant of Israel's mortal enemy, is given full range to kill all the Jews of Persia, only to be defeated by them in a reversal that celebrates the Jews' massacre of the Gentiles. In order to fulfill God's biblical commandment to blot out the memory of Amalek and take revenge on history, the Jews must kill the Amaleks of the future, Haman's descendants. The paradoxical words in Deuteronomy, that the Jews must not forget to forget Amalek ("you shall blot out the memory of Amalek from under heaven. Do not forget!" [Deut. 25:19]), is played out as well in the reading aloud of the scroll of Esther during Purim, when Jews customarily use noisemakers to blot out Haman's name—an act during which one must listen for Haman's name in order to drown it out.

* * *

LIKE A TRUE SATIRIST Mordecai engineers Haman's antagonism in order ultimately to triumph over him. Since Mordecai is fully aware of the dimension of his act against Haman, his severe response when he learns of Haman's revenge appears excessive: "Mordecai tore his clothes and put on sackcloth and ashes. He went through the city crying out loudly and bitterly, until he came in front of the palace gate; for one could not enter the palace gate wearing sackcloth." Mordecai's mourning, his wailing in the streets, seems an exaggerated and self-conscious reaction in a man who so boldly incited Haman's wrath. He is enough in control of his emotions to stop as is required at the palace gate—in fact his public display seems more a theatrical ploy designed to attract Esther's attention. Indeed, although Esther's attendants apparently do not yet know her relationship to Mordecai, they clearly find his behavior outrageous enough to inform her of his antics, and she immediately sends a messenger to investigate.

That so much of the story's action takes place at Mordecai's post at the gate, the boundary between royalty and the populace, is significant in a satire, where the relationships between law and anarchy, power and impotence, action and subversion, are unstable. This marginality grants Mordecai a privileged position, aligning him with the narrator, whose hand in the story is similarly heavy in shaping its events. When Mordecai later tells Esther that if she does not risk her life to save her people, "relief and deliverance will come to the Jews from another quarter," he may, as tradition has it, be referring to God, but his absolute faith in the story's eventual satisfactory outcome may also hint at his awareness of the nature of satire.

AN EVER-OBEDIENT STUDENT, Esther will surpass her teacher in satire's subtle art. Unlike Vashti, who refuses to appear before the king, Esther arrives unbidden to plead for the lives of her people— and yet she breaks the king's law out of her obedience to Mordecai, who challenges his reluctant cousin to intercede. Rather than banishing Esther for her boldness, Ahasuerus extends his golden rod, indicating his favor, and "Esther approached and touched the tip of the scepter." The golden rod, with its overt sexual innuendo, stands in for any real physical relation the king and Esther have and indicates in whose hands the true power lies.[3] But although the king asks Esther what troubles her, promising her "even to half the kingdom,"

Esther does not reply. Instead she asks the king and Haman to a wine banquet, where the king again offers her anything she desires. She extends an invitation to another wine party.

While Haman boasts of his exclusive invitation, the sleepless king looks through his records to discover that Mordecai has never been rewarded for saving the king's life. In Ahasuerus's perpetual inability to think for himself, he asks Haman—who at that moment happens to enter the court—how he might reward the man the king would like to honor; and Haman, who, with impeccable timing, has come before the king to request a stake on which to impale Mordecai, in his egotism assumes the king is referring to Haman himself. In a fitting comic reversal, Haman must lead Mordecai through the streets upon the royal horse.

Throughout the story Haman reveals himself to be the unwitting court fool whose every scheme recoils " 'al rosho," on his own head. In this respect he resembles Shakespeare's Malvolio, whose unwillingness to partake in the revelry of Twelfth Night casts him as the unsuspecting object of ridicule. Like Malvolio, who shares a pompous faith in his position of subordinate authority, Haman backs up his foolish yet dangerous plots with the law, which he holds absolute. And like Malvolio's, his self-love leads to a delusional sense of his virility, which in turn leads to his downfall.

IN RISKING HER LIFE to deliver an invitation to a banquet, Esther departs from a literal execution of Mordecai's wishes. But while her actions belie common sense and Mordecai's urgent command, they reveal that in improvising from his script, Esther is acting in a manner surprisingly consistent with Mordecai's own modus operandi.

Esther's plan for a two-day wine party in order to fulfill her duty to her people is hardly realistic—after fasting for three days she is in no shape to drink for two. Yet this postponement heightens the story's suspense and allows the banquet to serve as an appropriate satiric setting for the most dramatic moment of the story. Haman's exuberant pride—in his wealth, his many sons, his elevated position, and his prized invitation to the queen's private banquet—is given time to swell before it bursts: his wealth will be given to Esther, his sons will be killed and then impaled on the very (large) stake he builds for Mordecai, and Mordecai will be honored in his place.

While Vashti refuses to parade her sexuality before the king and his consorts, at her second banquet Esther plays hers for all it's worth—which is nothing less than the survival of her people. She exposes Haman's plot to Ahasuerus, who is furious to learn the identity of Haman's victims and not in the least distressed to learn that his wife is a Jew. But even if Haman had earlier informed the king of his intention, Ahasuerus could not have known the Jews were Esther's people. His anger at Haman is misdirected, for he himself is to blame for delegating his power so freely and with such ignorance. At this point in the story a king of true nobility and inherent graciousness would feel shamefully aware of his failure as a ruler; yet Ahasuerus merely retreats to the palace garden, and when he returns to find Haman prostrate on the couch on which Esther is reclining, he misunderstands Haman's ostensible plea for forgiveness and cries, "Does he mean to ravish the queen in my own palace?"—and only then does he condemn Haman to his death.

Ahasuerus's jealous rage, his misreading of Haman's slavish desperation, betrays his insecurity in his authority and in his manhood, in this respect echoing his hasty punishment of Vashti. But even if the king is right to suspect Haman, he displays his inability to behave on a human level in issuing an executive condemnation to avenge a personal slight.

Ironically, King Ahasuerus, the embodiment of the law, is at the mercy of Persian law, which, once formed, is irrevocable, even by the king. Throughout the story, Ahasuerus is portrayed as a passive prop who is not even in command of his own authority: his swift condemnation of Haman's perceived seduction is the first legal decision we see him make on his own. The edict displacing Vashti is drawn up by an adviser, and for an exaggerated sum (reckoned at two-thirds the annual income of the Persian Empire) he allows Haman to exterminate an entire people whose identity he never questions. Yet even while the narrator pokes fun at Ahasuerus's dependence on the law to resolve personal matters, this dependence reveals the shaky foundations of the law itself. When the king and Haman feast to celebrate the edict ordering the extermination of the Jews, their action hints at deeper saturnalian undercurrent in the story. The sinister complicity of their private celebration suggests the dubious moral authority of the law, shown here to be solely in the interest of the personal rather than of society at large.

The unnatural, imposed order of Persian life is in constant tension with the triumphant natural moral sense of Mordecai, Esther, and the Jewish people, whose laws, it is implied, come from a higher, unquestionable authority. The artifice inherent in satire, its overt narrative manipulation, contributes to our understanding that almost everything in the Book of Esther's vision of life in Babylonian exile is unnatural—from its laws, to its sexuality, to its extravagant materialism, to its exaggerated sense of proportions, to its contrived use of time itself.

The story's pacing, its odd blending of the imminent and the long-range, bears this out, adding to the book's farcical effect. While the beauty treatment for the virgins lasts a year, Hegai hastens to supply Esther with cosmetics and attendants; Haman's edict is sent out almost a year in advance of his intended massacre, yet his couriers rush to promulgate it; and when the king, after a considerable time, remembers Mordecai's good deed, Haman is told to hurry to reward him. While Jewish life emphasizes that there is a proper time for every action to coincide with the natural order, the king of Persia does not give himself over to the conventions of carnival time, and banishes his queen. And Haman's appearance in court and his plea to Esther are disasters of bad timing. Even his drawing of lots to determine the date on which to massacre the Jews relies on chance rather than a more natural system. In contrast Mordecai thrives on timely coincidences; Esther too proves herself a master at using time and circumstance to her advantage when she exposes Haman to Ahasuerus.

The most striking use of the manipulation of time in Esther is the contrast between the half-year-long banquet at the beginning of the story and the two-day slaughter at the end, which makes the Jews' battle for survival all the more urgent and momentous. The irrevocability of Persian law will finally empower the Jews of Shushan: because Ahasuerus cannot call off the slaughter, Esther insists that he authorize a self-defensive counterattack. When Mordecai receives the king's signet ring, the Jews are encouraged by law to destroy, slay, and exterminate ("*l'ha-shmid la-harog u-l'abed*")—the very same words Haman uses in his edict. Esther's new law is just as inherently meaningless as the king's edict regarding Vashti. Do the Jews need a law to allow them to fight for their endangered lives? Yet in a world in which assimilation is both a threat to and an insurance of survival, the new law allows for the story's greatest triumph and most ironic reversal: many of the Persian people, afraid for their lives, profess to be Jews.

In contrast, by the end of the story Mordecai and Esther are firmly entrenched in Persian life. Mordecai is promoted to Haman's former rank and leaves the king's presence "in royal robes of blue and white, with a magnificent crown of gold and a mantle of fine linen and purple wool," colors that echo those in the opening scene; and the Jews celebrate the new edict with "a feast and a holiday" of their own. Although the Jews are allowed to plunder, the story states three times that they do not, an implied reference to Saul's mistake in keeping the choice Amalek flocks. The ancient commandment to blot out all memory of Amalek from generation to generation is by implication replaced at the end of Esther by the instruction to celebrate the holiday of the Jews' victory throughout all generations.

IN THE SPIRIT OF carnival, the Book of Esther is a kind of fun-house mirror to reality, whose distortions can make us laugh, but whose recognizable reflections make its contortions all the more disturbing. Yet the one image it reflects in full natural beauty, a beauty impervious to artifice or contrivance and at comic odds with Ahasuerus's need to have his virgins scented, oiled, and cosmetically treated for an entire year, is that of Esther. It is not merely Esther's beauty, however, but her sexuality to which the Jews owe their salvation—and this distinction is what is so startling and powerful about the story, even to modern readers. Inborn and natural, Esther's sexuality is presented as the embodiment of Jewish virtues. In this sense the story is truly utopian, for its world remade—through Esther's intervention—hearkens back to an unselfconscious, unfallen female sexuality. It also demonstrates that the subtle, indirect workings of a woman can be more effective than the brash carryings-on of a man. And all this explains why as a girl I couldn't understand the supposed heroism of Esther—for it is not one that many teachers might want to teach to uncomprehending children.

But we are left with one more question. Why does Esther, the paradigm of natural Jewish virtues, order the most unnatural act of all, the impaling of Haman's sons, who have already been killed in battle? Both gruesome and farcical, an assault upon the natural order, this double killing recalls Falstaff's stabbing of Hotspur's corpse. Just as Falstaff, the life force of Shakespeare's play, conquers death by killing a dead man, the impaling of Haman's dead sons ultimately keeps alive a memory. The just irony of Haman's hanging on the stake he has built for Mordecai reveals Esther's canny ability to turn the unnatural Persian order against itself—to the advantage of her people.

While the Book of Esther ends with a tribute to Mordecai's "mighty and powerful acts," his benevolence and popularity, Esther gets the last word, outperforming her cousin yet again. For while "Mordecai recorded these events," Esther then "wrote a second letter of Purim for the purpose of confirming with full authority the aforementioned one of Mordecai the Jew." And, in the self-referential manner so common to satire, it is her observances of Purim that are recorded in a scroll—which becomes her book, the Book of Esther itself.

Job: He's a Clown

❦

ELIZABETH SWADOS

A couple of years ago I translated the book of Job into a live, musical circus of clowns. But before doing so, I studied the texts and commentaries on the text. I started by reading the King James translation and was struck by the Beckett-like fairy-tale feeling of the prose and the contrast of the dark end-of-the-world quality of the lamentations. Most important I spent many hours with clowns, improvising on themes resonated in the biblical poetry. We didn't restrict our style of clowning to what might seem "respectful" to Job. We explored everything from the ridiculous Three Stooges type of slapstick to the more classical venue of mime. We excerpted small sections from the text and tried out our interpretations in front of different audiences. We didn't discriminate. We showed our work to everyone from Asian and Afro-American children to Jewish scholars. The interpretation of Job held its own, and I forged ahead to create a musical clown show.

Setting certain texts to music offered new problems. When should the music evoke liturgical sounds and when should it reflect the more popular feel of clown routines? These questions could only be answered by what was happening on stage in response to the ancient words themselves. Often the results were odd and unexpected, but quite thrilling.

Biblical quotations are adapted from the King James Version; the "fairy tale" sections were written by Nessa Rapoport.

After many months of work, Job opened Off-Broadway, had a successful run, and has played in many arenas ever since. As I look back on my notes, I'm aware that Job as a clown is not the only Job. Job as a clown is not the definitive interpretation. There was a helpless, human spirit inside of him that beckoned me, and I took the metaphor as far as I could. The character of Job remains a rich and personal one for all of us who want to know why innocent people suffer. He is confused; he is a fool. He looks for answers in the wrong places. But he keeps asking "why?" My Job is a man with a bright red nose and cream pies melting down his face. The fact that he would appear very differently to others is exactly what makes the Bible such a rich, creative source for theatrical ritual and musical composition.

The following essay describes what inspired me to write Job. *It also delineates the various characters in the Book of Job and how I saw each as a clown type.*

THE STORY

There was a man in ancient land, his name was Job-Iov.
A perfect righteous honorable man, a man who feared his God.
He turned away from evil, he sought only the good.
A perfect righteous honorable man, a man who feared his God.
Now Job had ten children, three daughters and seven sons.
Seven thousand sheep in flock, camels three thousand strong.
Hundreds of oxen, hundreds of mules and servants manifold.
The richest man in all the land, the greatest man of all.
His sons would make a grand, grand feast, each in his own way.
And they used to send for their sisters and eat and drink all day.
When the days of feasting ceased, then Job rose early to sanctify
With sacrifices to offset any evil in their hearts or eyes.

I TRY TO SPEND EVERY NEW YEAR'S EVE WATCHING THE BEAUTY AND antics of the Big Apple Circus. Unlike the larger and more flamboyant Ringling Brothers, the Big Apple has only one ring and an eccentric virtuoso array of ensemble performers. The animals are healthy and tolerant (the elephant pours champagne into a glass at midnight). The acrobats double as jugglers and stilt walkers. There's a family feeling. The ringmaster is an educated, strict father. His rebellious and hilarious children are, of course, the clowns.

Several years ago the Big Apple Circus introduced a master clown I'd never seen before. His name was Dimitri. Dimitri entered the ring during a blackout with only a sharp, angular spotlight shining on him. He pushed a cart full of boxes of instruments. He was dressed somewhat like a hobo, and his face had an orange, muddy pallor. He wasn't a sad sack. He seemed curiously serene. Every time he tried to move forward, the boxes on his cart fell to the dirt. He'd patiently rearrange them and they'd fall again. It took Dimitri a long time to get to the center of the ring, and once he arrived, his troubles had just begun. He unpacked the different instruments, but he had only parts of instruments—the mouthpiece of a trombone, the horn of a trumpet, the stem of a clarinet. He earnestly tried to put the parts together. He'd play and get a horrible honk or toot. He'd try the puzzle again and get a bray like a donkey or a wail like an elephant. Dimitri never lost patience. He ignored the laughter and the odds, which seemed stacked against him. When he finally got the trombone, trumpet, clarinet, tuba, and flute assembled, he began to play an eerie, beautiful melody, moving rapidly from one instrument to another, never losing a beat. His melancholy and soulful tone reminded me of another clown I'd seen. At the end of Fellini's documentary *The Clowns* an elderly clown talks about his dead partner and how he summoned him by standing in the middle of the ring playing a trumpet duet they once used as a finale for their act. The film ends with a clown standing alone in front of empty bleachers in the mess left from a wild show. He plays a tune full of longing and humor. Another trumpet answers him from the darkness. He never questions the mystery. I copied down the notes just to see how the music came to have such an ethereal, calling melody. Of course there were no hints to the magic I'd heard in the bare musical notes. Years of experience and belief lived inside the old clown and his trumpet.

Watching Dimitri that New Year's Eve and hearing the Fellini music in my head, I found myself thinking of Job. This was a clown who sat in a spotlight, abandoned by all the others, left to deal with seemingly arbitrary tricks and hardships that were never resolved. He was patient, then frustrated, determined to solve his travails to the point of insanity, and his isolation was striking. I wondered if there wasn't some way to portray the story of Job as a clown show. Job and a clown had much in common. Disaster came for no apparent reason. The harder a clown tried to extricate himself from a catastrophe, the worse it got. Clowns were often scorned by ringmasters or other clowns for getting into trouble. Anyone who tried to help the beleaguered clown usually managed to aggravate the situation. "Friends" got fed up and left the exhausted clown to his own salvation. A clown had to exhibit enormous patience. If his pants kept falling down, he'd just have to keep pulling them up. A clown had to be tolerant. If he got ten pies in the face, he had to endure ten more. If he asked why, he'd get no answer. There didn't seem to be an answer as to why an elephant stepped on his foot and wouldn't move. If the pies stopped or the other clowns stopped hitting him with a big rubber bat, the timing of his redemption was as inexplicable as his persecution. A clown, it seemed to me, was a character of great faith. He lived in a haphazard, cruel world and yet he made no attempt to escape. He endured. It was his destiny to suffer. He had much in common with Job.

What kind of clown was Job? A low clown? Pies and rubber bats, raspberries and seltzer bottles, or a more elevated Pierrot? Was he a Charlie Chaplin fighting the monster of an urban civilization? Or was he a Beckett character, a prisoner of a spotlight? Was he condemned to call out to characters who passed through his life, tempting him and scolding him but never stopping to offer salvation? Was he a Ringling Brothers clown, run over by a fire truck, squirted by seltzer, furious with his predicaments, unable, even in his rage, to get the abuse to stop? Or was he a passive target, a clown who set himself up to be the foil of "smarter clowns," accepting their taunts and oversized boxing gloves, too punch-drunk to fight for his dignity. Job was, at different times and for different reasons, all these clowns and more.

GOD AND SATAN

Now, there was a day when the angels of God stood before the
  Lord.
And Satan came within their midst.
God said to him: "From what chaos do you come?"
Satan answered and he said: "I am from the place of no rest.
To and fro upon the earth, walking up and down."
God said to him: "Have you set your sights on my servant named
  Iov?

For there is none like him on earth, a perfect righteous good man.
   A perfect man.
Fearing God, refuting ill, fearing God, refusing evil."
Then Satan answered God and said: "Why shouldn't Job fear you?
Look at the way you've buffered him with his house and all his
   goods,
Blessing the work of his hands, his worth increasing in all the
   land.
Stop, with your great hand smite all he has and you'll see:
Job will curse you to your face."

Job was the object of a practical joke. He was the patsy in a wager
between God and Satan. Satan tells God, "I can get that goody-
goody Job to lose faith in you." God says, "No, you can't." Satan
says, "Oh, yes I can. Let me just take away his physical comforts and
a few choice loved ones. He'll turn on you." God says, "Go, try."
And the bet of the millennium begins. Job is a perfect setup for a
foil. Innocent Job tends to his farm, family, and prayers and then suddenly, seemingly for no reason, messengers begin arriving. Each messenger brings worse news than the one before: "Your oxen are dead."
"Your sheep are slain." "Your cattle stolen." "Your servants murdered." "Your house burned down." "Your children all crushed to
death." The messengers arrive in rapid succession, and each one is
the only one left to tell his macabre, ridiculously gory story. Job
watches this Indianapolis 500 of cruelty and keeps waiting for the
racers to stop running over him. And you want to say, "So what's the
punch line?" But there is none. It's a merciless shaggy-dog story.
   Job's wife becomes a shrew clown. She could wear a red wig and
wield an oversized bowling pin. "This is ridiculous," she seems to say,
"Curse God and die." Bam! She hits him over the head with the
bowling pin. But Job, though off balance and disoriented, is a patient
clown. Tattered, blown apart, and humiliated, he sticks to his little
place in the ring. He savors the quiet after the mad production
number. He grieves to the audience, tearing off his tie and coattails,
trying to get his high hat back on his head. He does what he can
with his broken props. "Naked I came from my mother's womb," he
says, "And naked I'll return. God gave. God has taken. May the
Lord's name be a blessing."

THE BOILS

Again the day came when the angels of God stood before the Lord. And Satan, too, came in their midst, he too before his God. God said to him: "Where are you coming from?" And Satan answered him to say: "To and fro, to and fro. Up and down, up and down."

God said to Satan: "Have you set your heart on my servant named Iov? None like him in all the land, a perfect righteous honorable man. Fearing God, resisting evil, holding fast to his purity. Despite your setting me against him within and without reason."

Satan replied to God and said: "His faith is just skin deep. A man will give all he has to breathe, just to save his life. Put forth your hand, smite bone, tear flesh and he will curse you to your face."

Satan and God witness Job's resiliency, and Satan ups the ante in this heavenly bet. He explains to God that Job will stay faithful until his own physical well-being is threatened. Now the method of clown technique must change. We have used simple methods until now, employing mostly bad dancing, tasteless melodrama, and goofy "corpses" falling over Job like sacks of flour. Now, however, the slapstick has to get more disgusting. We have to combine horror movies and the Three Stooges. We must combine the relentless physical abuse of Abbott and Costello with the scatalogical excesses of Jonathan Swift. We stop the narrative here and ask, "What horrendous, disgusting thing can Satan do to Job's body?" Children have no qualms about participating in the fantasies of really uncensored torture. We've seen it all in wrestling matches, in wars, in famine, in natural and man-made catastrophes and ancient and modern plagues. So we twist Job's nose, hack at his limbs, pull out his hair, elbow his private parts, operate on his belly button with a chain saw, pound a stake into his heart, turn his head 360 degrees, push a drumstick in one ear and out the other, and he screeches and hops and gags and does a pratfall. In the Bible Job ends up with a nasty case of boils all over his skin. Big balloon boils filled with water, tied all over him and ripe for popping. But despite the abuse and his extreme physical discomfort Job simply must endure. He has to keep the show going for reasons he can't understand. Despite all that's happened, Job's horrible nightmare has barely begun. He's only at the end of his first act. For him there's no sense of absolute time. No beginning. No end. A clown lives to survive the present. Each second is as full as a whole life. Each moment is so important, it seems as if it will never pass. A clown never knows when his ordeal will be over. By being a clown he's relinquished the control of his life to the unknown forces.

The attacks on him come from every direction, but the clown can't uncover a central force that gives the orders. He can complain his heart out, but each stranger to whom he brings his complaint doesn't understand, or is repelled by his hideous physical state. The line between nightmare and comedy can become very thin. Job the clown can ask *why* his life is in shambles, but his chances of getting an answer from a source he trusts are probably nonexistent. He doesn't know what he did that made the bucket fall on his head. He doesn't know why the bucket is there or if it's ever coming off. Some clowns don't even know they have buckets on their heads and therefore can't figure out why they keep walking into walls. Some clowns don't know how scary their bizarre infirmities are and why they bring screams from other clowns who see them. If they chance upon a mirror, they'll cry out in terror and run from their own reflection. They've become so bulbous or withered—the gag is they don't recognize themselves.

THE FRIENDS

> Call now; is there any one who will answer you? To which of the holy ones will you turn? Surely vexation kills the fool, and jealousy slays the simple. I have seen the fool taking root, but suddenly I cursed his dwelling. His sons are far from safety, they are crushed in the gate, and there is no one to deliver them. His harvest the hungry eat, and he takes it even out of thorns; and the thirsty pant after his wealth. For affliction does not come from the dust, nor does trouble sprout from the ground; but man is born to trouble as the sparks fly upward.

Job isn't a one-man clown show. There are other characters written into the text who have their entrances and exits with the specific purpose of making a really bad situation worse. These characters are like early sitcom clowns—"I Love Lucy," Jackie Gleason, Burns and

Allen clowns of the Bible. They have lots of passion, a million ideas, and they get hot under the collar if Job doesn't see their point of view. These "friends" want to help Job get past his sorrow, get rid of his ugly boils, reconcile his relationship with his wife and regain his riches. They're so determined to help Job that they have no desire to listen to what he has to say. His opinions can't be worth much anyway—if he got himself in such a predicament. These friends fall under the category of bulldozer clowns—they're bound and determined to get Job off the window ledge even if it means pushing him off. They're going to pull his head out of the potted plant even if it means stretching him like a rubber band. They're going to get Job to stop crying even if it means scaring him to death and replacing the tears with hiccups. They're the kinds of friends whose sympathy is rooted in disapproval, mild distaste, and in some cases downright fury. Job needs them like a hole in the head, but since he's been assigned the role of the dupe, he must willingly or even unwillingly take the advice of each of them and be put through the ordeal of each "cure."

ELIPHAZ

> Behold, happy is the man whom God reproves; therefore despise not the chastening of the Almighty. For he wounds, but he binds up; he smites, but his hands heal. He will deliver you from six troubles; in seven there shall no evil touch you. In famine he will redeem you from death, and in war from the power of the sword. You shall be hid from the scourge of the tongue.

Eliphaz is the first friend. He is the car mechanic, physician, fix-it clown. His beliefs seem to be rooted in the notion that Job has something fundamentally wrong with him, or he wouldn't have lost everything and be caught in this tragic drama. To Eliphaz Job is like a defective car or a broken-down human machine. Look inside, check the oil, bounce the springs, pull out the engine, electrocute him by charging his battery, poison him by giving him gasoline, slam his hood, kick his tires, staple a bill to his chest, and send him on his way. Eliphaz is a friend who believes strongly in cause and effect. If he gives Job a tune-up, if Job's mechanism runs according to the fundamental laws of mechanics, he won't break down. Job might try to tell Eliphaz that there's nothing fundamentally wrong with him—he did nothing *wrong*. But no doubt Eliphaz has his rubber flashlight stuck so far down Job's throat, he can't hear. When he pulls the sausage and the telephone from Job's innards, he is convinced Job's parts are tainted. Eliphaz would like to wrench the very heart from Job, but despite Eliphaz's huge chain saw and blowtorch, Job's exhausted heart stubbornly stays in place. The frustrated mechanic doesn't regard Job as a very cooperative or high-class specimen.

This is a case where the operation becomes much more important than the patient. As a "friend" Eliphaz is a well-meaning clown and doesn't realize he's nearly killing Job in the search to find out what's wrong with him. Eliphaz tries to have compassion—or at least pity—but these are not emotions that last long in clowns like Eliphaz. If Job can't cough up enough proof of his sin, Eliphaz isn't going to listen to Job's cries of pain. Better to sodder his teeth together. This loyal friend decides that if Job continues to insist there's nothing wrong with him, it's time to dump him in the human junkyard.

BILDAD

> How long will you say these things, and the words of your mouth be a great wind? Does God pervert justice? Or does the Almighty pervert the right? If your children have sinned against him, he has delivered them into the power of their transgression. If you will seek God and make supplication to the Almighty, if you are pure and upright, surely then he will rouse himself for you and reward you with a rightful habitation. And though your beginning was small, your latter days will be very great.

The second "friend" who appears is Bildad. Bildad is not worried about the past or Job's fundamental make-up. Bildad is a discipline freak. He knows how Job should behave. He has the formula to turn a terrible, sinful life into a four-star redemption. Job tries to tell Bildad that he hasn't lived a terrible life and there's no *reason* to partake in bizarre purification rituals and punishing exercise to become a more zealous, patriotic person. Bildad, however, seems to be dedicated to the notion of punishment before the crime. He's a cross between an army commander and an aerobics instructor gone mad. He's the fascist clown. He wants to teach Job how to be a man, how to take his punches and how to be aggressively holy. He has Job run laps, push-ups, march with his chest out, pull in his abdomen till it juts out his back. Bildad extinguishes a burning cigarette in Job's bare palm and warns him not to cry. He teaches him to do lethal rifle maneuvers while making vicious guard dogs out of balloons. Bildad is busy being paranoid—watching Job's every position and move. He's totally immersed in rules, regulations, CV, body building, manliness, preparedness, and violence. He is God's little drill sergeant. He thinks he should train the wimpiness out of Job in one session. Once Bildad sees that Job is nearly dead from overexertion, he's overjoyed and encouraged. But after further testing Bildad feels a sense of hopelessness about Job's testosterone. The exhausted clown can only make a little duck out of his balloon, not a ferocious rifle.

Whereas Bildad thrusts, Job can only quack. Bildad knows that those who are less physically pure and perfect are not worthy of God's attention. Job's intellectual whininess forces Bildad to stomp on Job's head for his own good.

ZOPHAR

> Can you find out the deep things of God? Can you find
> out the limit of the Almighty? It is higher than heaven—
> what can you do? Deeper than She'ol—what can you
> know? It's measure is longer than the earth, and broader
> than the sea. If he passes through, and imprisons, and calls
> to judgment, who can hinder him? For he knows worthless
> men; when he sees iniquity, will he not consider it?

The third visiting ally is Zophar. He's calm about Job's predicament. He seems less emotionally involved. He doesn't care about Job's mechanical diseases or his inability to follow specific rules. Zophar surmises that Job is genetically inferior. Most human beings by nature come with defective cells, inferior nerves, and faulty electronic fields. Zophar is the guru-scientist clown. He advises that Job abandon any notion of his own importance and see himself as a recipe of mixed-up molecules. His pain is not pain—it is a gross misunderstanding of science. Job can't feel better because it is useless to try to be a weak human. Feelings are so low on the scale of things. Even worms know that messy emotions have nothing to do with God. God likes props, advanced word processors, and Nintendo games. Man is a glorious calculation. And Job is nothing more than a severely miscalculated mathematical equation. Zophar—as scientist—will use computers and electronic inventions to rearrange Job's atoms and circuitry. He decides to join him genetically with a brainless surfer from northern California and find the right mix of DNA and SPAM for both of them. The Zophar clown is obsessed by the big picture. He has no time for the little puzzle parts of human beings. What he cares about are the data of his experimentation. Whatever is sacrificed toward the final mathematical proof is a gift to science. Zophar's scientific device short-circuits, and he ends up with the surfer's brain while the surfer goes off to Big Sur to contemplate genetic engineering. The computers blow up. Body parts fly all over. Job is left as unchanged and as frazzled as an overcooked french fry. His clothes are burned. He's in shock. His "friends" are exhausting whatever was left of his endurance. He has only his same tears and prayers. He's even more desperate and alone.

ELIHU

> I am young in years, and you are aged; therefore I was timid and afraid to declare my opinion to you. I said, "Let days speak, and many years teach wisdom." But it is the spirit in a man, the breath of the Almighty, that makes him understand. It is not the old that are wise, nor the aged that understand what is right. Therefore I say, "Listen to me; let me also declare my opinion." Behold, I waited for your words, I listened for your wise sayings, while you searched out what to say. I gave you my attention, and, behold, there was none that confuted Job, or that answered his words, among you. Beware lest you say, "We have found wisdom; God may vanquish him, not man." He has not directed his words against me, and I will not answer him with your speeches.

Elihu makes no pretense about being Job's friend. He lets us know that he disdains the filthy, old, beaten-up has-been of a clown. Elihu is young and handsome, a lady-killer who knows magic tricks. He's the show-off clown. If there is anyone who would provoke Job to feel envy—it would be Elihu. Elihu's the type of guy who claims to have seen God. Elihu can catch bubbles on the end of his tongue and turn them into crystal balls, while Job gets a mouthful of soap. Elihu can transform his cape into a cane and dance a dazzling tap dance. Job's rags remain rags and his oversized shoes cause him to fall. Elihu is a fire eater. He breathes fire like a dragon. Job breathes dust and has an asthma attack. Elihu is young. Job is old. Elihu is cocky. Job can't keep up with his hip-hop dance steps. Elihu claims to be loved by God and understands perfectly why God does what he does. It is the young who take over God's love because the has-beens no longer know how to listen. Worst of all, Elihu doesn't care one way or another about Job. Elihu's the future. He's got the present in his finger-tips (colored confetti, sparks, streamers) and he is the future. If Job can't pull himself together, well, that's too bad, Elihu's got Job's act covered with God. Elihu is the performer's worst nightmare. Life goes on without us. Someone steps in who is as good as we were—maybe better. There's no evidence that we'll be remembered or missed. The scariest part of watching Elihu perform his Romeo-clown magic is that, by comparison, Job's suffering seems very dull. "It's been done." Elihu seems to say, "You haven't had a hit in years. You give others nothing with your doubts and lamentations. It's time for some entertainment. I've got the funding from God and I know what show he wants to see. My sold-out show is being extended. Your closing notice is long overdue."

JOB'S LAMENTATIONS

Let the day perish wherein I was born, and the night which said, "A man-child is conceived." Let that day be darkness! May God above not seek it, nor light shine upon it. Let gloom and deep darkness claim it. Let clouds dwell upon it; let the blackness of the day terrify it. That night—let thick darkness seize it! Let it rejoice among the days of the year, let it not come into the number of the months.

In between each visit of Eliphaz, Bildad, Zophar, and Elihu, the Job clown tries to figure out how he ended up in the middle of this circus ring ducking pies and being hitched up to the contraptions of his "friends." He doesn't just weep and moan. Like any good clown, he attempts to make the best of his situation. He tries, like Red Skelton, to chase the spotlight that keeps evading him. He begs for a way to end his misery. He offers to make bargains and deals and, looking like a madman, babbles to the nothingness around him. He loses his temper, regains control, and loses his temper again. Like the mythological clowns of ancient Africa and Native American tricksters, Job's body and mind fight within him. He is a creature forced into a war with himself—his right hand fighting his left, his fingers tearing at his hair as if he was a foreign enemy.

In the Bible, Job's lamentations are exquisite, dark poems of suffering. They might not seem appropriate as texts for the songs of a clown. But clowns are not the stereotypical buffoons that many audiences imagine. There's a reason why many children are as afraid of them as love them. The white-faced, red-nosed clown is as potent a nightmare image as an entertaining bozo. He's an extreme. He's on the edge of what's real. No one knows what he really will do. Or what will be done to him. You push a funny routine one step beyond the ridiculous and you may end up with real cruelty. You take a pratfall and keep the clown's body prone for one minute too long and he could be dead. You shoot him out of a cannon and he could go too high and float forever in weightless darkness. A child's mind knows this. A child also knows that the clown's mask covers a human face. The mystery of the relationship between the clown's painted mask and the flesh underneath can be as haunting as the masks of a Greek drama or an African masquerade. Into what world are we going? What is this creature who leads us? What is the relation between my dreams and this odd, distorted, beautiful face?

Therefore, the lamentations of Job introduce another kind of clown to the stage. He's the same man, but he inhabits a markedly different world of clowns. These are the victims of ancient tricksters. They've been seduced, duped, and tormented as innocents in mythology for centuries. They show up in Indian, Native American, Balinese and African ritual. This behavior is not unlike characters related through parables as told by the Baal Shem Tov or the creators of classic fairy tales. They have the resigned wisdom of Lear's fool. Their human counterparts suffered and endured, convinced and transcended in war zones and camps everywhere, including Eastern Europe, Germany, Cambodia, Central America, Somalia, and Ethiopia. Wherever men and women have been victimized by unspeakable evil, there are characters who faced their undoing as hero-clowns. With concrete weapons or abstract literary meditations, these clowns fight against impossible odds. Simply by fighting they try to advance the cause of goodness. They refuse to let evil prevail, and sometimes eloquent suffering is their only defense. It's the impossible, overwhelming odds that make them clowns. It's the seeming arbitrariness of the cruelties they encounter that transform them into symbols of David-like "smallness" or "nothingness" as compared with the omnipresent forces of fate or the gods they face. Universal images bring these clowns to mind: the tiny, weakened worker bent under a crushing load; the last man on the bread line, who waits and waits only to arrive at the front to find the bread all gone; the slave who lifts rocks from one side of the road to another, only to turn around and lift them back over the road again; the farmer who plants the single fruit and watches it plucked by his greedy overseer; the beaten man who attacks a lurking shadow and finds it is his own reflection; the single woman who storms an army of men for taking her sons; the starving child searching through garbage; the slave singing under the whip of the overseer; the woman who sings the lullaby to the broken child, half knowing the child can't hear her, her face frozen in an immortal clown mask of grief. This is a very different style of mine. Job the clown becomes witness and participant in these and other photographs of disaster, which come to life and haunt him.

An unexpected illness or injury can come off like a bad joke. A mourner can feel like the victim of a conspiracy of invisible forces. The "conspiracy" feels like a bet between Satan and God. Job had no clue he'd become the central player in an unfathomable show about pain and loss. He was the leading man and he hadn't known he'd been cast. He's an unwilling guest at a party in which all the other guests are mad. Or he is the only madman in a village where it doesn't seem moral to remain sane. But although he contemplates suicide again and again, he never acts on his threats. It isn't hope that keeps him going. He keeps going because that seems to be his assignment or fate. Clowns are innately stubborn. They may not consciously challenge their oppressors. Few clowns openly declare war on the forces that make shambles out of their simple lives. Nonetheless they hang on. They endure insult upon insult, beating upon beating, loss upon loss. Their energy for accepting humiliation is indefatigable, and therefore they turn humiliation into something noble. The well of their tears is deep. When you watch a great clown, you feel as if he's lived out his battle with the rubber bat, the bucket, and the pie forever. You sense that it will go on forever. This is the clown's service. He's a shaman for the audience, taking on their worst fears, accepting derision for their mistakes. He grieves the audience's grief and takes in the pain an audience has suffered. When the night is over, the audience experiences relief from tension and anger spent from laughter. No one knows what a clown feels. You'd never get a straight answer from a real clown.

Of course clowns do scream for relief. By the time thirty pies have been thrown in Job's face, he would demand an explanation. "Why me? Why not Eliphaz, Bildad, or the clown on the unicycle or the one on the donkey?" The silence that meets Job's entreaties makes his temper seem all the more ridiculous. A lonely clown shaking his fist in an empty tent yelling at the empty sky is a perfect image of madness. But Job can't lose his mind completely, because then he wouldn't feel the excruciating pain he's meant to feel. If he went insane, he'd enter a new reality, and it seems he's doomed to suffer without illusion. His desolation and confusion never overwhelm him to the point where he loses his ability to describe clearly what's going on. He can't withdraw—the spotlight's on him. He sinks as low as any human being can go, but he must rally. The show must go on and on and on.

THE VOICE OF GOD

Where were you when I laid the foundation of the earth? Tell me, if you have understanding. Who determined its measurements—surely you know! Or who stretched the line upon it? Have you commanded the morning since your day began, and caused the dawn to know its place, that it might take hold of the skirts of the earth, and the wicked be shaken out of it? Have you entered into the springs of the sea, or walked in the recesses of the deep? Have the gates of death been revealed to you, or have you seen the gates of deep darkness? Have you comprehended the expanse of the earth? Declare if you know all this. Where is the way to the dwelling of light, and where is the place of darkness?

Can you lift up your voice to the clouds, that a flood of waters may cover you? Can you send forth lightnings, that they may go and say to you, "Here we are?" Who has put wisdom in the clouds, or given understanding to the mists?

Finally Job receives the biggest pie in the face of all. Without introduction, warning, trumpets, angels, or reason, God pops out of nowhere and speaks to him. The lights change, and the whole set is overtaken by a booming voice. Job isn't even given the benefit of smoke, flashpots, or a burning bush. God just resonates like a huge rock 'n' roll speaker. Furthermore God isn't giving any clear-cut answers for the bizarre events that have discriminated Job's existence. God in effect shouts at Job through a megaphone saying, "You can't know the universe, clown, so don't try to understand where you fit into it." God is like the ringmaster, rushing onstage, ready to bring on the horses and elephants, and he finds, to his surprise and dismay, that there's still one clown left mopping the floor. The ringmaster is impatient and unsympathetic. He has a whole circus to get going. The curtains are opening, the orchestra starts to play, and the ringmaster wants to restore the stage to its original, colorful, active chaos. The clown's lonely spotlight is snapped off, and he's expected to resume his place among his large family of entertainers.

Job is supposed to accept this change in reality without question. He is after all only a clown. He goes where he's directed. Maybe it takes a couple of kicks in the pants by the ringmaster, but he has a whole night ahead of him. He must juggle, walk on stilts, dance to the accordion exactly as he did before. Maybe he is rewarded by getting to watch his friends, Eliphaz and the others, fall in the mud instead of him. Maybe the ringmaster gives him balloons, a short bow, and some whistles from the audience. But Job's personal travail is over. This transformation occurs as inexplicably as it began. Job has no choice but to accept these startling changes. He can't ask about the timing of his redemption or even if the idea of bad and good have anything to do with it. He simply has to move with the flow of the action. He will take his part in the lovely parade of acrobats and animals as fully as he did when he railed against his broken suspenders or blown-up tricycle. His painted mouth will turn upward, with its sad smile glowing toward the girl on the trapeze. And the smile will be as real as his grimace when he caught the dead dummy someone shot at him from a cannon. The smile doesn't seem to remember the frown. Job no longer seems to have any passion to fight God's ways. Satan isn't even mentioned. Maybe he was paid by the hour. The wisest choice for Job is not a choice at all. He's relinquished his desire for control. The universe is far more cruel and complex than the logic of a tiny man with a painted face. He travels through a dangerous and arbitrary expanse of time never knowing what will happen to him or when. He keeps facing the unknown. This is what makes him a hero. And this is why many heroes are clowns and why Job lives inside any person who has innocently suffered.

But Job lived for many years—a hundred and another forty—and saw his sons and his sons' sons, four generations procreating. The daughters, each in her own way, were stunned by that which once befell him. And no one knew if they would marry, or if they ever would bear children. Despite the fact that Job did die at a great and venerable age, his daughters knew what the sons forgot: That all you have can be whirled away. Naked we stand before our God, naked born and then return. Made of earth, days like grass, and all we own returns with us. The portion of the righteous thus: Comfort that we are but dust.

The Paradox of the Psalms

KATHLEEN NORRIS

"Pain—is missed—in Praise."
—EMILY DICKINSON

CHURCH MEANT TWO THINGS TO ME WHEN I WAS LITTLE: DRESS-ing up and singing. I sang in choirs from the time I was four years old and for a long time believed that singing was the purpose of religion, an illusion that was rudely swept away by the rigors of cathechesis. Church was also a formal affair, a matter of wearing "Sunday best" and sitting up straight. Like the girl in Anne Sexton's "Protestant Easter, 8 years old," I knew that "when he was a little boy / Jesus was good all the time," and I made a confused attempt to connect his story with what I saw around me on Sunday morning: "they pounded nails into his hands. / After that, well, after that / everyone wore hats ... / The important thing for me / is that I'm wearing white gloves."

I have lately realized that what went wrong for me in my Christian upbringing is centered in the belief that one had to be dressed up, both outwardly and inwardly, to meet God, the insidious notion that I need be a firm and even cheerful believer before I dare show my

Biblical quotations are taken from *The Grail Psalter*.

face in "his" church. Such a God was of little use to me in adolescence, and like many women of my generation I simply stopped going to church when I could no longer be "good," which for girls especially meant not breaking rules, not giving voice to anger or resentment, and not complaining.

Not surprisingly, given their disruptive tone, their bold and incessant questioning of God ("How long, O Lord, will you hide yourself forever?" [Pss. 89:46]) the Psalms were largely excluded from Sunday worship when I was a girl, except for a handful of the more joyful ones selected as suitable for responsorial reading. The wild and often contradictory poetry of the Psalms is still mostly censored out of Christian worship in America, though Catholics, Episcopalians, Lutherans, and other mainstream Protestants hear snippets every Sunday. In such churches one hears much less of the exacting music of poetry than lax, discursive prose that provides the illusion of control over what happens in church, and in the human heart. And the Pentecostal churches that allow for emotional response in their worship try to exercise control by allowing only acceptable emotions. Their "Psalms" are likely to be schmaltzy pop tunes about Jesus.

Not having been to church for twenty years, I rediscovered the Psalms by accident, through an unexpected attraction to Benedictine liturgy, of which the Psalms are the mainstay. A Benedictine community recites or sings psalms at morning, noon, and evening prayer, going through the entire Psalter every three or four weeks. My involvement with a monastery near my home in South Dakota led eventually to a year-long stay at the Institute for Ecumenical Research in Collegeville, Minnesota, where much of my research consisted of immersing myself in the daily liturgy at Saint John's Abbey and the Convent of Saint Benedict. I found that I was also immersed in poetry and was grateful to find that the poetic nature of the Psalms, their constant movement between the mundane and the exalted, means, as British Benedictine Sebastian Moore has said, that "God behaves in the Psalms in ways he is not allowed to behave in systematic theology," and also that images of the Psalms, "roughhewn from earthy experience, [are] absolutely different from formal prayer."

During my year among the Benedictines I found that as their prayer rolls along, daily as marriage or doing dishes, it tends to sweep away the formalities of systematic theology and church doctrine. Experience is what counts, and experiencing the Psalms in this way allowed me gradually to let go of that childhood God who had set an impossible standard for both prayer and faith, convincing me that religion wasn't worth exploring because I couldn't dress up and "do it right." I learned that when you go to church several times a day, every day, there is no way you can "do it right." You are not always going to sit up straight, let alone think holy thoughts. You are not going to wear your best clothes, but whatever isn't in the dirty-clothes basket. You come to the Bible's great "book of praises" through all the moods and conditions of life, and while you may feel like hell, you sing anyway. To your surprise you find that the Psalms do not submerge or deny your true feelings, but allow you to reflect on them, right in front of God and everyone.

Benedictine liturgy made me aware of three paradoxes in the Psalms: that in them pain is indeed "missed—in Praise"; that though of all the books of the Bible the Psalms speak most directly to the individual, they cannot be removed from a communal context; and that the Psalms are holistic in insisting that the mundane and the holy are inextricably united. The Benedictine method of reading psalms, with long silences between them rather than commentary or explanation, takes full advantage of these paradoxes, offering almost alarming room for interpretation and response. It allows the Psalms their full poetic power, their use of imagery and hyperbole ("Awake, my soul, / awake lyre and harp, / I will awake the dawn" [Pss. 57:8]), repetition and contradiction, as both tools of wordplay and the play of human emotions. For all of their discipline, the Benedictines allowed me to relax and sing again in church; they allowed me, as one older sister, a widow with ten children, described it, to "let the words of the Psalms wash over me, and experience the joy of just being with words." As a poet I like to be with words. It was a revelation to me that this could be prayer, that this could be enough.

But to the modern reader the Psalms can seem impenetrable: how in the world can we read, let alone pray, these angry and often violent poems from an ancient warrior culture? At a glance they seem overwhelmingly patriarchal, ill tempered, moralistic, and often seem to reflect precisely what's wrong with our world. And that's the point, or part of it. As one reads the Psalms every day, it becomes clear that the world they present is not really so different from our own; in fact the fourth-century monk Athanasias wrote that they "become like a mirror to the person singing them." The Psalms remind us that the way we judge each other, with harsh words and vengeful acts, constitutes injustice, and they remind us that it is the powerless in society who are overwhelmed when injustice becomes institutionalized. Psalm 35, like many psalms, laments God's absence in our unjust world, even to the point of crying, "How long, O Lord, will you look on?" (v. 17).

This is not comfortable reading, and it goes against the American grain. A writer whose name I have forgotten once said that the true religions of America are optimism and denial. The Psalms demand that we recognize that praise does not spring from a delusion that things are better than they are, but rather from the human capacity for joy. Only when we see this can we understand that both lamentation ("Out of the depths I cry to you" [Pss. 129:1]) and exaltation ("Cry out with joy to the Lord all the earth" [Pss. 100:1]) can be forms of praise. In our skeptical age, which favors appraisal over praise, the Psalms are evidence that praise need not be the fruit of optimism. But Benedictine communities draw their members from the world around them and naturally reflect its values to some extent. Women in American society are conditioned to deny their pain, and to smooth over or ignore the effects of violence, even when it is directed against them. As one sister said, "Women seem to have trouble drawing the line between what is passive acceptance of suffering and what can transform it." This is the danger that lies hidden in Emily Dickinson's insight that "Pain—is missed—in Praise": that we will try to jump too quickly from one to the other, omitting the necessary but treacherous journey in between, sentimentalizing both pain and praise in the process.

One Benedictine sister, speaking of the women she counsels— displaced homemakers, abused wives, women returning to college after years away—says, "It doesn't help that the church has such a lousy track record. We've said all these crappy things to people, especially to women: 'Offer it up,' or 'Suffering will make you strong.' Jesus doesn't say those things. He says, 'This will cost you.'"

Anger is one honest reaction to the cost of pain, and the Psalms are full of anger. Psalm 39 begins with a confident assertion of self-control: "I will be watchful of my ways / for fear I should sin with my tongue" (v. 1). The tone soon changes in a way familiar to anyone who is prone to making such resolutions and watching them fall apart: "The prosperity [of the wicked] stirred my grief. / My heart was burning within me. / At the thought of it, the fire blazed up / and my tongue burst into speech" (vv. 2–3). Typically, though judgment is implied in calling another person wicked, the psalmist's anger is directed primarily at God, with the bitter question "And now, Lord, what is there to wait for?" (v. 7).

Many Benedictine women seem to find that the Psalms provide an outlet for such anger; the Psalms don't theologize or explain anger away. One reason for this is that the Psalms are poetry, and poetry's function is not to explain but to offer images and stories that resonate with human experience. Walter Brueggemann, a Lutheran theologian, writes in *Israel's Praise* that in the Psalms pain acts both as "the locus of possibility" and "the matrix of praise." This is a dangerous insight, as risky as Dickinson's. There's a fine line between glorifying or idolizing pain and confronting it with hope. But I believe that both writers are speaking the truth about the Psalms. The value of this great songbook of the Bible lies not in the fact that singing praise can alleviate pain but that the painful images we find there are essential for praise, that without them praise is meaningless. It becomes the "dreadful cheer" that Minnesota author Carol Bly has complained of in generic American Christianity, that blinds itself to pain and thereby makes a falsehood of its praise.

People who rub up against the Psalms every day come to see that while children may praise spontaneously, it can take a lifetime for adults to recover this ability. One sister told me that when she first entered the convent as an idealistic young woman, she had tried to pretend that "praise was enough." It didn't last long. The earthy honesty of the Psalms helped her, she says, to "get real, get off the holy talk and the romantic image of the nun."

In expressing the contradictions of human experience the Psalms act as good psychologists: They defeat our tendency to try to be holy without being human first. Psalm 6 mirrors the way in which our grief and anger are inextricably mixed; the lament that "I am exhausted with my groaning; / every night I drench my pillow with tears" (Pss. 6:6) leads to rage: "I have grown old surrounded by my foes. / Leave me, you who do evil" (vv. 7–8). Psalm 38 stands on the precipice of depression, as wave after wave of bitter self-accusation crashes against the small voice of hope. The Psalm is clinically accurate in its portrayal of the symptoms of extreme melancholia: "the very light has gone from my eyes" (v. 10), "my pain is always before me" (v. 17), and its praise is found only in the possibility of hope ("it is for you, O Lord, that I wait" (v. 15). Psalm 88 is one of the few that ends without even this much praise. It takes us to the heart of pain and leaves us there, saying, "My one companion is darkness" (Pss. 88:18). We can only hope that this darkness is a gift, a place in which our deepest wounds can heal.

The Psalms make us uncomfortable because they don't allow us to deny either the depth of our pain or the possibility of its transformation into praise. As a sister in her fifties, having recently come through both the loss of a job and the disintegration of a long-term friendship, put it to me, "I feel as if God is "binding up [my] wounds" (Pss. 147:3) but adds, "I'm tired, and little pieces of the Psalms are all I can handle. Once you've fallen apart, you take what nourishment you can. The Psalms feel to me like a gentle spring rain: You hardly know that it's sinking in, but something good happens."

The Psalms reveal our most painful conflicts, our deep desire, in Jungian terms, to run from the shadow. In the Psalms the shadow speaks to us directly, in words that are hard to hear. In recent years some Benedictine houses, particularly women's communities, have begun censoring the harshest of the Psalms, often called the cursing psalms, from their public worship. But one sister, a liturgist, said after visiting such a community, "I began to get antsy, feeling *something is not right*. The human experience is of violence, and the Psalms reflect our experience of the world."

The Psalms are full of shadows—enemies, stark images of betrayal: "Even my friend, in whom I trusted, / who ate my bread, has turned against me" (Pss. 41:9). Psalm 10 contains an image of a lion who "lurks in hiding" that calls to mind the sort of manipulative people whose true colors come out only behind the doors of their "lairs." Psalm 5 pictures flatterers, "their throat a wide-open grave, all honey their speech" (Pss. 5:9). As C. S. Lewis has noted in *Reflections on the Psalms*, when the Psalms speak to us of lying and deceit, "No historical readjustment is required. We are in the world we know."

But all-American optimism, largely a middle-class and Protestant phenomenon, doesn't want to know this world. We want to conquer evil by being nice, and nice people don't soil their white gloves with the gritty anger of a cursing psalm such as 109, in which the psalmist is driven to cry out against his tormentor, "He loved cursing; let curses fall upon him. / He scorned blessing; let blessing pass him by." The imagery roils like a whirlpool, drawing us in and down: "He put on cursing like his coat; / let it soak into his body like water; / let it sink like oil into his bones" (vv. 17–18).

Evidently in the Hebrew it is clear that this breathtaking catalog of curses, according to one commentary, "should be understood as the curses of the psalmist's enemy against him." The intent is to show the bully what it's like to have "no one show any mercy" (v. 12), how it feels to be hated. But the poem also shows us how it feels *to* hate: its curses are not just a venting of anger, but a devastatingly accurate portrait of the psychology of hatred. Though the psalmist starts out praying for his enemies, he fails, as we tend to do when beset by evil, to keep the love foremost.

The psalmist finally reaches out of this paranoiac maelstrom by saying, "Let the Lord thus repay my accusers" (v. 20) and recalling his own true condition: "I am poor and needy / and my heart is pierced within me" (v. 22). This most painful of psalms ends with a whisper of praise, an exhausted plea for help from a God "who stands at the poor one's side / to save him from those who would condemn" (v. 31).

It is good to fall back into silence after reading this psalm out loud, to recall that it is a true prayer in that it leaves ultimate judgment to God. But it also forces us to recognize that calling for God's judgment can feel dangerously good. It became clear to me in Benedictine liturgy that, as one sister explained, the "enemies" vilified in the cursing psalms are best seen as "my own demons, not 'enemies out there.'" But, she added, noting that the Psalms always resist an attempt to use them in a facile manner, "you can't simply spiritualize all the enemies away."

In fact Benedictine liturgy is too down-to-earth, too daily to allow this to happen. It establishes a rhythm to one's life that, as more than one sister told me, "becomes like a heartbeat." The Psalms do become a part of a Benedictine's physical as well as spiritual life, acting on the heart to slow it down, something I came to know as I often came to noon prayer with my mind still racing with the work I'd interrupted. Beginning to recite a psalm such as 62, which begins, "In God alone is my soul at rest," I'd feel as if I were skidding to a halt. Like many of the Psalms, it laments human falsity, those who "with their mouth . . . utter blessing / but in their heart they curse" (Pss. 62:4). But the next line—"In God alone be at rest, my soul"— offers not only a pleasurable poetic repetition but a shift from pain into hope, a widening of horizons that is not only healthy but comforting.

But daily exposure to the Psalms also makes it possible to become numb to them, to read even the most stunning poetry ("By God's word the heavens were made, / by the breath of God's mouth all the stars" [Pss. 33:6]) in such a way that you scarcely notice what you've said. What often happens is that holiness reasserts itself, so that even familiar psalms suddenly infuse the events of one's life with new meaning. One sister told me that as she prayed the Psalms aloud at the bedside of her dying mother, who was in a coma, she discovered "how perfectly the Psalms reflected my own inner chaos: my fear of losing her, or of not losing her and seeing her suffer more, of saying good-bye, of being motherless." She said that the closing lines of one psalm of trust, Psalm 16—"You will show me the path of life, / the fullness of joy in your presence"—consoled her. "As I saw my mother slipping away, I was able to turn her life over to God."

Internalizing the Psalms in this way allows contemporary Benedictines to find personal relevance in this ancient poetry. Paradoxically it also frees them from the tyranny of individual experience. To say or sing the Psalms aloud within a community is to recover religion as an oral tradition, restoring to our mouths words that have been snatched from our tongues and relegated to the page, words that have been privatized and effectively silenced. It counters our tendency to see individual experience as sufficient for formulating a vision of the world.

The liturgy that Benedictines have been experimenting with for fifteen-hundred-plus years taught me the value of tradition; I came to see that the Psalms are holy in part because they are so well used. If so many generations had found solace here, might I also? The holiness of the Psalms came to seem like that of a stone that has been held in the palm by countless ancestors, illustrating the difference between what the poet Galway Kinnell has termed the "merely personal," or individual, and the "truly personal," which is individual experience reflected back into community.

Recent scholarship regards the Psalms as primarily liturgical poems that were used in ancient Israel's communal worship. Even individual laments such as Psalm 51, it is believed, were incorporated into a public-worship setting. But praying the Psalms is often disconcerting for contemporary people who encounter Benedictine life: raised in a culture that idolizes individual experience, they find it difficult to recite a lament when they're in a good mood, or to sing a hymn of praise when they're in pain.

But communal recitation of the Psalms works against our narcissism, our tendency in America to turn everything into self-discovery. One soon finds that a strength of the monastic choir is that it always contains someone ready to lament over a lifetime of days that tend toward "emptiness and pain" (Pss. 70:10) or to shout with a joy loud enough to make "the rivers clap their hands" (Pss. 98:8). Though, as one sister says, "we're so different, I sometimes think we live in different universes, the liturgy brings us back to what's in the heart. And the Psalms are always instructing the heart." This is not a facile remark. Among other things the vow of "conversion of life," which is unique to Benedictines, means that you commit yourself to being changed by the words of the Psalms, allowing them to work on you and sometimes to work you over.

A cursing psalm such as 52, "Your love lies more than truth . . . you love the destructive word" (Pss. 52:3), might occasion self-recrimination, demanding that we pray it for someone who is angry with us, and also reflect on how justified that person might be in leveling such an accusation. Psalm 22, which moves dramatically from pain ("My God, My God, why have you forsaken me?" [v. 1]) to prophetic praise ("All the earth shall remember and return to the Lord" [v. 27]) might pose a challenge to the rational mind. What if there is no one to hear such a prayer? What if one is simply too exhausted by despair to pray it? Herein lies the gift of communal worship. "In the really hard times," says one sister, "when it's all I can do to keep breathing, it's still important for me to go to choir. I feel as if the others are keeping my faith for me, pulling me along."

It helps that the Psalms themselves keep moving. In a monastic choir they inevitably pull a person out of private prayer, into community and then into the world, into what might be termed praying the news. The newspapers contain countless illustrations of Psalm 74's lament on the violation of sacred space: "Every cave in the land is a place where violence has made its home" (Pss. 74:20). Watching television footage of the Los Angeles riots of early 1992 gave me a new context for the words of Psalm 55:9: "I see nothing but violence and strife in the city." Hearing Psalm 79 ("They have poured out water like blood in Jerusalem / there is no one left to bury the dead" [Pss. 79:3]) as I read of civil war in the Balkans forces me to reflect on the evil that tribalism and violence justified by religion continue to inflict on our world.

But the relentless realism of the Psalms is not depressing in the way that television news can be, though many of the same events are reported: massacres, injustices to those who have no one to defend them, people tried in public by malicious tongues. As a book of praises, meant to be sung, if for no other reason, the Psalter contains a hope that "human interest" stories tacked on to the end of a news broadcast cannot provide. The Psalms mirror our world but do not allow us to become voyeurs. In a nation unwilling to look at its own violence, they force us to recognize our part in it. They make us re-examine our values.

When we want to "feel good about ourselves" (which I have heard seriously proposed as the purpose of worship), when we've gone to all the trouble to "get a life," current slang suggesting that life itself is a commodity, why should we say, with the psalmist, "I am poor and needy" (Pss. 40:17) or "my life is but a breath" (Pss. 39.5)? It seems so damned negative, even if it's true. How can we read Psalm 137, one of the most troubling of the Psalms and also one of the most beautiful? The ultimate song of exile, it begins, "By the waters of Babylon / there we sat and wept, / remembering Zion."

In a line that expresses the bitterness of colonized people everywhere, the psalmist continues,

> For it was there that they asked us,
> our captors, for songs,
> our oppressors, for joy.
> "Sing to us," they said,
> "one of Zion's songs."
>
> O how could we sing
> the song of the Lord
> on alien soil?   (Pss. 137:3–4)

These lines have a special poignancy for women: All too often, for reasons of gender, as well as poverty and race, we find that our journey from girlhood to womanhood is an exile to "alien soil." And how do feminist women, who often feel as if we're asked to sing in the midst of an oppressive patriarchy, asked to dress pretty and act nice, read such a psalm? We may feel, as radical feminists do, that the very language we speak is an oppressor's tongue. How, then, do we sing?

If the psalm doesn't offer an answer, it allows us to dwell in the question. And as one encounters this psalm over and over again in Benedictine liturgy, it asks us to acknowledge that being uprooted and forced into servitude is not an experience alien to our "civilized" world. The speaker could be one of today's refugees or exiles, an illegal alien in America working for far less than minimum wage, a slave laborer in China. When one reads the Psalm with this in mind, the closing verse, containing an image of unspeakable violence against Israel's Babylonian captors, comes as no surprise: "O Babylon, destroyer, / he is happy who repays you the ills you brought on us. / He shall seize and shall dash / your children on the rock!" (vv. 8–9).

These lines are the fruit of human cruelty; they let us know the depth of the damage we do when we enslave other people, when we blithely consume the cheap products of cheap labor. But what does it mean to find such an image in a book of prayer, a hymnbook of "praises"? The Psalms are unrelenting in their realism about the human psyche. They ask us to be honest about ourselves and admit that we, too, harbor the capacity for vengeance. They ask us to consider our true situation and to pray over it. This psalm functions as a cautionary tale: such a desire, left unchecked, whether masked as "niceness" or violently acted out, can lead to a bitterness so consuming that even the innocent are not spared.

What the Psalms offer us is the possibility of transformation, of converting a potentially deadly vice such as vengeance into something better. What becomes clear when one begins to engage the Psalms in a profound way—and the Benedictines insist that reading them communally, every day, is a good place to start—is that it can come to seem that the Psalms are writing *us*. This concept comes from an ancient understanding, derived from the Hebrew word for "praise," *tehellim*, that, in the words of the Benedictine Damasus Winzen, "comes from *hallal* which does not only mean 'to praise' but primarily means 'to radiate' or 'to reflect.'" He states that the "medieval Jewish poet Jehuda Halevi expressed beautifully the spirit of the Psalter when he said: 'Look on the glories of God, and awaken the glory in thee.'"

I never felt particularly glorious at morning, noon, or evening prayer in my time with the Benedictines, but I did begin to sense that a rhythm of listening and response was being established between me and the world of the Psalms. I felt as if I were becoming part of a living poem, a relationship with God that revealed the holy, not only in ordinary words but in the mundane events of life, both good and bad. As I was plunged into mysteries beyond my understanding—the God the psalmist has exhorted to speech ("O God, do not keep silence" [Pss. 83:1]) suddenly speaking in the voice of the *mysterium tremendum* ("from the womb before the dawn I begot you" [Pss. 110:3])—I recognized the truth of what one sister told me. She compared Benedictine liturgy to "falling in love, because you don't enter into it knowing the depths. It's a relationship you express *until* you begin to understand it."

In the dynamic of this liturgy one rides the Psalms like a river current, noting in passing how alien these ancient and sophisticated texts are, and how utterly accessible. When I encounter Psalm 61, which asks God to "set me on a rock too high for me to reach"

(v. 2), I often think of the dying girl in Robert Coles' *The Spiritual Life of Children*, who said as she slipped into a final coma, "I'd like to go to that high rock." When I read Psalm 131, with its image of the soul as "a weaned child on its mother's breast" (v. 2), I remember the Benedictine sister retired from a university professorship on account of a debilitating illness who said, "For so many years, I was taught that I had to 'master' subjects. But who can 'master' beauty, or peace, or joy? This psalm speaks of the grace of childhood, not of being childish. One of my greatest freedoms is to see that all the pretenses and defenses I put up in the first part of my life I can spend the rest of my life taking down. This psalm tells me that I'm a dependent person, and that it's not demeaning."

There is much beauty in the Psalms to stir up childlike wonder: the God who made whales to play with, who calls the stars by name, who asks us to drink from the stream of delight. Though as adults we want answers, we will sometimes settle for poetry, and we can begin to see how it is possible to say, "My soul sings psalms to God unceasingly" (Pss. 30:12), even if that means, in the words of one Benedictine nun, "I pray best in the dentist's chair."

The height and depth of praise urged on us in the Psalms ("Let everything that lives and that breathes / give praise to the Lord" [Pss. 150:6]) can heighten our sense of marvel and awaken our capacity to appreciate the glories of this world. One sister told of herself and another nun getting permission from their superior, in the days before Vatican II, to don army-surplus parkas and ski-patrol pants and go cross-country skiing in the early spring. Coming to a wooded hill, the women sank in waist-deep snow and discovered at their feet a patch of hypatia blossoms. "There'd been an early snow that fall," she said, "and those plants were still emerald green, with flower buds completely encased in ice. To me this was 'honey from the rock' [Pss. 81:16]. It was finding life where you least expect it."

Sometimes these women who live immersed, as all Benedictines do, in the poetry of the Psalter are granted an experience that feels like a poem, in which familiar words that have become like old friends suddenly reveal their power to bridge the animal and human worlds, to unite the living and the dead. Psalm 42, like many psalms, moves the way our emotions do, in fits and starts: "Why are you cast down, my soul, / why groan within me? / Hope in the Lord, I will praise God still" (Pss. 42:5). But its true theme is a desire for the holy that, whatever form it takes, seems to be part of the human condition, a desire easily forgotten in the pull and tug of daily life, where groans of despair can predominate. One sister wrote to me, "Some winters ago, when ice covered all the lands surrounding our priory, deer came close in search of food. We had difficulty keeping them from eating our trees and even the shrubs in our cemetery." Having been at the convent for many years, she had known most of the women buried there. One morning she woke to find that "each deer had selected a particular tombstone to lie behind, oblivious to us watching from the priory windows. The longing for God expressed in Psalm 42:1, 'Like the deer that yearns / for running streams, / so my soul is yearning / for you, My God,' has stayed with me ever since."

The Preacher

❧

LOUISE ERDRICH

I encountered Ecclesiastes most recently in a small ranch-style house by a nameless river, where I went to retrieve a misaddressed package. I was admitted by a quiet and neurasthenically grim blond woman, who left me in the living room while she went to get my mail. While she was absent, the phone rang. She fell into a low and heated conversation, and I was left alone to regard my surroundings. Brown shag carpeting. Walls of dimpled sheetrock. All was normal, unless you counted the life-size crucifix suspended over the couch. Nothing out of the ordinary, except for the yellow Post-It squares adhering to walls, to lampshades, television, doors. I stepped close to one above the light switch by the entry and read the fourth verse of chapter six of Ecclesiastes: *For he cometh in with vanity, and departeth in darkness, and his name shall be covered with darkness.*

I stepped away, looked around me. Above the phone extension resting on a side table: *Be not rash with thy mouth, and let not thine heart be hasty to utter any thing before God: for God is in heaven, and thou upon earth: therefore let thy words be few.* Upon the arm of that brown couch: *By much slothfulness the building decayeth; and through idleness of the hands the house droppeth.* Everywhere that I could see, a quote from Ecclesiastes appropriate to the proper use of the instru-

Biblical quotations are taken from the King James Version.

ment or piece of furniture, or simply a general admonition, was pasted. Not just the room. I couldn't help taking a quick look down the hall. The walls fluttered with yellow bits of paper. A strange thrill gripped me, a curiosity, and when my sour-mouthed hostess came back holding the package she was returning, I begged her, with as much diffidence as seemed appropriate, for a tour.

"Ecclesiastes is my favorite book," I explained, intent on seeing what quotes decorated the bathroom medicine cabinet, the bedroom, the rest of the house.

Her answer to me was a shrug of refusal, a hand waved at the walls. She lit a cigarette and tapped a bit of tobacco off her tongue. "I don't know the first thing about the Book," she said, "My sister put this shit up to get me in the right mind-set." She gestured at the crucifix.

I tend not to look very closely at the faces on crucifixes, so I hadn't noticed that over the features of the suffering Christ a man's clean-jowled photo obviously cut from a studio portrait had been pasted. He stared out into the empty, stale air of the living room, his eyes long-lashed, his mouth half open in expectation, his expression bland. Over his head the misogynistic chapter of the seventh verse, altered for the gender blamed in this particular instance, was printed in bold. *And I find more bitter than death the man whose heart is snares and nets.*

ECCLESIASTES SPEAKS TO PEOPLE in tough binds, people with vendettas, a bone to pick, no dog to kick, the sour-grapers, the hurt, those who've never shucked off their adolescent angst. In general tones the preacher speaks to the bummed-out. *All is weariness, the soul cannot utter it.* The book speaks to the audiences of the high school choirs throughout the land and the recipients of cards of bereavement, every other one of which compellingly includes the pieties of chapter three: *To every thing there is a season, and a time to every purpose under heaven. A time to be born, and a time to die; a time to plant, and a time to pluck up that which is planted,* a passage that not only states the obvious but that offers no consolation. When bad things happen, what comfort is there in being told it was "the time" for it to happen? One's response is: Who said so, who determined the time, and how can I get even with the bastard?

Ecclesiastes is a mixture of sweet wisdom and pompous rage, of strikingly ornate nihilisms and self-pitying complaints. Often it seems to have been written by a mean-spirited academic, and then again there are those great-hearted turns of phrase, those moments that show a shining poetic intelligence that spoke to Edith Wharton: *The heart of the wise is in the house of mourning; but the heart of fools is in the house of mirth.* And Henry James: *Or ever the silver cord be loosed, or the golden bowl be broken, or the pitcher broken at the fountain, or the wheel broken at the cistern. Then shall the dust return to the earth as it was: and the spirit shall return unto God who gave it.*

I'VE NEVER DEVELOPED AN attitude of mature acceptance, of heightened pleasantness, of genteel correctness about our uncertain lot, so I read Ecclesiastes. Within the strange and ragged verses the voice of Koheleth, the preacher, still zings with the wasp-whine of a man undergoing the universal human tantrum. I think Koheleth felt as desperate as we all do about the absolute paucity of real answers to a five-year-old's mind-boggling question, namely, Why are we here?

Why are we forced to think about eternity, when our lives are so damn brief? Why do we have to lose the ones we love? Except for the famous words to *Turn, turn, turn,* Koheleth rarely lapses into platitude. He contradicts himself, scorns joy, and then praises it as the one true response to empty fate. He is enigmatic, thought by some scholars to have actually been King Solomon, by others, a wealthy aristocrat, or perhaps not one person at all but a group of aphorists. Most think he lived in Jerusalem, a bachelor, and had few family connections. Certainly at the time of the writing he was not madly in love. The book was written in his lonely age.

Although Koheleth seems a basically sour sort of fellow, he comes to hard-won affirmation. He takes what he can get. In his youth and at the beginning of his quest, he says, *I gave my heart to know wisdom, and to know madness and folly: I perceived that this also is vexation of spirit.* He piles up wealth, beautiful lands, orchards, buildings, hits the bottle, eats a lot of darkness. His wisdom increases through grief, and he acknowledges the frustrating enigma that most of our deepest learning occurs when we are humbled by suffering. Knowledge itself acquired through such means is not pure enlightenment but a more complex portrait composed of extremes of shaded brilliance. And yet by the time I reach chapter 8, verse 16, and the Preacher coins the phrase "eat, drink, and be merry," I'm not sure I believe in his advice. For although there is an air of bitter acceptance accompanying the most discouraging verses, the joy that he espouses doesn't ring half as true as the relish he takes in castigating the wicked, the idle, the foolish, the laughers, the talkers, the vain, the small, and women.

There is misery in Koheleth's enjoyment of everything, but an inability to love or at least respect the opposite gender is an embarrassment to any complex intelligence. Somebody told this guy what, or he was jilted, let down royally. He used that as the excuse to write three self-righteous, arrogant, and mean little verses of diatribe. Men are made by God, he concludes, but there's not one good woman in a thousand. *I find more bitter than death the woman, whose heart is snares and nets, and her hands as bands: whoso pleaseth God shall escape from her; but the sinner shall be taken by her.* These words have stood through time in thought, no doubt been spoken from pulpits, used to punish uppity and opinionated women, been cited as God's actual credo on the female subject. These are words that have done historical harm, and yet they were probably written in the same short-sighted spirit that any gender uses in complaining about the other. That barstool spleen taken as divine revelation casts a sick pall upon the acquired wisdom of Koheleth, just as it did in my strange encounter.

In the house of bitterness I accepted my misaddressed package. We could have got into a long conversation, things were headed that way, more cigarettes were lighted. I accepted one even though I have given up smoking, except at high school reunions. I thought about it, but decided to take leave without the rest of the story—the betrayals, the deceits, the japing, mocking fights, all the shit that flies. If I were to choose a passage most valuable to me from Ecclesiastes, I wouldn't choose the face-to-the-wall, sulking *all is weariness, the soul cannot utter it, and there is nothing new under the sun.* I'd choose the line that has something to do with trusting an instinct for generosity, *Cast thy bread upon the waters.* For the image of a man or woman standing in a boat or on the shore and throwing bread at the waves makes no sense and yet speaks volumes, as does the best poetry. I'd choose the balanced passages where joy and realism coexist, or the following pieces of advice, which seem both ridiculous and important: *Let thy garments always be white and let thy head lack no ointment.* Words to live by.

The Women in the Balcony:
On Rereading
The Song of Songs

❦

DAPHNE MERKIN

I

EVERYONE LIES ABOUT SEX, MORE OR LESS, TO THEMSELVES IF
not to others, to others if not to themselves, exaggerating its importance or minimizing its pull.

Perfect sex is like some platonic essence, taking place only in our
heads, safe from the incursions of an always-blemished reality. Sexual
reality demands that we bury our erotic disappointments and leads us
to credit a moment's tremorous fulfillment with the whole earth-
shaking shebang. We cannot experience sex *in situ*, except as it is
acted upon us, and we can only imagine the erotic life of others. As
befits the workings of fantasy and guesswork, the mythology of
sex tends toward florid stereotypes: Men in general are supposed to
prefer their sex served straight up—like strong drink, without the
diluting agent of affection. Lower-class men are supposed to be
either quick and unsubtle or, like Lady Chatterly's lover and the
shepherd in the Song of Songs, unexpectedly gifted in the sensual
arts. Then there are rich men, gone soft with too many pleasures,
men on the order of King Solomon, who chase skirt frenetically,

Throughout my piece, I have referred to three translated versions of the Song of
Songs: the Anchor Bible, the Soncino, and the JPS. I alternated among them as the
specific translation struck me, purely subjectively, as more in the spirit of the original
Hebrew.

238

showering gold coins, but who ultimately lose out to poorer and more potent rivals.

Women, the whole lot of us, are a mystery, insistently confounding. (*"What do women want?"* Even Freud threw up his hands.) Supposedly incapable of sex without intimacy—of physical ardor without at least the whisper of love—we insist from time to time on following our baser instincts and thereby put the whole tentative patriarchal order in jeopardy. Just look at Eve. Ignoring the compliant Adam's lead, she bit covetously into the infamous apple and thereby sundered carnal and spiritual desires forever.

When speaking of erotic matters it seems we are always at pains to guard against gender anxiety, to differentiate between subject and object, between the *he* and the *she*: who's on top and who's on bottom. From biblical times through the present secular moment, the power play of lust—frivolous but telling—remains a constant if encoded theme. A strict division of behavior along male (designated as active) and female (designated as passive) lines runs like a hidden thread in the Judeo-Christian narratives that have been passed along, pulling them tight against homosexual and/or androgynous encroachment. (This is in distinct opposition to the construction of morality put forward by the ancient Greeks and Romans, wherein boys and women were treated as interchangeable objects of male desire, with the former culture glorifying homosexuality and the latter accepting it as a matter of course.) Thus down the slope of religious history it is unmanly to seek fulfillment where none is forthcoming, but it is just like a woman to long for what she cannot have.

Accordingly we have had in the Judaic formulation of the world—which was the only one of the archaic civilizations to prohibit homosexuality per se—clearly demarcated territories: the godhead is kept rigorously unanthropomorphized, while the sexes are kept in their places at opposite ends of the seduction equation as the sorely tempted male and the dangerously blandishing female. There have naturally been some lapses or detours along the way—most notably the Cabalistic strategy of investing the Jewish concept of divinity with erotic power, leading to a "restitution of primordial androgyny," as Elliot K. Ginsburg suggests in his essay "Jewish Mysticism."[1] But the Cabalistic mode, which embraced mysticism and its attendant sacral devices, calls attention to itself by the very audacity with which it went against the mandated principles of the religion it sought to invigorate.

Enter the Shulamite, whoever she be, love object or subject, bestride (or ridden by?) this frisky colt of a text—canonical glitch or deliberate oversight, Jewish original or Persian derivative, holiest of holies or pure, unadulterated smut—called, with arrant hyperbole, The Song of Songs. Enter the dusky-skinned Shulamite ("I am black but comely" [Song of Songs 1:5])[2] filled with boundless longing, just like a woman. . . .

Or is she in fact just like a man? The pinprick of gender anxiety haunts the reader almost from the moment one begins reading this most sacrosanct piece of erotica. Marcia Falk, a feminist biblical scholar, in the introduction to her audacious, albeit meticulously researched translation of the Song, points out that "there is hardly a trace of coherent plot" and that "the voices do not conform to masculine and feminine stereotypes."[3] All the ordinary mooring points of identity are so tentatively established in this famous love poem—a dramatic dialogue with remarkably diffuse boundaries—that the reader is left feeling deeply uncertain as to exactly *who* is doing the talking, much less what sex the person is.

This first sliver of doubt brings others in its wake, revolving around the basic dyad of Self and Other upon which the enigma of amorous choice is based: Are you me, am I you, are you there, are you gone, are you worthy, are you ridiculous, who is the male (i.e., dominant-aggressive) and who is the female (i.e, subordinate-receptive)? *Who is the lover and who is the loved?* Indeed the emotional lability of the writing—all in a dither over the Other, but the Other as representative of aspects of the Self—is so omnipresent that one could easily imagine it being presented, in another context, as psychiatric evidence of dangerous symbiotic yearnings on the part of two mental patients, the "David and Lisa" of biblical times.

It is one of the givens of literary interpretation that there will be, inevitably, almost as many perceived contexts as readers, and what looks like signs of pathology to one may seem indicative of the greatest psychological health to another: Turn unhealthy symbiosis on its head, in other words, and you end up with blissful mutuality. Feminist biblical critics, ever on the lookout for hidden textual persuaders, have been quick to adduce progressive—that is, antipatriarchal—signs from the Song's suppleness, or sexual amorphousness; there is, among this crowd, glowing talk of the narrative's "egalitarianism," as if its author, unbeknownst to him/her, was a hoary prototype of the contemporary jargon-infused orthodox-feminist redactor . . . er, reader.

So you have an academic reader like Ilana Pardes, in an essay full of opaque, Bakhtinian-inspired theoretical stratagems (" 'I am a Wall, and My Breasts like Towers': The Song of Songs and the Question of Canonization"), referring to the song's "metaphoric fluidity, whereby the lovers use the same vehicles to interpret one another in their cocourting [sic]."[4] With similar pyrotechnic ease at overlooking time warps and bending a given text to her will as a reader, the French psychoanalytic critic Julia Kristeva, in an essay entitled, "A Holy Madness: She and He," comments passingly on "the listless quality of the woman lover," only to go on, rather confusingly, to hold said listless lover up as a domestic woman warrior: "The amorous Shulamite is the first woman to be sovereign before her loved one. Through such a hymn to the love of the married couple, Judaism asserts itself as a first liberation of women[!]"[5]

Of course the hunger of female Bible scholars to find some trace of their own predicament in the onion-peel layering of the Old Testament is entirely understandable. Marcia Falk, in her author's note, explains that her "growing need . . . as a woman and Jew, for sources more directly connected to my own origins led me in search of Hebrew literature that included the authentic voices of women."[6] This need helps explain why Falk seems compelled to locate in this perplexing artifact echoes of her own concerns—although she's just gotten through admitting that the poems don't offer much in the way of gender specificity, much less validation. To this wishful end she distorts, however eruditely, parts of the original material beyond recognition on more than one occasion. There is for instance the implausible opening line of stanza 13 as Falk renders it—"At night in bed, I want him"—which suggests the zipless fuck was invented way before Erica Jong came along to coin the phrase. It also explains how like-minded readers have managed to hear a sanguine "collective female voice" in the "daughters of Jerusalem" to whom the Shulamite addresses her warnings about love, in spite of the fact that these unwilling soul sisters are as likely to jeer at the Shulamite's advice as to applaud it: "What is your beloved above another, / O fairest of women, / What is your beloved above another, that you thus adjure us?"[7]

Perchance one can discern in the Shulamite's predicament an early case of sexual harassment, replete with unconscious racist overtones. . . . So long as we are merrily throwing caution and credibility to the winds, we might as well go a step farther. Who knows but that biblical times had their wily subversives just as we do, their Princes and Madonnas who had a say along with the clean-living, God-fearing Pat Boone types. What if this most famous of love poems, preserved in the alembic of a deeply paternalistic tradition that is yet canny enough to give the opposition its due, constitutes a stab to the heart of the very androcentric religion in which it nestles? "His hands are rods of gold, / studded with beryl / His belly a tablet of ivory, / Adorned with sapphires."[8] Any putatively male love object described with such a decided lack of virility and such a decidedly female sense of adornment presents ripe territory for study. Could it be that what we have before us is nothing less than a daringly prescient ode to bisexuality? *The Male Lover as Odalisque: Gender Inversion in the Song of Songs*. Chills run through one at the exegetical possibilities such a hypothesis would open up, whole graduate departments trained to spot the semiotics of kinky doings in the late biblical period.

II

There is, patently, nothing straightforward about the Song of Songs. Even before you get to the text itself—one of the five *megilot* included in the *Ketuvim*, or writings, section of the *Tanakh*—you encounter controversy. While the late historian Gerson D. Cohen argues that "the Song of Songs has suffered basic neglect in modern scholarship,"[9] Marvin Pope begins his introduction to his thickly appended translation for the Anchor Bible series with the following observation: "No composition of comparable size in world literature has provoked and inspired such a volume and variety of comment and interpretation as the biblical Song of Songs."[10]

Then there is the vexed issue of authorship. The time-honored conservative view, which attributes the poems to King Solomon, has an undeniable (if unprovable) logic to it. Who better to pen poems with a prurient undertone than the Bible's own homegrown voluptuary? Less tradition-bound scholars have tended toward a looser theory of authorship, though there is little consensus as to which reconstruction is the most persuasive. In the past generation or two, as the field of biblical criticism has come into its own and its methodology has been refined, a wide variety of historical influences have been discerned in the poems, each in turn cast aside as soon as a tantalizing new lead presents itself. Parallels have been found with Syrian nuptial customs (specifically the mode of celebratory description known as the *wasf*), Mesopotamian fertility cults, Tamil love poems (which feature another swarthy beauty at their center), the Gita-

Govinda, Hindu hymns celebrating the dark-skinned goddess Kali, and a brief Akkadian text. Then there is the smorgasbord approach, alluded to by Pope, which views the Song as "a syncretistic torrent from a variety of springs from different cult areas, Canaanite, Byblian and Babylonian."[11]

Along with Ecclesiastes, Proverbs, and Psalms, this slim collection of verses—also known as the Canticle—occupies a much-disputed position in the biblical canon; the book has inspired a flurry of interpretive strategies bent on controlling if not outright dousing the fiery passion contained within. These strategies have themselves been looked upon with a suspicious eye: Gershom Scholem, for instance, in his *Origins of the Kabbalah*, cites one Meir of Narbonne, who, in the 1240s, thought that "the commentary on the Song of Songs deserved to be destroyed in order to prevent simple souls from being ensnared by it."[12]

The response of simple souls has occasionally surfaced in stray remarks—such as the one by Samuel Ibn Tibbon, who is said to have heard from his father, Moses (himself the author of an elaborate commentary on the Song, written sometime in the Middle Ages, which explained the text as representing a union of active and passive intellects), that the Song of Songs was merely a love poem. Still, fears of the common reader's misjudging the book are rife: "He who trills his voice in chanting the Song of Songs in the banquet house and treats it as a sort of song has no part in the world to come."[13] Staunchly defended as the "holiest of holies" by none less than Rabbi Akiba (also known for indulging himself in the farther shores of mystical speculation and emerging with his belief unscathed), the book remains a strange contender for inclusion and has generally been conceded to be a bit rich for less-than-sophisticated palates. "It is like a lock," observed Sa'adya Gaon in the early tenth century, "whose key is lost or a diamond too expensive to purchase."[14]

Reader, in other words, beware. But who can resist a challenge? The intelligentsia least of all. Precisely because of the difficulties it poses, the Song of Songs is beloved of theorists, traditional and nouveau alike. The postmodernists, especially, warm to its "charming confusion," as Pope calls it. And with good reason: If ever there was a narrative cut to fit the current fashion in dense literary speculation, this one qualifies. Various special-interest groups—be they religious, deconstructionist, or feminist—have tried to get in on a piece of the heterodoxical action, all laying claim to a unique relationship with this avowedly independent-minded text, all attempting to fudge the question: How did so conspicuously ungodly a composition—a piece of undeniable erotica, filled with enough sexual punning ("Your lips drip honey, bride," or, "Let my love enter his garden. / Let him eat its delectable fruits" [Song of Songs 4:11,16])[15] to make Shakespeare blush—slip by the defenders of the faith, the old men with beards?

And then, like dominoes toppling, a whole slew of questions comes in the wake of that first one: How could the rabbis of the first and second centuries have failed to sound the alarms and allowed the Song to secure for itself a sanctified niche, right up there with the creation of the world and the destruction of the Second Temple? Were they duped into stretching the category of sanctity wide enough to let in a bastard text? Or did they discreetly look away, recognizing that a religion based on 613 commandments could do with a little leavening, a welcome touch of sensuality?

What is clear in any event is that it is well-nigh impossible for the contemporary reader to approach the Song of Songs in a virginal spirit; the book's fame—or, more rightly, infamy—as the "I Am Curious, Yellow" of Jewish literature precedes it.

III

The notion of the taboo in Jewish thought has always struck me as hazy, underdeveloped in its implications. Unlike Catholicism, a religion that comes with a firmly entrenched sense of sin—and a concomitant sense of atonement—Judaism makes, perhaps, insufficient fuss about the mysteries of the flesh. In the Old Testament everything is handled in a matter-of-fact, so-called "naturalistic" fashion, from Noah's drunken near-incest with his daughters, to David's wandering eye, to Koheleth's sexual malaise. This inclination to regard the promptings of the id with a certain bemused tolerance is true of rabbinic literature as well: If a man can't handle his urges, advises the Talmud, he should go to a neighboring town and seek relief.

It is important to note, in any discussion of the Judaic treatment of eros, that it is the only religion that historically had no specific sexual rites. As Gerson D. Cohen has been credited with noting, the love of the couple *sanctified by the law*[16] has always been at the core of the Jewish stance toward lust and its consequences. This emphasis on demystifying the erotic by placing it in an ongoing conjugal context is a canny and subtle one; without fully disavowing its power, the focus on situating sexuality within marriage works toward weakening the hold of the unattached woman, as well as the hold of the carnal in general. Yael S. Feldman, in an essay that maps out a psychoanalytic reading of the Bible, argues along these lines: "It is therefore no accident that the domestication of the sexual drive is a major theme throughout Genesis, rivaled only by the analogous gradual sublimation of the aggressive drive."[17] If Judaism can be said to be about the contextualization of problematic drives, then anything that is inherently outside the law of religion—the wild landscape of eros for instance, a region without recognizable markings—must be brought inside and given boundaries.

Yet with all its emphasis on the connubial satisfaction of libidinal claims, there is in Jewish tradition a shrewd recognition that marital life and the business of ritual observance will not fully tame the stirrings of desire. So it seems entirely in keeping with this sense of *realpolitik* to allow the unrulier passions some representation. Which goes a long way to explaining the acceptance not only of the crazy-for-your-body lyrics of the Song but the groanings of the eponymous Koheleth, who, with his nihilism and decadence, might have found greater outlet for his frustrations had he lived in the latter half of this century.

But leave it to the rabbis to gyp us hapless readers. See them wink knowingly at one another behind their s'*forim*, their big black books of learning, getting ready to renege on their offer. Watch as they pat themselves on the back for their sense of embracing irony about the human animal, stuck forever between the worldly and the transcendent. The rabbis—of whom it can be said, as the critic George Steiner said of Freud, that they had "a mastering bias toward solutions"—were, after all, stuck themselves between appeasing the more absolutist among their constituency and keeping the less inflexible of their followers within the fold by attending to their wishes. And so we are handed a bill of exchange in which a Shulamite virgin is meant to stand in for Israel and a tumescent Solomon is meant to stand in for God, their passion to be acknowledged but never gratified. (Renunciation as a form of holiness is something those sniffy non-Jews Henry James and Edith Wharton would surely have cottoned to.) What at first might have appeared to be a blistering piece of amatory literature turns out to be, via the magic of hermeneutics, a dutiful homiletic; instead of gaping at a skin flick we find ourselves watching a video made for the annual synagogue dinner.

How like a people who have God in the head to insist that God is in their loins too!

IV

I have never been a true believer, not even as a child brought up in an Orthodox Jewish family. For one thing I never understood my role in the religiously ordained hierarchy, other than to mutely observe and admire. I think of myself on Saturday mornings, standing in the women's balcony with my mother and two sisters, at a careful remove from the men's club going great guns downstairs. All those patriarchs and their sons busily thumping around with the Torah, carrying it aloft and singing its praises, opening and closing the curtain of the *Aron Hakodesh*, the Holy Ark, where the Torah scrolls were stored, or officiously dispensing *aliyahs*, calling up young and old to the *bima*, the raised platform in the center, for a bit of momentary glory. That club included my father and three brothers, included anyone who wasn't female and excluded anyone who was: me, for instance, blusher carefully applied (rub it *in*, my mother would insist on the way to *shul*), the essence of self-conscious, unblossomed girlhood.

At what point did I stop listening to the text of the service, my years of Jewish day school and immersion in Hebrew endured for naught, the better to concentrate on the subtext—the palpable sexual tensions I sensed around me in the synagogue? All those dolled-up women, dressed and made up to kill, *their eyes like doves', their hair as black as goats, their teeth like a flock of ewes all shaped alike, their lips like woven threads of crimson silk, their breasts like twin fawns.* Why did they gleam and glisten so, I wondered, only to be cordoned off from the objects of their ministrations: the men downstairs, who cast appreciative glances upward and then went back to their noisy activities?

The burden of sexuality—both its allure and its danger—is placed on women, this much I see. Can it be that if the men venture upstairs, come too close to the expensive scents wafting through the women's balcony, they'll be bewitched, throw their marital vows out the window? Perhaps they'll cheat or, worse yet, leave their wives and families altogether; perhaps they'll go crazy with fleshly greed. Down the corridors of my mind, doors open upon a flurry of long-ago, briefly glimpsed images, scenes from a synagogue on the Upper East Side of Manhattan: sudden divorces and shamefully short marriages; older, prosperous husbands paired with younger, blond wives; trade-ins and -ups. The doors close, and order is restored. All is once again as it should be: We are here, the matriarchs and their daughters, stuck behind the *mechitza*, that inviolable dividing wall, whether balcony or curtain, consigned to an attitude of expect-ant readiness.

There are other questions that go unanswered because to ask them would be to imply that the bourgeois verities of life are up for grabs and thus their very asking is taboo. How interesting, really, is *fulfilled* desire? What happens, that is, after you get the girl, find yourself ac-tually bedding the Shulamite? How sustainable is erotic passion once you place a ring upon its finger? How sustainable is erotic passion, period?

The Song of Songs is read aloud in synagogue at the end of the long eight-day Passover holiday. It is doubtful I was present to hear it at an age when I could most have appreciated its uniquely un-theological nature; once I had put in an appearance in my spring fin-ery on the first two mornings of the holiday, I generally forswore further *shul* duty. But even if I was to be found in my seat in the women's balcony, I doubt I was listening anymore by the time I could have grasped its message, the secret it clutched to itself, behind its reputation for smuttiness.

It would be years before I stumbled upon a true consideration of what that secret was, before I teased out that sexual desire is a lie we tell ourselves, more or less. Romantic enamorment is a fabrication that serves to conceal the immense relativity of all passion and the virtual invention of the love object. "How sustainable is erotic pas-sion?" *It was a question nobody asked because nobody wanted to know the answer.* Tell the truth about it and you did so at your own peril, as I discovered when I heard the tale of my great-uncle, Raphael Breuer. Simple artistic soul that he was, he undertook in 1912 to write an interpretation of the Song based on a literal rather than al-legorical reading: It was, as Samuel Ibn Tibbon had hinted centuries before, merely a love poem. So strong was the reaction of the Ger-man Jewish community of which he and his family were an influen-tial part that Breuer not only had to rescind the introduction to his commentary but the gaffe is said to have cost him one of the most prestigious chief rabbinates in Germany.

AND SO, BURDENED BY my particular history as a woman, I come to reacquaint myself with this infamously titillating text. How well will it live up to its reputation as the dirty, red-hot book of Jewish liter-ature? I must admit that, after several readings to make sure I haven't somehow missed the climactic moment as I used to do when I read the late novels of Henry James, I don't find the poem particularly sexy. Resoundingly lyrical, yes; intimate and charming, undeniably; in the nature of an aphrodisiac, hardly. Perhaps it is the overwhelming rusticity of the amorous imagery—love that is like the crocus of the plain, the lotus of the valley, the apple in the wood; love that leaps over mountains and bounds over hills—that leaves me, a constitutionally urban creature without much direct experience of flora and fauna, at a loss. Perhaps it is all those trailing flocks of goats and ewes come up from the washing that give the narrative a faint whiff of barns and cow manure. I muse upon the possibility that allusions to the bestiary once carried a greater erotic charge than they do now. At any rate a zookeeper's vision of loveliness is not mine. Nor, for that matter, is a banker's; otherwise the persistently mercantile notion of comeliness that the Song advances—the lover's beauty is compared to gold, gems, ivory, sapphires, and marble—would undoubtedly move me more.

I find myself without sufficient frame of reference in the jumble of other metaphors as well. Lebanon. The tents of Qedar. Carmel. Clusters of grapes. More Lebanon. True, there is praise for a vulva that smells, improbably, of apples, but what is one to do with *that* piece of information?

Which leads me to the tale itself, rather than the telling. Goethe was supposed to have viewed the Song as "the most tender and inimitable expression of passionate yet graceful love that has yet come down to us." Nice words, although they still don't help me get a grip on the story. Like, what exactly *happens* in it? I look ahead a couple of centuries and come upon this, from Kristeva: "The Song of Songs gives Judaism the unique trait of being the most erotic of abstractions, the most ideal of sensualities."[18] Nice words again, although they leave me with a blurry feeling around the edges. All this obscure, high-flying description, and I'm beginning to feel like the proverbial Hollywood philistine who prefers his literary plots pitched in one sentence or less.

Here, for better or worse, is what I've made of this "enigmatic parable," as it's been called. Once you've put the credos aside, you're left slipping around in the liquid atmosphere of the text without a foothold. Interestingly enough, what almost all of the readings of the Song have in common is a notion of union, marital or merely consensual, presumed to be implicit within the poem itself. This interpretive bias can be discerned as much in the various secularist stances as in the religious-allegorical approach, which raises the bawdy goings-on of the poem to a spiritually correct level by treating Israel as the symbolic bride and God as the symbolic husband—a familiar sacral conceit, used by the prophets Hosea and Jeremiah.

But to this reader the whole predicating idea of a union is never quite persuasive, perhaps because the Shulamite never comes across as an actual breathing specimen of womankind, just as Solomon and his lowly shepherd rival never emerge as fully embodied malehood. The verses, I propose, speak not to the idea of union, either literal or metaphorical or, God help us, "depatriarchalized," but rather to its virtual opposite: the solitary, wholly interior churn of ambivalence, expectant desire entwined with melancholy longing. Inherent in the very nature of erotic presence is absence—the looming loss of the lover even as he/she is glimpsed. How to "own" the love object, how to pin down another beyond the fleeting moment: the possibility of sexual gratification is at least as threatening as it is pleasing, with its inevitable shadowy denouement of withdrawal and further longing.

I choose, then, to think of the Song of Songs as a story about the risks of passion—about being a fool for love and all of that. A particularly overlooked aspect of the text, to my way of thinking, is its recognition of the lover's vulnerability. To fall in love is to open oneself up to potential ridicule. The Shulamite's thrice-repeated bleak admonition about the dangers of falling in love seems most significant in this regard: "I adjure you, O / daughters of / Jerusalem, / by the gazelles, and by the hinds of the field, / That ye awaken not, nor stir up love, / Until it please." (Song of Songs 8:4).[19] Under its Zen-like absolutism this refrain points to the fear of rejection implicit in all extensions of self. There is, too, the implied fear that once you've gone ahead and fastened your hopes on some designated other, the world will rush in with scabrous comparisons and invidious remarks of the *Who, him?!!* variety.

Radical as its inclusion in the canon of Holy Scriptures may appear to be, I suggest it is less surprising if one sees this amorous dialogue in the form of a warning—a prophylaxis, as Gerson Cohen calls it[20]: Caution, ye seekers of passion, lest you end up lost and wandering, in a city with no name, reduced to calling on the help of anonymous and hostile "watchmen." Caution, in other words, lest you end up lovesick, shades of Truffaut's *Adele H.*, the woman consigned to an unfulfillable longing for the absent, ever-fleeing male.

V

The final section of the Song begins by alluding to the yearning for a preeroticized period in life in which a young boy is free to suckle on his mother's breast and a prepubescent girl ("Our sister is young / And breasts she has none") is free to kiss her brother without risk: "none would scorn me" (Song of Songs 8:8).[21] It is a curious scenario for a purportedly heavy-breathing amorous dialogue to end on, but an entirely reasonable conclusion for the conflicted, push-me/pull-you recitation—a monologue in several voices—that I take this text to be. Perhaps, with just the smallest of shifts in emphasis, we might read the Song of Songs as an internalized argument *preceding* the taking of romantic action, a sort of amplified version of Hamlet's famously indecisive soliloquy: To love or not to love, that is the question.

At the core of the Song of Songs, under all its waffling, is an erotics of restraint, even of stasis. Someone, a woman perchance, longs; someone else, a man perchance, responds, but is ultimately unattainable. It is a game, a lie, an elaborate ruse: A case for adult heterosexual passion is presented in the guise of two amorphously defined lovers who never come close to consummating their relationship. Once the dust the poem is designed to kick up has settled, its stark secret is revealed: Stay upstairs in the balcony, Shulamite woman, for withheld consummation is the best kind.

But even as I write this, it becomes clear to me that I am writing out of my own idiosyncratic tastes. As such, it must be pointed out that my imagination is drawn more to the prospect of erotic doom than to sensual rapture, to Jean Rhys and her abandoned boarding-house creatures than to daredevil dames astride one stallion-lover-husband after another. It is, in the end, a matter of personal accounting whether any passion is worth the price of that passion. So, too, in the end, the Song throws one—in the most parodied of postmodernist theories of reading—upon oneself as Author.

It would seem, finally, that one brings to a text about love all that one was taught to read into it, an amorous imprint stretching back for generations: unto mothers and grandmothers, and behind them ancestors galore. Some of us are destined to exalt love and others to demonize it; some rise to its occasion and others shy away for reasons unknown even to themselves. Lineage counts—Noah was the son of *x*, the son of *xx*, the son of *xxx*—even in matters of the flesh and heart. What you recognize as the siren call of love I may fear as the siren call of imminent abandonment. Someone must have scared off the author of the Song of Songs in the porousness of childhood, whispering sweet messages of caution: "Bolt, my love / Be like a buck, / Or a young stag, / On the spice mountain" (v. 14).[22]

The Poetry of Isaiah

❧

AMY CLAMPITT

No cozy tales about being fed by ravens like Elijah, no fabulous ones of being swallowed up like Jonah: The Book of Isaiah, for the child I was, amounted to nothing but bad news. My notion of it came presumably by way of Sunday-morning sermons, and the figure of the prophet himself was inseparable from the most forbidding of the Old Ones who sat there, Sunday after Sunday, nodding dour agreement. Isaiah is undoubtedly for grown-ups; and I was myself exceptionally and protractedly resistant to my elders and all they stood for. On what they stood *against*, the words of the prophet were unmistakable:

> In that day the Lord will take away the bravery of their tinkling ornaments . . . , the rings, and nose jewels, the changeable suits of apparel, and the mantles, and the wimples, and the crisping pins. (Isa. 3:18, 21–22)

Wanting to look pretty was all wrong; going out and having fun was the road to perdition:

Biblical quotations are taken from the King James Version.

252

> Woe unto them that rise up early in the morning, that
> they may follow strong drink; that continue until night,
> till wine inflame them! And the harp, and the viol, the
> tabret, and pipe, and wine, are in their feasts. (Isa.
> 5:11–12)

It was in the face of such strictures that I came to envision being
taken to a nightclub as a kind of *summum bonum*. The figure, in
beautiful, wicked decolleté, or Lena Horne emerges from a sodden
blur; a flirtatious sally is rebuffed ("Go 'way, I don't like white girls"):
this was the world, I was in it, at the drunken heart of it.

Toward such excitements the child in me has grown sufficiently
blasé that I now return to the Book of Isaiah at least as often as I do
to *Alice in Wonderland*, my favorite book for as long as I can remember. If one lives to a sufficient age, the day is bound to arrive for discovering a kind of bedrock delight in the curmudgeonly I-told-you-so
of the Hebrew prophets, when the rhetoric of the King James Version has the aspect not of a stumbling block but rather of a bulwark,
and the ring of it becomes almost contemporary:

> Woe unto them that decree unrighteous decrees, and that
> write grievousness which they have prescribed; to turn
> aside the needy from judgment, and to take away the right
> from the poor of my people, that widows may be their
> prey, and that they may rob the fatherless! (Isa. 10:1–2)

In the approximately two and a half millennia since Isaiah lived, human nature can hardly be said to have pulled itself out of such crass
unconcern for the victims of misfortune. A society that goes on arguing over entitlements and curtailments, as of the right to beg on
subway platforms, seems to have come no nearer to what could be
called social justice. Nor have we very noticeably advanced beyond
the mayhem and the hypocrisy of organized religion:

> Your new moons and your appointed feasts my soul hateth:
> they are a trouble to me; I am weary to bear them. And
> when ye spread forth your hands, I will hide mine eyes
> from you: yea, when ye make many prayers, I will not
> hear: your hands are full of blood. (Isa. 1:14–15)

The message is clear enough, with hardly any adjustment of perspective. Nevertheless, the strangeness inhering in the messenger himself is not to be minimized.

Who was he? According to biblical scholars, the writings that make up the Book of Isaiah both are and are not the work of a historical person. Like so much else in the Bible, they are a handed-down and patched-together bundle, its chronology addled and its meaning blurred in the processes of copying and translation. They date roughly to a period when the smaller states of the Palestinian region were being jostled and menaced by superpowers—by Egypt to the west and, more alarmingly, Assyria and Babylonia to the east. In the time of Isaiah the northern kingdom of Israel had already been snuffed out, and numbers of its populace deported eastward as a safeguard against future uprisings. The southern kingdom of Judah continued to hold out, unsteadily, until the invasion under Sennacherib in the year 701 B.C.E. That event is presumably the one referred to in the opening chapter of the Book of Isaiah:

> Your country is desolate, your cities are burned with fire: your land, strangers devour it in your presence, and it is desolate, overthrown by strangers. And the daughter of Zion is left as a cottage in a vineyard, as a lodge in a garden of cucumbers, as a besieged city. (Isa. 1:7–8)

It would appear that the aim of the compilers was to seize their readers' attention by beginning *in medias res.* But this is surmise. The identities and circumstances of those compilers have vanished beyond retrieval, barring some latter-day discovery such as that of the Dead Sea Scrolls. According to current scholarship, the first thirty-nine chapters are ascribed to or directly associated with the man Isaiah. Those beginning with chapter 40 are by a person or persons of a later period, referred to by some as Second or Deutero-Isaiah. Since chapters 56 through 66 refer to a still-later period, some scholars split them off into a Third or Trito-Isaiah. There is, at any rate, sufficient unity of tone throughout to suggest that whosoever they may have been, the later voices belong to successors or disciples of the earlier prophet.

As for who and what he was, this outspoken counselor, fearlessly addressing kings as his equal, has no modern counterpart. How could he—this deliverer of messages who spoke, more often than not, in the voice and person of the One who sent him?

Hear, O heavens, and give ear, O earth: for the Lord hath
spoken. (Isa. 1:2)

What he tells us of himself and in his own voice is hardly less strange
and remote:

In the year that King Uzziah died I saw also the Lord sitting upon a throne, high and lifted up, and his train filled
the temple. Above it stood the seraphim: each one had six
wings; with twain he covered his face, and with twain he
covered his feet, and with twain he did fly. (Isa. 6:1–2)

I think I am not alone in finding something barbaric about the images here. Such winged hybrids, monsters really, are frequent not
only in the art of Assyria but in that of Greece and Egypt as well.
They inhabit the Temple of Solomon, as described elsewhere:

And he set the cherubim within the inner house: and they
stretched forth the wings of the cherubim, so that the
wing of the one touched the one wall, and the wing of the
other cherub touched the other wall; and their wings
touched one another in the midst of the house. And he
overlaid the cherubim with gold. And he carved all the
walls of the house round about with carved figures of cherubim and palm trees and open flowers, within and without. (1 Kings 6:27–29)

That "inner house" was the home of the Ark of the Covenant—a
place beyond nature, the dazzling antecedent of Yeats's Byzantium.
The visions of Ezekiel, a deportee to the banks of the Euphrates,
would have been fed by the memory of that same Temple, the scene
of Isaiah's own vision of the seraphim:

And one cried unto another, and said, Holy, holy, holy, is
the Lord of hosts: the whole earth is full of his glory. And
the posts of the door moved at the voice of him that cried,
and the house was filled with smoke. (Isa. 6:3–4)

The house was filled with smoke from the altar of sacrifice—an offering not fundamentally different from those itemized in the *Iliad*—
but those moving doorposts suggest an earthquake, which in its turn

is linked with supernatural intervention: the nightly pillar of fire, the daytime pillar of cloud, brought indoors.

Some idea of ritual uncleanness, of the need for an act of propitiation or expiation, must underlie any animal sacrifice. But for Isaiah the feeling associated with the barbaric occasion was one of transcendence:

> Then said I, Woe is me: for I am undone; because I am a man of unclean lips, and I dwell in the midst of a people of unclean lips: for mine eyes have seen the King, the Lord of hosts. (Isa. 6:5)

The idea of the Holy, of something beyond either fear or dread, all but confounds definition. From the etymological root *kailo-* are derived not only the English word *holy* but also *whole, hale, hallow,* and *health.* On the other hand, the Hebrew word *k'dosh,* for which *holy* is offered by most translations as a likely equivalent, conveys a meaning so different as almost to seem its opposite. The Latin word *sanctus,* with its English cognates (*sanctity, sanctify,* and—yes—*sanctimonious*) may come closer to the intended meaning: an unapproachable exaltation, along with an outraged abhorrence of whatever is unclean or untrue. Implicit in it is what Isaiah himself called righteousness, an attribute scarcely acknowledged by the pragmatic Greeks, who coped with the Furies by lodging them in a cave underneath the Areopagus, renaming them the Eumenides ("beautiful, good, delightful") and asking only—as Victor Hugo noted during a lull in his own chronicle of miseries—to be left alone. Throughout much of Greek tragedy a pusillanimous relief not to be called upon to act is the mood of the chorus. The ritual will go forward—that is what everybody is here for—but a comforting solidarity among the common folk is the ground of that ritual: historically, we're told, the chorus came before the actors. Not so in the Book of Isaiah. Absolutely and scathingly other is the relation between the prophet and the people:

> Then flew one of the seraphim unto me, having a live coal in his hand, which he had taken with the tongs from off the altar: And he laid it upon my mouth, and said, Lo, this hath touched thy lips; and thine iniquity is taken away, and thy sin purged. And I heard the voice of the Lord, saying, Whom shall I send, and who will go for us?

Then said I, Here am I; send me. And he said, Go, and
tell this people, Hear ye indeed, but understand not; and
see ye indeed, but perceive not. (Isa. 6:6–9)

To be condemned in advance as a backslider of whom no good is to
be expected, and by a remote, unbending, punitive deity, is a very
different thing from the Greek notion of a public assembly: Isaiah
volunteering with such alacrity for such a being is on the face of it
unattractive.[1] Only the most odiously precocious of young people
could be otherwise than put off by so zealous a response. And not
only the young. Emily Dickinson, late in her career, calling the Bible
"an antique Volume— / Written by faded Men," drew her own contrast with the Greeks:

> Had but the Tale a warbling Teller —
> All the Boys would come —
> Orpheus' sermon captivated —
> It did not condemn.[2]

She was, just here (at past fifty), being waggish for the benefit of her
nephew. If pressed, she could hardly have disagreed that a "warbling
Teller" might after all be found even in the Book of Isaiah. There is
indeed something Orphic in such a passage as this often-quoted one:

The wolf also shall dwell with the lamb, and the leopard
shall lie down with the kid; and the calf and the young
lion and the fatling together; and a little child shall lead
them. And the cow and the bear shall feed; their young
ones shall lie down together: and the lion shall eat straw
like the ox. And the sucking child shall play on the hole
of the asp, and the weaned child shall put his hand on the
cockatrice's den. They shall not hurt nor destroy in all my
holy mountain: for the earth shall be full of the knowledge
of the Lord, as the waters cover the sea. And in that day
there shall be a root of Jesse, which shall stand for an en-
sign of the people; to it shall the Gentiles seek: and his
rest shall be glorious. (Isa. 11:6–10)

Even in the absence of such pacific and utopian content, the balanced rhythms, the parallels and repetitions, have a way of settling
into the very texture of memory, where what arrived as unwelcome

comes in due course to be not only tolerated but treasured. Absorbed early and unwittingly, it is ineradicably a part of oneself, as what I later came to know of Greek masterpieces could never be. The latter were works I had come to know and admire without having wrestled with the nemesis of their being there. Looking back, I see that wrestling as integral to the process of growing up, of finally accepting the sense of responsibility I had put off for so long. The nature of that unwanted responsibility was neatly summed up, just lately, by Václav Havel:

> Genuine conscience and genuine responsibility are always, in the end, explicable only as an expression of the silent assumption that we are being observed "from above," that "up there" everything is visible, nothing is forgotten.[3]

Who *is* in charge of conscience? According to the scheme I thought I wanted, nobody was. The likely consequences of such an assumption would become clear eventually, after having been given a fairly convincing demonstration in various quarters and at various levels, over the past two or three decades. Offers to take charge of the national conscience have by now, of course, awakened a set of increasingly raucous constituencies and counterconstituencies.

As for Isaiah's seeming contemporaneity, one look at the docket of the U. S. Supreme Court, or at any page of the *Congressional Record*, is enough to challenge the supposition that nothing at all has changed. The debate over school prayer would have meant nothing to Isaiah; the possible separation of church and state had not yet been thought of. As for freedom of religion, the prophet's fulminations concerning idolatry are enough to dispose of *that*. His views on abortion can be readily imagined. On First Amendment rights I don't suppose that he would have differed materially from Jesse Helms. The actual Isaiah begins to have a troubling resemblance to the Ayatollah Khomeini. Would he have subscribed to the *fatwa* against Salman Rushdie? One makes one's way painfully, in fear and trembling, through such a mine field. Just how indispensable *is* the freedom we keep saying we believe in—and then try to curb when it takes a form we feel threatened by?

Isaiah was, after all, only a man. His predictions were not always accurate; his advice often went unheeded; and much of what he wrote has since been misread, by accident and/or for purposes more or less wrongheadedly doctrinaire. Out of blandly pious habit, certain passages have become familiar in just such mistaken and wrong-headed contexts. For me it is unlikely that the seventh chapter of Isaiah, in whatever translation, can ever be heard without the rolling bass of the setting Handel gave it:

> Behold, a virgin shall conceive
> and bear a son . . . (Isa. 7:14)

In text as well as context this is all wrong. Not only is *virgin* a mistranslation—a "maid" or unmarried woman, as Jewish and Christian scholars now agree, is expressed in Hebrew by the word *bethulah*, whereas the word *almah*, used here, "means no more than a young woman of age to be a mother, whether she be married or not"; and what is more, the equally familiar lines that follow in the text of Handel's *Messiah*—

> For unto us a child is born,
> unto us a son is given (Isa. 9:6)

—are more correctly rendered as "unto us a child *has been* born—unto us a son *has been* given" [italics supplied], "the reference being not to any future Messiah, nor to anyone yet unborn."[4]

There is, in other words, nothing more proto-Christian in this passage (or, for that matter, the one from Isaiah 11:10, which I've already quoted) than there is in Virgil's Fourth Eclogue, whose wishful thinking reaches out to color the flocks on the hillside in hues of saffron and vermilion. It is perhaps inevitable that such visionary passages should be seized upon by all-too-eager misinterpreters. As David Slavitt phrases it in his poignant rereading of that Eclogue:

> Someone must come along
> to get us out of this mess, to make it right,
> to save us from what we have been, from what we are.[5]

Such a longing is not far, indeed, from what Isaiah himself, in his more utopian passages, sought to convey—Isaiah the man having been also and above all a poet. And not only Isaiah himself, but certain of his followers:

> Who is this that cometh from Edom, with dyed garments
> from Bozrah? this that is glorious in his apparel, travelling

in the greatness of his strength? I that speak in righteousness, mighty to save. Wherefore art thou red in thine ap-
parel, and thy garments like him that treadeth in the
winevat? (Isa. 63:1–2)

Who wrote these lines we do not know. They have been absorbed
into the liturgy of Holy Week, where I must have heard them first;
but they transcend that occasion as they do every other, and as only
the greatest poetry can do. The Old Testament is studded with such
passages, and nowhere are they more sublimely recurrent than in the
Book of Isaiah. W. H. Auden has written somewhere of the peculiar
delight taken by poets in images of catastrophe, to the point of being
ready to invite them. Here is an example from Isaiah:

Oh that thou wouldest rend the heavens, that thou
wouldest come down, that the mountains might flow
down at thy presence, as when the melting fire burneth,
the fire causeth the waters to boil, to make thy name
known to thine adversaries, that the nations may tremble
at thy presence! (Isa. 64:1–2)

The truth is, of course, that nobody is immune to apocalyptic excitements. An entire genre of moviemaking (of which, or so I gather,
Raiders of the Lost Ark is merely one of the pricier examples) amounts
to a homage to such gratuitous sublimity. But given the usage to
which the human craving for extremes has been put, we experience
the sublimity mainly as a succession of purple passages. What we're
able to hold onto of the Bible, as of all great literature, is unavoid-
ably in fragments. For me the Book of Isaiah is peculiar, if not indeed
unique, in the frequency with which these passages occur.

Have ye not known? have ye not heard? hath it not been
told you from the beginning? have ye not understood from
the foundations of the earth? It is he that sitteth upon the
circle of the earth, and the inhabitants thereof are as
grasshoppers; that stretcheth out the heavens as a curtain,
and spreadeth them out as a tent to dwell in: that
bringeth the princes to nothing; he maketh the judges of
the earth as vanity. (Isa. 40:21–23)

Very different is the note struck by passages like this:

Who hath believed our report? and to whom is the arm of the Lord revealed? For he shall grow up before him as a tender plant, and as a root out of the dry ground: he hath no form nor comeliness, and when we shall see him, there is no beauty that we should desire him. He is despised and rejected of men; a man of sorrows, and acquainted with grief: and we hid as it were our faces from him; he was despised, and we esteemed him not. Surely he hath borne our griefs, and carried our sorrows: yet we did esteem him stricken, smitten of God, and afflicted. But he was wounded for our transgressions, he was bruised for our iniquities: the chastisement of our peace was upon him: and with his stripes we are healed. (Isa. 53:1–5)

Nobody knows who the author of this passage was, nor is it clear just what figure—past, present, or future—is being represented. Though generations of annotators have invoked it for often tendentious and occasionally demagogic purposes, as a figure of inexhaustible power the Suffering Servant ranks with Lear, Oedipus, and Jean Valjean, and its unnamed author among the greatest of poets.

Plato was right: Poets are always a nuisance, and often dangerous. On public matters they are anything but the last word. That is in a way their virtue—that what gives them their power comes from somewhere beyond allegiance to any system of belief or behavior. By nature they are unstable, sometimes unruly, now and then giving way (as in Alice's Wonderland) to subversive fits of merriment, as well as to an uncensored sublimity. Without them, who is there to tell us the best, along with the very worst, about ourselves?

The Wind of Judgment and the Wind of Burning: The Holy One of Isaiah

(ISAIAH 1–39: PROTO-ISAIAH)

CHRISTINA BÜCHMANN

I didn't read the book of Isaiah from beginning to end until I was an adult, but was jolted by it as if I still believed in a Sunday school God. Expecting messianic promises like those I knew from hymns— behold, a Virgin shall conceive, the desert shall rejoice and blossom as a rose—I was instead terrified after reading a page. When one hears little bits from this book in religious services, the longing for justice or redemption turns the prophecy into pleasingly vivid imagery. But taken all together, Isaiah has the impact of the morning newspaper, with death, disaster, and broken faith on every page.

THE 2,700 YEARS BETWEEN ISAIAH AND OURSELVES ARE NOT the only reason it's so difficult to know what to make of the God revealed in Isaiah's prophecies. Nor is it that God is just an intellectual problem—something too great to be encompassed by our thoughts.

Biblical quotations are taken from *The New Jerusalem Bible* (New York: Doubleday, 1985). Since scholars divide the collection we call Isaiah into sections written centuries apart (Proto-, Deutero-, and Trito-Isaiah), I am limiting myself to the sections thought to be written mainly by the original prophet who gave rise to the Isaian school.

There are psychological reasons why he's beyond being thought about. We can't bear to believe we're in the power of a God who says, "I shall make people scarcer than pure gold, human life scarcer than the gold of Ophir. . . . I am going to shake the heavens . . . the earth will reel on its foundations, under the wrath of Yahweh Sabaoth, the day when his anger ignites" (Isa. 13:12–13).

He who wields the world, according to Isaiah, is the author of our calamities. Even as he tells us that the Assyrian will come down like a wolf on the fold, he insists that the king of Assyria is only God's instrument.

To a modern reader it might seem an unnecessary complication for Isaiah to be so insistent that the calamities of the world are God's doing and grounds for praise. If we're willing to praise God nowadays, we'll do so despite the evidence against him, or by distinguishing him from what we've noticed about the world. At least since the Enlightenment we've resolved the problem of a perfect God and a terrible world by assuming that God made the world and then withdrew his protection, although we vary the details of what kind of connection he nonetheless might keep up. By claiming that God is present in the world, Isaiah gives us grounds for hating or indicting God, not for praising him, yet one of the few certainties we have about Isaiah as a historical man is that he considered his compositions religious.

Is he writing out of a need to explain human suffering and divine injustice? Even if that might not be how he himself would have described his work, on some level, surely those are his topics, although he sets them in a relation very different from what we are used to. He wrote a few generations before the composition of the Book of Job, which raises these questions explicitly and which shows influences from the prophetic writings of Isaiah's period, particularly of Jeremiah and Ezekiel, who in turn drew on Isaiah. It is as if there's a line of descent in the Bible that sometimes wearily and sometimes indignantly presents the wrongness of the world and sometimes settles for human sinfulness as an explanation—exculpating God—and sometimes offers no resolution except that we cannot understand.

As modern readers, with the threatening army long dead, we may accept the downfall of Judah as fair punishment; but although this is one "solution" Isaiah gives us, he doesn't let the problem lie there. So far removed from the calamity, it's easier not to question how something like this could have been allowed to happen. If we add a religious context, it is even easier to accept these terrible, past events as morality, since religion generally assumes that God is good and usually also that this goodness is to be shown toward us.

Isaiah's prophecy connects—or reconnects—God to the world in at least two, contradictory ways as he shuttles between different views of God. At times Isaiah, on God's behalf, inquires into our spiritual constitutions, accusing us of shallow religion, and then, in his fervor to establish Yahweh as lord of all, doesn't give a damn about what we're like. On the one hand he presents us with a God who cares about the states of our souls and thus to some extent takes our own experiences, even of ourselves, into account. God "thinks" in terms of our psyches. He is the personal god of everybody, who by a miracle can pay attention to everybody's soul. On the other hand Isaiah shows a god that no one could love, who doesn't love us, and to whom love is irrelevant. Either of these versions of God might destroy us, but they'd be doing it in different spirits, one as a father who's lost patience and now chastises his brood, hoping to save as many as possible even if some must be sacrificed; another because to create and destroy is what a god does. For him there are no psychological explanations—either both humans and God have psyches, or neither do in any way that matters.

Prophecy is an outgrowth of God's covenants with Israel, particularly his promises when he gave his laws, so one would expect prophecy to reflect the same convictions that we humans are responsible for our actions and can hear correction from God. When Moses explains the covenant to the children of Israel, in Deuteronomy, he says, "Until today Yahweh has not given you a heart to understand, eyes to see, or ears to hear" (Deut. 29:3). Surely we wouldn't be reproached for not heeding the law and not hearing the prophecies except in a context where God takes our inner lives into account, since only if we have something like souls could we be expected to change and even improve. This is religion that we can live with, but only because we don't imagine that we must. The essence of the covenant is that God commands, we listen, we disobey. Prophecy can be seen as the second half of the covenant, what happens once we have disobeyed: God reminds us, we listen, and at long last we change our ways. A holy life is held out as available to us, since the law to be followed is "not in heaven ... nor is it beyond the seas; No, the word is very near to you, it is in your mouth and in your heart for you to put into practice" (Deut. 30: 12–14). That is how Moses can speak of the covenant as a matter of (momentous) choice: "I am of-

fering you life and prosperity, death and disaster. . . . If your heart
turns away, if you refuse to listen . . . you will most certainly perish. . . . I am offering you life or death, blessing or curse. Choose life,
then, so that you may live . . . obeying his voice" (Deut. 30: 15–19).

But one has to wonder: by the time Isaiah prophesies, the children
of Israel have sinned against the covenant so long that it seems that
part of a prophet's task is to speak unheard. An exasperated, sarcastic
Yahweh instructs Isaiah to

> Go and say to this people,
> "Listen and listen, but never understand!
> Look and look, but never perceive!"
> Make this people's heart coarse,
> make their ears dull, shut their eyes tight,
> or they will use their eyes to see,
> use their ears to hear,
> use their heart to understand,
> and change their ways and be healed. (Isa. 6:9–10)

God is blaming us, but as the many reproaches make clear, our of-
fenses are so habitual that they might as well count as part of our nature, making his reproaches seem disingenuous. If we cannot
improve, aren't the conditional threats to kill us disguised statements
of intention?

The prophecies generally start with an accusation, for example
that Zion's daughters are proud. We may flinch, but this kind of
charge seems manageable; relatively speaking, the accusation is reassuring, because we can answer it. We can admit to a number of sins
in a context of negotiation, where God addresses us with promises at
the same time that he mentions our sins:

> "Come, let us talk this over . . .
> Though your sins are scarlet,
> they shall be white as snow;
> though they are red as crimson, they shall be like wool.
> If you are willing to obey . . ." (Isa. 1:18–19)

On some level surely we agree that we're guilty and deserve all the
disasters the prophets heap up. But the reproaches boil over, and not
only punishment but relentlessness itself becomes the theme:

> Look, the Day of Yahweh is coming,
> merciless, with wrath and burning anger,
> to reduce the country to a desert
> and root out the sinners from it. . . .
> All those who are found will be stabbed,
> all those captured will fall by the sword,
> their babies dashed to pieces before their eyes,
> their houses plundered, their wives raped.
> Look, against them I am stirring up the Medes
> who care nothing for silver,
> who set no value by gold. (Isa. 13:9–17)

The information that the Median army is incorruptible goes straight to quench our instinctive hope that we, at least, might escape, that one little exception might be arranged. Then comes the climax, which makes love of righteousness seem almost a pretext:

> Never again will anyone live or reside there
> for all generations to come. . . .
> But beasts of the desert will make their haunt there
> and owls fill their houses,
> there ostriches will settle their home,
> there goats will dance.
> Hyenas will howl in its towers,
> jackals in its delightful palaces,
> for its doom is about to come
> and its days will not last long. (vv. 20–22)

What's the point—if you're not the King of Judah being warned against an alliance with Egypt—of imagining so much destruction in detail? Will it improve us? Take the compressed story of two palace stewards, Shebna and Eliakim, for instance. Shebna is at the height of his power when Isaiah is told to take him a message. In a single speech Isaiah is to tell Shebna of his fall, of the rise of his successor, Eliakim, and then of the calamitous fall of Eliakim. That speech soars out of the particulars of eighth century (B.C.E.) politics, as extravagant as if Yahweh were besting a competitor in a speech duel or a cursing contest. Was the point ever really Eliakim's ascendance over Shebna? Yahweh instructs Isaiah,

Go and find that steward,
Shebna, the master of the palace. . . .
"Yahweh will throw you away, strong as you are . . .
I shall hound you from your office . . .
I shall summon my servant
Eliakim son of Hilkiah.
I shall dress him in your tunic. . . ."

"I shall drive him [Eliakim] like a nail into a firm place;
and he will become a throne of glory for his family.

On him will depend all the glory of his family, the
descendants and offspring, all the vessels of small capacity
too, from cups to pitchers. That day declares Yahweh
Sabaoth, the nail driven into a firm place will give way,
will be torn out and fall. And the whole load hanging on
it will be lost. For Yahweh has spoken." (Isa. 22: 15–25)

What was high will be brought low, and what's to replace it will also
be brought low; if seeing one turn of the wheel of fortune is to de-
tach us from this world, how much stronger is the effect of two revolutions. Eliakim's glory is surely given praise so that we'll marvel at
its destruction—like a tower of building blocks raised by a baby
solely for the clatter it will make when it falls.

Apparently it is not enough to remind us that we are mortal; we
should know that about the world too. As far as one can tell, Shebna
provoked Yahweh by hewing himself a tomb in the palace rock—
making a double mistake by wanting to give himself a permanent
place in something he should not have thought of as permanent (v.
16). The assumption that nature would remain apparently dishon-
ored Yahweh as much as the more glaring forms of idolatry. The
Lord—not a rock—should be Shebna's rock and his salvation.

Convincing us of his power, Yahweh quickly overshadows moral
considerations. Look what happens in this speech, despite its mention of guilt:

So the Holy Ones say this,
"Since you have rejected this word
and put your trust in fraud and disloyalty
and rely on these,
for you this guilt will prove to be

> a breach opening up,
> a bulge at the top of a wall
> which suddenly and all at once comes crashing down.
> He will shatter it like an earthenware pot,
> ruthlessly knocking it to pieces,
> so that of the fragments not one shard can be found
> with which to take up fire from the hearth
> or scoop water from the storage-well." (Isa. 30:12–14)

Strictly logical reading reveals our sinfulness and lack of trust in God as the nearly unidentifiable *it* that is to be shattered. But the comparisons to other things that can be destroyed are so many and so drastic in their own right that the passage reads as if breach, bulge, earthenware pot, or a nail in a firm place were interchangeable with Eliakim ben Hilkiah and also (incidentally) with the sin of not trusting in God. Our guilt is to be shattered? We are to be shattered for our guilt? Everything—the world—is to be shattered? Is the world guilty? Here, as with Shebna and Eliakim, the original, "real" situations don't keep priority over the images that succeed them; Isaiah works his way through the real disasters until he ends in a metaphor, as if to suggest that what is truest is the version that is least liable to rational, delimiting interpretation.

According to Isaiah's messages, sometimes a town, sometimes a people, and sometimes the very landscape is to be blasted—hardly a sign of condemnation for specific wrongs. The curses, too, go from war and devastation by Judah's contemporary enemies, to natural disaster, to annihilation. And the worse it gets, the more often Yahweh bears his title of honor, Yahweh Sabaoth, "the Lord of Hosts." Considering how literal-minded we tend to be—certainly when anything important to ourselves is in question—this ability to look at our world and see large, impersonal patterns is already a disturbing sign of God's detachment from human reality. What we're attached to he rises above, including our preoccupation with staying alive.

Everything that makes up our world might be different from how we know it, without affecting God. This seems to be the deeper lesson and the reason why Isaiah's lists of God's destructions are matched by numerous lists of substitutions:

> Then, instead of perfume, a stink;
> instead of belt, a rope,
> instead of hair elaborately dressed, a shaven scalp,

instead of gorgeous clothes, sacking around the waist,
brand marks instead of beauty. (Isa. 3:24)

When that day comes, wherever there used to be a thousand
    vines
worth a thousand pieces of silver,
all will be brambles and thorn-bushes. (Isa. 7:23)

The few comforting passages also promise that the world will be
made the opposite of what it is now:

water will gush in the desert ...
the lairs where the jackals used to live
will become plots of reed and papyrus. (Isa. 35:6–7)

Whichever direction the transformation works in, the emphasis is on
God's power. Isaiah forces on us the vision of another reality, where
God acts on a far larger scale, more or less oblivious of us, making
and unmaking. The beauty of Isaiah's lyrical descriptions of our end
suggests that we are reading hymns of praise, a reversed theodicy,
where God is praised not for being good but for being as he is—for
being God. This is unpleasant enough to make us avoid believing
what we read.

Circular as it sounds, and is, our human definitions of God also define us, because they name our place in the world—his precious
nurselings or expendable bits of his creation. The way we see God,
if we are trying to be accurate, and the way we see ourselves are mu-
tually exclusive, like the famous picture of the duck-rabbit, where
the same line defines the two animals: You can see them one at a
time but never both at once. We can only take in one kind of reality
at a time, they are on such different scales. Believing in him is done
at our expense, the idea of God makes us less than nothing, unless
we bring in ingenious compromises that humanize God and deify
ourselves, a little here, a little there. The alternative to our being
nothing is that we—along with God—remain undefined or never
brought together in our minds, that is, we take care not to see him
in any relation to ourselves.

A comprehensible name for a god like this would be absurd;
Isaiah's coinage, the Holy One of Israel, defers the problem, since we
cannot say what holiness is, any more than what God is. Holiness
does not have to do with virtue; it is a word that applies to God. It

is not anchored by a reference to anything we already know and is not so different from medieval mystical names that express the ineffable nature of God such as *All That Is, Yet Nothing*, or *Invisible, All-Resplendent Light*, or from modern, post-Enlightenment classifications such as *Mysterium Tremendum*. All of these are attempts to get around the problem of something inaccessible not only to language, but also to thought. Otherwise perhaps as good a name for God as any is Friday's definition for Robinson Crusoe of the islanders' deity: *He to Whom All Things Say Oh*. As flat and irreducible as that. A god who is so absolutely master even makes it impossible to say, accurately, "a god"; it would have to be "God."

I think we usually forget that *he* would have to consider himself God too; this is not a relation where he would respond politely, "Oh no, unto *you* all honor and worship is due." Mutuality—which we're taught to consider basic to decent behavior—is out of the question. In these assertions of God's primacy there are no guaranteed rewards for good behavior, and yet his self-revelations are not grounds for complaint, since they define God's nature. Whether or not one believes in God, there is no appeal beyond him. The idea of God is savage and extravagant, as we see during the few moments that we might try to think about God without the humane guises of benevolent father, disappointed husband, merciful judge. Our imagination puts a hand over our eyes as God passes.

But unless we think of ourselves as utterly subject to him, we're not thinking of a real god. A definition of a god great enough to encompass all divine power, unlike the metaphors for him, is not friendly and does not change historically. The theologians are right: Monotheism is radical. If God can encompass everything and is omni-everything, the eclipse of human speculation, then his nature cannot be the subject of anthropology or any comparative science, but of inference, so that twentieth-century humans, and their psyches, are in the same position vis-à-vis God as Isaiah's audience. Although God does not have to earn our subordination, we have a kind of veto power because we can refuse to believe. True, now we have new stock ideas to ward him off with: Our notions of God have changed through history along with our ideas of a good ruler until, as suggested in the beginning, arbitrary rule even by God has become unimaginable.

IT'S NOT OUR SINS we don't want to think about; it's God. His greatness is uncomfortable to contemplate, reducing us to tininess.

His power is an awful thing to imagine, since it means that we are continuously at his mercy. But still worse is the idea of his being so different from us in other ways too. It borders on the unacceptable for God to consider himself so important.

Isaiah gives God's power two parallel but distinct names: *the wind of judgment* and *the wind of burning* (Isa. 4:4). The wind of burning is the transcendent God who manifests himself by creating and destroying, compared with which the wind of judgment is practically anthropomorphic: The humanized God of laws and morality cares what we do. Even as a thunderously stern judge, this kind of God is preferable to an impersonal force. If one must be killed, wouldn't one rather have it happen by the hand of someone who knows that it is Me? Most societies think so, reserving certain executions and forms of burial for honored criminals—compare the old European ceremonious beheadings of noblemen by sword to their poor-men's hangings, for instance.

With a judge there is the hope of getting around his judgment. If God really knew it was Me, surely he couldn't let me die. To know all is to forgive all, and we praise him as omniscient. Modeling God on earthly ideals of justice gives humans a relatively good deal: To weigh our worth by the method we consider fair, he would have to take our individual circumstances and consciousness into account. Every time the word *righteous* occurs in the Bible, it asserts that God cares about the individual soul. Paying that kind of individual attention, he'd be halfway to seeing us as we see ourselves, and we are after all quite fond of ourselves. These are the terms we want to get God thinking in. Articulated rules, paradoxically, bring with them the possibility of reprieve and exceptions that might be made. Earlier, thanks to the idea of right judgment, he agreed to haggle with Abraham over Sodom's fate—fifty righteous men, then forty-five, then forty, thirty, twenty, ten. Sodom wasn't saved, but three lives were. If God really looks at us, we might bargain—from fifty good qualities to some redeeming circumstances.

Even in the Bible's first account of thorough devastation, the Flood, God the moral judge paused in his disgust and distinguished one man from everyone else: "Yahweh saw that human wickedness was great on earth. . . . Yahweh regretted having made human beings on earth and was grieved at heart. And Yahweh said, 'I shall rid the surface of the earth of the human beings whom I created—human and animal, the creeping things and the birds of heaven—for I regret having made them.' But Noah won Yahweh's favor" (Gen. 6:5–8).

But God the creator of the material world is the one who shuts up the protesting Job, who invokes justice. God's answer automatically puts a stop to human opinions on his actions: "Where were you when I laid the earth's foundations?" (Job 38:4)

Far from being pedagogical, the human suffering Isaiah prophecies will be too great to be a learning experience, even to us in our arm-chairs. One prophecy closes with God's remark "Nothing but fear will make you understand what you hear" (Isa. 28:20), but the only lesson we are taught is about the relative positions of Creator, Master of the Universe, and us, pots that are not allowed to question the potter's ways—a preoccupation that explains Isaiah's emphasis on God's actions instead of ours. If that God, representable only by his effect on the physical world, is the mysterious, inmost God that Isaiah reveals to us only sometimes but with greater urgency than his other versions of Yahweh, what would Isaiah have wanted citizens of Jerusalem in the eighth century B.C.E. to take to heart? In what way would he have wanted to be believed? Would it have been enough if they shivered and repented? He also wanted to tell them about God; he spends a lot of time distinguishing Yahweh from the "gods" of other nations.

Apocalypse, which is Isaiah's medium for this, is an artistic genre, but is it religious? Does it tell us about God? Perhaps it does but seems incomprehensible because we can't bear to understand. Apoc-alypse surfaces again and again in the Bible, and through the ages and in various civilizations, sometimes introduced with a semblance of a rationale, but always inherently enigmatic: depictions of horizon-to-horizon atrocities, untamed by commentary or by any in-dication of respect for our souls. The material Isaiah uses—horrors that have made war poets and artists question the existence of God—nonetheless differs in a single, all-important respect from what inspired Goya's *Disasters of War* or H. D.'s *Trilogy*, for example: Isaiah describes devastation before the fact. He's using it to express some-thing else, as having metaphoric value; for later poets and artists, who weren't prophets, events like these were facts one could not, and maybe should not, get over. Sharing God's perspective, and even making us see it if we are to make sense of what we're reading, Isaiah forces a revelation of God on us by making us see deaths as ideas to be contemplated in a light other than as the phenomenon of mortal-ity. This is the most terrifying brutality in all his writing.

Apocalypse isn't tragedy, which is imbued with human meaning; it

gives us no psychological foothold. It gives us no heroes, no person-
alities, no painful choices being made. The deaths we see raise no
one to a higher plane of existence—not the dead, not the living—
which is the difference between annihilations and martyrdoms. We
can identify with the corpses insofar as we remember that we also
have skulls to be cracked, but there are no complicated feelings,
only intense gratitude at not being the person in question.
Nothing learned except that we might have been dead. And yet
Bruegel's *Massacre of the Innocents* against the snow, for instance,
is such a beautiful sight that it can be downright consoling. As Isaiah renders it, the end of the world can give one pleasure to
think about too:

> He has vowed them to destruction,
> handed them over to slaughter.
> Their dead will be thrown away,
> the stench will rise from their corpses,
> the mountains will run with their blood,
> the entire array of heaven will fall apart.
> The heavens will be rolled up like a scroll
> and all their array will fade away,
> as fade the leaves falling from the vine,
> as fade those falling from the fig tree.

For my sword has drunk deep in the heavens. (Isa. 34:1–5)

How could one not admire this? Its grandeur matches that of the
Creation:

Now the earth was a formless void, there was darkness over the deep,
  with a divine wind sweeping over the waters.
God said, "Let there be light . . ."
God said, "Let there be a vault through the middle of the waters to
  divide the waters in two. . . ."
God said, "Let the waters under heaven come together into a single
  mass, and let dry land appear. . . ."
"Let there be lights in the vault of heaven to divide day from
  night. . . ."
Thus heaven and earth were completed with all their array. (Gen.
  1:2–24, 2:1)

During these sections of Isaiah the perspective can grow luxuriously vast, so that the enemy's conquest of the world is comparable to a stroll through the countryside:

> My hand has found, as though a bird's nest,
> the riches of the peoples.
> Like someone collecting deserted eggs,
> I have collected the whole world
> while no one has fluttered a wing
> or opened a beak to squawk. (Isa. 10:14)

God teaches Isaiah, and Isaiah tries to teach us in parallel ways, and the cost of hearing prophecy would be as devastating for us as it was for him, if we did hear it. A prophet bent on shocking his audience would have to use something that had not already been relegated to the category of material suitable for religion. He would need to get at whatever we considered our real lives, both to make an impression and because his subject really was the relation of human reality to divine reality.

By making Isaiah live in both realities at once—still in this world although claimed by God—Yahweh achieves his dramatic effects. A well-educated man, a witty, accomplished poet, close to the king, had something to lose. Isaiah even had the anchor in this world that rabbis later were to insist on as necessary for the study of Cabala: family, to pull the visionary back into his own life no matter what he might see in his ecstasy. These qualifications set him up for Yahweh's service, making it possible for Isaiah to say:

> His hand seized hold of me
> and he taught me not to follow the path of this people. . . .
> Look, I and the children whom Yahweh has given me
> shall become signs and portents in Israel on behalf of
> Yahweh Sabaoth who dwells on Mount Zion. (Isa. 8:11–18)

Isaiah's second son was named Speedy-spoil-quick-booty because Yahweh intruded into domestic life to connect the baby to political history by prophesying, "Before the child knows how to say 'mother' or 'father', the wealth of Damascus and the booty of Samaria will be carried away while the king of Assyria looks on." Then Yahweh raised the stakes even further. One day he said,

"Go, undo the sackcloth round your waist and take the sandals off your feet." And he did so, and walked about, naked and barefoot. Yahweh then said, "As my servant Isaiah has been walking about naked and barefoot for the last three years as a sign and portent for Egypt and Cush, so the king of Assyria will lead the captives of Egypt and the exiles of Cush, young and old, naked and barefoot, their buttocks bared, to the shame of Egypt. Then they will be afraid and ashamed of Cush their hope and Egypt their pride . . ." (vv. 3–4)

"Yahweh then said" is an understated allusion to Isaiah's three years of absolute, uncomprehending obedience. Until Yahweh's explanation came, how were the people of Jerusalem—or Isaiah himself, or his wife—to know that he represented a defeated Egyptian or Ethiopian, not a mad former prophet? The price of being dislodged from one's ordinary life is suggested by the fragment that follows immediately after Yahweh's instructions to Isaiah:

Oppressed and starving, he will wander the country;
and, once starving, he will become frenzied
and curse his king and his God; turning his gaze upward,
then down to earth, there will be only anguish,
gloom, the confusion of night, swirling darkness. (vv. 21–22)

With horror we see God acting from his own perspective as he disposes of us, helping himself to his creation, quite willing to use up what he has made. Being dislodged, for us, might mean not thinking that our perspective is the ultimate one.

Judging by the prophets' complaints, it goes against human nature to believe in a god who can't be appeased, so that earlier people also would have exercised the power of simply not believing, in whatever ways they could find. Why should we think that such a God was easier for the ancient Israelites to imagine? We usually attribute our modern lack of faith to secularism or rationalism, forgetting that we're rarely rational, and not particularly skeptical either. Yet we imagine other ages to have been as religious as we're ashamed of not being.

There cannot have been a time when people could read Isaiah without hiding from what he says and from his God. Occasionally, among the prophecies directed at us, Isaiah tells a story about his working conditions. These stories are bursting with realistic psychological characterization—fittingly, since they are about psychological defenses. When he prophesies to King Hezekiah, for instance, what is the king's response? Isaiah tells him, "Listen to the word of Yahweh Sabaoth. 'The days are coming when everything in your palace, everything that your ancestors have amassed until now, will be carried off to Babylon. Not a thing will be left. . . . Sons sprung from you, sons begotten by you, will be abducted to be eunuchs in the palace of the king of Babylon.' " And Hezekiah answers, "This word of Yahweh that you announce is reassuring," for he was thinking, "There is going to be peace and security during my lifetime" (Isa. 38:5–8).

The king hides from taking in what Isaiah means by concentrating on the wording, not the message, and revealingly he does this by emphasizing his own perspective: "security during *my* lifetime." He has saved himself from getting the point and trivialized Yahweh's pronouncement by treating it as one would a contract, looking for loopholes, looking out for oneself. In this way Isaiah's reports on human nature, applying to us as well, accuse us as much as the direct reproaches do.

Hezekiah's dodge presumably comes out of terror: It's an elaborate form of denial that reconstructs the threat to one which he can answer. This seems to me to be the greatest temptation for a modern reader of Isaiah, a misreading that's a combination of literal-minded sensationalism and concern for one's own survival. Prophetic threats can be taken *too* seriously: taking in the message enough to consider the situation an emergency—which means one must save oneself—and thereby never having to contemplate the implications, which are even more terrifying, since they mean that one is not safe even when one has got away. We can use our self-interest both to make ourselves deaf and to hear so oversensitively that we miss the larger point, namely that we inevitably are in God's power. Reading Isaiah's words imaginatively, or impressionably, isn't enough, then; that's too personal, like Hezekiah's interpretation.

Compare this to another period often assumed to have been more religious than ours, the Middle Ages. Think of what it would have cost medievals to imagine themselves and their children in the hellfires that were so vividly painted and preached. Soon enough they also thought up intercession, purgatory, indulgences. And during the Counter-Reformation someone who followed Ignatius Loyola's instructions to imagine the smell of sulfur or hold a finger in a candle flame and then multiply that pain in order to understand the hell one deserved to burn in—surely such a person would have a particularly urgent motivation to find a way to believe himself exempt? We ourselves do our best to ignore prognoses that the ozone layer will be gone by next week. (True enough? Name a plausible disaster that we do not also discount.)

We're still benefiting from the ancient Israelites' way of taming the thought of God's perspective: God was contextualized by religion; prophecy was estheticized by literary sensitivity; prophets were institutionalized by being assigned a place in society. Religion, sooner or later, becomes part of social existence and allows one to think about these dire subjects in a regulated way—often, but a little at a time. We are not the first to read the Bible as literature; Isaiah was admired for his style, particularly his imagery, which was imitated, and thereby diffused, by a school of Isaian writers that lasted for centuries, some of whose work was combined later into the book we know as Isaiah's prophecies. What Isaiah said was turned into culture. Once sackcloth had become recognized as the professional garb of religious professionals, it would remind one not of desolation but of prophets. So God commands Isaiah to take off his sackcloth.

Small wonder most audiences are deaf to prophecy; even the prophets often don't want to deliver their messages. It's as if we instinctively know that taking in the message would be like seeing God himself, and that if it didn't kill us, as seeing him would, it would mean losing or giving up something, because it would change us in uncomfortable ways. The story about the contemporary reaction to having Elijah so much as staying in one's house seems separated from our own evasions of the idea of a strong god only by being a less inhibited and more concrete response: "It happened that the son of the mistress of the house fell sick; his illness was so severe that in the end he expired. And the woman said to Elijah, 'What quarrel have you with me, man of God? Have you come here to bring my sins home to me and kill my son?'" (1 Kings 17:17–18). As God's messenger, the prophet often represents the terrible power to destroy that God himself has.

On the other hand the suffering that Isaiah threatens his contemporaries with is already a part of our world that we nearly take for granted, so that we have a stake also in believing. The inconsistencies in Isaiah's formulations of God reflect the use humans have for the idea of God: something about him is to be the explanation for our experiences of the world, and as these fluctuate, so does he, a crystallization of the experience of being human. Without the idea of God as judge, the world would still be subject to acts of God.

Burning the
Book of Lamentations

❦

NAOMI SEIDMAN

Lamentations describes the fall of the kingdom of Judah and the sacking
of Jerusalem in 587–586 B.C.E. The laments have been traditionally
ascribed to Jeremiah, who prophesied the ruin of the kingdom and
lived to see his prophecies fulfilled. The formal structure of the
laments, however, contrasts with Jeremiah's direct style—the verses
of each of the first four chapters begin with successive letters of the
Hebrew alphabet in what is known as the acrostic form. For all
the symmetry and attention to form of these poetic laments, their
description of the starving and destroyed city is powerfully graphic,
suggesting that Lamentations was written by a witness to
these events.

   Jews read from the Book of Lamentations on the ninth day
of the Hebrew month of Av (sometime in midsummer), traditionally
the date when both the first and the second temple of Jerusalem were
destroyed. Other historical catastrophes associated with the Ninth
of Av are the expulsion of the Jews from Spain in 1492 and the
beginning of the Second World War.

Biblical quotations are taken from the King James Version.

TISHA B'AV, THE NINTH DAY OF THE MONTH OF AV, COMES AT
the claustrophobic center of the tightening chokehold of the siege of
Jerusalem, 587 B.C.E.—first the Three Weeks, and no weddings, no
trips to the Bronx Zoo, no music; then the Nine Days, and no meat,
no showers either. The walls of Jerusalem have been breached, the
fires rage; boorish and lustful Babylonian troops tramp down the narrow streets toward the Holy of Holies. In the dining rooms of the diaspora, women set the table for the final meal before the long fast.
As the summer dusk falls, the mournful cadences of the Book of
Lamentations will begin to fill synagogues and float across bungalow-
colony lawns. Wooden benches will be turned over so the mourners
can sit on their splintery backs, low to the ground. The curtain of
the Ark will be taken down and folded, stripping the Torah scrolls of
their velvet cloaks, their gold-embroidered lions.

For me, having almost forgotten Jerusalem, there is only the mo-
notonous stretch of summer days melting in the blurry heat rising
from the city sidewalks. I walk in a haze of unmemory, my tongue
dry, if not cleaving to my palate. But even broken clocks are right
twice a day, and sometimes I catch myself where I thought I would
never return. One summer evening, around twenty-five hundred
years after the Babylonians had packed up and gone, I take the F
train toward Coney Island and let myself into my parents' house just
in time to see my mother pull two pairs of sneakers from the back
of the closet. For a second I have the absurd thought that my parents have started some sort of exercise regimen. But then I remember Tisha B'av, and the heat outside makes a certain kind of sense
now, as if someone had told me that the next neighborhood was
in flames.

I may need to explain the sneakers. My Orthodox parents were re-
fraining from wearing leather because leather, for the first barefoot
Jewish exiles, meant comfort and the good life. In the absence of
sackcloth and ashes and dung heaps, they remember Jerusalem
through thin rubber soles and in the splinters of upended benches
and their proximity to the floor. Every once in a while it's important
to touch bottom.

For me it's a little different. Wearing sneakers or going barefoot
and sitting on the floor, that's what I do year-round. In my parents'
book maybe this makes me a perpetual mourner.

"Come to shul with us," my mother says, a far-from-innocent invitation.

I mutter something about being on my way to a poetry reading. Of all possible non-synagogue-going activities, this is among the least reprehensible.

My mother chuckles. "This *is* a poetry reading."

I grumble, but mostly for form's sake. I joke to my friends that I get religion around Purim and Simchas Torah, when piety and partying go hand in hand. But the truth is that Tisha B'av sometimes brings me home, too, whether I actually make it to a synagogue or not. Tisha B'av, for the Orthodox, is also Holocaust Memorial Day, set in the context of the destruction of the First Temple, the Second Temple, and the long chain of national catastrophes since. In short, Tisha B'av is about Jews first and God only a distant second. I take this as a kind of boarding pass.

The synagogue is only half full. The younger couples are in the country, in bungalow colonies, their kids in camp. The seasonal migration has swept them into the shade, leaving behind only the older people in the sweltering New York streets among the radios and firecrackers. My mother introduces her baby daughter to the three women in identical wigs sharing our bench as if my awkward presence needed no comment; she insists that they must remember me, and I remember them, from the bungalow colony, the dress shop, the candy store. The women have tucked Kleenex into the wrists of their dresses, though no one makes a show of being somber. They talk about what they cooked their husbands for the last meal, nothing too heavy on such a hot fast day. The woman from the dress shop swears by fruit soup. In a few minutes we will be in a different landscape altogether, one that is announcing itself in the dread that tightens my chest. I hope my mother won't cry. This is not an unselfish wish. I know full well that I am bound to figure somewhere in the list of grievances my mother airs on Tisha B'av and on every Friday night as she stares into the candles, beckoning the flames toward her heart. The complaints may begin with the destruction of the Temple, but they go on from there, in jagged spirals of shrapnel and disgrace, getting closer and closer to home.

My mother has brought me a copy of the latest Artscroll edition of the Tisha B'av prayers, with an English translation and commentaries and a historical introduction. Until I turned twelve, I would arrive at shul on fast days with an emergency care package—a small Baggie filled with raisins and pretzels and sour candy to eat out of sight of adults. We gobbled handfuls in furious overanticipation of our imminent initiation into the rites of hunger. One Tisha B'av someone's mother came out to the concrete rectangle of the synagogue courtyard to tell us a story. In a certain small town in Poland, right after they broke the fast, the Jews would light an enormous bonfire. They would throw the Tisha B'av liturgy with all its sad poems about the destruction of the Temple into the fire and dance and sing the midsummer night away. You see, they didn't have any use for them anymore, since this was sure to be the year the Messiah would come and take all the Jews off to the Land of Israel, and instead of fasting and sitting on the floor there would be juicy portions of the Leviathan all around. But it was only a story. Those books, I knew even then, had gone up in a different kind of bonfire, and still the Messiah had failed to show up. And when we were finished for this year, the Artscroll Lamentations in my lap would go right back onto the bookshelf until next year.

From the other side of the sheet, strung across the archway that separates the men from the women, an invisible fist pounds an invisible lectern, and the women quiet down and open their books. I know the first lines by heart: *"eicha yashva badad ha'ir,"*

> How doth the city sit solitary, that was full of people! how is she become as a widow! she that was great among the nations, and princess among the provinces, how is she become tributary! (Lam. 1:1)

Movie child that I am, I watch the sheet to see the shifting silhouettes of my father and his friends. The shadows on the curtain reward my attention, forming for a second the monstrous shape of a lopsided-breasted woman, as if we were seeing our own reflections mutated into a single enormous female figure. Jerusalem sways and shakes her big skirts, crooning in the hoarse voice of the old stockbroker or diamond cutter on the other side of her veils. Then she splits into two amorphous bodies, black hats, a lectern in between.

He-she sings a mourning dirge, falling empty and flat at the end of each phrase. The tune has no resolution, accrues no meaning. This is not Yom Kippur—the tune, the overturned benches, the fasting are not meant to spiritualize. Tisha B'av is an event of the body, creaking bones settling down on splintery wood, hard pavement under thin soles, the rumble and gnaw of an empty belly. Even the naked Torah scrolls remind us of their participation in the cruelties of physical existence, their vulnerability to violation and debasement. And Lamentations, I understand now, reinvents the picture-perfect princess, Zion as God's beloved daughter or bride, as a physical woman, a woman with all her fleshly sorrows. Whatever the Babylonians did to turn Jerusalem the city into rubble, it is the Jewish poet, I can't help feeling, who rips the bride Jerusalem's jeweled veils from her forehead, stripping the embroidered robes to flash us a glimpse of her genitals, *"ervatah,"* translated by the squeamish or modest translator as "her nakedness":

> Jerusalem hath grievously sinned; therefore she is removed: all that honored her despise her, because they have seen her nakedness: yea, she sigheth, and turneth backward. Her filthiness is in her skirts. (Lam. 1:8–9)

My mother sways as she murmurs along, a ready sorrow propelling her words. My own spine is rigid with insult and distance, my thighs clenched with the usual impotent rage. I know full well that I take offense the way a woman might grab a robe to cover herself, and my proud impiety is only a makeshift dam against the insistent words of the reading.

Reciting the R-rated shots of the naked Jerusalem from two sides of a white sheet strung across an archway, we sweat through more layers of clothes than most New Yorkers would dream of wearing past Memorial Day. Nevertheless the words have an accuracy that belies the long-sleeved shirts, the shiny-black jackets. Underneath them we (they, I) inhabit a nakedness these clothes cannot begin to cover. Inside the synagogues, within the circles of singing voices, in the midst of the comforting or stifling refrains of dress and speech there are those unfortunate spaces where grandparents and cousins should be, where parents throw dishes at ghosts of the enemy, where the mother and father in their strange old-fashioned accents speak to children with even stranger ones, where the shapes of family and neighborhood warp and curl at the edges like an old photo. It's not just me, a foot taller than the woman who is my mother, one-and-a-half missing generations younger than the old man who is my father. To say we are a community of survivors and children of survivors is only half true. Survivors maybe; community—that is something else altogether. The voices in unison, the thigh next to mine on the bench, the crowded room takes us to where we are most alone; where we are alone is where the shapes of those others, called for or not, unfailingly press.

King James calls the account of the destruction of Jerusalem "Lamentations." In Hebrew, though, it is "The Book of How," "*megilat eicha*," because of its opening. "How doth the city sit solitary, that was full of people! how is she become as a widow!"

Behind the declarative *how* lurks an interrogative one, questioning the means, the possibility of telling a catastrophe that evades description or comparison: "What thing shall I take to witness for thee?" the poet asks, "what thing shall I liken to thee, O daughter of Jerusalem?" The ragged structure of the book tells us that the poet found no ready words. Not knowing how to speak of what he has seen, he begins and stops, begins anew, three times in all. First his unrecognizable hometown appears to him to have sunk as low as only a woman could, widowed through her bad luck or abandoned because of her loose morals. Then, in the central portion of the book, the poet abandons his bitter combination of pity and revulsion, compassion and blame, and speaks in his own voice of what he has suffered. The city-woman is gone, and now the story is of an anonymous and solitary survivor in a landscape that is the nightmarish opposite of the green fields through which God the Shepherd led the Psalmist:

> I am the man that hath seen affliction by the rod of his wrath.
> He hath led me, and brought me into darkness, but not into light. (Lam. 3:1–2)

Only in the final chapters does the poet step back far enough to see the destruction of Jerusalem through the misery of the community of survivors:

> They that did feed delicately are desolate in the streets: they that were brought up in scarlet embrace dunghills. (Lam. 4:5)

I imagine the poet of Lamentations, moving from the empty streets of the first morning after the siege, waking only weeks later to his own bruises, brushing the soot from his eyes to witness the survivors crawling out of caves and from underneath piles of rubble. My father says that he emerged from hiding the morning the Nazis left, alive enough to think of reciting the blessing for he "who has granted us life and sustained us and brought us to this day." My father, looking around at an emptiness I can only imagine, did not recite the blessing, he says, because it was in the plural. I think of him now, mourning his own losses across the curtain. Has he moved to the plural yet, as the poet of Lamentations does in the final chapter?

The three versions tell the same story, but they also do not. The solitary city-woman segues into the isolated survivor who gives her voice. The city-woman Jerusalem contains the women, is the women who roam through the deserted streets in search of food for their children. But how many of those women walked with outstretched necks and painted their eyelids in shades the prophets so abhorred? As many as were later laid low? The sin written large catches too much, and too little, in its broad outlines. We are like and unlike the myths of our destiny, we are given voice and betrayed by the poets and prophets and leaders who share our fate, we are determined but not explained by these terms: Jew, survivor, woman.

In the synagogue the raspy baritone of the reader floats over the curtain, and the murmured voices of all of us mourners, men and women, come together in the words of the city-woman and the words of the man-survivor. But the city-woman and the poet who repeats "I am the man" are separate, and not only because each is as necessarily isolated as the individual suffering human must be. I refuse to see that the menstrual blood on Jerusalem's skirt is just a way of saying that her inhabitants have committed murderous acts. The city-woman's disgrace is a poor allegory for the sins of her men who take cover in these skirts:

For the sins of her prophets, and the iniquities of her priests, that have shed the blood of the just in the midst of her,
They have wandered as blindmen in the streets, then have polluted themselves with blood, so that men could not touch their garments.
They cried unto them, Depart ye; it is unclean; depart, depart, touch not. (Lam. 4:13–15)

The blood of the priests and prophets is the trace of what they have done; the blood of Jerusalem, who is "as a menstruous woman," tells us nothing more than that she has a woman's body. However much the poet may imagine the city to be his larger self, he also lets us know that her blood is something utterly alien. There may be men, and even women, for whom nakedness is beauty or truth, Adam and Eve before the Fall. Adam and Eve, though, were not Jewish, and even they covered up eventually. To be a naked Jew, a naked woman, a naked Jewish woman, may be something else altogether. Reading

Lamentations in the divided synagogue, hearing a male voice intone the complaints of the widowed Jerusalem, are we really a community of mourners, the men and women who recognize how much a woman's truth has to say about the broader experiences of national degradation? Or is Lamentations itself yet another outrage, heaping a man's distaste for women onto the already painful enough outrages of Jewish history?

But if the poet's identification with the stricken city is sometimes stretched thin, his relation to her marked by her revulsion and horror, maybe it's because catastrophe not only brings us back to what we most fundamentally are but also shows us ourselves as alien. The body in disease and hunger pits us against ourselves, and the vision of extreme suffering can never seem other than inescapably foreign. For the poet the unreality of horror created a monstrous woman; how different would it be for any of us, inhabitants of female or male bodies that can become, given the right or wrong circumstances, the most nightmarish of enemies.

The sickening waste, the dirt and garbage, people's bad behavior and the madness of hunger, even the dread that fills me as I listen to each new grim verse are familiar enough. They are mine, but also not mine, as the city-woman both was and was not the prophet. If I feel my own distance from the twisted wreck of Jerusalem as a kind of comfort, there is also discomfort and danger in this distance. If I am also a broken-down, lonely survivor of a disgraced city, if I can feel the shame of her nakedness, feel myself caught with a telltale patch of blood on my skirt, the equally terrible possibility exists that my part in the story is also the revolted lover slamming the door, the jeering witness. Worse, I am the stupid child bawling for her supper while the city burns. I am the wicked child who wants to know why I was dragged here, what all this twisted stuff has to do with my life. Is Lamentations my story, as a woman or as a Jew? I don't know. Until I was twelve or so, I thought I would be exempt, both from history, which meant Nazis, and from being a woman, which meant menstruation. In summer camp the Kaplan girls and I set up a fort in an old shed at the far end of the lake, where a few mattresses and a rusty canoe had found their final resting-place. If the Nazis came to the Catskills, we were ready. The twins had a Swiss army knife, and I had a week's supply of chocolate. We talked about which of the other girls at camp we would save and for what price. There was room for one more at the very most. The summer I was twelve, I was always hungry and always afraid, afraid of my first fast, afraid of getting fat. I couldn't believe that after all *that*, adults would fail to put food on the table for me. Naturally I checked to make sure I had a bag of Goldenberg's Peanut Chews in my closet right before Tisha B'av started. I wasn't completely stupid.

The play that summer was *The Wall*, and the Kaplan twins were in it. I sat on the floor in front of the first row of seats and watched jealously as they stomped across the stage in their galoshes and arm bands. A divider, painted to look like peeling bricks, set them off from the right half of the stage, where five or six Jews huddled and cowered. One of the girls from Bunk 6, her hair covered in her kerchief, hushed the sniveling teddy bear she held in her arms so that the sound wouldn't betray them. The twins looked cloddish and stupid. Couldn't they hear the crying? Couldn't they see how flimsy the wall was? The girl with the kerchief clutched the teddy bear tighter until, from somewhere behind the curtain at the back of the stage, it gave its final, strangled gasp.

The story of mothers killing their children is what we remembered about the Warsaw Ghetto and what we remember from Lamentations. The horrors of the devastated city reach their anguished crescendo in the poet's question, "Shall the women eat their fruit, and children of a span long?" And later, sharpening the focus on this image, he relates that in the madness of hunger, "The hands of the pitiful women have sodden their children: they were their meat." The figurative fruit of women's wombs become the literal fruit they consume, reversing the sacred direction of birth, of feeding a child from the mother's body. Lamentations, in its most grotesque vision, transforms the prescribed generosity of parents toward their children that we all take utterly for granted into a parody of the life cycle, where mothers eat their children and it is the dying body that feeds the ravenous earth.

> They that be slain with the sword are better than they that be slain with hunger: for these pine away, stricken through for want of the fruit of the field. (Lam. 4:9)

> Even the sea monsters draw out the breast, they give suck to their young ones: the daughter of my people is become cruel, like the ostriches in the wilderness. (Lam. 4:3)

In this logic of the body women are to blame for the end of domestic life, for the drying up of the sources of sustenance, since they were the ones who provided the food when it was there to be gotten, who sent their children off to school with packed lunches. The descriptions of female cannibalism not only set the outer limits of the horror, show the lengths to which even "compassionate women" can be driven, they also stand in for the catastrophe as a whole. If the survivor has rejected the loathsome city-woman, it is because she rejected him first.

The rabbis attempted to explain the apparent contradiction between compassionate maternity and cannibalism otherwise. The mothers boiled their already dead children to feed those still living. Or the mothers didn't actually boil their children, they just allowed their souls to burn because they were *too* compassionate with them, letting them sleep late and miss the morning prayers. Having saved the women from one charge, they plea-bargained for a lesser one. Obviously there was no way these women could get off altogether.

Are all of us caught in the center of this twisted web of logic, this terrible cycle of effect and cause? Having cooked their husbands a meal, did the women tuck a roll of tissue into their sleeves and walk into the shul as into a tribunal? Was fasting penance for the madness of hunger, past or future? Is it a humbling reminder of how few hours away we are from hunger, and how few days away from madness? Or does our ability to look away from the life of the stomach reassure us that the Messiah may not come this year, but neither will our hunger escape its limits? A cake for after the fast is already cooling in the refrigerator. Tomorrow night my mother will need a hot drink to help it go down. My fasting is different, easier because I am young enough to imagine myself free of the restraints of nutrition, harder because I fast loosed from the comforting bonds of law. And having felt them once, I could never believe in fasting to "clean my system out," or as a spiritual therapy, or in invisible solidarity with people who need food rather than symbolic acts. There is a diner at the corner where I can sneak a burger after synagogue, though I still haven't decided if I will or won't. In the meantime we have a language in common, my mother and I, in the faintest beginnings of a rumbling in our bellies.

The reader is coming to the hopeful, humble end. We join in with relief, the men more loudly, the women softly.

> Thou, O Lord, remainest for ever; thy throne from generation to generation.

> Wherefore dost thou forget us for ever, and forsake us so
> long time?
> Turn thou unto thee us, O Lord, and we shall be turned;
> renew our days as of old.
> But thou hast utterly rejected us; thou art very wroth
> against us. (Lam. 5:19–22)

The tone of this coda is utterly different from what has gone before, a sign that the madness of devastation has begun to cede to the necessary unconsciousness of survival, the restrained complaints and humbled pleas of a dissipated rage. We have come back to the realm of piety and rhetoric. We are "we" again, collective-bargaining with a God whose terrible powers make such actions mostly symbolic. If we forgive him, it is because we are too exhausted to do otherwise.

A group of my mother's friends walk back with us toward the house. Their faces show the signs of what the Greeks understood to be the pleasure of tears. Me, I haven't cried and so haven't earned the comfortable talk about daughters-in-law who aren't fasting because they are still nursing, or the problem with getting a decent exterminator in the neighborhood. Even so it is rare, even festive, to be walking down the street with a group of adults in sneakers.

My mother cheerfully turns to me. "That wasn't so bad, was it?"

"No," I answer reluctantly. Not nearly bad enough, meaning that indifference and recognition, guilt and rage, had combined to keep me there, to keep me away.

In the distance fireworks light up the still not completely dark sky. In Brooklyn the Fourth of July hangs on at least until Labor Day. I hold my mother's elbow so that I can walk with my neck flung all the way back, the way she would lead me when I was very young. The streetlights cast shifting shadows against the low clouds. I think of the bonfire in that little town in Poland. I wish we could have one now. I wish we could all, in our wickedness and in our faith, throw in the books we carried under our arms and join in the end-of-lamenting dance, the dance of the olden days, spinning and whirling the New York night away.

In the Belly of the Whale

PATRICIA HAMPL

SHE WAS BEGGING ME TO LET HER OUT. "I'M SCARED," SHE whimpered. "I'm scared of the dark. No kidding, I really, really, really am." She held to the word, clinging to the long vowel like a life ring: *ree-ee-lly, ree-ee-lly, ree-ee-lly*. No anger, no outrage. Just that panicky voice, clutching sincerity.

This was the voice of Sheila Phalen, my best friend. I had pinned her in Sister Immaculata's broom closet, an airless cube at the back of our second-grade classroom, next to the cloakroom. The hempy, not-quite-dead smell of wet wool rose from the jackets hanging on pegs in the cloakroom; black slush puddled on the floor from the boys' rubber overshoes. *I'm really, really scared. Really.*

Anyone would have taken pity on this voice, limp with fright. Not me. I hove in, drove my shoulder harder against the narrow closet door, put some real muscle into it: *You just stay there till you're good and scared. You just stay there.*

I had my reasons.

MAYBE I TAKE NATURALLY to the Book of Jonah, having lived fretfully over the years with this memory of casting Sheila Phalen into

Biblical quotations are taken from the New Jerusalem Bible, unless otherwise indicated.

the belly of darkness. Yet the parallel is not exact: Sheila never struck me as a Jonah, and I had no godly lessons to teach her, just a grudge to work out. But Jonah's whale-cave and the awful black hole of that broom closet where I meant for Sheila to stew have remained linked darknesses.

There is another connection: Jonah has always seemed a bigger story to me than the space it occupies in the Bible, just as that endless moment with my shoulder slammed against the door of Immaculata's broom closet has refused to become unimportant as it recedes in time.

Some stories, like certain memories, are strangely vivid precisely because their narrative is smudged and incomplete. The meaning in such instances becomes elusive and therefore oddly demanding. The Book of Jonah is like that—perhaps most Old Testament stories have this incomplete, haunting quality. It is the curious tone of myth, a capacity to enchant in the ageless storytelling way while refusing the satisfaction of a fully finished drama. Such stories and such memories don't want to entertain or even simply edify you. They mean to bother you. They draw to the surface half-finished memories with their own bothersome details. Jonah in his whale has always flashed before me Sheila in her closet.

Sheila and I were best friends. She knew it, I knew it. Every morning we walked down Oxford Street together on the way to Saint Luke's, and back again after school when I walked the two extra blocks beyond my house to the corner of hers. Then she walked back with me a full block to the midpoint of the distance separating our houses. We had devised this method to put off to the last moment the geographic imperative that severed us until the next morning.

We shared the bond of first friendship and the soupy union of being Sister's favorites. Once, during lunch hour, we had gone into the closet, two teacher's pets fetching fresh erasers for Sister's blackboard. There in the darkness we had discovered a cardboard box almost as tall as ourselves, filled with reams of paper tossed every which way. We fished out the papers—weeks' and months' worth of discarded classwork. It was a scandal, we saw that right away. We understood that Sister Immaculata, who made much of collecting our work each day, had simply dumped all those Palmer exercises, all those poems to the Holy Family—everything—without ever casting an eye upon any of it. We had stumbled upon a shocking scholastic waste site.

It was a political moment, the beginning of institutional mistrust, primal disillusion rooting against the established order.

With such a history of intimacies and corporate secrets between us, how had it come to pass that Sheila had fallen under the spell of Helena Eldridge, new girl from Chicago? Helena Eldridge with her blond ponytail that really did swing and snap like the tail of a bold and frisky pony. Helena, who took ballet lessons and made a showy habit of walking back from the drinking fountain with her feet pointed outward. How had Sheila succumbed to the false values of this parvenu with her arty ways, in recent weeks giving over wholly to Eldridgian modes of speaking and thinking, even to the point of pestering her mother for ballet lessons? *We don't take ballet lessons, Sheila. We go skating!* I expostulated to no avail.

The day before had broken me entirely. We had left school together as usual, Helena Eldridge nosing along beside us. But at the point where Helena should have sheared off, turning down Lincoln Avenue to her house in a lonely new-girl sort of way, Sheila, unbelievably, had turned with her. *We have ballet stuff to talk about.* They toe-pointed their way along Lincoln together, leaving me slouching down Oxford toward home alone.

HOW MANY PEOPLE RECALL the first time they heard of the cowardly man swallowed by the big fish? He's always been there. Like all abiding tales that carry heavy psychological freight, Jonah is not a story you merely read or hear, but one into which you are born, as into a family, recognizing the blood relation.

The Book of Jonah is the Rhode Island of the Old Testament, a snapper of a tale whose minimalism is fundamental to its power. There are other lean books in the Old Testament. But who knows them—Nahum, Haggai, Obadiah? Like Jonah, they are tucked roughly in the middle of the Jewish Tanakh; in Christian Bibles these books are crammed up close to the detailed narratives of the New Testament's Synoptic Gospels. But most of them are warnings and alarms, cries and even curses. Only Jonah carries the ancient force of story. And Jonah, unlike its slender neighbors, is the story known in the bones, the story you can't remember ever not knowing, like a memory so old, it isn't a memory but an ounce of yourself.

"Up!" Yahweh commands Jonah, son of Amittai, in the book's first line. "Go to Nineveh, the great city, and proclaim to them that their wickedness has forced itself upon me."

Our hero's response? "Jonah set about running away from Yahweh, and going to Tarshish. He went down to Jaffa and found a ship bound for Tarshish; he paid his fare and boarded it, to go with them to Tarshish, to get away from Yahweh."

It is worth pausing to note the perfect pitch of the writing in these lines. The caged, circular feel of panic is rendered with utter conviction. The statement begins with Jonah "running away from Yahweh, and going to Tarshish"; at its fevered finish he is still frantically boarding the ship, "to go with them to Tarshish, to get away from Yahweh." The repetition of action is masterful, the once, twice, thrice charge to the safe barricade of Tarshish, the no-exit breathlessness of the prose.

It is appropriate that the story's style should be so subtly nuanced. After all, Jonah is a writer—what else is a prophet? At this point he is a writer with writer's block, fleeing his vision. Later he must contend with being a writer *manqué*, a prophet whose words don't prove true. But that's on the next page, a world—and half the plot—away.

The nature of Jonah's instinctive fear remains unspecified: Is he afraid of what the inhabitants of "the great city" will do to a bearer of stern news? Or does he fear the grandeur of the enterprise itself? We don't know. Which is as it should be. For Jonah's fear is the great fear, the nameless one at the core of each of us. It must not have a defining *reason*. This is no place for analysis. The thing must be felt.

Once aboard the ship bound for Tarshish, Jonah falls asleep. He is seeking, like the faint-hearted soul he is, an even deeper safety: the sanctuary of unconsciousness. No luck. "Yahweh threw a hurricane at the sea, and there was such a great storm at sea that the ship threatened to break up."

The sailors, all Gentiles of unspecified animist faiths, take fright, and "each of them called on his own god." They also throw cargo overboard to lighten the ship's load. To no avail. They are astonished to discover that Jonah is actually sleeping through the tumult. They wake him, beg him to pray to *his* God as they have to theirs. The storm thrives on.

In desperation the sailors cast lots to see who aboard the ship is the negative charge among them. Stripped of its superstition, their casting of lots is telling. *They* know, low-level Gentiles though they are, that *somebody* has to take responsibility for things. Jonah's plan is to sleep it away, forget, repress, and sail on to sweet dreams of yes-teryear. But the sailors determine to live the real storm, to achieve real peace. They know they must *do* something, find the source of trouble.

No surprise when the lot points to Jonah. Now here is the surprise: The sailors do not instantly haul him to the gunwales and toss him overboard. They settle in for a little colloquy there on the heaving ship in the midst of the tempest. "Tell us," they say, "what is your business? Where do you come from? What is your country? What is your nationality?"

Jonah comes clean. "I am a Hebrew," he says, "and I worship Yah-weh, God of Heaven, who made both sea and dry land." He confesses that he is fleeing Yahweh and that this flight has angered his God.

A moment of truth, of allegiance. Jonah, for the first time, is not a coward in flight. He is a man living his fate.

The sailors still hesitate, loathe to do what clearly needs to be done. They seem to have an inbred repugnance against doing harm to another being. This first shred of mercy in the story emanates from these foreigners, men with no reason to spare the life of an alien. Nor is their rudimentary compassion allied to generosity. It be-longs to the balancing act of justice. Theirs is a stony, but real mercy, grounded in their fear of punishment: "Do not hold us responsible for causing an innocent man's death," they cry to God. The sailors' bedrock decency sees Jonah as "innocent" even though the lot has come up against him (a fact that would seem to give them their proof, or a certain justification).

The sailors' decency roots compassion not in individual choice but in the nature of life itself. Compassion *feels* like an emotion; it is ex-perienced as an intensely personal, individual thing. But its first ap-pearance here in Jonah's story, in the voice of the Gentile sailors, plants it in a fundamental natural order more basic, more immutable, than human feeling. True, this first flash of compassion does not carry the day—but it's not supposed to. This isn't the moment for compassion.

Jonah himself makes this plain: "Take me and throw me into the sea, and then it will calm down for you. I know it is my fault that this great storm has struck you." Still the sailors demur. They row hard, trying to reach the shore, still unwilling to cast him into the deep. "But in vain . . ."

Finally they must do as fate and Jonah direct: They toss him overboard . . . "and the sea stopped raging." This makes converts of the sailors, who offer sacrifices to Yahweh and make many vows to him.

FOR ALL ITS MYTHIC drama—calamitous storm at sea, high-stakes divine threats, the cameo appearance of the monster whale—Jonah is a story with a lot of white space. It is a setup for reflection, for the supreme human act: contemplation. It is a story that intends for you to keep writing it on the remaining blank of its third, and final, page.

The filling in of blank space that Jonah invites—or positively requires—is not more action of a whale-swallows-man variety. By tale's end the secret preoccupation of the story has etched itself sharply into each gesture of the action. That preoccupation or obsession or longing (it is all of these) is revealed clearly only at the end and comes there—as all good endings must—as a revelation. But the obsession is threaded through the whole text. Enter, on my own stage, Sheila Phalen.

For the story's obsession, first hinted at by the sailors loath to save themselves at a stranger's expense, is compassion: who gets it, who gives it. Who withholds it. I'm slammed up against Immaculata's closet door again, Sheila Phalen whimpering inside. The lesson begins to come home: At the heart of the refusal of mercy is not cruelty—but fear.

Sheila appears to be the frightened one. But her fear is straightforward, a natural terror of the dark, just as the sailors have an appropriate fear of the raging storm. Jonah lacks this appropriate fear; he sleeps right through the storm. His fear is abject, chronic. It is a fear of his fate, his calling. Which is to say, a fear of reality. And my fear is—of Sheila, of all things. The real Sheila, who is a free Sheila. I'm afraid to let her out, for I must release the ballet-loving Sheila, disciple to Helena Eldridge. Looking back, I've always thought I was punishing her, though I have the distinct memory of being mystified as I threw my weight against the closet door: *why am I doing this?* I wasn't punishing Sheila, after all. I was holding her, hanging on to her former self, fearful of the real Sheila. *You just stay there till you're good and scared—like I am,* was the unspoken end of that threat.

I don't remember letting Sheila out of the closet. I don't remember how I came to slam the door against her to begin with. Yet this shard of memory remains suspended like a judgment over my head (amazing how often I think of it, even as an adult): the raw evidence of my cruel streak. The transparent tableau, still palpable: my shoulder planed against the closet door, Sheila's voice a riot of blameless sup-plication. The heady, abstract sensation of refusing mercy. The icy satisfaction of it. The, yes, pleasure. Really.

Cruelty belongs, then, to fear, and compassion belongs to justice. It is necessary to learn these relationships, to trace the integuments that bind us to our actions. Once he is cast into the belly of the whale, Jonah makes no mention of being afraid, except retrospec-tively. In fact the whale is a kind of underwater safehouse, a submerged hermitage. The usual Christian association is the Jonah-Christ equation: Jonah's three days in the belly of the whale = Jesus' three days in the tomb.

But Jonah's three days are no death. Alone within the big fish, he finally smashes through his block. He becomes a writer. And not a polemicist, not a preacher. But a poet—and specifically a lyric poet in the memoirist mode, writing from his own immediate experience:

> The waters round me rose to my neck,
>   the deep was closing round me,
>   seaweed twining round my head.
> To the roots of the mountains,
>   I sank into the underworld,
>   and its bars closed round me for ever. (Jon. 2:6–7)

The beautiful psalm Jonah composes in the dark of his living subma-rine is a telegraphic account of being cast overboard. He describes the experience literally as his close call with death, but also meta-phorically as a larger spiritual death:

> All your waves and billows passed over me;
>   then I thought, "I am banished from your sight;
> How shall I ever see your holy Temple again?" (v. 5)

The poem is also a pledge, a promise whose language is as open and buoyant as the earlier language of his attempted flight to Tarshish was coiled and tight:

> . . . I shall sacrifice to you
>   with songs of praise.
> The vow I have made I shall fulfil! (v. 10)

This is a confident man, free at last to make a pledge, assured he can keep it, for he is promising simply to live his fate, to be a singer of songs.

THE BOOK OF JONAH is a tour de force that manages to shoehorn two stories into its few paragraphs. The first is Jonah's story, the second is God's story *for* Jonah. Both are suffused with the mystery of compassion. That's the thing about compassion: It's a wild card, an enigma, love's most elusive variation. You can't understand it, you can only taste it. This is the cup Yahweh is determined Jonah will accept.

Once vomited (or spewed—the verbs favored by Scripture) onto dry land, Jonah is given Yahweh's commission again. Same words, same job: "Up! Go to Nineveh, the great city . . ."

This time Jonah lives up to his poetic pledge. He makes the arduous journey to the great city, gives the populace the bad news, and with a stroke of beginner's luck this first-time prophet is heard. The people of Nineveh put on sackcloth without argument; they fast and renounce their evil ways. God, seeing their efforts, relents. He spares Nineveh from his wrath and leaves the city in peace and prosperity.

This is bad news for Jonah. In fact, "This made Jonah very indignant; he fell into a rage." Yahweh's mercy has rendered him a false prophet. God has caused him to proclaim the destruction of Nineveh—but Nineveh is doing very well, thank you. Jonah is appalled at how badly Yahweh has used his messenger. His assignment has come to nothing—as if God, like Sister Immaculata, had simply dumped his careful, brave words into a trash box and gone willfully about his business, leaving Jonah with egg on his face.

Jonah is furious at God for being compassionate, the very quality the supposedly "stern" God of the Old Testament is usually accused of lacking. Jonah had always suspected God of having a soft spot. Jonah's anger has a telltale crabbiness as well as the fury of one betrayed: "Isn't this what I said would happen when I was still in my own country?" he cries to God. "That was why I first tried to flee to Tarshish [note the revisionist history here], since I knew you were a tender, compassionate God, slow to anger, rich in faithful love, who relents about inflicting disaster."

He ends by playing the same high card he played with the sailors:

"So now, Yahweh, please take my life, for I might as well be dead as go on living."

Yahweh, like a mellow Rogerian therapist, merely murmurs, "Are you that deeply grieved?"[1] Jonah, denied even the glory of death, goes off to sulk.

JONAH LEAVES NINEVEH AND sits to the east of the great city, waiting "to see what would happen to the city."

But Yahweh is done with Nineveh. He trains his new story on Jonah himself. It is a parable of a single paragraph, the final one in the Book of Jonah (in the Tanakh it is two brief paragraphs). God ordains a castor-oil plant to grow over Jonah to shade him from the sun and to "soothe his ill-humor." It works. Jonah perks up for the first time since his great public failure: he loves the plant, glories in its shade and comfort.

But the next day God causes a worm to destroy it. The plant withers and dies. In the morning God sends a scorching east wind, and the sun beats down on Jonah's head. For the third time in the book Jonah begs for death: "I might as well be dead as go on living."

"Are you right to be angry about the castor-oil plant?" Yahweh asks.

"I have every right to be angry, mortally angry!" cries the sweating, aggrieved hero.

Then Yahweh, reserving the last word for himself, strips off his modest Rogerian mask, proving just how stern his compassion is: "You are concerned for the castor-oil plant," he says, "which has not cost you any effort and which you did not grow, which came up in a night and has perished in a night. So why should I not be concerned for Nineveh, the great city, in which there are more than a hundred and twenty thousand people who cannot tell their right hand from their left, to say nothing of all the animals?"

A strange argument. The oddity of God's parable lies in its off-kilter logic. He has not set up a situation in which Jonah experiences sympathy for another being that is an obvious parallel to God's tender-heartedness toward Nineveh. Rather, God arranges for Jonah to experience a dumb object, the castor-oil plant, giving *him* comfort. And this is no pet, no other-self—it's just a mute plant, hardly more than a piece of environmental furniture. Yet its loss, allowing the sun to bake down on him, causes Jonah to let out his death-wish wail.

At this point Yahweh comes in for the kill. He hammers home his fundamental point about compassion, making it look very much like a law of nature. Compassion, as the parable has it, is not generosity, it is not born of fond feeling, nor is it mercy, though we tend to use the words interchangeably. Compassion is the acknowledgment of connection, the refusal to see the world as divided into distinct units that can do without one another. It is, literally, a "suffering together with" (*com*, "with" + *pati*, "suffer"). It is primal union. Interesting, too, that the Hebrew word for "compassion," *rachmanes*, derives from the root *rechem*, meaning "womb." There could be no more human origin for a word—and of course the whale's belly is the womb where Jonah is re-made, and from which he is re-born.

For the truth is that all creation is connected, attached, together, intertwined—compassionate. Jonah needed that plant. His fury at its destruction is anger at *his* loss, not at the plant's loss of life. If Jonah is inspired at all by something that might be called kindness, it is only in the most archaic source of the word: he recognizes the plant as being of his own *kind*, or his sort somehow. But that's the point: compassion is not a personal form of enlightened social welfare for everybody else. It is reality, it is how things fit together in the universe. To lack compassion is not merely to lack a human quality, it is to not quite exist, to be missing an essential working part of reality.

To Jonah's liberal soul Yahweh plays the radical teacher with a flair for drama. He does not try to convince Jonah to feel for the other, but to find the astonishing root of compassion within himself, for himself. The key to the lesson is that the separating boundary between self and other is understood—in a blaze of scorching sun—to be illusory.

The parable makes God's compassion decisive. Jonah must acquiesce to this compassion now that he has lost a creature that pleased *him*. He knows now the God-like sensation of possession, the pleasure of it, the comfort. He knows the urgency of attachment and can never upbraid God again for being slow to anger, rich in faithful love.

The great city is full of fools—"more than a hundred and twenty thousand people who cannot tell their right hand from their left," as a somewhat exasperated Yahweh puts it. If Jonah mourns a dead plant, "Why should I not be concerned for Nineveh, the great city," Yahweh asks, ". . . to say nothing of all the animals?"

With this final question, Yahweh seems to introduce class discussion rather than snap the story shut. But then, the parable of the castor-oil plant proves, if there was ever a doubt, that this is a teaching book.

Jonah, being a writer, is a slow learner, stubborn, self-righteous, not given to trust. And who is this Yahweh? Jonah has told the sailors he worships Yahweh. But he talks to God as if he were a rival author, part of the competition, forever a book ahead of him. The Book of Jonah ends on Yahweh's question. Jonah does not reply. It is never clear if our hero gets the message, if he does bend, finally, to Yahweh's stern compassion there in the broiling scriptural sun.

BUT I MUST NOT leave my own broken-off story unfinished, seeing that recently I've come into possession of an ending. I saw Sheila Phalen's father's death notice in the paper about a year ago. Name of funeral parlor, time of visitation. I hadn't seen Sheila in twenty-five years, a million years, forever. She had married, I knew that. Had moved away from Saint Paul years before, had five children, or six— some large Catholic number. I'm not sure how I came to know even these few details, maybe from my mother, who still lives in the old neighborhood. Sheila and I had never exchanged so much as a Christmas card across the span of our adulthood, but I was in my car, headed at the appointed hour toward the address given in the death notice. Instinct was driving me there, certainly not friendship anymore.

I recognized her right away, very thin, almost austere, her thin father laid out on ecru satin behind her. He had been a book lover, always lying on the couch in the living room, reading, when I came over to visit. It was almost less strange to see him lying still in a coffin than to see him lying there without a book open in his folded hands.

Sheila detached herself from a group of women and came right toward me the minute I stepped into the room, as if she'd known I was coming, both of her hands out to grasp mine, a great serene smile shining from her severe face.

We all live a version, not a story. Even a memory with parts missing or lost has as many readings as there are players in the action. Who knows how Sheila came to her version? But with her reader-father laid out behind us, she gave it to me, my old friend whose cries of terror I had refused to honor all those years ago. "You came," she said, looking into my eyes the way someone does who knows every door in your house and can go anywhere. "I knew you'd come. You always were so kind."

Prophecy and Poetry

ALLEGRA GOODMAN

Prophetic poetry has always drawn me. The reading of the Haftorah, the weekly selection from the Prophets, is my favorite part of Saturday-morning services. Long after the congregation moves on, I am still reading and rereading Isaiah, Micah, or Jeremiah. Prophecy is challenging. The prophets do not stroke us with familiar images or tell us what we want to hear. They do not soothe us, or play to our moods, providing easy listening. Prophecy is not ingratiating poetry, and I like that.

HOW DO WE SPEAK TO GOD? HOW DO WE APPROACH HIM? WE plead with him directly. We praise his work in the world. We develop doxologies and apologetics in our prayers: "Poor am I in worthy deeds," the reader chants on Yom Kippur. But in Scripture the question of approaching God is cast differently. In the Torah God approaches man. He speaks to us. He speaks through us. The prophets speak consciously of God's approach to them, the infusion of God's voice in their language. Amos cries out, "The lion hath roared, / Who will not fear? The Lord God hath spoken, / Who can but

Biblical quotations are taken from J. H. Hertz, ed., *The Pentateuch and Haftorahs Hebrew Text, English Text, and Commentary,* 2nd ed. (London: Soncino Press, 1979).

301

prophesy?" (Amos 3:8). God's words demand human expression. As Amos describes it, prophecy is as instinctive and immediate as fear. The prophet raises his voice not in response to God but as God's instrument. The prophet's poetry is not mimetic; it manifests God's presence. No apology is made for art's inadequacy, because it is assumed the words come from God.

When Amos asks, "Who can but prophesy?" his words have a double meaning: prophecy is an imperative. Who can avoid lifting up his voice when he hears God? But prophecy is also the province of every person. No one can turn from God's voice, and no one is excluded from prophetic language. Continually the raised voice and charged language of prophecy break through the historical biblical narrative. Out of extraordinary experience comes profound, mystic language. Images take shape, and a voice expounds their meaning. The chronicle of events pauses, and a name in the record of generations becomes a person with a prophetic voice, a voice divinely inspired. And yet, although prophecy might be possible for every man or woman, few speak as prophets. We read the prophets and we ask ourselves, Is there some social or cultural criterion for choosing prophets? They say of course that they are chosen by God. Do they mean by this that they are the imaginative artists of the nation, or its political leaders? Must they be men? Searching for a rule or cultural pattern reveals the diversity of prophetic voices in place, time, vocation, gender, occasion. We might say that the prophets speak out of a political nationalist vision, but we must also take into account the intense personal experience expressed in prophecy. Jonah lifts up his voice from within the great fish, and he speaks of divine power as he experiences it, from the depths of God's creation, from the midst of the layers of the world: "the flood rolled round me" and "the waters surrounded me, endangering my life; / The deep rolled round me, seaweeds wrapped my head. / I sank to the very roots of the mountains." We might say that prophetic language is overwhelmingly reserved for men—but women are not silent in the Torah. The prayers of Hannah, the songs of Miriam, the public prophecy of the judge Deborah preserve their voices. The prophets do not speak in a vacuum; they raise their voices in a specific culture, and like all artistic expression, their language is grounded in particular social circumstances. And yet prophecy defines itself in opposition to the everyday world and the common social experience. Gideon and Jonah and even Moses cling at first to their accustomed lives and social roles, and only finally do they voice—and act on—their prophetic visions.

Prophecy is a poetry of change, social, political, moral, spiritual. It was with the prophetic model in mind that Shelley wrote of poets as the unacknowledged legislators of the world.

What makes prophetic poetry so startling and, even now, so new? It is the immediacy of the prophet's lyric voice. Even as Jonah thanks God for his rescue from the sea, he speaks from the midst of its waters, praising God from within the fish. Jonah is still lying in the deep at the roots of the mountains; he is still being rescued. This is no emotion recollected in tranquillity; it is the instant of present experience.

The same immediacy is voiced in the songs of victory throughout the Torah. After battle is over, the prophet takes up a battle song, fierce, proud, triumphant—not a reminiscence but an expression of the struggle as it happens. "I will sing unto the Lord, for He is highly exalted" (Exod. 15:1), Moses sings with his people after crossing the Red Sea. The poetic use of the verb "I will sing," or *ashira*, has always served as a point for discussion and elaboration among commentators. Why does Moses say that he will sing unto the Lord when he is already actually singing to him? He speaks of the future because he places his song within his experience of God's act. He speaks as if he were calling to God during the flight from the Egyptians, as if he were looking up from the seabed and crying out, "When we are saved, I will thank the Lord." To begin with "I will sing" brings back the moment at which Moses called out to God. It collapses the time between the event and the expression of it. Throughout the Song of the Sea, Moses, Miriam, and Israel speak from within the moment of escape, and they speak of God, not as a distant power but as the active force in their triumph. Thus they figure God as a warrior: "The Lord is a man of war, / The Lord is His name" (v. 3), and this image provides the outward parallel to the more inward-looking declaration: "The Lord is my strength and song" (v. 2). God is for his people the source of power and artistic expression. Indeed he *is* their power and their inspiration.

The prophet and judge Deborah also situates her victory song within the battle that has passed. She diffuses her own narrative voice among the events, places, and people in the battle against Sisera. She speaks in the past tense: "The mountains quaked at the presence of the Lord" (Judg. 5:4); in the future tense: "There shall they rehearse the righteous acts of the Lord" (v. 11); and in the present tense: "And Dan, why doth he sojourn by the ships?" (v. 17). Deborah addresses God; she addresses herself: "Awake, awake, Deborah; Awake, awake, utter a song" (v. 12), and she addresses the tribes of Israel, the brave tribes of Zebulun and Naphtali, and the tribes who evaded the risk of battle. Positioning her song within the battle itself, Deborah even takes the voice of Sisera's mother waiting at home during the battle: "Why is his chariot so long in coming? / Why tarry the wheels of his chariots?" (v. 28). Deborah imagines the battle in its complexity, in multiple places and perspectives—even from the perspective of the enemy. This sublimation of the narrative voice is a triumph of imagination, a virtuosic flight of negative capability. The prophet sings from within the swirling battle, and she takes her listeners in with her as if to the eye of the storm, where God's will is visible.

Both the Song of the Sea and the Song of Deborah evoke, and even invoke, God's violence on behalf of the Israelites. At the sea God throws back the waters to allow Israel to pass and then lets the waters fall upon the pursuing Egyptians. Miriam sings, "Sing ye to the Lord, for He is highly exalted: The horse and his rider hath He cast into the sea" (v. 19). Deborah addresses God: "Lord, when Thou didst go forth out of Seir, / When Thou didst march out of the field of Edom, / The earth trembled, the heavens also dropped, / Yea, the clouds dropped water" (Judg. 5:4). God is an active presence in the world, and the prophets speak as witnesses to his deeds; they speak of God because they must, because they cannot deny what they have seen and heard.

The pagan prophet Balaam provides one of the clearest expressions of the overwhelming imperative to speak God's will. Called by the Moabite king, Balak, to curse Israel as they enter Canaan, Balaam rides up to the hills and prepares his sacrifices. Yet he cannot curse Israel. When he lifts up his voice, he hears himself blessing the people. The king demands, "What hast thou done unto me? I took thee to curse mine enemies, and, behold, thou hast blessed them altogether" (Num. 23:11). The prophet answers with another question: "Must I not take heed to speak that which the Lord putteth in my mouth?" (v. 12). Balaam is the mouthpiece of God. Twice more Balaam tries to go up and curse Israel, and each time he finds his curses overwhelmed and reversed into blessings. Out of this experience he redefines his prophecy and himself as "The saying of him who heareth the words of God, Who seeth the vision of the Almighty, Fallen down, yet with opened eyes" (Num. 24:4). The prophet is overwhelmed by God's message, prostrate before it. Yet he is not numbed or silenced but awakened into action. His eyes are open to God's vision.

These are God's battles of which the prophets sing, and these are his songs. What are we to make of this kind of poetry, these cries of certainty? We can distance ourselves from the assertions of divine inspiration and examine the language of the Song of the Sea, the imagery in the Song of Deborah: "Then did the horsehoofs stamp / By reason of the prancings, the prancings of their mighty ones" (Judg. 5:22)—a line worthy of Homer. But it is impossible to separate these images from the theme that generates them. These are glimpses of God's acts in the world. The elevated voices of the prophets' song is their fitting record and pronouncement. Such poetry seems dangerous because it claims so much. Yet if we are to examine this poetry without apology, we must take its claims seriously.

When we hear or read these cries of divine inspiration, we want a measure and standard of comparison. We want to know how to judge the poetic voice of the prophet, how to hold up and study the claim of authenticity. We want to put the prophet's words in context. One context is provided in the surrounding narrative of the Torah. Some scholars think that the prose narrative is written as the setting for the more ancient and oracular poems. Whether written first or second, the prose narrative mediates: it helps to situate the prophetic voice within the record of a historical, national experience. While the elevated voice of a prophet rises up out of the historical narrative, it is still part of that larger chronicle. Each of the great leaders in the Torah is mortal, and his death is recorded. Moses goes up to the mountains and dies without entering the promised land. Granted a vision of the land from afar, Moses dies exiled like the poets in Plato's *Republic*.

Woven into the biblical narrative, prophetic, spiritual language is inextricably connected to the particulars of the history of Israel. Balaam's vision of Israel as a perfect, whole, and ordered community is juxtaposed against the narrative record of a people doubting themselves and the promises made to them, at times courageous, at times frightened and cynical. The Song of the Sea with its affirmation of God's love for Israel is woven into the prose record of Exodus—a record that reveals the divisions, dissensions, and pettiness of the children of Israel. The thanksgiving to God—"I will sing unto the Lord, for He is highly exalted"—he contrasts with the other voices and emotions of which Israel is capable, among them the voice that complains to Moses and refers ironically to the great Egyptian tombs:

"Were there no graves in Egypt that thou hast taken us away to die in the wilderness?"(Exod. 14:5). In the context of a larger history, the Song of the Sea is triumphant, but not triumphalist. It takes its moment, but cannot stand alone as the sole image of the exodus.

A second point of reference for the claims of prophetic poetry is provided by the prophets themselves. The prophets use a language that expresses God's will, but they speak against an idolatry of language. The words do not capture, contain, or coerce divinity. The poetry is complete in the moment of utterance. Yet woven through the mystic language are exhortations to action. The prophets speak self-consciously of God's desire for deeds instead of words, ethical action instead of ritual demonstrations of piety. Figurative language and the figurative action that is ritual cannot stand alone as substitutes for righteousness of action. Thus Isaiah chastises Israel for its pleas to God: "Why seest thou not, they ask, when we fast? Why heedest thou not when we afflict ourselves?" The fast and the pleas to God are insufficient. God answers Israel with questions of his own:

> Can such be my chosen fast, the day of man's self denial?
> To bow down his head like a bullrush, to sit in sackcloth and ashes?
> Is that what you call fasting, a day acceptable to the Lord?
> Behold, this is the fast that I esteem precious:
> Loosen the chains of wickedness, undo the bonds of oppression,
> Let the crushed go free, break all yokes of tyranny! (Isa. 58:5–6)

Ritual obeisances and the submission of momentary denial are inert signs. God requires righteous action.

The prophets do not present themselves solely as ecstatic poets. Continually a social program emerges from their incantatory rhythms: "loosen the chains of wickedness, undo the bonds of oppression." The social program voiced in their lyric manifestos becomes a vision of God and Israel. Prescriptive and lyric language fuse and temper each other in prophetic poetry. Amos holds up the transgressions of Israel:

> . . . they sell the righteous for silver,
> And the needy for a pair of shoes;
> That pant after the dust of the earth on the head of the poor,
> And turn aside the way of the humble;

And a man and his father go unto the same maid,
To profane My holy name. (Amos 2:6–7)

Avarice, oppression of the poor, incest, lewdness, blasphemy—Amos
catalogs the broken laws. Then in searing mystic language he announces the punishment for these transgressions: "Saith the Lord . . .
Behold, I will make it creak under you, As a cart creaketh that is full
of sheaves" (vv. 11–13). God will not punish as a human judge does,
and God's sentence is not to be measured in legal or social terms.
Amos can express God's response to moral and civil violation only
with a layered metaphor, an image of the fragility of human enterprise piled up like sheaves in a rickety cart, a vision of impermanence
and motion, heading for breakdown. Summer ends; the harvest is
gathered and piled precariously in a shaking, trembling world.

The multiple voices and genre forms in the Torah mingle narrative
and poetry and, on a smaller scale, build prophetic poetry from the
dynamic play of historical narrative and lyric vision. In the Song of
the Sea the children of Israel link glimpses of their flight from the
Egyptians with a mystic visualization of God's power—the work of
his "right hand." They picture the Egyptian army, "Pharaoh's chariots and his host" and "his chosen captains" (Exod. 14:4), and then
catch God's wrath in a simile: "it consumeth them as stubble" (v. 7).
Throughout the song the narrative of the escape is fragmented. Visionary language interrupts and scatters the details of the story, just
as God overwhelms Pharaoh's army.

Like the Song of the Sea, the Song of Deborah is a fugue of narrative detail and lyric metaphor. Deborah tells of the tribes joining in
rebellion: "The kings came, they fought; / Then fought the kings of
Canaan, / In Taanach by the waters of Megiddo" (Judg. 5:19). She
describes exactly who composed the alliance against the Canaanites
and identifies the battlefield. Then Deborah raises her voice:

They fought from heaven,
The stars in their courses fought against Sisera.
The brook Kishon swept them away,
That ancient brook, the brook Kishon.
O my soul, tread them down with strength. (vv. 20–21)

The battle is joined in cosmic terms that echo the events of human
history. The specific site, the brook Kishon, is mirrored and matched
by the stars. The prophet's narrative record gives way to a mystic vi-

sion of destiny figured by the stars. And the third-person narrative is broken by the first-person exclamation "O my soul" as the lyric voice of the prophet enters the history of the battle.

The play of narrative and visionary modes in these songs expresses a complex relation between God and historical events. On the one hand, men and women shape history with the choices they make. Yael determines to kill Sisera; the tribes of Naphtali and Zebulun choose to join the rebellion. There is murmuring and dissension among the tribes of Israel, together destined by God to be a nation, but divided and freely choosing separate futures among themselves. Yet Deborah figures God as an active force in battle, a warrior who "didst march out of the field of Edom" (v. 4). The prophet figures God as moving and controlling nature and armies. Divine and human agency act together in Deborah's battle song—the one figured by balladic narrative and the other by the lyric voice. It is impossible to separate the interwoven voices, and together they provide a history in which human agency and God's will coexist, neither one completely upstaging the other.

God's will and man's will shape history together. The prophet Moses provides the most important expression of this nexus between God and man. Moses' great song after the giving of the law begins with an appeal calling to witness both heaven and earth, and evocation of divine and human realms: "Give ear, ye heavens, and I will speak; / And let the earth hear the words of my mouth" (Deut. 32:1). Moses' final prophecy concludes and culminates his recitation of God's commandments. He takes the detailed, prescriptive language of the law into a new key as he raises his voice and proclaims God's commandments in poetic terms:

> My doctrine shall drop as the rain,
> My speech shall distill as the dew;
> As the small rain upon the tender grass,
> And as the showers upon the herb. (v. 2)

Moses mingles images from the natural and social worlds. He describes the legal doctrine he has developed as rain. His speech will nurture growth like dew. God allows the tender grass to grow and provides rain for young plants. In the same way God's law will fall among the children of Israel and give them life. The law comes from the heavens like rain, but it takes a gentle form on earth. It is not designed for punishment, storms, and floods, but for light showers and growth. If the law has prescriptive content, it also has poetic form. Moses has prescribed a code of action, but now he speaks of this ethical code as a gift. If the law is structured, it is also natural. Together in Moses' prophecy, the prescriptive and lyric voices define the active reciprocity of Israel and God. God commands Israel, and when Israel acts according to his law, the nation will flourish as the tender grass springs up in the rain.

The law is like rain; prophetic speech like dew. One falls from above and the other springs up mysteriously in the night. Rain is an image of God's intervention in the world. Dew is an image of God acting on the imagination.

Our Dream of the Good God

LORE SEGAL

This essay searches the Bible stories for the character we call God, Lord, Yahweh. What are his characteristics? Do the stories agree in what they tell us about him? Is it his nature, for instance, to forgive the sinner, or to visit the sins of the fathers upon the children, or the sins of the children upon the fathers? He is a God who sometimes changes his mind, who tells us he is jealous as well as faithful. He is a war god who destroys nations down to the baby suckling at the breast, as well as an ever-merciful and tender father. The God created by the stories in our Bible tells us about our own balked desire for perfection, our dream of goodness.

THIS ESSAY MEANS TO DISOBEY THE BEAUTIFUL ADVICE OF THE Book of Job that tells us to refrain from questioning the moral character of the Lord's activities, reminding us of our ignorance of him at whose creation of the world, and of ourselves, we were so particularly absent.

Biblical quotations are taken from Lore Segal, *The Book of Adam to Moses* and *The Story of King Saul and King David* (New York, Schocken Books, 1987 and 1991), respectively, unless otherwise indicated.

I want to question God's behavior as it is related in the Bible, the source of which one may call God, if one has the talent for belief. Remember the old lady in the joke: She walks into a bookshop and wants a Bible. "What version of the Bible, madam?" asks the clerk. "Why, the Bible," the old lady says, "as God wrote it." The rest of us are answered by another joke addressed to those who can't believe Shakespeare wrote Shakespeare's plays: "Shakespeare's plays were written by Shakespeare, or by somebody called Shakespeare."

It is our brilliant good fortune that the Source was bound to communicate itself through human agency—through a number of human agencies, some of whom happened to be the world's greatest narrative artists; nor could they help leaving upon him the thumbprint of their human propensities. I want to read the Bible not as the production of J, E, D, or P, but the product of two of these human propensities: One is precisely the propensity for storytelling, and the other is our dream of the good God. I will argue that these two propensities are in a different business from, and at cross-purposes with, each other.

THAT HUMANS TELL STORIES is demonstrably so. The Bible means by means of stories. That we, ancients and moderns both, yearn for goodness may require substantiation. The late George P. Elliott has said that when Jean Genet cries, "Evil be thou my good!" good is his criterion. Cecil Day Lewis asserts that the man who crashes a queue and lies, "I was here first!" shows he knows wrong when he does it, and thereby proves God's existence.

The very words *goodness* and *virtue* make us itchy, and with reason. They smack of the old repressions: they sound anti-intellectual, antiscientific, ignorant of what we have internalized of Freud, and of our developmental history. We say that we don't use words like that; we don't think in terms of good and bad, we think, and I think that we are wrong. Suppose I accuse you of some of the old-fashioned venalities. You lie, I say, and you are envious and lazy. Don't you experience me as suddenly disagreeable? Don't you wish I would go away and not come back? How, if you care nothing about virtues, could I trouble you by saying that you don't have them? You say it isn't virtue but the reputation for virtue that we desire? Isn't hypocrisy proof that we value virtue? Why would we pretend to have a thing for which we have no value? Does the value that I say we have for goodness make us good? Not at all. It has as much effect as a New Year's resolution. Perhaps goodness is like belief—a talent, and talent is exceptional.

What we have is not goodness but a dream of goodness and we continue dreaming it against reason and despite the evidence of our daily experience. We keep demanding that our leaders have it. We react with unsophisticated shock every time our presidents prove to be crooks and clowns. We experienced a sharp regret when we learned Martin Luther King had plagiarized his examinations. "Say it ain't so!" the little kid famously begged his baseball hero who had cheated. We remember the day we discovered our parents did things that were wrong, and didn't know, half the time, *what* they were doing. Better keep our heroes inside their myths where they can't be cross-questioned: "Are you certain, Hercules, that you got the dirt out of all those Augean corners?" Do we doubt Superman's ability to clean the bad guys out of our metropolis? How clever of religion to locate paradise in a time past of the past, and heaven in a future the far side of that bourne from which no traveler returns to tell us it ain't necessarily so.

If there is a God in heaven, he must, please, be all those things nothing in the world can ever be—just and merciful and consistent. The atheist is caught in the same dream: If even God is not perfect, we prefer our heavens empty.

DOES THE BIBLE GIVE us a God who is just, merciful, and who always knows what he is doing? Read what the Bible stories say. Here are some things they tell.

Standing and talking to the burning bush, Moses asks who this God is who is sending him on a mission impossible. He says, "What if I go to the children of Israel and say to them: The God of your fathers has sent me to you!—and they ask me, What God? What is His name?—What shall I say to them?" (Exod. 3:13). The Lord replies with his two classic answers: He says, "I am the Lord, the Almighty God," that is to say everybody's only God; and he says, "I am the God of Abraham, Isaac, and Jacob" (v. 16), that is to say the tribal God of the children of Israel.

The second name is the one that Moses is to tell the children. God adds, "But it is to you that I make known My name: I AM THAT I AM" (v. 14), an answer as broad and as long as eternity backward and forward. The Hebrew verb is in a narrative future tense: "I have (always) been and will (always) be what I am." And it is an answer that has the circumference of the head of a pin: I exist (and that is all you are able to know about me). It invites the most rigorous apprehension of a God so holy we may not take his name into our mouths, whose nature is to be inapprehensible. Any modifier we add to the belief in God's sheer existence is, by definition, a human and inapplicable idea.

This is the grandest, purest concept of God, and one which story can do nothing with, which the human imagination constantly betrays: Rabbi Adin Steinsaltz began a recent lesson on Talmud with a midrash meant to warn his New York lay audience not to do what I am presently doing—thinking about God. The God in the midrash says, "I wish my people would forget me and observe my Torah." But in order to tell us not to think about God, the midrash has to think about a God who speaks, is witty, and has a preference.

An ancient and recurring theme in story shows mankind—or more usually womankind—as prone to vulgar curiosity, wanting to uncover mystery, to name its name and know its nature. In folk tale, which tends to side with the human, the miller's daughter who learns Rumpelstiltskin's name has the imp in her power; henceforward he must do her bidding. In myth the mortal woman who uncovers her divine lover's identity earns death, or the withdrawal, at any rate, of his divine favor.

The Grimm tale called "Mrs. Gertrude" gives an exemplary warning to those of us who want to know:

> Once upon a time, there was a little girl and she was obstinate and willful and did not obey her parents when they spoke to her. Can such a child come to any good? One day she said to her parents, I've heard so much talk about Mrs. Gertrude that I want to go and see her. People say her house is very strange and they say there are such queer goings on there that I've become curious. Her parents strictly forbade her and said . . . If you go there you are no longer our child.[1]

But the little girl goes to visit Mrs. Gertrude and sees "the witch in her true ornament," that is to say, in the devil's several iconographical selves. Hereupon Mrs. Gertrude

> changed the little girl into a log and threw it into the fire. And when it was at full glow she sat down beside it, warmed herself and said, "There now, isn't that nice and bright!"[2]

The biblical character called God, too, prefers obedient to intelligent and nosy children. The desire for knowledge equals hubris. "This human has become like one of us in the knowledge of good and evil," says the Lord (Gen. 3:22), and makes us mortal. When we acquire the skill to raise a tower so high that we could peer into heaven, God comes right down and puts a stop to it.

At Sinai Moses asks the Lord for yet more revelation. "Lord, let me look upon the glory of Your Presence!" The Lord is stern and gentle with him:

> You may not see My face. No man may see Me and live. Look! Here is a place by Me. Stand on this rock and when My glory passes by you, I will put you in a cleft of the rock and cover you with My hand till I have passed. Then I will take away My hand, and you shall see My back, but My face may not be seen. (Exod. 33:18–23)

God has many means by which to manifest himself to his children. He is Lord of visual metaphor. As a bush he burns without consuming himself. As a cloud by day and a pillar of light by night, God leads his children out of slavery. By placing himself between them and the pursuing Egyptians, he keeps the armies apart, remaining visible to his chosen, his dark side turned to their enemies.[3] And he is God of the word. He speaks the world into existence. He talks to his children through his priests and prophets, via visions, and in dreams. The Lord alone, says Joseph, is the dream interpreter. God is the oracle one consults in domestic, political, military, and judicial crises. The Lord's lot, the Urim and Thummim, confirms the election of kings and fingers the oath breaker.

In the early stories he and his words are grammatically inextricable from the messenger-angels. "The Lord appeared to Abraham in Mamre. . . . Abraham raised his eyes and there, in front of him, stood three men" (Gen. 18:2). The three men bathe their feet, eat, ask Sarah's whereabouts, and the Lord says, "I shall return. . . . your wife Sarah will have a son" (v. 10), and asks why Sarah is laughing. It is the men who rise and whom Abraham, like a good host, accompanies on their way, and the Lord who says to himself, "Shall I hide from Abraham what I am going to do?" (v. 17) and tells him his plan for the destruction of Sodom and Gomorrah. "And the Lord went away as soon as he had finished speaking with Abraham, and Abraham returned home. In the evening two angels arrived at Sodom"

(Gen. 18:33–19:1). It is an angel, for good measure, who stands in the path of Balaam's ass, and the Lord who meets Balaam night after night to teach him the words with which to bless Israel and curse the enemies.

To Abraham God talks directly and repeatedly, and to Moses "mouth to mouth, like a man speaking to his friend" (Exod. 33:11).

The Lord is one of the few biblical characters to whose thoughts we are privy. This is a literature that does not deal in the stock-in-trade of realist fiction. We are not told, and are not invited to imagine, what it feels like when the Lord of Israel has locked the wheels of your carriage in the middle of the dry bed of the Red Sea just as the two walls of water rejoin to drown you. The story tells what the characters do and what they say: Joseph leaves the room, weeps, washes his face. The story does not explain—and does not need to explain—that he is moved by the presence of his little brother, Benjamin. David retains Uriah in Jerusalem over two nights. The story does not comment on the king's need for the husband to sleep with his wife to legitimize the king's baby. The story does not say, "the Egyptians felt . . . ," or "Joseph knew . . . ," or "Abraham saw . . . ," or "David thought. . . ." But it tells us what God saw when he looked at the world he had made and that it grieved him, and how, afterward, he "smelled the sweet smell" of Noah's sacrifice (Gen. 8:12). We know how God feels because he tells his heart, and we overhear the conversation.

God has several ways of expressing his disappointment. He can give us the silent treatment. "The Lord's word was rare and there were few visions" (1 Sam. 3:1) in the time of the priesthood of the well-meaning, ineffectual Eli, who shares with the future king, David, an inability to control grown sons. Eli keeps misunderstanding what goes on in front of his eyes—an old man going blind to the Lord's purposes. It is with the new little prophet, Samuel, who, like Moses, does not know who this is talking to him, that the Lord reopens his ongoing conversation with his people, Israel. He foretells to the reluctant child the destruction of Eli's priestly dynasty, which will visit the sins of the children upon the father.

It is an anthropomorphic God who walks in the garden in the cool of the evening to catch our first parents in their guilt and nakedness. After Sinai his Presence makes itself known in—or is it on?—the tent of the congregation, causing the skin of Moses' face to shine so that it must be veiled from common sight. To the people, who cannot bear very much reality, God appears as brightness, or as weather and trumpets, which the sonorous King James Version of the English Bible works hard to render transcendently: "It came to pass on the third day in the morning, that there were thunder and lightning and a thick cloud upon the mount, and the voice of the trumpet exceedingly loud" (Exod. 19:16). When Samuel wants to awe the children of Israel into guilt and obedience, he relies on the Lord for a demonstration:

> Stand before me and you will see a great thing that the Lord is going to do right before your eyes. Isn't this the dry time of the wheat harvest? I will call upon the Lord and He will make it thunder and rain. . . . And Samuel called upon the Lord and the Lord made it thunder and rain and that day the people were very much afraid of the Lord and of Samuel. The people said, Pray to the Lord your God so your servants shall not die because on top of all our sins we asked for a king! Then Samuel said, Don't be afraid! (1 Sam. 12:17–18)

There's reason to fear a Lord who is also a war god with a temper.

> The earth shuddered and shook and the foundations of the heavens quaked and shuddered because He was angry. Smoke rose up from His nostrils, and a consuming fire out of his mouth; it kindled the living coals. He bent the heavens and came down; darkness was under His feet. Mounted on a cherub He flew; He was seen on the wings of the wind. . . . Out of the brightness before Him living coals kindled. The Lord thundered out of heaven. . . . He loosed His arrows to scatter them [the enemy] and His lightning to confound them. The bedrock of ocean was laid bare, the foundation of the world was disclosed with the Lord's chiding, with the breath of the wind from His nostrils. (2 Sam. 22:8–9)

He is the origin of nature's cataclysms, the great flood, the fire and brimstone over Sodom and Gomorrah. It is he, and he never tires of reminding us, who sent those ten plagues that finally forced the Egyptian slaver to let us go free.

It is not only the enemy who feels his draconian displeasure. The Lord sends plagues, snakes, and famines to punish his own stiff-necked, disobedient children, who keep despairing and grumbling and are always about to slide into the worship of foreign gods. They grumble once too often.

> The Lord said ... as My Presence fills the earth, not one of those whose eyes have seen the Glory of My Presence and the wonders that I have done for them in Egypt and who have tried Me ten times over and have disobeyed Me and railed against Me, not a single one shall see the land I promised to their fathers. ... This is what you shall say to them: Your carcasses shall rot in the wilderness! (Num. 14:20–25)

There is not a little resemblance, in certain passages, between the biblical God and the Greek models on whom the human imagination conferred its own propensities raised to a power. Like the Olympians, our God quarrels with the other gods, except that he can always prove all except himself to be impostors. There is the witty story in which Dagon pays unwilling homage to this idea. Having captured the ark of the Lord in battle, the Philistines carry it triumphantly into their pantheon.

> When the Ashdodites woke early next morning, and came to the house of Dagon, what do you know! There was Dagon and he had fallen face down on the ground before the ark of God. So they picked Dagon up and set him back in his place. They woke early next morning, and there he was again—Dagon flat on his face before the ark of God, and his head and both his hands lopped off on the threshold, and only the stump of Dagon left in one piece. (1 Sam. 5:2–4)

And anyone who has tried to barbecue appreciates the famous contest in which Elijah and the Lord beat Baal and his lot of worshipers. Four hundred and fifty of Baal's prophets praying morning to noon cannot get the fire started under their sacrifice, but Elijah calls upon the name of the Lord of Abraham and Isaac and Israel, and fire consumes wood that has been doused with three times four barrels of water. All the renegades fall on their faces and proclaim, "The Lord, He is God, the Lord He is the God!" (1 Kings 18:39).

What does the Lord mean when he says he is a jealous God? He means what you and I mean: Love me and me alone. The metaphor extends: The unfaithful "whore" after the other gods.

Like the Greeks the Lord likes his fame and glory. He manipulates his world constituency with Machiavellian skill. The Lord hardens Pharaoh's heart in order, says the story, to be obliged to loosen the ten plagues and give himself the opportunity for a public demonstration of the power of his hand. He says,

> I shall send down all My plagues upon you and upon your court and upon your people. I shall show you there is no one like Me in all the world. Don't you understand that I could stretch out My hand and wipe you and your people off the face of the earth? I have preserved you in order to show you the greatness of My might, and to make My name known upon the earth. This time tomorrow I shall send down a very great hailstorm. (Exod. 9:14–16)

His vanity, as well as his personal affections, can be manipulated.

> Oh, Lord [says Moses]. Why does Your anger rage against Your own people, whom You brought out of Egypt with the might of Your great hand? Do You want the Egyptians to say, It was to do them mischief that He brought them out, so He could slay them in the mountains and wipe them off the face of the earth! Remember Your servants Abraham, Isaac, and Jacob. (Exod. 32:11–13)

And the Lord relents.

There are moments when he wields that same mighty hand with a fatherly—a motherly—tenderness. Before sending Adam and Eve into the bitter outside world, the Lord "made tunics out of skins for Adam and his wife, and dressed them" (Gen. 4:21). Before drowning the violent and wicked world, the Lord makes sure everyone inside the ark will be safe and dry, and "He closed the door behind them" (Gen. 7:16). It is the hand that made the plagues that the Lord of the World puts over Moses in the cleft of the rock to shield him from His murderous glory. And he promises to care for David's children like a human parent:

I shall be a father to him and he shall be a son to Me.
When he does wrong I shall punish him with the rod the
way men beat their children, but I shall never withdraw
my love from him as I withdrew it from Saul whom I removed out of your way. (2 Sam. 7:14–15)

The story has accumulated the character called God out of contradictions—how else could one God encompass everything? Harold
Bloom calls him an imp.

WHERE DO WE GET this notion of justice by which we judge the justice of God, which we take to be our birthright, encoded in our national declarations, ingrained in our language: "That's not fair!" we cry
in outrage; "So and so didn't deserve this or that!" Human courts enact
morality plays for which there is no precedent: it is not from nature
that we learn that right is rewarded and wrong punished. We did not
observe the justice of which we dream in our personal autobiographies
nor our national histories. It was Torah that taught us justice.

HOW JUSTLY DOES THE Lord judge his children?
    The 37th Psalm denies life's unfairness. It says, "I have been young
and now am old; yet have I not seen the righteous forsaken nor his
seed begging for bread" (Pss. 37:25). When observant Jews recite the
blessings after meals, they add, "Praise the Lord for He is good; His
love endures for ever. He opens His hand and satisfies every living
thing with favor. . . . I have been young and now I am old; yet I have
not seen the righteous so forsaken that his children were begging for
bread."4 In the prayer books of the past this passage came with a del-
icate stage direction: "Whisper to avoid offending anyone present
who might be poor or hungry."
    King David is confident that God responds appropriately. "To the
faithful You will be faithful; with the perfect You will be perfect.
With the pure You will be pure, and cunning with those who are
crooked" (2 Sam. 22:27). He looks back upon his own fortunate life
and, leaving out of the equation the sick baby who died, the rapist
son who was murdered by the son who dethroned his father and was
killed in battle, deduces that he has been good:

    The Lord repaid my righteousness. He rewarded the clean-
    ness of my hands, for I have kept the Lord's ways and have

not wickedly turned away from my God. All his laws have
I kept before my eyes; I did not turn from His statutes. I
was perfect before Him, and kept myself from sin. Therefore the Lord repays me. (vv. 21–25)

In another place God annunciates his divine freedom from the constraints of justice. "I show favor to whom I show My favor, and My
mercy to whom I show My mercy" (Exod. 33:19). Christianity calls
this grace by which God favors without reference to human desert.
To the unbeliever the phenomenon presents as luck.

THE BOOK OF JOB is a meditation on ill luck when God gives the
devil leave to visit misfortune upon a righteous man. Job, never having heard of the Christian doctrine of original sin, insists on his own
perfection, and the story caves in, out of kindness to the reader,
I think, and reinstates Job in a happiness commensurate with
his deserts, not with our human experience of the probabilities.
Job's comforters, adherents of the just-God theory, are bound to argue that Job's misfortune proves that he, or someone belonging
to him, has by intention or inadvertence done something to deserve it.

The children of Israel make the same deduction whenever the enemy wins a battle and takes back the cities that the children of Israel
had taken from them, and they must pay the enemy tribute instead
of exacting it from the enemy. The text always assumes the children
of Israel must have "done what displeased the Lord." Better to blame
misfortunes on our sins, which we plan to amend next Yom Kippur.
To believe ourselves innocent of our past disasters makes for a helpless future.

WHAT ARE THE SINS God punishes? Whom does he reward?
What did Adam and Eve do to get us bumped out of paradise and
condemned to mortality? Was it appetite succumbing to what looked
beautiful and tasted delicious? Was it intelligence lusting to know?
Was it the ur-woman's propensity not to accept the prohibitions of
authority without prior discussion? Was it disobedience? Cain receives the same penalty—exile and suspended mortality—for the ur-
murder and survives to father the race that invents our fratricidal
cities.

The Bible fails, consistently, to calibrate sin according to the standards that we think it has taught us.

What is it that the Lord punishes? Gathering wood on the Sabbath; the children of Israel hesitate, but the Lord tells them to stone the man to death. The insurgents, Korah, Dathan, and Abiram, die theatrically. For sinning with the golden calf some three thousand are cut down.

> Moses went and stood by the gates of the camp and said, All those on the side of the Lord come here. . . . And all the sons of Levi gathered around Moses and Moses said, This is the word of the Lord, the God of Israel: Let everyone of you gird on his sword and go through the camp from one end to the other and slay his brother, his neighbor, his kin. —And they did as Moses said. (Exod. 32:26–27)

The ill-gotten cousins who make war against the Lord's chosen children get killed by the edge of the sword. Instant death punishes a human touch upon a holy object. Man and beast are warned under threat of destruction to keep their hands and hoofs off Sinai so long as the Lord is on it. Remember Uzza:

> They carried the ark of God out of the house of Abinadab, who lived on the hill, and set it on a new cart, and his sons Uzza and Ahio went down the hill with the new cart. Uzza walked alongside and Ahio walked ahead, and David and all the House of Israel danced with all their might. . . . But as they came to the threshing floor of Nachon, the oxen stumbled and Uzza reached for the Ark of God to hold it steady, and the Lord's anger broke against Uzza because he had reached his hand to the ark and he died there, beside the Ark of God. (2 Sam. 6:3–7)

Even King David is horrified. "David was angry because the Lord had broken out against Uzza and had broken him. . . . On that day David was afraid" (v. 8). The king does not want to bring this holy and dangerous ark into Jerusalem; he diverts it to the house of a neighbor.

Bible stories not infrequently decline to satisfy us in the matter of

motive. Just what *was* the matter with Cain's sacrifice? Why is his offer, why is *he*, rejected, and why are Abel and his offer favored? We
would not have kept Moses out of the promised land because of what
he did at the waters of Meribah!

Did Saul lose God's favor and his kingdom for failing to wait for
Samuel, who is late for their appointment? Isn't it sensible, when you
see the enemy about to attack and your soldiers beginning to desert,
to sacrifice to the Lord and make yourself battle-ready? Samuel has
the answer:

> Do burnt offerings and sacrifices please the Lord as much
> as obedience to His word? To listen is better than to sac-
> rifice, and to hear better than the fat of rams. Disobedi-
> ence is as sinful as sorcery, and rebelliousness as wicked as
> idolatry. (1 Sam. 15:22–23)

Obedience and faith are the virtues that the patriarchs share with
every one of the Lord's favorites, who don't, in other matters, necessarily act according to our own ideas of what is right and wrong. The
story says that Noah is the only righteous man in a wicked world, but
gives no evidence beyond his prompt and unquestioning obedience
to the Lord's word. Nor does the Lord, later in the story, fault Noah's
drunkenness or nakedness.

Disobedience is one sin father Abraham fails to commit. But, fearing the lecherous and violent Egyptians, he has Sarah say she is his
sister and pimps her to Pharaoh to save his own skin, and, in the
event, grows richer. The heathen behaves like a gentleman—an irate
gentleman, it's true.

> For her sake Abraham was treated well and got sheep and
> oxen. . . . But the Lord afflicted Pharaoh and his house-
> hold with great plagues because of Abraham's wife Sarah.
> Pharaoh sent to Abraham and said, What have you done
> to me! . . . Why did you say, She is my sister, so that I
> took her to be my wife? Here! Here is your wife. Take her
> and go away. . . . and he sent him away with his wife and
> with all his possessions. (Gen. 12:16–19)

In another story the Lord encourages Abraham to let the hurt and
spiteful Sarah send his lover, Hagar, and their young son, Ishmael,

into the desert. On the Lord's say-so Abraham will raise the knife in his hand to kill his beloved son Isaac. Jacob takes advantage of a brother's hunger and his father's blind affection and cheats and lies for his blessing,[5] yet the Lord appears to him at the head of a ladder full of angels and allows Jacob to wrestle him for his blessing also.

Faith, obedience, and bad behavior are all in the service of the Lord's business. God insists on moving, as the hymn has it "in mysterious ways His wonders to perform." If Ham abuses his father's nakedness, it is in order to be cursed and father a tribe of Godless children for God to use as an instrument with which to punish his children of Israel's future disobedience. In the cognate story of Lot, God's cleansing of Sodom and Gomorrah leads Lot's daughters to engender from *their* drunken father another set of cousins with whom to scourge Israel's backsliding. If the French court attended royal births to certify their future king, the Bible invites our witness at the coitus from which will spring our future enemy.

As for Joseph, that obnoxious child with the megalomaniacal dreams, he tattletales on his brothers so that they will sell him into Egypt, so that he can save the region from starvation (in the course of which he manipulates Egypt's independent farmers into vassalhood to the Pharaoh) in order to install the family in the lushest Egyptian neighborhood (failing to take every opportunity to relieve his gray-haired father's lifelong mourning, for the sake of a more suspenseful narrative and a more deliciously happy ending). The happy ending will be temporary, for the Lord is preparing for his children four hundred years of enslavement so that, eventually hearing their howls of despair, he will send Moses to take them on that forty-year death march into the wilderness.

ONE THEORY ARGUES THAT the two books of Samuel were written at the court of King Solomon to whitewash the usurpation of the House of Saul by the reigning House of David. Observe how the story glamorizes David, the rosy-cheeked young giant-killer, and portrays Saul as a paranoid would-be killer. Story and history know the same political trick: Insist on the lovable side of the characters on your own side, and the moral sleaze on the other's. The story manipulates the reader to compare David's grace under the pressure of defeat with the manipulations of the treacherous son, Absalom. Observe Absalom outside the city's gates:

> Absalom got himself a chariot and horses, and fifty men to
> run ahead of him. He would get up early in the morning
> and stand in the road.... If anybody came along with
> some matter of justice to bring before the king for judg-
> ment, Absalom would call him over and say, What town
> do you come from?—The man would say, Your servant is
> from such and such a tribe of Israel! Then Absalom would
> say, Look, your case is right and just, but none of the
> king's people are going to listen to you.... Or if someone
> approached to prostrate himself before Absalom, Absalom
> would reach out his hand and take him and kiss him.
> That's how Absalom behaved to all the Israelites who
> came to the king for judgment. That is how he stole the
> hearts of the people of Israel. (2 Sam. 15:1–6)

Now watch David halted by the city's last house to see his army and
his loyalist friends marching out before him.

> The king said to Ittai the Gittite, Why, are you coming
> with us too? Go back and stay with the new king, for you
> are a stranger; you, too, are an exile from your own land.
> It was only yesterday that you came, and today I should
> make you wander who knows where with us? I must go
> where I can. Turn back and take your kin with you and
> may the Lord's mercy and truth be with you! (vv. 19–20)

But the good Ittai says, "Wherever my lord the king will be, whether
to live or die, that's where your servant will be too" (v. 21), and becomes one in the spy ring that, with God as ally, returns David to his
throne.

STORY HAS A MIND of its own and tells things sometimes it might
have preferred us not to know. Stories operate like dreams; both veil
what is to be uncovered; neither is capable of the cover-up.

 If it is true that the story sets out to do a whitewash, it tells incon-
venient truths: How clean are David's hands? Forget Bathsheba and
the fact that the king, having cuckolded his lover's husband, sends
him to be killed in the front lines. He says he's sorry, God punishes
him with the illness and death of the baby, and forgives him.

(Whether we forgive God for the death of the baby is the question Job has advised us to refrain from asking.) There are other things David does, and they appall the modern reader of a certain cast of mind: After David has exiled himself in Philistia to escape Saul's persecutions, King Achish grants asylum to him, to his guerrilla army of malcontents, and to David's father and mother. He gives them the city of Ziklag to live in. (Perhaps King Achish is benevolent. Also it's to his advantage to keep the great Hebrew warrior under his eye; he would like to induct him into his own army.) How does David, the Lord's favorite, spend time in the Diaspora?

> David and his men would go out and raid the Geshurites and the Gazirites and the Amalekites, who had always lived in the region. . . . Achish asked him, Where did you raid today? David would say, In the Southland of Judah and the Southland of the Jerahmelites, or the Southland of the Kinites. And David left not a man or woman alive to bring the story to Gath, for he said, They might betray us and say, This and this is what David did while he lived in the land of the Philistines! (1 Sam. 27:8–11)

David is operating in *imitatio dei*. Doesn't the Lord tell Samuel to tell Saul,

> I remember Amalek and what he did to Israel, and how he lay in wait when Israel came up from Egypt. Go and kill Amalek! Accomplish the sacred massacre upon all that is his. Have no pity. Kill man and woman, the weaned child and the baby at the breast, the ox and the sheep and the camel and the ass. (1 Sam. 15:2–3)

Saul seals the fate of his dynasty when he fails to accomplish the sacred massacre and lets his Amalekite brother king and the fatter animals live.

David is a better killer. When Saul asks him for a bride price of one hundred Philistine foreskins, David harvests two hundred. After he becomes the king of both Israel and Judah, he mops up the Canaanite cities.

> The Moabites, too, he defeated and he made them lie on the ground and measured them with a cord; he measured

off two cord's lengths and that many he put to death, and
one full cord's length and that many he let live, and the
Moabites became David's vassals and paid him tribute. . . .
for the Lord gave David victory wherever he went.
(2 Sam. 8:2–6)

Who are we to complain! These are our enemies on the ground, being measured, being put to death, or made to make bricks, even as
we used to be made to make bricks in Egypt. The Amalekites, whom
Saul failed to finish off, had ambushed us, generations ago—as we
were fleeing Egypt. Our father, whose favorite children we are, is
only visiting their sins upon *their* children. It's to *us* he has promised
a house of our own in our own land—it's true that we need to throw
the Kenites, the Kennizites, the Kadmonites, the Hittites, Perizzites,
the Rephaims, the Amorites, and the Canaanites, the Girashites,
and the Jebusites, who have always lived there, out of their house
and land, but not to worry because they're a bad lot and include our
accursed and our incestuously born cousins, and they worship false
gods. In fact the reason we had to be enslaved four hundred years
was to give them time to fulfill their wickednesses so as to deserve to
be thrown out.[6]

WHY ARE WE CROSS-QUESTIONING this ancient text for its good
behavior and justice? We don't ask the *Iliad* which of its characters
and which of their actions are or are not righteous. Why do we raise
the question in the case of the Bible? Because it is this same Bible
that has taught us what justice is, because by the fourth verse of the
first chapter of the first book, Torah has already raised the question
of goodness. God creates light and sees that it is good, creates land
and water, self-reproducing vegetation, the divisions of time and the
seasons, fish, fowl, and the variety of land-dwelling beast, six more
good things; the whole, when it is finished, he pronounces to be very
good.

Whether the Creator means that his workmanship is good or that
creation is good for mankind, we understand that all things were
from the moment of their genesis to be judged and that they were
judged to be good until the creation of man and woman. We are the
spoilers. The seventh "good" applies to the taste of fruit, and the
eighth comes as a paired set, with evil as the second term. The Hebrew phrase for "good and evil" is synonymous with the word for

"everything." Translate "the Tree of the Knowledge of Good and Evil" or "the Tree of the Knowledge of Everything" and take it that everything, henceforward, is one or the other. Torah has set us helplessly down into a moral world.[7]

Get the truism out of the way: What is good or bad changes. Taboos pass and we create ourselves new ones. The Grimms' nosy, disobedient, enterprising child that the nineteenth-century story burned to a cinder in the devil's fireplace is today's heroine of *Free to Be You and Me*, only she's not free to be modest and obedient, for how can such a girl come to any good?[8] What remains constant is our propensity to judge things to be one or the other and to desire them to be good.[9]

We cannot bear God to fail to be perfect, and when the stories in our truthful Bible tell it as it lays, we quarrel with them:

A perfect God cannot, by definition, be unfair to Cain, and we look to exonerate him. Maybe the adjective *fattest* attached to Abel's offering means Abel offers the best, that is to say from the heart, so that the absence of an adjective in respect to Cain's offering must mean he offers a shabby sacrifice, as a mere formality. A good try, except that the text does not say Abel offered a shabby sacrifice. Try again. Maybe the story is not *about* God; it's about the quarrel between Cain and Abel and refers to the ancient rivalry between the resident farmers and the nomadic cattlemen?

Perhaps Sarah really *was* Abraham's sister?

There is an industry engaged in excusing the Lord for ordering Abraham to sacrifice Isaac. Maybe the story doesn't mean, "Don't sacrifice Isaac!" but "No more human sacrifice!" Or is it a realistic story about all the fathers and mothers, past and present, who willingly sacrifice their sons for God and country? Kierkegaard says the story of Abraham and Isaac means that we cannot have our sons till we have given them up.

It is not at all original of us to worry. There are Bible scholars in the business of harmonizing what won't jibe. For two millennia the rabbis have been telling midrashim to justify God's ways to themselves.

At the Seder we can choose to relate the midrash in which God rebukes the angels who are applauding Israel's rescue from the pursuing Egyptian. How, God asks them, can you rejoice when my children are dying? There is a midrash that says Moses dies because of the Egyptian he killed, back in the beginning of the story. Midrash can enlighten, enlarge the scene, nudge the imagination. It can explain away what troubles us, but only as long as it keeps talking. When it stops, we discover the original question intact, and that is why we tell ourselves always more and other midrashim.

WITNESS THIS SAME YEARNING for God's perfection, goodness, and competence in the Bible itself. When the story tells something it doesn't like, it quarrels with itself. Here the Lord tells Moses, and tells Moses to tell us, that he is a just and merciful God; he says,

> I will let My goodness pass before your eyes and I will proclaim to you the name of the Lord. The Lord, the Lord God, merciful and gracious, slow to anger, full of love and faith for a thousand generations, forgiving iniquity and transgression, who will not let the guilty go free but shall bring the sins of the fathers upon the children and the children's children to the third and fourth generation. (Exod. 34:6–7)

"Wait, just a moment, God," we want to say to him. "Didn't you just contradict yourself there?" God does not wait. He says, "Write down these words, for according to these words I make my covenant with you and with Israel" (v. 28).

The biblical God has a human dilemma: Justice and mercy are, as often as not, actually exclusive.

Meanwhile there is, in Deuteronomy, a benevolent heart and a liberal mind whose God legislates mercy and imagination. In the King James Version it says,

> If thou at all take thy neighbor's raiment to pledge, thou shalt deliver it unto him by that the sun goeth down: for that is his covering only, it is his raiment for his skin. Wherein shall he sleep? (Deut. 24:10–13)

It commands us to know that even for the fellow who owes us the nights get cold. It makes it our business that people are hungry.

> When thou cuttest down thine harvest in thy field and hast forgot a sheaf in the field, thou shalt not go again to fetch it: it shall be for the stranger, for the fatherless, and for the widow. (Deut. 25:14)

The law applies not only to the "neighbor" of our own blood, but to the stranger within the city gates, for "Remember [what it felt like] when you were a bondman in the land of Egypt" (Deut. 15:15). Perhaps it is this same congenial soul who flatly contradicts one of the Lord's pronouncements when he says:

> The fathers shall not be put to death for the children, neither shall the children be put to death for the fathers: every man shall be put to death for his own sin. (Deut. 24:16)

Why is it that often, after some ferocity on the part of the Lord, the text tells us he is full of mercy, and after he has changed his mind, that he never changes? The Lord tells Samuel, "I am sorry that I made Saul king" (1 Sam. 15:10), and proposes to tear the kingdom of Israel out of his hand in order to give it to David. Samuel responds, "The Everlasting of Israel will not lie or regret, because He is not a man and does not regret" (v. 29). But of course he does so regret. He regrets making the world and drowns it, and regrets drowning it. Like the rest of us the Lord learns as he goes along. Poor God! He has to learn what our idealistic revolutionists learn over and over, or refuse over and over to learn: Wipe out one irredeemably rotten society and there's a likelihood another will rise in its place that will be rotten, too, and irredeemable. No sooner is the world washed clean than Noah gets drunk and Ham becomes guilty of that unspecified sexual uncleanness. Nor do the Lord's best-laid plans work out, for the children of Israel will never deserve Canaan, nor will Canaan ever be cleared of all the cousins. History bears witness that we remain pricks in each other's eyes and thorns in each other's sides.

As for the Lord's justice, it is Abraham who famously and forever raises the issue. It is sweet and good of the Lord to allow himself to be so questioned and argued and bargained with. Abraham is very nervous. "You see how I have taken it upon myself to speak to my Lord—I who am dust and ashes!" he says (Gen. 22:27), but cannot let it alone: "Lord don't be angry because I am still talking" (v. 30), and "Now that I have dared to take it upon myself to speak to My lord" (v. 31), and, finally, "Don't be angry if I say one more thing!" (v. 32). In the new world where a nation is in the act of being created and chosen to be the Lord's own favorite, where nations are favored and punished *as* nations, Abraham raises the issue of the individual inside the nation: Should an innocent member be punished for the sins of the members who are wicked? "Could you, the judge of all the earth, judge so unjustly and kill the good with the wicked, as if there were no difference between goodness and wickedness?" asks Abraham (v. 23).

We moderns might have given Abraham's argument a different construction: Abraham does not talk about the pain to human flesh of the coming destruction. He has two agendas—to keep clear the distinction between good and wicked and insist that they deserve differently; and to keep the Lord honest.

God avoids the theoretical difficulty when there turn out to be no innocent members.

I once brought my quarrel with the Lord to the late Rabbi Wolfe Kelman. I complained that the Lord who invented the Noahide laws that say "You shall account to Me for every life—for your own life and for the life of your brother" (Gen. 9:5), and forbids any man to shed any other man's blood, is the same Lord who orders the death of the Egyptian firstborn "from the firstborn of the Pharaoh, who sits upon his throne, to the firstborn of the prisoner in his dungeon" (Exod. 11:5). Wolfe Kelman lifted both shoulders and turned out his hands in the gesture I remember my grandmother making when she meant "True! So? What can you do?" which, in its refusal to deny, or harmonize, or finesse, or rationalize, has the heroism of Job, who acknowledges the difficulty and our human helplessness before it.

She Unnames Them

❦

URSULA K. LE GUIN

[*What better way to close our book than by returning to Eve. Ursula K. Le Guin's classic story lets Eve have the last word.*
—C.B. and C.S.]

MOST OF THEM ACCEPTED NAMELESSNESS WITH THE PERFECT indifference with which they had so long accepted and ignored their names. Whales and dolphins, seals and sea otters consented with particular grace and alacrity, sliding into anonymity as into their element. A faction of yaks, however, protested. They said that "yak" sounded right, and that almost everyone who knew they existed called them that. Unlike the ubiquitous creatures such as rats and fleas, who had been called by hundreds or thousands of different names since Babel, the yaks could truly say, they said, that they had a *name*. They discussed the matter all summer. The councils of the elderly females finally agreed that though the name might be useful to others, it was so redundant from the yak point of view that they never spoke it themselves and hence might as well dispense with it.

331

After they presented the argument in this light to their bulls, a full consensus was delayed only by the onset of severe early blizzards. Soon after the beginning of the thaw, their agreement was reached and the designation "yak" was returned to the donor.

Among the domestic animals, few horses had cared what anybody called them since the failure of Dean Swift's attempt to name them from their own vocabulary. Cattle, sheep, swine, asses, mules, and goats, along with chickens, geese, and turkeys, all agreed enthusiastically to give their names back to the people to whom—as they put it—they belonged.

A couple of problems did come up with pets. The cats, of course, steadfastly denied ever having had any name other than those self-given, unspoken, ineffably personal names which, as the poet named Eliot said, they spend long hours daily contemplating—though none of the contemplators has ever admitted that what they contemplate is in fact their name, and some onlookers have wondered if the object of that meditative gaze might not in fact be the Perfect, or Platonic, Mouse. In any case, it is a moot point now. It was with the dogs, and with some parrots, lovebirds, ravens, and mynahs, that the trouble arose. These verbally talented individuals insisted that their names were important to them, and flatly refused to part with them. But as soon as they understood that the issue was precisely one of individual choice, and that anybody who wanted to be called Rover, or Froufrou, or Polly, or even Birdie in the personal sense, was perfectly free to do so, not one of them had the least objection to parting with the lowercase (or, as regards German creatures, uppercase) generic appellations "poodle," "parrot," "dog," or "bird," and all the Linnaean qualifiers that had trailed along behind them for two hundred years like tin cans tied to a tail.

The insects parted with their names in vast clouds and swarms of ephemeral syllables buzzing and stinging and humming and flitting and crawling and tunneling away.

As for the fish of the sea, their names dispersed from them in silence throughout the oceans like faint, dark blurs of cuttlefish ink, and drifted off on the currents without a trace.

NONE WERE LEFT NOW to unname, and yet how close I felt to them when I saw one of them swim or fly or trot or crawl across my way or over my skin, or stalk me in the night, or go along beside me for a while in the day. They seemed far closer than when their names had stood between myself and them like a clear barrier: so close that my fear of them and their fear of me became one same fear. And the attraction that many of us felt, the desire to smell one another's smells, feel or rub or caress one another's scales or skin or feathers or fur, taste one another's blood or flesh, keep one another warm—that attraction was now all one with the fear, and the hunter could not be told from the hunted, nor the eater from the food.

This was more or less the effect I had been after. It was somewhat more powerful than I had anticipated, but I could not now, in all conscience, make an exception for myself. I resolutely put anxiety away, went to Adam, and said, "You and your father lent me this— gave it to me, actually. It's been really useful, but it doesn't exactly seem to fit very well lately. But thanks very much! It's really been very useful."

It is hard to give back a gift without sounding peevish or ungrateful, and I did not want to leave him with that impression of me. He was not paying much attention, as it happened, and said only, "Put it down over there, OK?" and went on with what he was doing.

One of my reasons for doing what I did was that talk was getting us nowhere, but all the same I felt a little let down. I had been prepared to defend my decision. And I thought that perhaps when he did notice he might be upset and want to talk. I put some things away and fiddled around a little, but he continued to do what he was doing and to take no notice of anything else. At last I said, "Well, goodbye, dear. I hope the garden key turns up."

He was fitting parts together, and said, without looking around, "OK, fine, dear. When's dinner?"

"I'm not sure," I said. "I'm going now. With the—" I hesitated, and finally said, "With them, you know," and went on out. In fact, I had only just then realized how hard it would have been to explain myself. I could not chatter away as I used to do, taking it all for granted. My words now must be as slow, as new, as single, as tentative as the steps I took going down the path away from the house, between the dark-branched, tall dancers motionless against the winter shining.

Introduction

1. Elizabeth Cady Stanton. *The Original Feminist Attack on the Bible (The Woman's Bible)*, with an introduction by Barbara Welter (New York: Arno Press, 1974), pp. 11–12.
2. Gerda Lerner, *The Creation of Feminist Consciousness from the Middle Ages to Eighteen-Seventy* (New York: Oxford University Press, 1993), p. 162.
3. Lerner's observations have interesting resonance in the case of the *Tze'enah U-re'enah*, a Yiddish version of the Bible. Written in 17th–century Eastern Europe by a man, Jacob ben Isaac Ashkenazi, it was used not only by women but also by men who could not manage the original Hebrew. It was nonetheless known informally as the "women's bible." The *Tze'enah U-re'enah* contains both less and more than the standard biblical text: emphasizing story over law, it includes the Pentateuch without the Prophets or Writings, but is so embellished with legend, folk tales, and commentary from an abundance of sources that Cynthia Ozick has called it the first Jewish novel. Ozick suggests that by entering the unofficial world of women, Ashkenazi gained imaginative license and could play freely with the stories that were part of the holy canon. See "Notes Toward Finding the Right Question" by Cynthia Ozick in *On Being a Jewish Feminist*, edited and with an introduction by Susannah Heschel. (New York: Schocken Books, 1983).
4. Katie Geneva Cannon in "The Emergence of Black Feminist Consciousness" in Letty M. Russell, ed., *Feminist Interpretation of the Bible* (Philadelphia: Westminster Press, 1985), p. 38.

A Meditation on Eve
BARBARA GRIZZUTI HARRISON

1. Dante, *Paradiso*, translated by Philip H. Wickstead (New York: Modern Library/ Random House, 1932), Canto 9:103–105, p. 458.

Looking Back at Lot's Wife
REBECCA GOLDSTEIN

1. Rabbi Moshe Weissman, *The Midrash Says: The Book of Beraishis* (Brooklyn, N.Y.: Benei Yakou Publications, p. 197).
2. And it's only right to remember that even Abraham might, on occasion, try to get God to *change* his word, as he did when he was informed that Sodom was imminently to be destroyed. Abraham had argued that there must surely be at least fifty righteous inhabitants who should not be killed because of the sins of the others. God agreed, but there were no such fifty—nor forty-five, nor forty, nor thirty, nor even ten. When Abraham learned that there were not even ten righteous Sodomite men, he accepted the city's doom and was silent. But it was Abraham's pleading that subsequently won Lot and Lot's family their lives.
3. For this last insight I am indebted to Esti Fass, who, in private conversation, connected Isaac's love of Esau with his own close brush with death.
4. Impersonal, that is, as compared with the more personal conception of transcendence represented in the notion of God. It's left open of course that the truth might very well *include* the existence of God.
5. In the *Republic* Plato attempts to construct a society in which the force of the ties of blood will be effectively neutralized, with children being held collectively and the facts of who is the biological relation of whom concealed.
6. Rev. Dr. S. Goldman, trans. (London: The Soncino Press), p. 223.
7. Ibid., p. 225.

Rebekah and Isaac: A Marriage Made in Heaven
NORMA ROSEN

1. Louis Ginzberg, *The Legends of the Jews*, vol. 5 (Philadelphia Jewish Publication Society, 1925), p. 42.
2. Ibid., p. 286.
3. I owe this dramatic turn to Robert S. Rosen, who as a small boy in Vienna in the 1930s was imprinted with its pathos in a Yiddish theater production of Goldfadden's play, *Akeydus Yitzhak*. The theater version may itself be related to a midrash cited in Ginzberg, in which Satan is the messenger.
4. *Yitzhak* (Hebrew): Isaac.
5. *Yitzhak*: from the same root as the Hebrew for "laughter." Kafka's name means "crow" in the Czeck language.
6. Eric Averbach, *Mimesis* (New York: Doubleday Anchor Books, 1957), p. 7.
7. Ginzberg, p. 249.
8. Ibid., p. 244.
9. Ibid., p. 254.

Rachel's Dream of Grandeur
ILANA PARDES

1. Gabriel Josipovici, *The Book of God: A Response to the Bible* (New Haven: Yale University Press, 1988), p. 70.
2. My approach to patriarchal specular dynamics thus differs from that of Luce Irigaray. In *Speculum* Irigaray suggests that woman is outside of representation in Western culture. She is the negative required by the male subject's specularization, the Other whose main function is to bolster the "subject's" position; she is "his faithful polished mirror, empty of altering reflections." Irigaray's critique of Western thought, though persuasive, fails to take into account the heterogeneity of specular dynamics, the moments in which specular hierarchies are called into question. See *Speculum of the Other Woman*, trans. G. Gill (Ithaca, N.Y.: Cornell University Press, 1985), esp. p. 136.
3. See Zvi Jagendorf, " 'In the Morning, Behold, It Was Leah': Genesis and the Reversal of Sexual Knowledge," in *Biblical Patterns in Modern Literature*, ed. David Hirsch and Nehama Ashkenazy (Providence, R.I.: Brown University Press, 1984), pp. 51–60.
4. As Robert Alter argues, the annunciation type–scene is constructed upon a tripartite schema: initial barrenness, divine intervention, and the birth of a son. In some cases "the distress of the barren wife is accented by the presence of a fertile, less loved co-wife" (compare with Gen. 22 and 1 Sam. 1). See Alter, "How Conventions Help Us Read: The Case of the Bible's Annunciation Type–Scene," *Prooftexts* 3 (1983): 115–130, esp. p. 119.
5. Henry James, *The Portrait of a Lady* (New York: Penguin Books, 1986), p. 53.
6. See J. P. Fokkelman, *Narrative Art in Genesis* (Amsterdam: Van Gorcum, Assen, 1975), p. 140.
7. See Mieke Bal, *Death and Dissymmetry: The Politics of Coherence in the Book of Judges* (Chicago: The University of Chicago Press, 1988).
8. See E. A. Speiser, "Genesis," *The Anchor Bible* (New York: Doubleday, 1964).
9. See Mieke Bal, "Tricky Thematics," *Semeia* 42 (1988): 133–55.
10. See Adin Steinsaltz, *Biblical Images: Men and Women of the Book*, trans. Yehuda Hanegbi and Yehudit Keshet (New York: Basic Books, 1984), pp. 49–54.
11. See Pirke de Rabbi Eliezer 36; Agadat Breshit 51, Tanhuma, *parashat va-yetse*.
12. The story of Jephthah is well known: "Jephthah vowed a vow unto the Lord, and said, if thou shalt without fail deliver the children of Ammon into mine hands, Then it shall be, that whatsoever cometh forth of the doors of my house to meet me, when I return in peace from the children of Ammon, shall surely be the Lord's, and I will offer it up for a burnt offering" (Judg. 11:30–31). The first "thing" he ends up meeting, upon his triumphal return, is his own daughter. Bath-Jephthah thus turns out to be the victim of her father's promise. Mieke Bal persuasively suggests that "If we use the well-known realistic-psychological argument, we may say that this ritual [of women greeting the victor with dance and song] was well enough known for Jephthah to possibly have been aware of the risk he was taking; but obviously, his unawareness is precisely the point" (*Death and Dissymmetry*, p. 45).
13. Michal is another example of a rebellious daughter whose end is rather tragic. In a fascinating evocation of Rachel's move, Michal covers David's escape from

her father's eyes by placing the household gods (the *terafim*) in bed. Later on, however, she will be rejected by David and will disappear from the stage (2 Sam. 6).

14. I am grateful to Jonathan Rosen for this last point.
15. Erich Auerbach, *Mimesis: The Representation of Reality in Western Literature,* trans. Willard Trask (Princeton, N.J.: Princeton University Press, 1974), pp. 17–18.
16. Sigmund Freud, "The Relation of the Poet to Day-Dreaming." In *On Creativity and the Unconscious: Papers on the Psychology of Art, Literature, Love, Religion,* trans. John Riviere (New York: Harper and Row, 1958), p. 50.
17. Ibid., p. 51.
18. Gabriel Josipovici, *The Book of God,* p. 193.
19. Nancy Miller, "Emphasis Added: Plots and Plausibilities in Women's Fiction" *PMLA* (1981) 96:36–48, p. 40.

The Nursing Father
ALICIA OSTRIKER

1. *Eyheh asher eyheh,* the name God tells to Moses in Exodus 3:14, may be literally translated either "I am who/what I am" or "I will be who/what I will be"; it is commonly translated "I am that I am," but commentators agree that the meaning is intended to remain elusive.

In Search of Pharaoh's Daughter
PATRICIA J. WILLIAMS

1. C. Stansell, *City of Women,* p. 175.
2. "Arson Damages Disputed Foster Home in Queens," *New York Times,* April 22, 1987, p. 1 and p. B5.
3. "Infants, Anger and Fire Engines in the Night," *NYT,* April 22, 1987, p. B5.
4. "Arson Damages . . . ," p. B5, col. 3.

Reflections on Hannah's Prayer
MARCIA FALK

1. We know from the biblical texts that priests gave the priestly blessing in sanctuaries and that King Solomon prayed at the Jerusalem sanctuary (the First Temple); the Bible also records multiple instances of prayers said by individuals in other settings. But Hannah's prayer is a unique instance in the Bible of an ordinary person's prayer offered in the cultic setting—the sanctuary in which sacrifices were offered. As such, Hannah's prayer was a historical point of nexus for the rabbis, who sought to replace sacrifice altogether with "the prayer of the heart." In our terms her act is noteworthy as a personal, spiritual action that, *in context,* implicitly challenges the hierarchized social and religious order.

Infant Piety and the Infant Samuel
MARGARET ANNE DOODY

1. Charlotte Brontë, *Jane Eyre*, ed. Richard J. Dunn (New York: W. W. Norton & Company Inc., 1971), pp. 27–28.
2. *Hurlbut's Story of the Bible for Young and Old: A Continuous Narrative of the Scriptures Told in One Hundred and Sixty-eight Stories* (London: Ward, Lock and Co. Ltd., 1958). There are variations in subtitles and title-page information. I believe that the version in our home was probably the 1947 American edition, but that copy has long disappeared.
3. "Hush'd Was the Evening Hymn" is presented in the version printed in *Hymns Ancient and Modern for Use in the Services of the Church*, standard ed. (London: William Clowes and Sons Limited, 1924), p. 497.
4. I take this information from the commentary by Peter R. Ackroyd in the volume entitled *The First Book of Samuel*, one of a series in *The Cambridge Bible Commentary on the New English Bible* (Cambridge, Eng.: Cambridge University Press, 1971), p. 26.
5. The *New English Bible* (NEB) has "they lay with the women who were serving at the entrance to the Tent of the Presence." The *Cambridge Bible Commentary* notes that "The Tent of the Presence" is an older term from the time before the sanctuary building existed, "while the reference to the women may be a late addition," perhaps designed to allude to the religious prostitution practiced "in the later Graeco-Roman world" (p. 36). Neither the biblical narrative nor the commentary is interested in whether the women were willing or unwilling participants in the sexual activities of Eli's sons; they may have been slaves bound to household service in the Temple, with no real choice in the matter.
6. Euripides, *The Bacchae and Other Plays*, trans. Philip Vellacott (Harmondsworth, Eng.: Penguin Books, 1973), p. 44. Other quotations from the *Ion* will be given in this translation, with page numbers supplied and no further annotation.
7. Eli's contemptuous reference to Hannah as drunken, and his sons' outrageous use of women around the Temple area create links to the world of Creusa, in which forced sexuality is part of religious ritual, stimulated and excused by the drunkenness of both parties. Eli is metaphorically the spiritual father of Hannah's child, endorsing her prayer while she is intoxicated by praying—which at one level may seem a polite reshaping of material more like Creusa's story.
8. *Jane Eyre*, pp. 26, 53, 57.

The Psychopathology of King Saul
DEIRDRE LEVINSON

This essay was informed by the following reference works: W.O.E. Oesterley and T. H. Robinson, *An Introduction to the Books of the Old Testament* (Cleveland and New York: The World Publishing Company, 1962); Bernhard W. Anderson, *Understanding the Old Testament* (Englewood Cliffs, N.J.: Prentice-Hall Inc., 1966); and Yohanan Aharoni and Michael Avi-Yonah, *The Macmillan Bible Atlas* (New York: Macmillan Publishing Co. Inc., 1977).

1. Leo Tolstoy, *War and Peace*, tr. Louise and Aylmer Maude (New York: Norton Critical Edition, W.W. Norton & Co., 1966), p. 670.
2. The researches of modern biblical scholars show conclusively that the compiler of this text has drawn upon at least two major sources. The earlier of these is more sympathetic to Saul than the other, later, presumably Davidic source, which makes up the larger part of the narrative. However, since the character of Saul, as it emerges from these disparate sources, is a self-consistent one, I shall in general treat the text as a coherent whole.
3. See Rivkah Kluger's *Psyche and Bible* (New York: Analytical Psychology Club of New York, Inc., 1974) to which I am indebted for this observation. It is reinforced by the twofold meaning of the Hebrew verb *nava*: "to prophesy" or "to rave" (in prophetic ecstasy or lunatic frenzy, according to the context).

The Judgment of Women
ANNE C. DAILEY

1. The phrase literally translated from the Hebrew means "her bowels were in a ferment." See John Gray, *I & II Kings: A Commentary*, (Philadelphia: Westminster Press, 1963), p. 125. As Gray explains, "The bowels . . . , also 'womb,' were the seat of the emotions in the reckoning of the ancient Hebrews." Phyllis Trible explains that the original Hebrew comprehends both the concrete meaning "womb" and the abstract meaning "compassion." See Phyllis Trible, *God and the Rhetoric of Sexuality* (Philadelphia: Fortress Press, 1978), p. 33.
2. This interpretation of the Solomon story is often associated with the "best interests of the child" standard used in making child-custody decisions. See K. Bartlett, "Rethinking Parenthood as an Exclusive Status: The Need for Legal Alternatives When the Premise of the Nuclear Family Has Failed," 70 *Virg. L. Rev.* 879, 891 n. 68 (1984).
3. "Solomon's test rested on a simple ploy: he threatened to destroy what was most precious to the women. This is the tactic of the terrorist, here practiced by the wisest king and judge. Because of his unique position, because of his wisdom, Solomon's use of power was not challenged." M. Minow, "The Judgment of Solomon and the Experience of Justice," in *The Structure of Procedure*, ed. R. Cover and O. Fiss (Mineola, N.Y.: Foundation Press, 1979), p. 450.
4. I would like to thank Jeannie Heifetz and Rick Kay for bringing the Abraham story to my attention.
5. See R. Cover, "Violence and the Word," 95 *Yale L.J.* 1601 (1986).
6. I am indebted to Nina Pillard for helping me articulate this insight.
7. See Marie Ashe, "Abortion of Narrative: A Reading of the Judgment of Solomon," 4 *Yale J. of L. and Feminism* 81, 87–88 (1991).

In and Out of the Fold:
Wisdom, Danger, and Glamour in the Tale of the Queen of Sheba
MARINA WARNER

1. See for instance the catalog *Distant Worlds Made Tangible. Art and Curiosities: Dutch Collections, 1585–1735*, Amsterdam Historisches Museum, 1992.
2. I am not counting the interpolation of verses 11–12, speaking of the army of Hiram, which complemented the wealth of tribute Solomon received.
3. "Solomon to Sheba," in W. B. Yeats, *Collected Poems of W. B. Yeats*, ed. Richard J. Finneran (New York: Collier Books, 1983, 1989), p. 138.
4. "The Ant," *The Koran*, trans. N. J. Dawood. (Harmondsworth, Eng.: Penguin Classic, 1972), pp. 82–4.
5. Ibid., p 84.
6. H. St. John Philby, *The Queen of Sheba* (London: Quartet Books, 1981), pp. 94–96.
7. "The Legs of the Queen of Sheba," in *The Mermaids in the Basement: Stories 1982–1992*, Marina Warner (London: Chatto & Windus, 1993).
8. *The Queen of Sheba's Legs*, music by Julian Grant, English National Opera, London, 1991.

The Odd Couple: Elijah and Jezebel
PHYLLIS TRIBLE

1. Sidon was a city-state in the territory of Phoenicia, which lay north of Canaan along the Mediterranean coast. See Brian Peckham, "Phoenicia, History of," *The Anchor Bible Dictionary*, ed. David Noel Freedman, vol. 5 (New York: Doubleday, 1992), pp. 349–57.
2. For the classical statement, see Martin Noth, *The Deuteronomistic History* (Sheffield, Eng.: JSOT Press, 1981); cf. Frank Moore Cross, "The Themes of the Book of Kings and the Structure of the Deuteronomistic History," *Canaanite Myth and Hebrew Epic* (Cambridge, Mass.: Harvard University Press, 1983), pp. 274–89.
3. For translation of the Ugaritic texts, see Michael David Coogan, *Stories from Ancient Canaan* (Philadelphia: The Westminster Press, 1978). Note that Canaan and Phoenicia shared the same religion. See John Day, "Canaan, Religion of," *Anchor Bible Dictionary*, vol. 1, pp. 831–37; Philip C. Schmitz, "Phoenician Religion," *Anchor Bible Dictionary*, vol. 5, pp. 357–63.
4. For a discussion with ample bibliography, see Mark S. Smith, *The Early History of God* (San Francisco: Harper and Row, 1990), pp. 80–114, esp. p. 94.
5. No documents attest to the goddess Asherah in Phoenicia during the Iron Age, the larger setting for these stories. The reference to her in 1 Kings 18:19 is thus historically implausible, probably a gloss added for polemical purposes. See Smith, *The Early History of God*, pp. 89ff.
6. Stanley B. Frost, "Judgment on Jezebel, or a Woman Wronged," *Theology Today* 20 (1964): 503–517.

7. Alexander Rofé, "The Vineyard of Naboth: The Origin and Message of the Story," *Vetus Testamentum* 38 (1988): 89–104.

8. For a similar judgment, see Peter R. Ackroyd, "Goddesses, Women and Jezebel," *Images of Women in Antiquity*, ed. Averil Cameron and Amelie Kuhrt (Detroit: Wayne State University Press, 1983), pp. 245–59. Cf. Athalya Brenner, *The Israelite Woman: Social Role and Literary Type in Biblical Narrative* (Sheffield, Eng.: JSOT Press, 1985), pp. 20–28; Claudia V. Camp, "1 and 2 Kings," *The Women's Bible Commentary*, ed. Carol A. Newsom and Sharon H. Ringe (Louisville, Ken.: Westminster/John Knox Press, 1992), pp. 103–104.

9. See Burke O. Long, *2 Kings: Forms of Old Testament Literature*, vol. 10 (Grand Rapids, Mich.: William B. Eerdmans Publishing Company, 1991), pp. 23–32.

10. The words of the unnamed prophet alter the syntax of Elijah's prediction. They put the object *Jezebel* before the verb *eat*, thereby emphasizing her and her fate. On the alterations in these prophecies, see Peter D. Miscall, "Elijah, Ahab and Jehu: A Prophecy Fulfilled," *Prooftexts* 9 (1989): 73–83.

11. See John Gray, *I & II Kings* (Philadelphia: The Westminster Press, 1970), pp. 368, 551; Gale A. Yee, "Jezebel," *Anchor Bible Dictionary*, vol. 3, pp. 848–49.

Chosen Women
RACHEL M. BROWNSTEIN

1. "Sarah Maria Jones" copyright © 1950 by Charlotte Hochman.

The World Remade: The Book of Esther
CELINA SPIEGEL

1. From Aristophanes' play "The Birds," *Three Comedies*, ed. and trans. William Arrowsmith (Ann Arbor: University of Michigan Press, 1969), p. 26. I would like to thank Gardener Stout for pointing out this useful phrase to me.

2. See Michael André Bernstein's discussion on the relationship between satire and carnival in *Bitter Carnival: Ressentiment and the Abject Hero* (Princeton, N.J.: Princeton University Press, 1992).

3. See Robert Alter's discussion of the king's impotence in *The World of Biblical Narrative* (New York: Basic Books, 1992), pp. 30–34.

The Paradox of the Psalms
KATHLEEN NORRIS

1. "Protestant Easter" in *Live or Die* by Anne Sexton (New York: Houghton Mifflin Co., 1966).

The Women in the Balcony: On Rereading The Song of Songs
DAPHNE MERKIN

In addition to the works listed below, this essay was informed by Raphael Patai's *The Hebrew Goddess* (Detroit: Wayne State University Press, 1990).

1. Elliot K. Ginsburg, "Jewish Mysticism" in *The Schocken Guide to Jewish Books*, edited by Barry W. Holtz (New York: Schocken, 1992), p. 165.
2. Song of Songs 1:5, from *Soncino Books of the Bible: The Five Megilloth*, Hebrew text and English translation with introductions and commentary by the Rev. Dr. A. Cohen (London: The Soncino Press, 1977).
3. *The Song of Songs: A New Translation*, translated and edited by Marcia Falk (New York: HarperCollins, 1990), p. xiii.
4. Ilana Pardes, *Countertraditions in the Bible: A Feminist Approach* (Cambridge: Harvard University Press, 1992), p. 118.
5. Julia Kristeva, *Tales of Love*, translated by Leon S. Roudiez (New York: Columbia University Press, 1987), p. 85.
6. Falk, p. ix.
7. Song of Songs 5:9.
8. Song of Songs 5:14. *Tanakh: The New JPS Translation According to the Traditional Hebrew Text* (Philadelphia: The Jewish Publication Society, 1985).
9. Gerson D. Cohen, *Studies in the Variety of Rabbinic Cultures* (Philadelphia: JPS, 1991), p. xv.
10. Pope, p. 17.
11. Ibid., p. 42.
12. Gershom Scholem, *Origins of the Kabbalah* (Princeton, N.J.: Jewish Publication Society and Princeton University Press, 1987), p. 374.
13. Pope, p. 19.
14. Pope, p. 17.
15. Song of Songs 4:11/4:16. From Pope, *Song of Songs: A New Translation*.
16. Kristeva, p. 96.
17. Yael S. Feldman, "Recurrence and Sublimation: Toward a Psychoanalytic Approach to Biblical Narrative" in *Approaches to Teaching the Hebrew Bible as Literature in Translation*, edited by Barry N. Olshen and Yael S. Feldman (New York: Modern Language Association, 1989), p. 81.
18. Kristeva, p. 99.
19. Song of Songs 2:9. *The Soncino Books of the Bible: Five Megillot*.
20. Cohen, p. xv.
21. Song of Songs 8:8. Pope, *Five Megillot: A New Translation*.
22. Song of Songs 8:14. Ibid.

The Poetry of Isaiah
AMY CLAMPITT

1. To be quite fair and judicious, some scholarly caveats should be noted. Isaiah's alacrity "is enough to make him a rather unique prophet" as compared with the reluctance of Moses, Jeremiah, Ezekiel, and Jonah. "The words of Yahweh's

commissioning . . . are some of the most difficult to understand in the Old Testament. . . . We should recall that the call narrative most probably reflects some of the circumstances of his ministry. . . . Does Isaiah think he alone is wise? The response to the question is found in the reference to the blinding and hardening: it is precisely those who should most especially perceive and understand, the counselors who surround the king and the king himself, whom Isaiah thinks of as having been blinded and hardened and made unperceiving." (Joseph Jensen, O.S.B., in *Isaiah 1–39*, Old Testament Message series, Vol. 8, [Wilmington, Del.: Michael Glazer, Inc., 1984], pp. 88–89).

2. Emily Dickinson, Poem #1545 from *Life and Letters of Emily Dickinson*, ed. Martha Dickinson Bianchi (New York: Houghton Mifflin Co., 1952).
3. Václav Havel, "Paradise Lost," *New York Review of Books*, April 9, 1992, p. 6.
4. Thus J. H. Hertz, sometime Chief Rabbi of the British Empire, in *The Pentateuch and Haftorahs . . .*, vol. 1 (New York: Metzudah Publishing Co., 5701 & 1941, pp. 202, 305). The Christian scholar Joseph Jensen concurs: "In all probability this poem looks forward not to a physical birth but the succession to the throne of a new king." (*Isaiah 1–39*, Old Testament Message series).
5. Adapted from *Eclogues and Georgics of Virgil*, David Slavitt, (Baltimore and London: The Johns Hopkins University Press, 1990), pp. 15–16.

In the Belly of the Whale
PATRICIA HAMPL

1. Translation taken from *Tanakh* (Philadelphia: The Jewish Publication Society, 1985).
2. Ibid.

Our Dream of the Good God
LORE SEGAL

1. *The Juniper Tree and Other Tales from Grimm*, trans. Lore Segal and Randall Jarrell (New York: Farrar, Straus & Giroux, 1973), p. 310.
2. Ibid., p. 313.
3. Were the children of Israel spoiled so that the absence, in a later generation, of the Lord's personal leadership made them urgent for a human king "to go before" them?
4. The *Siddur Sim Shalom*, trans. R. Jules Harlow.
5. He gets his comeuppance when he is outcheated, in turn, by that arch-cheat, his Uncle Laban.
6. See Gen. 15:13–16: "and they [the Egyptians] shall afflict them [the children of Israel] four hundred years; . . . But in the fourth generation they shall come hither [to Canaan] again; for the iniquity of the Amorites is not yet full."
7. The word *good* appears forty-five times in the book of Genesis. Its citation in the Concordance fills seven full columns, not counting *better, best, goodly, goodliest,* or *goodness*.

8. The good girls in the soap operas of the fifties gave their illegitimate babies up for adoption. Today's good girls keep the babies; the bad girls give them up.
9. I recall an old English teacher who, with anxious brilliancy, subverted the text of *Hamlet* to prove that Hamlet never intended Rosencrantz and Guildenstern to die. My teacher loved Hamlet and couldn't bear it that he plotted murder.

CONTRIBUTORS' BIOGRAPHIES

RACHEL M. BROWNSTEIN is professor of English at Brooklyn College and the Graduate Center, CUNY, and a native New Yorker. She was educated at Hunter College High School, Barnard College, and Yale University. Her ideas about women and fiction are elaborated on in her books *Becoming a Heroine: Reading About Women in Novels* and *Tragic Muse: Rachel of the Comédie Française*.

CHRISTINA BÜCHMANN is a Ph.D. candidate in English literature at the University of California, Berkeley. She is writing her dissertation on how John Donne and George Herbert render religious experience in their poetry.

AMY CLAMPITT was born in rural Iowa, graduated from Grinnell College, and has since lived mainly in New York City. She is the author of five collections of poetry, most recently *A Silence Opens*, and a collection of essays, *Predecessors, Et Cetera*. Her play, *Mad with Joy*, received a staged reading by the Poets' Theatre in Cambridge, Massachusetts, on March 1, 1993. She has been the recipient of a Guggenheim Fellowship, a literary award from the Lila Wallace–Reader's Digest Foundation, and a MacArthur Fellowship.

ANNE C. DAILEY is associate professor of law at the University of Connecticut, where her research and teaching focus on the areas of feminist legal theory, constitutional law, federal courts, and family relations.

MARGARET ANNE DOODY is Andrew W. Mellon Professor in the Humanities and professor of English at Vanderbilt University. Her publications include *A Natural Passion: A Study of the Novels of Samuel Richardson, The Daring Muse: Augustan Poetry Reconsidered, Frances Burney: The Life in the Works*, as well as two novels, *Aristotle Detective* and *The Alchemists*. She is at present the director of the Program in Comparative Literature at Vanderbilt.

LOUISE ERDRICH is the author of the novels *Love Medicine, Tracks, The Beet Queen, The Bingo Palace*, and, with her husband, Michael Dorris, *The Crown of Columbus*.

MARCIA FALK is a poet, scholar, and translator of Hebrew and Yiddish whose recent books include *The Song of Songs: A New Translation and Interpretation* and *With Teeth in the Earth: Selected Poems of Malka Heifetz Tussman* (translated, edited, and introduced). She has taught Hebrew Bible as Visiting Associate Professor of Religious Studies at Stanford University, and currently she is Affiliated Scholar at Stanford's Institute for Research on Women and Gender and at the Bain Research Group of the University of California at Berkeley.

REBECCA GOLDSTEIN graduated from Barnard College and received her Ph.D. from Princeton University. She was a member of the philosophy department at Barnard for ten years and now primarily devotes herself to the writing of fiction. She is the author of three novels, *The Mind-Body Problem, The Late-Summer Passion of a Woman of Mind*, and *The Dark Sister*, and a collection of stories, *Strange Attractors*.

ALLEGRA GOODMAN has published fiction in *The New Yorker* and *Commentary*. *Total Immersion*, a collection of her stories, appeared in 1989. She is writing a novel, as well as a new collection of stories, while studying for a Ph.D. in Renaissance literature at Stanford University.

PATRICIA HAMPL is the author of two memoirs, *A Romantic Education* and *Virgin Time*. She has published two collections of poetry, *Women Before an Aquarium* and *Resort and Other Poems*. Her short fiction, poems, reviews, essays, and travel pieces have appeared in numerous publications, including *The New Yorker*, *The Paris Review*, *The New York Times Book Review*, *Antaeus*, *Granta*, *Ms.*, *The Iowa Review*, and *The Best American Short Stories*. Ms. Hampl has been the recipient of fellowships and awards from the Guggenheim Foundation, the Bush Foundation, the National Endowment for the Arts, the Ingram Merrill Foundation, and the MacArthur Foundation. She is professor of English at the University of Minnesota, and lives in Saint Paul.

BARBARA GRIZZUTI HARRISON is the author of seven books, including, most recently, *The Astonishing World*, *The Islands of Italy*, and *Italian Days*, which won the American Book Award. She is a contributing editor to *Harper's Magazine*, a contributing writer to *Mirabella*, and has published essays and fiction in *The New York Times*, *The New Republic*, *The Nation*, *Mademoiselle*, *Vanity Fair*, *The Paris Review*, *Commonweal*, *Esquire*, *Condé Nast Traveler*, *European Travel & Life*, *Town and Country*, *New York*, *Life*, and *The Iowa Review*, among other publications.

JUNE JORDAN is a poet and professor of African-American studies and women's studies at the University of California at Berkeley. Her most recent book publications are *Technical Difficulties: New and Selected Political Essays* and *The Haruko/Love Poetry of June Jordan: New and Selected Love Poems*. She is a regular columnist for the *Progressive Magazine*.

URSULA K. LE GUIN writes both poetry and prose, and in several modes or "genres," including realistic fiction, science fiction, fantasy, young children's books, books for young adults, screenplays, essays, verbal texts for musicians, and voicetexts for performance or recording. She established her reputation in science fiction with the Hanish novels, which include *The Left Hand of Darkness* and *The Dispossessed*, and in fantasy with the first three of the Earthsea series: *A Wizard of Earthsea*, *The Tombs of Atuan*, and *The Farthest Shore*, as well as the last book in the series, *Tehanu*. Her most recent books are *Searoad*, stories of the Oregon coast, two picture books, *A Ride on the Red Mare's Back* and *Fish Soup*, a collection of stories, *Half Past Four*, as well as a new poetry collection, *Going Out with Peacocks*. She has received many awards, including five Hugos, four Nebulas, a Pushcart Prize, a Newbery Honor Medal, a National Book Award, and the Howard D. Vursell Award from the American Academy and Institute of Arts and Letters.

DEIRDRE LEVINSON lives and teaches in New York. Her last novel was *Modus Vivendi*.

DAPHNE MERKIN is a writer and editor who lives in New York City. She is the author of a novel, *Enchantment,* which won the Edward Lewis Wallant Award in 1986 for best Jewish-American novel. She contributes articles and reviews to a wide range of publications, including *The New York Times,* the *Los Angeles Times Book Review, Mirabella,* and *Tikkun.* Her essays on Jewish themes have appeared in *Congregation* and *Testimony,* anthologies about the Bible and the Holocaust, respectively. She is at work on a second novel, *The Discovery of Sex.*

KATHLEEN NORRIS is the author of *Dakota: A Spiritual Geography* and two volumes of poetry, *The Middle of the World* and *Falling Off.* She is a Benedictine oblate and part-time lay preacher for the Presbyterian church and has twice been a resident of the Institute for Ecumenical and Cultural Research in Collegeville, Minnesota. She has received awards for her writing from the Guggenheim Foundation and the Bush Foundation. She lives in Lemmon, South Dakota.

ALICIA OSTRIKER has published seven volumes of poetry, most recently *The Imaginary Lover,* which won the 1986 William Carlos Williams Award from the Poetry Society of America, and *Green Age.* Her poetry appears in *The New Yorker, The Nation, American Poetry Review, The Atlantic Monthly, Ontario Review,* and other magazines. As a critic she is the author of *Vision and Verse in William Blake* and editor of Blake's *Complete Poems* and has written two books on American women's poetry, *Writing Like a Woman* and *Stealing the Language: The Emergence of Women's Poetry in America.* Her most recent critical work is *Feminist Revision and the Bible.* Ms. Ostriker has received awards from the New Jersey Arts Council, the National Endowment for the Arts, the Rockefeller Foundation, and the Guggenheim Foundation. She teaches English and creative writing at Rutgers University.

CYNTHIA OZICK's fiction and essays have appeared in most of the major magazines and journals in this country, and her work has been translated into seventeen languages. Her most recent novels include *The Shawl* and *The Messiah of Stockholm*; her most recent collections of essays are *What Henry James Knew and Other Essays on Writers* and *Metaphor & Memory*. Among her many awards and grants are those from the American Academy and Institute of Arts and Letters, the Guggenheim Foundation, and the National Endowment for the Arts. Her work has appeared in numerous anthologies, including *The Best American Short Stories, The Best American Short Stories of the Eighties, The Best American Essays,* and the *O'Henry Prize Stories.*

ILANA PARDES, lecturer in the departments of Comparative Literature and English at the Hebrew University of Jerusalem, has also taught at Princeton University. She is the author of *Countertraditions in the Bible: A Feminist Approach.*

NORMA ROSEN's most recent work is a collection of essays, *Accidents of Influence: Writing as a Woman and a Jew in America.* Her fiction includes *John and Anzia: An American Romance, At the Center, Touching Evil, Green,* and *Joy to Levine!* Her short fiction and essays have appeared in *The New Yorker, The New York Times Magazine, Commentary, Ms., Lilith,* and *Congress Monthly,* and her essays have been included in *Testimony: Contemporary Writers Make the Holocaust Personal* and *Congregation: Contemporary Writers Read the Jewish Bible.* She is currently teaching fiction at the Tisch School of Dramatic Writing at New York University.

LORE SEGAL's latest novel, *Her First American,* parts of which were published in *The New Yorker,* earned her an American Academy and Institute of the Arts and Letters Award. Her translations include *The Book of Adam to Moses* and *The Story of King Saul and King David.* Her essays have appeared in *Testimony: Contemporary Writers Make the Holocaust Personal* and *Congregation: Contemporary Writers Read the Jewish Bible.* Lore Segal lives in New York and teaches at the Ohio State University.

NAOMI SEIDMAN is a Mellon Postdoctoral Fellow and Visiting Assistant Professor in the Department of Comparative Literature at Stanford University. Her academic research has focused on the sexual politics of Hebrew–Yiddish relations in the Eastern European

Jewish community. She is currently translating the Hebrew and Yiddish short fiction of the seminal turn-of-the-century writer Devorah Baron, as well as working on her own fiction.

CELINA SPIEGEL, an editor at a New York publishing house, first became interested in literary biblical criticism while doing graduate work in Comparative Literature at the University of California, Berkeley.

ELIZABETH SWADOS has composed, written, and directed productions including *Runaways, Nightclub Cantata, Alice in Concert, The Red Sneaks, Dispatches, The Greek Trilogy, The Beautiful Lady, Lullabye and Goodnight, The Mermaid Wakes, The New Americans, Groundhog,* and several Bible stories performed all over the world, including *Job, Jonah, Jerusalem, The Song of Songs, The Haggadah,* and *Esther.* She is the author of children's books and adult books; her most recent book is *The Four of Us.* She has written scores for film, ballet, and television, as well as videos for children, and has been commissioned to write two screenplays, *A Fine and Private Place* and an adaptation of *The Red Sneaks.* She is the recipient of a Guggenheim Fellowship, three Obie Awards, five Tony nominations, and a Ford Fellowship.

PHYLLIS TRIBLE is Baldwin Professor of Sacred Literature at Union Theological Seminary. Her books include *Texts of Terror: Literary Feminist Readings of Biblical Narratives* and *Rhetorical Criticism: Context, Method, and the Book of Jonah.*

MARINA WARNER was born in London, in 1946, attended convent schools in Egypt, Belgium, and England, and read French and Italian at Lady Margaret Hall, Oxford. Her books include *Alone of All Her Sex: The Myth and Cult of the Virgin Mary; Joan of Arc: The Image of Female Heroism;* and *Monuments & Maidens: The Allegory of the Female Form,* which was awarded the Fawcett Prize; as well as four novels, including *The Lost Father,* which was the regional winner of the Commonwealth Writers' Prize, a recipient of the PEN/Macmillan Silver Pen Award, and was shortlisted for the Booker Prize, and *Indigo, or Mapping the Waters.* She is also the author of a collection of stories, *The Mermaids in the Basement.* Erasmus University, Rotterdam, appointed her Tinbergen Professor in 1991. In 1993 she gave the Reith Lectures on the BBC on the uses of myth. She is currently writing a study of fairy tales, called *From the Beast to the Blonde*.

FAY WELDON was born in England and raised in New Zealand. Among her nineteen novels and short-story collections are *Affliction*, *The Life Force*, *Darcy's Utopia*, *The Cloning of Joanna May*, *Leader of the Band*, *Puffball*, and *The Heart of the Country*, winner of the 1989 *Los Angeles Times* Fiction Award. She lives in London.

PATRICIA J. WILLIAMS is professor of law at Columbia University and author of *The Alchemy of Race and Rights*. Her forthcoming book, *The Rooster's Egg*, is about the configuration of highly publicized trials and notions of civic identity. She is a regular contributor to *The Village Voice* and *Ms*.